Silent Film

Silent Film
Edited by Richard Abel

Silent Film offers some of the best recent essays on silent cinema, essays that cross disciplinary boundaries and break new ground in a varoety of ways. Some focus on the "materiality" of early cinema: the color processes used in printing nitrate film stocks, the choreographic styles of film acting, and the wide range of sound accompaniment. Others focus on questions of periodicity and nationality: on the shift from a "cinema of attractions" to a "classical narrative cinema," on the relationship between changes in production and those in exhibition, and on the historical specificity of national cinemas. Still others focus on early cinema's intertextual relations with various forms of mass culture (from magazine stories or sensational melodramas in the United States to the tango craze in Russia), and on the reception in silent cinema (from black audiences in Chicago to women's fan magazines of the 1920s). Taken together, the contributors to this volume suggest provocative parallels between silent cinema at the turn of the last century and "postmodern" cinema at the end of our own. This book is an important contribution to the study of silent film.

Richard Abel is Professor of the Humanities, Drake University, and the author of *French Cinema: The First Wave: 1915–1929; French Film Theory and Criticism: A History/Anthology;* and *The Ciné Goes to Town: French Cinema, 1896–1914.*

0 485 30076 1 pb

Edited and with an introduction by
Richard Abel

Silent Film

ATHLONE
LONDON

97000041 31

First published in Great Britain 1996 by
THE ATHLONE PRESS
1 Park Drive, London NW11 7SG

Reprinted 1999

British Library Cataloguing in Publication Data
A catalogue record for this book is available from the British Library
ISBN 0 485 30076 1

Printed and bound in Great Britain by
Short Run Press, Exeter

This one is for my parents, Owen and Ruth Abel

"My present?"

Piglet nodded again.

"The balloon?"

"Yes."

"Thank you, Piglet," said Eeyore. "You don't mind my asking," he went on, "but what colour was this balloon when it—when it *was* a balloon?"

"Red."

"I just wondered. . . . Red," he murmured to himself. "My favourite colour. . . . How big was it?"

"About as big as me."

"I just wondered. . . . About as big as Piglet," he said to himself sadly. "My favourite size. Well, well."

A. A. Milne, *Winnie the Pooh*, 1926

Contents

Theorizing a Cultural History of Silent Cinema

Intertextuality and Reception in Silent Cinema

Silent Film

Richard Abel

Introduction

"[Cinema] is the theater, schoolhouse, and newspaper of tomorrow."
                                        Pathé-Frères, 1905

As our own century approaches the point of turning into another, many of us find ourselves looking back to the last turn of the century, perhaps with fear and trepidation yet also with the surprise and even pleasure of (mis)recognition. Those of us interested in the cinema, of course, have an added stimulus because it was at the past century's turn that the cinema began to emerge as a new medium and venue of mass culture and, eventually, as a significant part of the "culture industry" worldwide. The current centennial celebrations of the cinema remind us that its earliest proselytizers, from Edmond Benoît-Lévy to Carl Laemmle, once heralded the twentieth century as "the age of moving pictures," a prophecy since born out, arguably, for at least half its length.[1] Some of these celebrations—such as the Gaumont film programs touring the United States (1994) and the Pathé Exposition on display at the Centre Pompidou in Paris (October 1994–March 1995)—pay homage to particular French companies that played a crucial role in the cinema's emergence as well as its continuing development over the course of the century. Others—such as the 1995 Society for Cinema Studies Conference in New York or the 1995 International Film Conference at Indiana University—cover a wider spectrum, focusing attention on "100 Years of Cinema: Writing Histories" or "European Cinemas, European Societies, 1895–1995." Still others are devoted exclusively to early cinema—for instance, the biennial conferences of Domitor, on "Nonfiction Films, 1894–1904" (New York, 1994) and on "Pathé and . . ." (Paris, 1996), or the international conference, "Celebrating 1895" (Bradford, 1995).[2] And it is particularly appropriate, at this turn of the century, to draw attention to those early decades of the cinema—and what has come to be called "silent cinema"—for if that cinema and its historical moment clearly are distinct from our own, the two moments also are far less dissimilar than one might suppose.

The recent renewal of interest in silent film, especially early cinema, has been spurred by several archaeological projects, archive restorations, special conferences and festivals, and published books and articles. It is impossible not to cite the impact of the 1978 Congress of the International Federation of Film Archives (FIAF), held in Brighton, England, which brought together archivists and academics for one full week to view and discuss nearly 600 fiction films made between 1900 and 1906, many of them newly rediscovered and printed. Nor can one forget such conferences as "Cinema Histories, Cinema Practices I" (Los Angeles, May 1981), organized by Patricia Mellencamp to initiate a reexamination of the premises of doing cinema history.[3] Likewise, there has been the revelatory effect of major silent film restorations, from the pioneering, well-publicized work of Kevin Brownlow and his associates (beginning with Abel Gance's *Napoléon*, 1927) to the no less important if perhaps less familiar work of, among others, Marie Epstein and Renée Lichtig at the Cinémathèque Française. For the past ten years, much of the best archive restoration work on film from around the world has been showcased at the annual Pordenone Silent Film Festival in Italy. The Pordenone Festival has given particular attention to national cinemas up to 1920 (American, Scandinavian, German, and Russian), "neglected" early production companies (Vitagraph and Eclair), and a variety of directors (Cecil B. DeMille, Frank Borzage, Maurice Tourneur, Emile Cohl).[4] But Pordenone is only the most visible of a host of festivals (such as those in Bologna and Paris), archive programs (such as those of the Nederlands Filmmuseum in Amsterdam and National Film/Television Archive in London), and special film exhibitions (for instance, the "Before Hollywood" series sponsored by the American Federation of the Arts), all promoting scholarly as well as public interest in silent film.[5]

Historical research on silent cinema has expanded considerably over the past two decades, as the bibliography at the end of this volume suggests. At least two previous books aimed at students and general readers have attempted to collect the best of that research, in English. The first, John Fell's *Film before Griffith* (1983), gathers together essays drawn from research done primarily in the middle and late 1970s, as cinema studies was being institutionalized within American universities. To some extent, those essays parallel the "Brighton Project" (to which the book never refers) by challenging the long-held notion that cinema really began with D. W. Griffith and the institution of Hollywood cinema. They also put in play what has proved a valuable range of methodologies for "doing history"—from examining unused sources to incorporating investigative tools from other disciplines. Yet the book's three-part structure simply mirrors the industry's own organization (with its sectors of production, distribution, and exhibition) and accepts a rather conventional sense of textual analysis. The second book, Thomas Elsaesser's *Early Cinema: Space, Frame, Narrative* (1990), brings together a good deal of superb research from the 1980s, much of which builds on the "Brighton Project" and extends the work collected by Fell. On the one hand, Elsaesser's aim is to resituate historical research on early cinema within what he calls a "cultural archaeology" of mass media at the turn of the century, in which the cinema serves as a crucial "media-intertext." On the other, as he himself admits, the three-part structure of the book as well as his own introductions to each tell a not unfamiliar "story" about the cinema, between 1896 and 1917—that is, the cinema's "turn to narrative as its main form of textual and ideological support" and "the industrialization and standardization of its standard product, the feature film." Yet Elsaesser also frames that "story" within a clear sense of our own historical moment (especially with its rapid transformation of audio-visual media, of storage and reproductive technologies, and of readership/spectatorship itself), a moment that, he suggests, may yet prove that the "classical cinema" is no more than a "transitional stage."

The present volume obviously builds on these previous books (including three of the same authors, with more recent essays), yet it does so, in part, by shifting the focus of historical work to subjects and questions that Fell and Elsaesser either opened up for further research or, for one reason or another, excluded. First, I have tried to collect some of the best essays on silent cinema done in the late 1980s and early 1990s—that is, after the international impact of Pordenone as well as the American "success stories" of Bordwell, Staiger, and Thompson's *Classical Hollywood Cinema* (1985) and of the initial volumes in Scribner's *History of the American Cinema* series (1990)—essays that break new ground in either the subjects they interrogate, the methods they deploy, the sources they uncover, or some combination of these. Second, many of the selected essays are informed by recent theoretical and critical developments that not only cross but problematize disciplinary boundaries.[6] At its most general, those include the poststructural critiques of textuality or discursivity, of representation and narration, of "truth claims" and evidence, and (using Michel Foucault as an example) of their institutional conditions, at a specific historical moment, of circulation, maintenance, and change. Just as significant, however, are those developments associated with programs that are reconceptualizing the American university—from Cultural Studies and Gender Studies to those, such as African-American Studies and Chicana/o Studies, embodying one or more versions of multiculturalism. Third, a good percentage of these essays falls within the category of historical reception study. That is, they redefine the cinema to privilege the point of reception, focusing attention on how different audiences and spectators experienced the cinema, on what use value the cinema had for them, and on how both that experience and use value may have changed over time. Finally, in keeping with the general principles of the "Depth of Field" series, I have sought to make several relatively inaccessible essays more readily available, including work written in languages other than English as well as work dealing with something other than the American cinema.

The thirteen essays in this volume have been selected and grouped according to a half-dozen general subjects that frame our current investigation and understanding of silent cinema. The first has to do with the materiality of that cinema, with its physicality, its corporality, its tangibility—with what historians, appropriating the methods of Marxism and/or archaeology, might call its "material culture."[7] That materiality can cover a good number of things: the various apparatuses involved in the production and exhibition of films, the permutations of film stock on which recorded images were composed, the human bodies and constructed decors involved in production, the documents and related materials (from trade press and local newspaper ads to posters, programs, or playbills, and "special gifts" or prizes) that both stimulated and mediated the distribution and exhibition of films, the design and spatial arrangement of different exhibition sites (conforming to several discourses of regulation), along with their varying temporal schedules, and the range of sound (music, voice, and sound effects) that either accompanied individual films or constituted significant parts of the program.[8] The materiality of silent cinema strikes me as particularly important because, in many ways, it has become so unfamiliar to us, so different from that of our own cinema in the late twentieth century, and because it changed so radically over the course of the early cinema's first three decades.

Of the growing research now available on the materiality of silent cinema, I have chosen three essays that address the subject in quite different ways—and included others that at least touch on it. First is a short piece by Paolo Cherchi Usai on the color processes most frequently used in both the United States and Europe for printing positive nitrate film stock during the silent period.[9] I chose this essay, rather than one of those better known on early apparatuses, because our current viewing experience of silent films so often comes from duped, black-and-white prints, either on 16-mm acetate film stock or on videocassette. That most of the silent film prints circulated throughout the world probably were colored in one way or another simply does not register in most existing film titles, whether available to the public for rental and purchase or accessible to researchers in archives. Cherchi Usai's essay reminds us of the significance for early cinema of color film processes (his example of Griffith's *The Lonedale Operator* [1911] is especially telling), from hand-coloring and stencil-coloring (a crucial Pathé trademark) to tinting and toning. And the significance of color contrasts (the idea comes from William Uricchio) may force us to reconsider our sense of early continuity editing. Implicitly, the essay also raises questions about the relative function of color to its use in other early twentieth-century forms of mass culture (for instance, illustrated magazines, postcards, and ads), as well as in the "high arts" of painting and theater. And it calls attention to a little used research source, the technical manuals issued by film stock manufacturers (Eastman Kodak, Pathé, Agfa Gevaert), which, in turn, can be linked to other manuals from the period—on film projection, cinematography, scriptwriting, and so forth—all of which acted as regulatory discourse in the cinema's industrialization.

The second essay, by Norman King, deals with a still largely ignored subject of research: the materiality of sound in early cinema. American researchers such as Gillian B. Anderson and Martin Marks recently have done excellent work in this area, but I have chosen King's essay for its relative brevity as well as for the range of questions it raises.[10] Although King offers a useful sketch of sound's presence throughout this period, his chief interest is in how "sound functioned *differently* in the silent era." Drawing on the filmmaker's own archives, he uses several Abel Gance productions to explore the range of sound-image relations in silent film, from a film's conception to its experience in the cinema.[11] Specifically, a film such as *La Roue* (1922) demonstrates that, during the process of scripting, shooting, and editing, a filmmaker's choice of music (whether or not specially composed for the occasion) could determine the "tonality" of a film's images as well as the "movement within the frame and cutting between frames." And, in France, this concept of musicality, of "the music of light," played an important role in some writers' and filmmakers' attempts to define a distinct aesthetics of film.[12] By contrast, the performance of *Napoléon* at the Paris Opéra in April 1927 demonstrates how music, dialogue, and declamation (in the "Marseillaise" sequence, for instance) could interpellate an audience, inviting them not to identify with a character but to participate, almost like extras, in an experience equating "production and performance." In other words, sound in the silent cinema could determine an audience's response to a film's images (as Marks has shown in his analysis of familiar lyrics and melodies used in specific American scores)[13] and could position the spectator as an active participant in a social event just as much as an absorbed, individualized observer. Moreover, such positioning would have been common, from the time when films were shown along with illustrated songs (and local singers) in nickelodeons.[14]

The third essay, by Mikhail Yampolsky, takes up a different kind of materiality in silent cinema, that of the actor's body. This subject has received a great deal of attention recently from those interested in the changing modes of film acting or the construction and circulation of film stars.[15] I have chosen Yampolsky's essay for several reasons: it exemplifies the fine work being done by Russian scholars on early cinema, as well as that in cross-cultural analysis, and it offers, by focusing on Lev Kuleshov, a model of how to negotiate the interface between film theory and film history. More specifically, it makes for a provocative comparison with Roberta Pearson's study of acting in Griffith's Biograph films, in that both

Griffith and Kuleshov take over a French theory of gesture and signification (drawn chiefly from F. A. Delsarte and J. Dalcroze), but much transformed within the context of two very different cultures. Yampolsky is particularly adept at tracing this "new anthropology of the actor" from the Russian theater (primarily through Sergei Volkonsky) to the postrevolutionary cinema and at situating Kuleshov, along with Vladimir Gardin, Valentin Turkin, and others, within the first Soviet film school (VFKO). And, in a detailed analysis of his writings and experiments, he convincingly shows how Kuleshov derived his theory of montage from a version of that "anthropology of the actor." Of the several issues that this essay raises, let me point to just one that demands further research: the Russian attempt to apply something like musical notation and segmentation to bodily rhythm, so that choreography not only became "a metamodel for the performing arts" but "an organizational principle in relation to montage." What are the implications of this linkage between music and movement (and, for some, emotion) for training actors as well as for educating viewers—that is, to borrow the language of Stuart Hall,[16] for the processes of encoding as well as decoding in the silent cinema?

Two other general subjects framing this volume are closely interrelated: the periodicity and nationality of silent cinema. As the essays just described suggest, the silent cinema was anything but homogeneous; its final commercial forms and practices in the late 1920s, for instance, looked almost nothing like those in the 1890s. The story of that transformation as narrated by historical writing on early cinema, however, has changed over the past twenty years. The evolutionary model of cinema history, which privileged either the European "art films" of the 1920s or the "classical Hollywood cinema" of the 1910s and 1920s, has been challenged by one of two models—that of "paradigm shifts" and "breaks" or that of uneven development (residual, dominant, emergent)—both of which tend to give value to what previously was marginalized.[17] According to these models, for instance, the "cinema of attractions" of the first decade is at least equal in interest to the narrative cinema that "supplanted" it, just as the one-reelers are to the feature-length films that began to predominate around 1914–1915. The same goes for the various "alternatives" that developed (as cultural practices rather than as "high art" forms) in parallel to the American continuity system. The worldwide dominance of the American cinema during the latter half of the silent era, of course, leads to the question of how pertinent the categories of "nation" and "national" (in the ideological as well as geographical sense) are for silent cinema. After all, the cinema often has been described as "international" in character before the Great War; yet it was then, arguably, that French films, especially those of Pathé-Frères, built up and then dominated an emerging global market. How did that French dominance play out within the historical context of rampant, competing nationalisms at the time, especially in the United States?[18] Was it any different, in the 1920s, when American dominance challenged countries such as France, Germany, and the Soviet Union to develop a national cinema through resistance or opposition? And in the related context of imperialism, how did the cinema emerge (and of what kind was it) in those countries that fell under one or more "colonial" spheres of influence?

Of the research concerned with questions of periodicity and nationality, again I have chosen four essays that take up those subjects in different ways—and included at least one other that touches on both. The first comes from Tom Gunning, who persistently has argued for a theoretical reconception of early cinema as a "cinema of attractions." This essay, one of his most recent, offers a summary of that argument over the past ten years, from the point when he and Gaudreault began to reformulate our assumptions about change and periodization in silent cinema history. The dominant, sometimes defining, element of early cinema before 1908, they argue, was not narrative or storytelling (however "primitive") but "attractions"—that is, spectacle or display. In other words, early cinema assumed venues of exhibition (from fairgrounds and parks to vaudeville houses and nickelodeons) that featured "novelties" foregrounding the act of display. Moreover, it assumed a particular form of address: rather than invoke a spectator's interest by posing and resolving an enigma, as narrative does, "the attraction directly address[ed] the spectator . . . seeking to quickly satisfy a curiosity." Yet Gunning's essay does more than recapitulate; it also extends this argument to explain how temporality functions differently in early cinema. Put simply, early cinema "arouse[d] a curiosity that [was] satisfied by surprise rather than narrative suspense . . . [by] a temporal irruption rather than a temporal development." In the cinema of attractions, consequently, the spectator's delight may have come "from the unpredictability of the instant, a succession of excitements and frustrations whose order [could] not be predicted by narrative logic and whose pleasures [were] never sure of being prolonged." Finally, Gunning also modifies his sense of a "rupture" between one kind of cinema and another around 1908 by arguing that silent cinema should be conceived as a perpetually shifting negotiation between "the desire to display" and "the desire to tell a story."

The second essay, by Charles Musser, posits a similar "break point," in 1907–1909, between what he calls the preclassical and classical cinema, but by focusing instead on "changing modes of film production." Here, Musser revises the ground-breaking typology of film production and its historical development in the United States offered by Janet Staiger in *The Classical Hollywood Cinema*.[19] Basically, Musser turns Staiger's four successive stages into two: a collaborative system in which cameraman and "stage director" worked in largely autonomous production units, and a central producer system that divided up the labor of production according to a hierarchy of organization (further division and reorganization, he agrees, follows that outlined by Staiger). Moreover, he contextualizes the change from one system of production to the other within a general transformation of the U.S. economy, from the structures of small-scale capitalism to those of modern corporate, industrial capitalism. And he, much like Gunning, not only aligns this "break point" with a "fundamental transformation in representation," in which the "self-sufficient narrative [film] text became dominant," but connects the representational techniques and collaborative filmmaking system of pre-1908 cinema with those of the various "avant-gardes" of the 1920s and beyond. Yet Musser's essay also makes an important distinction between the production of a film negative (which both his and Staiger's typology describe) and the delivery of that negative, as a commodity, to the consumer. For it was in the manufacture of positive film prints and in their projection in theaters that mass production, along with its standardization and "degradation of work," actually transformed the cinema. The real assembly-line workers in the industry (in contrast to those in the auto industry, for instance), whether female or male, were located in "the film laboratories, their finishing rooms, and the projection booths." With the coming of sound films, however, that too began to change, becoming more simplified and mechanized, particularly in the laboratory assembly of positive film prints.

Both Gunning and Musser, of course, concern themselves almost exclusively with the American cinema, implicitly writing the history of silent cinema within a national framework. But that writing will be different, depending on how we conceive of "national cinema" (as a viable epistemological category) and on which of the national cinemas we seek to map the coordinates.[20] The third essay, one of my own, tries to make a case for the historical specificity of early French cinema, but in ways that may be useful for mapping other national cinemas. First, there was the historical context of imperialism (or rival, expanding, "colonizing" economies), which put the emerging French and American cinema industries in competition, with the French economy setting certain conditions of policy and practice for its industries. Second, there were the specific social institutions and discursive systems that served to cement the social formation of the Third Republic into a nation-state, with a loosely related network of new mass cultural practices being unusually significant. Finally, and perhaps most uniquely, there were the contradictory categories that French law invoked to regulate the cinema, defining the production of film in terms of intellectual property but defining its exhibition in terms of *spectacles de curiosité* (subject to local censorship). That one of these definitions aligned the cinema with the theater and the other did not provoked "legitimizing" efforts within the industry to assert the cinema's autonomy as a form of mass culture and also give it a legal status commensurate with the "legitimate" theater. Supported by several prominent writers, these strategies of legitimation led to the adoption of a "theater analogy," which seems to have differentiated the French cinema from most other national cinemas. One thing this essay suggests, then, is that the discourses of regulation (for instance, those of censorship, the control of fire and illness, the organization of the labor force, the use and circulation of property or commodities) may crucially determine our conception of a particular national cinema during the silent era.

The fourth essay in this group, written by Heide Schlüpmann (and exemplary of recent work by German scholars on silent cinema), examines the German cinema industry during its point of transition (1909–1914) from a cinema of attractions to a narrative cinema. Schlüpmann first conceptualizes early German cinema as a site of negotiation between consumption (initially the dominant component) and production, between the discourse of moral reform (associated with the educated bourgeoisie) and that of mass culture. But this then is reframed so that the cinema becomes central to a clash of public "spheres" defined more precisely in terms of class and gender. Drawing implicitly on Oskar Negt and Alexander Kluge's reformulation of Jurgen Habermas's concept of the "public sphere" (most fully articulated elsewhere by Miriam Hansen), Schlüpmann argues that the German cinema during this period "took on the characteristics of an oppositional public sphere" in which "women and the 'little people' such as workers and office employees . . . constituted the [primary] audience."[21] Certain genres such as the *Autorenfilme* (adaptations from the theater) and melodramas in which "women appear[ed] as male projection" had the support of the moral reformers in their efforts to exercise some control over this audience. But others such as the social drama, which "accommodated women's interests in self-thematization" and "the thematization of domestic female life," could elicit desires and demands that ran counter to that control. In the social drama, then, an actress such as Asta Nielsen came to serve a dual role: although still "cultivat[ing] erotic attraction for the male gaze," she more importantly "placed herself on show in her social role" for women, even "standing in for the gaze of a female spectator." In its focus on genre, gender, and class within a national cinema, Schlüpmann's essay correlates well with several later essays in this volume, but it also points to other recent work in theorizing the history of a national cinema—perhaps most notably, *Streetwalking on a Ruined Map* (1993), Giuliana Bruno's elegant study of Elvira Notari and early Italian cinema.

The last two general subjects framing this volume also are closely connected: early cinema's relation to other contemporaneous cultural forms, and intertextuality and reception in silent cinema. As the previous two essays suggest, whatever the site of its emergence and the trajectory of its development, early cinema was enmeshed in a wide range of already existing cultural practices, perhaps most notably those of variety or vaudeville and melodrama theater. Rick Altman's essay offers a provocative introduction to the problems of theorizing such a cultural history of early cinema. His starting point is Sergei Eisenstein's famous essay, which used the work of Dickens and Griffith to create a theoretical paradigm of narrative construction linking the cinema to the nineteenth-century novel.[22] Repressed in this paradigm, Altman argues, was a much more direct link between the cinema and nineteenth-century theater, and specifically popular melodrama (which often included adaptations of novels), both in the United States and Europe. This essay does more than recover a lost moment of historical conjuncture, however, for it raises questions about how we, in cinema studies, have come to theorize the dominant mode of "classical" narrative cinema. Even those such as Thompson who acknowledge the influence of late nineteenth-century theater on early cinema, Altman writes, ultimately ignore the significance of popular melodrama theater, especially its mix of visual spectacle and narrative action, to the development of a "classical Hollywood cinema."[23] Indeed, the secularized, dualistic moral universe so characteristic of melodrama could be said to constitute a crucial precondition of Hollywood cinema, functioning as an "unconscious" determinant of the character-based causality and linear progression so familiar to recently advanced, widely accepted notions of film narrative. Altman's essay suggests then, together with Gunning's, a compelling need for further research "in tracing the interrelation of attractions [or spectacle] and narrative organization," especially in the classical cinema of the 1910s and 1920s.[24]

A second essay, by Ben Singer, offers a more specific, gender-based model of cultural history, focusing on the American serial-queen melodramas of the 1910s. Singer first situates these serial films in relation to nineteenth-century sensational melodramas as opposed to family melodramas, in the latter of which the mother serves as an emblem of domesticity.[25] But his principal task is to analyze the serial-queen heroine (who is anything but a mother) as a contradictory figure of female prowess and female imperilment. On the one hand, such heroines (exemplified perhaps best by Pearl White) embodied a radical transformation in the social construction of womanhood at the turn of the century, symbolized in the icon of the "New Woman." Moreover, they had an array of precursors, in all sorts of popular entertainments—dime novels, magazine stories, newspaper *fait divers*, and "stunt articles"—as well as in the feminist discourse of women's suffrage. On the other hand, these heroines also embodied, sometimes in graphic detail, the lurid victimization of helpless women by male villains so basic to the iconography of sensational melodrama. Yet there was a difference: the serial queen belonged to the upper or professional middle class (rather than the working class), and the violence or threat of violence that she endured seemed "necessary" to her emancipation. In other words, Singer argues, "the genre capture[d] the basically paradoxical nature of female experience" at the time, celebrating "the excitement of the woman's attainment of unprecedented mobility outside the confines of the home" as well as envisioning "the dangers of this departure." In its conclusion, the essay also raises questions about the reception of these films, suggesting that "present-day theoretical models of spectatorship" may not account fully for how they were read. Other models need to be theorized, then, to analyze the genre's largely female audience (perhaps in comparison with Schlüpmann's analysis of German social drama), as well as the differences within that audience, for it would have been far from homogeneous.

The essay by Yuri Tsivian explores a different kind of cultural history involving early Russian cinema.[26] Tsivian draws on a broad spectrum of observers, writing in 1913, to deftly sketch cinema's inscription into the "cultural landscape" of Russia during the decade preceding the 1917 and 1918 revolutions. Teasing out a web of interconnections within those writings, he constructs a cultural world in which historical coincidence— aligning the cinema with the popular variety theater, scandalous Futurist texts and performances, and the tango dance craze—turns into historical convergence "in the 'real space' of culture." The short-act format of variety theaters, for instance, was so conflated with that of cinemas that the two became nearly interchangeable between 1911 and 1916 (before the advent of feature films). Although jealously critical of the cinema's popularity, epitomized by Max Linder's visit to Saint Petersburg and Moscow in late 1913, Futurist writers such as Khlebnikov and Mayakovsky often found themselves tagged as mere perpetrators of "literary slapstick"; yet they were not above using the cinema "to challenge narrative time" in their own texts and to promote their trademark "face-painting." To crown his Russian tour, Linder also worked up a comic act culminating in an elaborate tango routine, inadvertantly importing the latest "fad fresh from Paris," which quickly became a featured attraction in both variety theaters and cinemas as well as the subject of public debates. Here, Tsivian is especially skillful in uncovering Russian interpretations of the tango's controlled sexuality (one of which surprisingly drew on Freud) and in suggesting the dance's pervasive effect on Russian film through a specific style of acting often associated with Evgenii Bauer—the so-called "braking school [of] pause-pause-pause acting." In the end, this tightly articulated essay sketches a cultural history strikingly different from that offered by Yampolsky's study of Kuleshov.

If all three previous essays touch on issues of intertextuality and reception in silent cinema, the last three in this volume take up the subject in earnest. Whether constituted as cultural "text" or "event," early cinema derived its meaning, at any specific historical moment, according to the sets of intertextual relations available to one audience or another (the nexus of knowledge and expectations they brought with them) as well as according to the "social text" of those audiences (with their differing desires and interests). Such a framework of inquiry into the silent cinema invites certain kinds of questions. Who actually went to the cinema, where and when, according to what social categories (class, gender, race or ethnicity, generation, religion), and for what reasons? In the practice of everyday life, what determined the range and availability of interpretive positions as well as the specific "choices" people made—whether those could be described either as "dominant or marginalized" or as "preferred, negotiated, and opposi-tional"? What use value did "going to the cinema" have for them, and how is that to be theorized, whether as pleasure, distraction, education, or communality (the neighborhood nickelodeon as "social center")? Doing history this way, Staiger reminds us, has as one of its tasks to produce "a historical explanation of the activities of interpretation" or an analysis of "historical *reading strategies,*"[27] whether one focuses on a specific film or set of films, a particular venue of exhibition or forum of discourse, or certain social categories of spectators.

The first of these last essays, by Uricchio and Pearson, aptly focuses on intertextuality as "an essential component of the conditions of recep-tion" in early American cinema.[28] It is from Tony Bennett and Janet Woollacott that the two writers chiefly derive their concept of inter-textuality—and the dialectical interaction of text, intertext, and context—to construct the "reading positions" or "interpretive stances" available to an audience at a particular historical moment. For their examples, Uricchio and Pearson use two 1908 Vitagraph "quality films," *Francesca da Rimini* and *Julius Caesar*, to explore first the interaction of text/intertext and then that of intertext/context. *Francesca da Rimini* allows them to tease out a network of intertexts (Dante's epic, plays, poems, paintings, public lectures, magazine articles, postcards, and calendars) that suggest an array of possible interpretive stances but "for a fairly restricted group of readers/viewers" defined largely by class. *Julius Caesar*, by contrast, because of the much wider circulation of Shakespeare intertexts and their centrality to turn-of-the-century American culture and education, lets the writers "look at the variations in particular intertexts . . . which circulated among different social formations" and conditioned the reception of particular social groups. In New York, for instance, "business- and leisure-class viewers" may have responded to the scenes of spectacle in the film, which imitated the current fashion of theatrical staging with which they were familiar. But the city's slum tenement viewers may have responded instead to the film's "key phrase, key image approach to Shakespeare," which dominated the public school system as well as the recitals and "bare stage" productions sponsored by the People's Institute and the Educational Alliance. Such films raise other questions as well, given the "Americanization" debate at the time: to what degree would *Francesca da Rimini*, for instance, promote the value of an Italian heritage (especially for certain immigrants) but also confirm anti-Italian feelings in others?

The final two essays extend this research on audience, spectator-ship, and reception into the 1920s. The first, by Mary Carbine, takes up the issue of black spectatorship during the silent era, a subject largely neglected by historians of cinema because, until recently, their theoretical models (unlike those dealing with contemporary mass culture) tended to "downplay the possibility that minority groups can use commercial entertainment in culturally specific ways."[29] Carbine focuses on the city of Chicago, to which southern blacks migrated in great numbers between 1890 and 1920, creating an "immigrant" urban population distinct from, yet parallel to, those of the widely discussed European immigrants in New York and elsewhere. Drawing on oral histories and the black press of the period (especially *The Defender*), she locates the black entertainment district, the "Stroll," on South State Street, and singles out the ways that people "exercised tactical consumption, incorporating motion pictures into specifically African-American cultural practices." Generally, it was the musical performances on stage that attracted black audiences to the movie theaters and vaudeville houses (which whites did not patronize), especially once Chicago became a major showcase for blues and jazz musicians. But the press discourse on that music also exposed class differences within the city's black community and questions about the relationship between that music and the projected films (nearly all of them commercial Hollywood products). Dave Peyton, a prominent pit orchestra leader, for instance, wrote a *Defender* column counseling "Race orchestras" on the principles of "correct performance" in movie theaters, including the use of the industry's cue sheets. His frequent criticisms of "inappropriate" music, however, reveals that many theaters "integrated" blues and jazz into the music accompanying their films, creating "reading positions" very different from those available in the mainstream cinemas as well as audiences whose active participation differed sharply from those described by Norman King for *Napoléon* in Paris.

Gaylyn Studlar's essay is one of the few to deal explicitly with the significance of the American cinema industry's assumption that, by the 1920s (if not long before),[30] women comprised its principal audience. Her strategy is to examine neither the films themselves nor the usual discursive traces of that audience but the fan magazine as "a neglected source [or intertext] for assessing how women were positioned as viewers/readers/consumers within discources specifically aimed at influencing women's reception of Hollywood film." In "selling stars" to women readers, of course, *Photoplay, Motion Picture Magazine, Picture Play,* and others were constructing and reconstructing notions of femininity and models of female subjectivity. The process of that (re)construction, however, was anything but simple. Although fan magazines, for instance, perpetuated an illusion of intimacy with the stars (with whom readers were encouraged to identify), they also offered a continual demystification of the star-making process. The sense of female subjectivity they inscribed, consequently, was "hardly passive and mindlessly consumerist" but distanced as well as intimate, skeptical as well as empathetic, and highly active—perhaps marked, much as the serial-queen melodrama had been before the war, "by women's growing economic and sexual emancipation" in the 1920s. In that it encouraged a "playful" kind of "masquerade," Studlar argues, this sense of subjectivity complicates the model of female spectatorship advanced by theorists such as Mary Ann Doane.[31] Ultimately, however, despite their willingness to address "controversial issues (flapperdom, bobbed hair, careers for women)" and satisfy certain transgressive desires and behavior, she concludes, fan magazines did tend "to channel women into ethnically, racially, and nationally normative models of heterosexual romance" or the "triple whammy," to quote Diane Waldman, of "marriage, romance, and consumerism."[32]

By way of a conclusion, let me summarize several points from a recent essay by Hansen that provocatively aligns the cinema of the past turn of the century with that of our own.[33] In line with that essay, this volume has sought not only to challenge the hegemony of "classical Hollywood cinema" and the construction of "canonical" film texts (a challenge now widespread, for instance, within the Society for Cinema Studies) but to recover the radical changes that marked early cinema to better understand those that have transformed our own cinema over the past two decades. For the preclassical cinema may be more closely related to a postclassical cinema than to a classical cinema, the parallels between them condensing most sharply around modes of film consumption and spectatorship.[34] Despite the historical differences between one turn of the century and the other, those parallels make sense, Hansen argues, "not only because of formal similarities in the relations of representation and reception . . . [but] because both moments mark a major transition in the development of the public sphere."[35] Here, the selected essays of Schlüpmann, Singer, Carbine, and Studlar can be linked with Hansen's in their suggestions of a potentially critical, utopian public sphere, a theorized space within which the cinema, however transformed, can "function as a matrix for challenging social positions of identity and otherness, a catalyst for new forms of community and solidarity." To study early cinema, and the different ways it could have developed, therefore, is to see more clearly that postmodern media culture may be characterized by a similar opening-up of new directions and possibilities and that it is imperative that we intervene on the side of promoting their development.

In closing, I want to thank in particular Tom Gunning, Miriam Hansen, Charles Musser, Roberta Pearson, Janet Staiger, and William Uricchio for their guidance in compiling a potential list of essays from which to choose for this volume and in debating various principles by which the essays could be selected and organized. I also want to thank Charles and Mirella Affron and Robert Lyons, the general editors of this series, for graciously agreeing to accept changes that I made in organizing the volume. Thanks as well to Leslie Mitchner and Marilyn Campbell, Editor-in-Chief and Managing Editor, respectively, at Rutgers University Press, for their generous unstinting support and to Peter Strupp and his team at Princeton Editorial Associates for coping so efficiently with the demanding task of copyediting. Regrettably, several essays that could and otherwise would have been reprinted have not been included here because of space limitations. For the same reason, some illustrations accompanying original essays had to be cut. Despite such inevitable restrictions, responsibility for the volume is mine alone. I only hope that these essays, whether taken singly or in combination, will encourage further research on the silent cinema as well as new strategies of intervention—around such issues as transmission and access, representation and reception—in our own present moment of media transformation.

NOTES

1. See, for instance, François Valleiry, "Les Cinématographes de Paris," *Phono-Ciné-Gazette* 49 (1 April 1907), 131; and "Moving Picture Industry Great," *Show World* 1 (29 June 1907), 28.

2. The proceedings of each Domitor conference are published by the time of the subsequent conference. See the bibliography at the end of this volume for the two already published in 1992 and 1995.

3. Patricia Mellencamp, "Introduction," in Patricia Mellencamp and Philip Rosen, eds., *Cinema Histories, Cinema Practices* (Frederick, Maryland: University Publications of America, 1984), pp. ix–xiv.

4. Annual catalogs and special issues of *Griffithiana* have been published in conjunction with the Pordenone Silent Film Festival at least since 1986. For a selected list of the catalogs, see the bibliography at the end of this volume.

5. In the United States, archives at UCLA, the Museum of Modern Art, the George Eastman House, and elsewhere frequently have showcased newly restored silent films.

6. In The Netherlands, for instance, both Thomas Elsaesser and William Uricchio are developing projects that cross disciplinary boundaries—see Elsaesser, "What Might We Mean by Media History?," *GBG Nieuws* 28 (Spring 1994), 19–25, and "New Professor in Film and Television History," *IAMHIST Newsletter* (Winter 1993/Spring 1994), 9–13.

7. Peter Burke, "Overture: The New History," in P. Burke, ed., *New Perspectives on Historical Writing* (London: Polity Press, 1991), 14.

8. Space limitations have kept me from including a general essay on silent film exhibition, but I can point to recent research by Douglas Gomery, Robert Allen (Manhattan), Gregory Waller (Lexington), and others in the United States as well as that of Jean-Jacques Meusy (Paris) and Nicholas Hiley in England. And I can single out work-in-progress by Ben Singer and Roberta Pearson (with Uricchio) on New York nickelodeons, along with that of André Gaudreault (studying the unique persistence of lecturers, and their function, in Québec).

9. Another more theoretical, wide-ranging essay on color and film is Jacques Aumont's "La Trace et sa couleur," *Cinémathèque* 2 (November 1992), 6–24. Color has been the subject of two recent events: the "Color and the Silent Cinema" Conference, Udine, Italy, 23–25 March 1995; and the 1995 Nederlands Filmmuseum Workshop, Amsterdam, the Netherlands, 26–29 July 1995.

10. Anderson, for instance, points to a glaring omission in scholarly work on film music, "*The American Organist*, a primary source for the study of the musical presentation of silent films [between 1918 and 1930]." See Anderson, "The Presentation of Silent Films, or Music

as Anaesthesia," *The Journal of Musicology* 5 (1987), 257–8. Rick Altman's current research also focuses on the standardization of sound practices during the silent period—see, for instance, "Naissance de la réception classique: La campagne pour standardiser le son," *Cinémathèque* 6 (1994), 98–111.

11. The Abel Gance Archives, along with those of René Clair, Jean Grémillon, Léon Moussinac, and others are housed in the Département des Arts du Spectacle of the Bibliothèque Nationale in Paris. Sound will be the primary subject of the Fifth International Domitor Conference in 1998.

12. For an extensive analysis of this and other French attempts to define a distinct aesthetics of film, see Richard Abel, *French Film Theory and Criticism: A History/Anthology, I, 1907–1929* (Princeton, N.J.: Princeton University Press, 1988).

13. Marks developed this analysis in remarks to questions following a paper presentation at the Society for Cinema Studies Conference, Los Angeles, 25 May 1991—remarks that did not get incorporated into "The First American Film Scores," *Harvard Library Bulletin* 2:4 (1991), 78–100. See, also, his *Film Music of the Silent Period, 1895–1924* (forthcoming from Oxford University Press).

14. In 1911, Mary Heaton Vorse also described nickelodeon audiences in New York as participatory, especially in the way spectators talked to one another during the screenings (is there a suggestive analogy to television audiences here?)—see Vorse, "Some Picture Show Audiences," *The Outlook* 98 (24 June 1911), 441–7. Thanks to Antonia Lant for drawing my attention to the Vorse essay.

15. See, for instance, Richard Dyer, *Stars* (London: British Film Institute, 1982); Miriam Hansen, "Pleasure, Ambivalence, Identification: Valentino and Female Spectatorship," *Cinema Journal* 26:3 (Spring 1987), 6–32; James Naremore, *Acting in the Cinema* (Berkeley: University of California Press, 1988); Gaylyn Studlar, "Discourses of Gender and Ethnicity: The Construction and De(con)struction of Rudolph Valentino as Other," *Film Criticism* 13:2 (Winter 1989), 18–35; Richard deCordova, *Picture Personalities: The Emergence of the Star System in America* (Urbana: University of Illinois Press, 1990); and Virginia Wright Wexman, *Creating the Couple: Love, Marriage, and Hollywood Performance* (Princeton, N.J.: Princeton University Press, 1993).

16. Stuart Hall, "Encoding, Decoding," in Simon During, ed., *The Cultural Studies Reader* (London: Routledge, 1993), pp. 90–103.

17. The model of "paradigm shifts" and "breaks" generally derives from either Thomas Kuhn or Michel Foucault; that of "uneven development," from Raymond Williams.

18. My own current research seeks to address this question: see Abel, "The Perils of Pathé, or the Americanization of Early American Cinema," in Leo Charney and Vanessa Schwartz, eds., *Cinema and the Invention of Modern Life* (Berkeley:University of California Press, 1996).

19. Staiger's typology of film production includes the "cameraman" system (1896–1907), the "director" system (1907–1909), the "director-unit" system (1909–1914), and the "central producer" system (1914–1931)—David Bordwell, Janet Staiger, Kristin Thompson, *The Classical Hollywood Cinema*, (New York:Columbia University Press, 1985) pp. 113–141. See, also, "Dialogue: Janet Staiger and Matthew Bernstein on Hollywood's Semi-Independent Production," *Cinema Journal* 33:2 (Winter 1994), 56–63.

20. Although Musser nearly erases Staiger's "director" and "director-unit" systems of production from the American cinema industry, for instance, those "modes of production" may characterize quite accurately the emerging industries in other countries—as I myself have tried to argue for French cinema, in Richard Abel, *The Ciné Goes to Town*, (Berkeley:University of California Press, 1994), pp. 21–22, 35–36, and 48. See, also, the special issue of *Quarterly Review of Film and Video* 14:3 (1993), entitled "Mediating the National" and edited by Marcia Butzel and Ana López.

21. See the bibliography at the end of this volume for specific references to Hansen's work.

22. Sergei Eisenstein, "Dickens, Griffith, and the Film Today [1944]," in Jay Leyda, ed., *Film Form* (New York: Harcourt, Brace, & World, 1949), pp. 195–255.

23. See, especially, Thompson, "From Primitive to Classical," in Bordwell et al., *The Classical Hollywood Cinema*, pp. 163–173. Others, of course, have focused on the relation between nineteenth-century theater and early cinema—see, for instance, A. Nicholas Vardac, *Stage to Screen, Theatrical Origins of Early Film: David Garrick to D. W. Griffith* (Cambridge, Mass.: Harvard University Press, 1949); and Peter Brooks, *The Melodramatic Imagination: Balzac, James, Melodrama and the Mode of Excess* (New Haven, Conn.: Yale University Press, 1976).

24. For two different trajectories of research on "the interrelation of spectacle and story" in American silent cinema, see Sumiko Higashi, *Cecil B. DeMille and American Culture* (Berkeley: University of California Press, 1994) and Ben Brewster and Lea Jacobs, *Pictorial Effect and Narrative Cinema: Early Filmmaking and Nineteenth-Century Theatre* (forthcoming from Oxford University Press).

25. See, also Singer's "Modernity, Hyper-Stimulus, and the Rise of Popular Sensationalism," in L. Charney and V. Schwartz, eds., *Cinema and the Invention of Modern Life* (Berkeley: University of California Press, 1995).

26. Tsivian wrote this essay for a special issue of *Griffithiana* 50 (May 1994), which was coordinated with the 1993 Pordenone retrospective of 1913 films.

27. Janet Staiger, *Interpreting Films: Studies in the Historical Reception of American Cinema* (Princeton, N.J.: Princeton University Press, 1991), pp. 95, 212.

28. See, also, R. Pearson and W. Uricchio's *Reframing Culture: The Case of the Vitagraph Quality Films* (Princeton, N.J.: Princeton University Press, 1993). For an equally fine introduction that formulates a slightly different concept of intertextuality and covers a fuller range of cinema history in the United States, see "Toward a Historical Materialist Approach to Reception Studies," in Staiger, *Interpreting Films*, pp. 79–97.

29. One of the only other exceptions to this neglect is Gregory Waller's analysis of Lexington, Kentucky, in "Another Audience: Black Moviegoing, 1907–1916," *Cinema Journal* 31:2 (Winter 1992), 3–25.

30. In the United States, the nickelodeon boom, for instance, had been attributed to "the patronage [of] women and children"—see "The Propriety of Film Subjects," *Views and Films Index* (11 May 1907), 3.

31. See, for instance, Mary Ann Doane, "Film and the Masquerade: Theorising the Female Spectator," *Screen* 23 (September–October 1982), 74–87; and *The Desire to Desire: The Woman's Film of the 1940s* (Bloomington: Indiana University Press, 1987). See, also, *Camera Obscura* 20–21 (1990)—a special issue, edited by Janet Bergstrom and Mary Ann Doane, entitled "The Spectatrix."

32. Diane Waldman, "From Midnight Shows to Wedding Vows," *Wide Angle* 6:2 (1984), 40–48.

33. Hansen's essay, "Early Cinema, Late Cinema: Permutations of the Public Sphere (1993)," can be found in another volume of the "Depth of Field" series, Linda Williams's *Viewing Positions: Ways of Seeing Film* (New Brunswick, N.J.: Rutgers University Press, 1994). For another provocative study that situates the emergence of cinema within the historical development of "a *mobilized virtual gaze*" now dominant in our own postmodern condition, see Anne Friedberg, *Window Shopping: Cinema and the Postmodern* (Berkeley: University of California Press, 1993).

34. For two particularly fine studies of postclassical cinema, see Timothy Corrigan, *A Cinema without Walls: Movies and Culture after Vietnam* (New Brunswick, N.J.: Rutgers University Press, 1991); and Jim Collins, Ada Collins and Hilary Radner , eds., *Film Theory Goes to the Movies* (New York: Routledge, 1993).

Richard Abel

35. Friedberg focuses on one of the primary challenges to Hansen's argument: once restricted to the public sphere, "the mobilized and virtual gaze" now has penetrated the private sphere (through the VCR and fiber optics cable or direct broadcasting satellites, through the home computer and the Internet communications "superhighway") and become "a fundamental feature of everyday life"—*Window Shopping*, pp. 2–5. For another version of this challenge, see David Trend, "Rethinking Media Activism: Why the Left Is Losing the Culture War," *Social Text* 23:2 (1993), 5–33.

The Materiality of
Silent Cinema

Paolo Cherchi Usai

The Color of Nitrate:
Some Factual Observations on
Tinting and Toning Manuals
for Silent Films

Blanche Sweet, playing the daughter of a station master, stands before two bandits in a train depot. Alone in one of the most isolated spots of the West, she must protect herself and the money that has been left to her charge. Her last chance is to try a stratagem. She turns off the light and hides herself, pretending that the nickel-plated monkey wrench she holds is really a gun, hoping to deceive the burglars in the semi-darkness. Her ruse succeeds. The glint of the metal object in the pale moonlight confuses the tramps, and their hesitation allows time for the girl's fiancé to arrive for the providential last-minute rescue. Such is the happy ending of THE LONEDALE OPERATOR (23 March 1911), the well-known one-reeler by D. W. Griffith, described by the Biograph Bulletin *as being "without doubt the most thrilling picture ever produced."*[1]

When viewing most of the existing copies of the film, one is puzzled by the climax of the plot. The tool in Blanche Sweet's hands is easily recognizable, and it seems absurd that her antagonists would fall for the trick. In fact, it is the modern viewer who is deceived. Most reference copies of *The Lonedale Operator* are in black and white and are therefore missing one fundamental detail. When the young woman turns off the light in the original version, the film is suddenly tinted a deep blue, which simulates the darkness of night. This *trompe-l'oeil* effect is pivotal to the plot and renders the heroine's quick-thinking improvisation credible.

From *Image* 34:1–2 (Spring/Summer 1991). Reprinted by permission of the author and *Image*, George Eastman House, 1994. Unfortunately, it has been too costly to reproduce the color illustrations.

Such visual invention was common during the age of silent cinema. As a matter of fact, it was estimated in 1920 that about eighty to ninety percent of all films produced in the United States toward the end of the 1910s were entirely or partially colored.[2] It is not surprising that, given the prevalence of color, most feature film scripts from the silent period contain precise instructions as to which scenes should be colored in order to clarify the narrative or enhance the dramatic situation. These colors had specific connotations: bright red was used for fire or a scene of passion; light amber, when a table light was turned on in a room; green suggested an idyllic rural life; and so on.

How can we begin to reconstruct the color in these early films when they are preserved in black and white and the technologies of tinting have long since disappeared?

Fortunately, primary documentation on this aspect of film production does exist. Technical manuals provide some of the best information. Volumes were published in France, Germany, and the United States in the late 1910s and throughout the 1920s, containing instructions on the techniques of film tinting during the silent era. Most of these books, published by the producers of film stock (Eastman Kodak Company, Gevaert, and Pathé), are preserved in the Richard and Ronay Menschel Library at George Eastman House. They contain not only technical information on the coloring systems used at the time by the motion picture industry but also include sets of illustrations made of actual pieces of original nitrate film. Through these fragments, it is possible to study in detail how production companies developed a true aesthetics of color.

The oldest known manual with color illustrations has no date on the title page, but it was probably distributed around 1916 by the Eastman Kodak Company of Rochester, New York, under the title *Tinting and Toning of Eastman Positive Motion Picture Film*.[3] This hardcover volume contains 31 pages and eight cardboard tables with forty-five double frames of 35mm nitrate film, arranged according to coloring technique and the shade of dye used. The success this book enjoyed with its specialized audience, along with the steady improvement of these techniques, led Eastman Kodak to produce three further editions of this work in 1918, 1922 (reprinted in 1924), and finally in 1927, at the twilight of the silent period.

The example of the Eastman Kodak Company manuals was followed by at least two other manufacturers of nitrate film stock. In Belgium and Germany, Agfa Gevaert distributed a table of illustrations containing a small number of film samples,[4] as well as a manual whose contents are similar to those in the Eastman Kodak books. Another volume, published in Paris in 1926, *Le film vierge Pathé* had wider distribution in Europe; only a relatively small section of the Pathé text deals with film coloring, but the three foldout cardboard tables of illustrations with 107 individual nitrate frames are the most complete ever published.

These books, together with a handful of other primary sources, constitute the basis of our knowledge of a relatively neglected topic in the study of early cinema: the effects achieved by coloring film stock.[5] Before the acceptance of Technicolor in the mid-1920s, there were four basic techniques of film coloring: hand coloring, coloring by stencil, tinting, and toning. A fifth method, mordanting, can be considered a modified version of the toning process. Other early attempts at additive color processes, such as George Albert Smith's Kinemacolor (1906–1908) and Gaumont's Chronochrome (1912), never moved from the experimental stage into the commercial market. Therefore the study of these four techniques yields an understanding of the basic technology of color during the silent era.

Hand Coloring
___

The earliest known example of a hand-colored motion picture is *Les Dernières Cartouches* (Georges Hatot, 1896–97). It was produced by the Lumière Brothers not long after their Cinématographe premiered on December 28, 1895, at the Grand Café in Paris.[6]

In this early film, the color was applied directly onto the print. This required a special bench fitted with an aperture the size of a single frame. The image was lit from below, viewed through the magnification of a lens, and advanced frame by frame by means of a foot pedal. An aniline dye was spread over the frame with a tiny brush. When the foot pedal was pressed, the next image appeared, and the worker repeated the same strike of color until the scene was finished. The film was then rewound, and another worker would begin to color another area of the film with a different dye.

A trained hand could move the brush rhythmically and very rapidly. The major problem was the fact that the spot of color had to follow the movements of the figure across the frame. It was also important to ensure that the shape and intensity of the brushstroke remained constant.

The films colored with such systems often had—and still do, insofar as they have been preserved—the flamboyant beauty of medieval miniatures. However, the production of these hand-tinted films could never be organized on an industrial basis. The cost of producing colored prints was only partially justified by the demand of the exhibition market. Thus, for some time, the most expensive films were sold in both black-and-white and color versions, especially in France.[7]

Stencil Coloring

In 1906 coloring by hand was gradually replaced by a mechanical system, similar to contemporary techniques of wallpaper and postcard color printing. This system, known as "stencil coloring," had two distinct steps. The first required cutting a different stencil for each color. These stencils were then used in a machine that automatically applied the color to the positive print.

Typically, a film required three to six stencils. At first, the cutting was done manually, using a cutting edge or a sharp needle on each frame. It was a difficult and time-consuming operation, but its advantage was that it needed to be done only once for each color to be applied. The stencils were then immersed in hypochlorite, which functioned as a degelatinizing agent. This treatment permitted the color to be applied more easily, without scratching the final print, or shrinking or embrittling the stencil.

Manual cutting rapidly became obsolete in favor of a semiautomatic device similar to a sewing machine, with the cutting needle operated by an A.C. electromagnet. At least two patents for this system are known. In a further stage of development, the technician no longer cut the matrix directly but worked instead on a parallel bench with a reference print. The area to be stenciled was traced with a stylus connected through a pantograph to a cutting needle that followed the identical contours on a strip of raw film stock. To ensure that the stencil cut precisely matched the actual shape of the area to be colored, the cutting needle worked only when the stylus was touching the film. A late development of this technique, relatively common around the mid-1920s, involved the use of a series of enlarged images instead of a reference print. These methods were widely used until the end of the silent period.

Such a complex system required the employment of highly specialized personnel. Several weeks of training were necessary to make sure that the technician could prepare the stencils in the most precise and effective way. Even then, the most skilled worker could not cut more than 3 feet of stencil an hour. Despite the fact that a stylus and a pantograph allowed for the use of raw stock, thus avoiding the degelatinizing process, it was periodically necessary to stop and verify the result. Moreover, when substantial portions of the frame were to be cut, manual cutting was still preferred. In such cases, alternate frames were cut from two separate stencils, because a single stencil would have been too fragile for repeated use.[8]

The second phase in the stencil coloring process, the application of color, was almost completely mechanical. In most coloring machines, a sprocket system matched the matrix to the black-and-white print. All the copies of a particular scene were joined and matched with the stencil, which rotated in a continuous loop. The aniline dye was then spread on the film by a loop of velvet moving in a direction opposite that of the advancing film. This band was fed past a rotating brush immersed in a tank of dye; the amount of dye transferred from the rotating brush to the velvet band was adjustable depending on the depth of the brush in the tank. In order to ensure uniformity, the velvet band colored three frames at a time.[9] As the film was rewound immediately, apparently no drying time was needed. If a mistake was made, the color could be washed out, leaving the base ready for another treatment.

This system was used throughout the 1920s[10] and survived until the dawn of the sound era. Less than 2 years after the invention of the stencil system, however, this method was combined with other techniques of film coloring, nowadays summarized under the terms *tinting* and *toning*. The earliest example I have found of this use of combined techniques is a nitrate fragment from a Gaumont film presumably made around 1908, tentatively identified as *Roi Midas*.[11]

Tinting

Tinting is a method of applying color to the surface of the film without altering the physical structure of the emulsion. Two details characterize a tinted nitrate print: the entire picture is colored uniformly, and the area around the perforations is also colored.

The oldest method of tinting is nothing more than a variation on the hand-coloring technique. Instead of applying the color to a portion of each frame, the whole print was brushed with color. This method can be recognized by the varying density of the dye on the print. An early example can be seen in the fragment of an unidentified Gaumont film. The distinctive shape of the frame and perforations, as well as other written evidence, indicates that this film may have been produced in late 1902 and certainly predates 1905. This demonstrates that the first attempts at tinting positive film stock in western Europe were made quite early.[12]

In most tinted films produced during the silent era, the color was applied on the emulsion side of the film, most often using aniline dyes in a solution of water. Aniline dyes are coal tar-based synthetic dyes that are water soluble and, unfortunately, light fugitive. Dyes were sought that would not affect the stability of the gelatin layer and were sufficiently stable to withstand the effects of heat and light from repeated projection.

Only carefully processed prints would yield a relatively permanent tint. Films to be tinted had to be printed with slightly more contrast. A rotating chassis system, tanks, or vertical tubes were used for applying the color. This last system was thought to provide the best control over the uniformity of the tint.

In some cases, it was even possible to provide a gradual transition from one color to another (for example, from blue to amber, in order to show the coming of daylight). Such a delicate operation, however, had to be supervised manually and always remained an exception. Usually, the transition from one tint to the next was abrupt and entailed splicing together two separate strips of film.[13]

When tinting was combined with other coloring techniques, for example, with toning or stencil coloring, technical difficulties often occurred. Since toning always preceded tinting, the process of tinting the film stock could sometimes alter the toning dye substantially. These inconveniences led the Eastman Kodak Company and Pathé to manufacture and distribute a new kind of tinting stock during the 1920s. Besides ensuring very uniform tinting, this stock proved to be very stable when immersed in fixing, toning, and mordanting baths. Furthermore, the colors were not altered by the heat and light of projection equipment, not even after several dozen screenings. In 1926 Pathé offered a choice of nine raw film stocks for tinting.

Toning

A more sophisticated range of color variations could be obtained through toning. The print was immersed in a chemical bath that substituted a colored compound for the silver in the emulsion. This dyed only the darker areas of the image, leaving the rest of the gelatin completely transparent. It is, therefore, easy to identify a toned print by the fact that the perforated edges are not colored and the light parts of the image appear white.

The toning dye was a colored metallic salt. Toning was accomplished either in a single dye bath (direct toning) or in two baths. In the latter case, the silver of the emulsion was replaced first by an uncolored salt, then by a pigmented salt. The original photographic image had to be extremely sharp; any haziness or nebulosity could jeopardize the final result.

Mordanting, or dye fixing, was a variation of the toning procedure. The silver emulsion was replaced by a nonsoluble silver salt. The metallic salt itself had no color or was very dimly colored; it acted as the mordant, fixing the pigment. The intensity of the final color was proportional to the amount of the mordanting material, which in turn corresponded to the original quantity of silver in the emulsion.

In a print colored by mordanting, as in a toned print, the transparent parts of the image are white, and the margins of the film have no color. This rule is particularly useful in identifying the processes involved in those nitrate prints colored with a system combining tinting with mordanting or toning; tinting leaves its traces around the perforation, while toning is visible only on the image.

Archival Implications

The 1922 edition of the Eastman Kodak tinting and toning manual cautioned that toning and mordanting were not advised for films that were to be preserved for a long time, because a chemical alteration of the emulsion was considered inevitable and the results were impossible to forecast. Therefore it was suggested that high-quality reference prints in black and white be made before a valuable film was altered by toning or mordanting. And indeed, many of the original colored versions of films have already been lost.

By and large, film archives today are forced to preserve duplicates of early films in black and white, both for financial and practical reasons. Even without considering the huge cost of restoring a film in color, the fact remains that current technology has proved unable to avoid the progressive decay of color film stock, even under the best possible conditions of preservation.

When color restoration is attempted, film archives usually follow one of two possible strategies. The most common approach is to reproduce the original tints and tones on a modern color negative. The result can be relatively satisfying, but technicians agree that the reproduction obtained is not completely faithful to the original. The materials employed at the beginning of the century (the nitrate bases and dyes) have a unique appearance that cannot be reproduced. A second and more rudimentary strategy involves reproducing tinted scenes by printing on color stock from black-and-white negatives, using a color filter. This system has the obvious practical advantage of not requiring the printing and preservation of a master color negative. The result, however, is not accurate in its color reproduction, as the tints obtained are usually rather cold and too bright. Furthermore, this solution cannot be used at all when the original print has any kind of toning, stenciling, or mordanting.

A few film archives[14] in the forefront of film restoration are trying to reproduce the actual techniques employed during the silent period, using machines and dyes that approximate as closely as possible those utilized in the early years of the century. The results obtained so far are tentative, and the work is extremely time-consuming. Given the current situation, with an overwhelming amount of nitrate film needing preservation and the relative lack of available time, money, and human resources, only a fraction of silent film will be restored according to these criteria. But there is little doubt that, following this direction of research, film restoration can acquire a scientific status comparable to the practices already established in other disciplines, such as painting and architectural restoration.

For those who work in the restoration of moving images, the importance of the original tinting and toning manuals is self-evident. Film archivists are often at a loss in knowing how a silent film looked at the time of its release. These books provide an extraordinary amount of primary evidence that is otherwise unavailable. All the volumes offer precise information about the chemical formulae used in order to prepare the dyes, the timing and methods of their use, the technical problems arising from inaccurate treatment of the film, and the possibilities of combining different coloring methods on the same positive print. Without these manuals, the ambitious enterprise of recreating the original techniques would be impossible.

Preservation and restoration are urgent tasks. Cellulose nitrate is a very unstable material whose estimated life barely reaches 100 years, according to the most recent scientific research. The phases in the process of decomposition are, sadly, well known in film archives. The cellulose base becomes brittle and shrinks so much that it cannot be projected anymore; the photographic emulsion fades; reels develop a layer of brown powder on the surface, then become so sticky that it becomes impossible even to rewind the film, and the image is lost. In the last stage of decay, nitrate film is reduced to a potentially explosive crystallized mass.

It is likely that within a few years, these tinting and toning manuals will be the only primary resource available for anyone trying to understand silent film's aesthetics of color and how it was shaped by a technology that was extremely complex for such a young industry.

But the same effects of nitrate decomposition are beginning to be apparent on the individual frames of nitrate preserved within these manuals. Even under the best storage conditions, the nitrate frames in these books are bound to disappear eventually. Fortunately, the samples of films contained in the Eastman Kodak and Pathé manuals have barely reached an early stage of decomposition. Most of their original beauty is still intact. If it is not possible to guarantee their existence for an indefinite future, we can at least undertake an accurate study and reproduce some of their characteristics. This is a scientific challenge and an ethical issue that involves the expertise and commitment of librarians and film archivists alike.

NOTES

1. *Biograph Bulletin*, 23 March 1911. Reproduced in *Biograph Bulletins, 1908–1912* (New York: Octagon Books, 1973), p. 284.

2. Richard Koszarski, *An Evening's Entertainment: The Age of the Silent Feature Picture, 1915–1928*, volume 3 of *A History of the American Cinema*, (General Editor, Charles Harpole) (New York: Scribner's, 1990), p. 127.

3. See the illustration on page 169 in Douglas Collins, *The Story of Kodak* (New York: Harry N. Abrams, 1990).

4. A copy is available in the film collections of the International Museum of Photography at George Eastman House.

5. The most widely used source on this topic is still Roger Manvell, ed., *The International Encyclopedia of Film* (London: Michael Joseph, 1972), containing a summary in four pages of the color techniques in use from the beginnings of cinema to 1960. Another useful reference tool is Steve Neale's *Cinema and Technology: Image, Sound, Colour* (London: Macmillan Education/The British Film Institute, 1985), pp. 109–58, with its two chapters on color in the silent period. The main focus, however, is the Technicolor system, developed from 1916 by Herbert Kalmus, Daniel Comstock, and Barton Prescott with the collaboration of Leonard Troland, Joseph Ball, and Eastman Weaver (see F. E. Basten, *Glorious Technicolor* [London: A. S. Barnes, 1980], and Robert A. Nowotny, *The Way of All Flesh Tones, A History of Motion Picture Color* [New York and London: Garland Publishing Co., 1983]). The most recent book on the subject was written in Germany by Gert Koshofer, *Die Farben des Films* (Berlin: Wissenschafts-verlag Volker Spiess GmbH, 1988) in cooperation with the 38th International Film Festival of Berlin; the quality of its illustrations is nothing less than outstanding as far as representing the color techniques used between World War I and II is concerned, but all information on pre-Technicolor techniques is squeezed onto a few pages. A more accurate idea of the complexity of early color techniques developed by the film industry can be drawn from the research of Harold Brown, a former curator of the National Film Archive in London. His conclusions have been summarized in an unpublished paper entitled "An Account of the Hand and Stencil Coloring Processes." I gratefully acknowledge Mr. Brown for having provided me with a copy of the original text. The only published version is available in Italian: "Tecniche di colorazione a mano e a pochoir," *Griffithiana*, 10:26–27 (September 1986), 72–73.

6. The Lumière catalog number of *Les Dernières Cartouches* is 745, but the numbering does not correspond necessarily to the chronological order in which the films were made. See Georges Sadoul, *Lumière et Méliès* (Paris: Lherminier, 1985; first published in 1964 and 1961 by Seghers as separate books, *Méliès* and *Lumière*), p. 137.

7. A good example is *Le Royaume Des Fées* (Star-Film, 1903). An original print of this film is held in the nitrate vaults of the National Film Archive in Berkhamstead, England.

8. A detailed description of these systems can be found in J. Marette, "Les procédés de coloriage mécanique des films," *Bulletin de l'Association Française des Ingénieurs et Techniciens du Cinéma* 7 (1950) 3–8.

9. Some technical drawings of the machines used for stencil coloring are reproduced in Esperanza Londoño's unpublished dissertation "Pour une histoire de la couleur au cinéma" (Paris: Université Sorbonne Nouvelle [D.E.R.C.A.V.], 1985).

10. The film collections of the International Museum of Photography at George Eastman House hold a print of *Cyrano de Bergerac*, made by Italian director Augusto Genina in 1923, that is extensively colored with the stencil system.

11. This fragment is now preserved at the Davide Turconi Archives, Pavia, Italy. The source of the tentative title is the catalog of the Josef Joye Collection in Zürich, where the material was found. It is reproduced in Paolo Cherchi Usai, *Una passione inflammabile. Guida allo studio del cinema muto* (Turin: UTET, 1991), Table of Colors, illustration 12.

12. The available evidence indicates that tinting and toning techniques were introduced in American films later. An analysis of the surviving nitrate prints shows that tinted and toned prints were far less common in the United States than in Europe. To my knowledge, tinting and toning remained a relatively uncommon technique in the United States until 1910, used only for the most ambitious projects. The exception to this is the production of the Vitagraph Company of America. The co-founder of Vitagraph, J. Stuart Blackton, often expressed his interest in new developments in coloring techniques for film, as is demonstrated late in his career with the films he produced in the United Kingdom such as *The Glorious*

Adventure (1922). An example of tinting in a Vitagraph split-reel before 1910 is *Princess Nicotine* or *The Smoke Fairy* (1909).

13. An early and outstanding case of gradual transition from one tint to another is the 1906 version of Pathé's *La Vie et la Passion de Notre Seigneur Jésus-Christ.* Many copies of this film exist. An original nitrate print is preserved in the film collections of the International Museum of Photography at George Eastman House.

14. For example, the Ceskoslovensky Filmovy Ustav in Prague and the Cineteca Comunale di Bologna. Some of the foremost specialists in film restoration have discussed similar issues at the first school for film restoration ever established on a permanent basis in Bologna, under the auspices of the Cineteca Comunale di Bologna. See also Ray Edmondson, "Towards a Philosophy of Film Archiving," *FIAF Bulletin* 41–42 (1991), 6–7.

Norman King

The Sound of Silents

We know that silent cinema was never actually silent—or hardly ever. The great movie palaces had large permanent orchestras with their own prestigious musical directors. Local cinemas might not be able to afford such lavishness, but they too would have at least a small ensemble of musicians. And so on down the "social" scale to the roadshow with its travelling pianist, a necessary part of the performance even, as *The Picture Show Man* reminds us, in the Australian outback. We know quite a lot too about what kind of music was played. Special scores for screenings of blockbusters such as *Birth of a Nation* in the major cities; a standard repertoire of popular classics in more downmarket cinemas; whatever the pianist could manage elsewhere. Mood music basically, making the images more atmospheric, intensifying the emotional impact, heightening the drama, underscoring the climaxes, providing a sense of complicity. It was there to anticipate, confirm, and reinforce. If the musical director of the Tivoli or the Empire didn't like the score sent along with the film or thought his orchestra couldn't manage it, he was at liberty to substitute something else that he thought would be suitable, and as cinema programmes show, he frequently did.

Music was, then, an essential ingredient of the cinema experience. But if sound is considered only on this level, it becomes merely an adjunct, subordinate to the images it was supposed to fit. What I want to do here, using the films of Abel Gance as examples, is try to shift the terms of reference, to examine sound as one of the major determinants in silent cinema.

Gance, it could be argued, is an exception, a privileged filmmaker given a relatively free hand and copious resources by producers who allowed him to experiment with new techniques. Certainly he was more inventive than most of his contemporaries and was able to draw on the expertise of a remarkably skilled team of technicians. But if, by the early 1920s, Gance was acknowledged as the great master of French cinema, it was not just as innovator but as filmmaker who blurred the distinction between the

From *Screen* 25:3 (1984). Reprinted by permission of the author and *Screen*.

"artistic" and the "popular," supplying pictures that were both prestigious *and* profitable. Because both factors were vitally important to a French industry struggling at the same time for recognition and survival, his films were heavily promoted and avidly discussed, with the result that there is a mass of documentation charting the progress of his more ambitious projects through from production to exhibition. And his work was at the centre of a debate about the function of cinema that frequently takes the equation of sound and image as reference point. It is for these reasons, plus the existence of a substantial archive, that Gance's films open out the possibility of a new approach to the sound of silents, the investigation not just of music but of speech and special effects as an integral part of film production and exhibition long before the arrival of the talkies.

Noel Burch[1] has demonstrated that from the beginning cinema aspired to have a "voice" as well as an image. At first it was the image that seemed to be the appendage—to the phonograph—and attempts to synchronise sound and image began with Edison. Léon Gaumont's Chronophone,[2] a system that used a rheostat to synchronise the speed of a projector with that of a gramophone, was introduced in 1902, and by 1912 he had produced several hundred Phono-Scenes, mostly popular songs or extracts from operas and ballets.[3] Sound effects were common in fairground performances, and in cinemas, actors would sometimes be concealed behind the screen, speaking in synchrony with the characters in the film. More important, in Burch's opinion, was the lecturer, who would explain and comment on the action, constructing a continuity out of a fragmentary narrative and indicating how the audience should respond.

Burch suggests that the lecturer disappeared around 1912–1914 with the arrival of continuity filming, but I would suggest that he continued in existence for rather longer, at least in rural areas where it was commonplace for the travelling projectionist to *present* his films. I did in fact encounter a survival of this tradition in a Provençal country town as recently as 1981. It was an open-air screening of silent films presented by an old man who had spent much of his life touring the local villages with a portable projector. There was no music, just live voice-overs that were amazingly eloquent.

Although they are hard to document, there seem to have been various other attempts during the 1920s to accompany silent films with spoken commentaries. There is, for example, a reference in Elie Faure's correspondence to a *commentaire* he was asked to write for Gance's *Napoleon*,[4] although nothing ever came of it, and there are other equally elusive references to live speech in the Gance archive, including references to the tonality of voice required in *Napoleon*.

By this stage, the use of sound in the studio was already a well-established practice. For big-budget films, directors could insist on a permanent ensemble of musicians to establish the mood for the actors. For cheaper pictures, there might be just one or two instruments, a violin or a piano, for example, or simply a gramophone. This was so much taken for granted that journalists invited to visit the studio didn't usually bother to comment on it unless something untoward happened. One such example is Marianne Alby's account[5] of the filming of *Au secours*, a comedy Gance made with Max Linder in 1923. Gina Palerme, the female lead, is supposed to be scared out of her wits by a masked man who comes into her bedroom. Filming of the scene begins well enough but is interrupted by a lighting problem. When shooting does eventually restart, Gina asks for *the music*, expecting *Danse macabre*. What she gets is an aria from *Tosca*. The director shouts instructions, there's the noise of the cameras and the inappropriate scratchy record of an operatic soprano. When Gina screams, it's as much to drown out all this extraneous din as to make her performance look convincing.

In the cinemas, too, music, speech, and sound effects were becoming commonplace. They were part of film's aspiration to be real. Reviewing the first screening of *La roue* in December 1922, Emile Vuillermoz reports that there were gasps of enthusiasm when the sound of "real" jets of steam were produced in synchrony with the images of a railway engine, although he goes on to admit that he would prefer there just to be music (on which he doesn't find it necessary to comment).[6] And when *La roue* was put out on release in Paris early in 1923, it was preceded in the programme by "an exclusive innovation," the Gaumont Chronographe—successor to the Chronophone—representing a talking picture, *Tombouctou la mystérieuse*, an illustrated lecture by Louis Forest with a commentary by M Saint-Yves. Around the same time, there were experiments of a different kind, such as those of Lordier who would stand in the wings singing one of his songs while on the screen there would be images to illustrate it. And singers would sometimes appear on stage, reproducing what was in the image.

Sound had, though, a more determinant effect on the image than the examples quoted so far might suggest. It wasn't just a question of appropriate music, convincing sound effects, or voices that made the image seem more immediate. Camille Saint-Saens had already conferred musical respectability on the cinema by agreeing to compose for it, just as Sarah Bernhardt had established "theatrical" credence by performing in front of the camera. Cinema, in its ambition to become the Art Form of the Twentieth Century and in its attempts to distance itself from the novelistic, saw music as a founding instance.

In *La dixième symphonie*, written and directed by Gance in 1917 but not released until November 1918, music is central. The film is about the composing of a symphony that is performed in the movie theatre, and at its high point the music takes precedence over the image.

Examining Gance's work in the context of the avant-garde, Henri Langlois sees *La dixième symphonie* as his first masterpiece.[7] It is basically, though, a conventional melodrama. Enric Damor, a gifted composer, suspects his wife of having an affair with the man her step-daughter wants to marry (she is in fact being blackmailed by him). But this breakdown of family relationships provides a new source of inspiration—art produced through suffering—his tenth symphony, which he performs on the piano for an invited audience of friends and admirers.

A working note dated August 1917[8] suggests that Gance initially planned to use recorded sound but instead *La dixième symphonie* became one of the first feature films to have a specially commissioned symphonic score, composed by Michel-Maurice Lévy. The orchestra in the cinema thus reproduces what is supposedly being played within the film. The evident disparity here, between the piano in the image and the orchestral sound in the cinema, is aggravated by the fact that many cinema orchestras could not cope with a symphonic score (the only programmes that I have seen do not in fact mention Lévy's music at all, suggesting that musical directors substituted something easier to play). The disparity is quickly effaced, however, because what we actually see on the screen is less the performance of the symphony than a series of images that illustrate it. There are locating shots of Damor playing and of the entranced listeners, but the sequence consists principally of tinted images of a ballet dancer superimposed on an idyllic garden setting with a frieze of dancers, flowers, and bunches of grapes at the top and bottom of the frame. The visual is thus an interpretation of the musical, breaking out from the narrative in which it is held. More precisely, music ceases to be simply the subject-matter of the film; it generates images that are presented as the visual *equivalent* of the musical.

The importance of *La dixième symphonie* is that it achieved within mainstream cinema what was to become one of the great preoccupations of the avant-garde, the liberation of the image from the narrative and the theatrical. It was a move toward non-narrative form, toward the expressive and the rhythmical. The title itself is significant here. Damor is assimilated to Beethoven by superimpressions, but his composition is also subsumed into the film as extension of the Ninth. After the Choral, the Visual. The supreme orchestrator is not the composer but the director: the first image is of Damor with the death mask of Beethoven in superimpression, but the final one is of Abel Gance taking a bow, thanking the audience for their appreciation.

La dixième symphonie illustrates, then, the extent to which cinema in its aspiration to be recognised as a popular *art* form was looking toward music as model and guarantee. They seemed to have a similar project, using rhythm, harmony, and tonal contrast as the basis of an appeal to feeling. Lyric poetry could also provide a parallel since it, too, played on the intuitive, but music seemed more appropriate and was more distanced from the literary. For Gance and many of his contemporaries in France, it opened out the possibility of a radically new theory of what cinema might become.

The idea of the symphonic was in fact to have an immense importance in French attempts to establish an aesthetics of film. The definition of
cinema as "the music of light," attributed to Gance but also claimed by
several others, including Emile Vuillermoz and Elie Faure, became an
accepted term in writings about film in the early 1920s. And for all its neat
oversimplifications, Henri Langlois' description of Germaine Dulac remains a pertinent characterisation of a dominant impressionist tendency:
"She sees music, she thinks music, she always considers film not as a fresco
but as a symphony of images in which each shot, through its tonality and
length, has the same value as a sound. She plays on montage as she would
play the piano."[9] As long as one doesn't eliminate poetry and dance, this
view could be applied to most of the French avant-garde, from Léger to René
Clair, Jean Epstein, and Blaise Cendrars. What they all have in common is
their reference to Gance as point of origin, especially to *La roue*, which
seemed to prove that cinema even in a proletarian setting and addressed to
a popular audience was an art for the future. It had elevated cinema
incontrovertibly to the status and dignity of music. This may seem to be an
argument in favour of the "musical analogy,"[10] and indeed Gance continued
to insist through to the late 1920s[11] that cinema had to equate itself with
music, to become a visual orchestra, performing symphonies in time and
space. But music was not *simply* an analogy, it was, as *La roue* further
exemplifies, a determinant of the image, providing a basis for tonality,
movement within the frame and cutting between frames, even though in
this instance the "source" of the music is not present in the image.

From its conception, *La roue* was mapped out in terms of musical
metaphors. It was to be a symphony in black and white or, more precisely,
"a white symphony following on from a black symphony."[12] A first part set
in the soot and smoke of marshalling yards and railway engines, a second
set high up in the Alps—contrasting worlds made for the cinema. Much
later Gance described the film as a poem in which each image counts, like
a note in music,[13] echoing Langlois' comments on Dulac. But as in *La
dixième symphonie*, music had a definite function within the film. His
project, she declared in a 1920 interview, was "to paint a visual opera," to
establish a direct relationship between the vibrations of sound and light, to
unite photography and Rachmaninov.[14] Like *La dixième symphonie* it was
a melodrama, not the "cathedral of light" he aspired to construct but a film
that would be understood by a popular audience and which would at the
same time have universal significance. The hero is an engine-driver called
Sisif (Sisyphus), but within this proletarian actualisation of myth, music
takes on a new function. It isn't something that is composed and performed
within a narrative from which it then escapes. Music and image are
conceived together.

Two examples may help to clarify. In the closing sequence, the
finale of the white symphony, Sisif and his adopted daughter Norma are at

last reconciled. Norma is invited by the mountain guides to join in their annual celebration, and as they dance higher and higher up the mountain above the snow-line, they gradually merge into a harmony with nature. Sisif, blinded by a railway accident, sits facing the window "listening" and as he dies achieves the same harmony. Shot 13,000 feet up in the Alps in the late autumn of 1920, this was an extraordinary piece of location filming. But Gance was particularly insistent on its musicality, on the construction of a filmic rhythm that exactly matched *Anitra's Dance*.[15] Similarly, in the opening sequence of *J'accuse* (1917–1919), he had used the Farandole from Bizet's *L'Arlésienne* as the basis for a village celebration, knowing that the increasing tempo and insistent rhythm of dancing and editing could be exactly matched by the performance of the same piece of music in the theatre.

Here, the music pre-exists an image that appropriates and exceeds it. In the other example, music provides a concept of rhythm that underpins one of cinema's most dynamic and historically significant innovations during the early 1920s, accelerated montage. Sisif is driving the train that is taking Norma to the city where she is to be married off against her better judgment to Hersan, the effete capitalist villain. And Sisif has resolved to crash the train to kill himself and Norma. Like most of Gance's rapid montage sequences, it begins slowly, gradually builds up to a crescendo with cutting that imitates musical notation and reaches a "paroxysm" of split-second shots before returning to the long takes and composition in depth of narrative. At the climax, the individual images are no longer clearly perceptible, there is only a compelling sense of rhythm.

This attempt to construct a visual equivalent of sound provoked one of the great pitched battles in film history. *La roue* was either an outrage, a bombastic, overblown and overlong piece of triviality, or the first cinematic *oeuvre* that demonstrated what the new art might become. Writing about the first performance nearly forty years after the event, the film director Henri Fescourt remembers it as a unique experience, a miraculous fusion of sound and image: "Thanks to the marrying of visual and aural rhythms each coinciding with the other, you had the impression that the noise was coming at you from the image. It was not at all music that tried to imitate but a music that suggested, that imposed on the ear the same effect as the impending catastrophe imposed on the nerves. The commotion of sound translated the turmoil, the soil of the locomotive into heart-rending notes, percussive explosions, breathless cadences. The image-sound complex created a sensation of total unity."[16] Fescourt, in his recollection, embroiders on the memory of an overall effect, but contemporary critics were similarly impressed. For Emile Vuillermoz, who was a musician as well as a prolific writer on cinema, *La roue* was the exemplification of the music of images, moving through from a slow indolent melody to a scherzo with abrupt modulations, fugal entries, leitmotifs, and a development into polyphony and polytonality. That, for him, was the mapping out of the cinema of the future.[17]

Fescourt is apparently mistaken in his recollections when he describes in detail the effect produced at the first screening of *La roue* by Arthur Honegger's abrasive score, and many critics (including myself) have followed him in supposing that Honegger supplied music for the whole film—programmes for the Paris release indicate that the original music was "borrowed" from Saint-Saens, Fauré, Mendelssohn, Massenet, and other composers. But Honegger did write special music for the rapid montage sequences, and this was subsequently performed as an independent orchestral piece that has entered the repertoire as *Pacific 231*. In fact, music and image become symbiotic here. Montage in *La roue* was based on musical notation, which was then taken over by Honegger in music that matched the rhythm of the images (figures 1–8).

Pacific 231 later provided the basis for a new sequence of images in a film made by Alexander Laszlo and released in Berlin in 1927. Hearing about this, Gance protested vehemently, claiming that he himself was planning to make a polyvision film that would be a new visualisation of the same music, an essay in visual counterpoint. Like many of Gance's projects of the late 1920s, the film was never made, but there is correspondence in his archive negotiating with the Paris-Orleans railway company for the use of tracks and locomotives.[18]

Honegger also wrote scores for *Napoleon* and for *La fin du monde*, Gance's first sound picture. The results were not an unmitigated success since the composer had to work quickly and it was not always easy to match the stark modernism of the music to the residual romanticism of the image. For *Napoleon,* the difficulties were insurmountable since Honegger had to write music for a film that kept changing its length (from, at the extreme, 3,700 to 11,000 metres) and had to blend original themes in with settings of Revolutionary songs dictated by the screenplay. The result, Moussinac states, was a mish-mash.[19] It was, even so, a claim staked out by cinema to be modern too, as original as the *Groupe des Six* but more accessible to the popular imagination.

So far I have looked mostly at music and want now to address the issue of speech. Although for many critics silent cinema seemed to have reached its peak in those films of Chaplin in which speech was superfluous, we have seen that the spoken word was a central preoccupation from very early on. Over and above the experiments with recorded sound, it is clear that implicit speech was already an accepted convention in European cinema by the early 1920s, with scripted dialogues even though these might not be reproduced in intertitles. In Germaine Dulac's *La souriante Madame Beudet,* for example, there is a long telephone conversation with frequent close-ups of the principal actress who is clearly speaking her lines. There are very few intertitles, and only a lip-reader would be able to make out

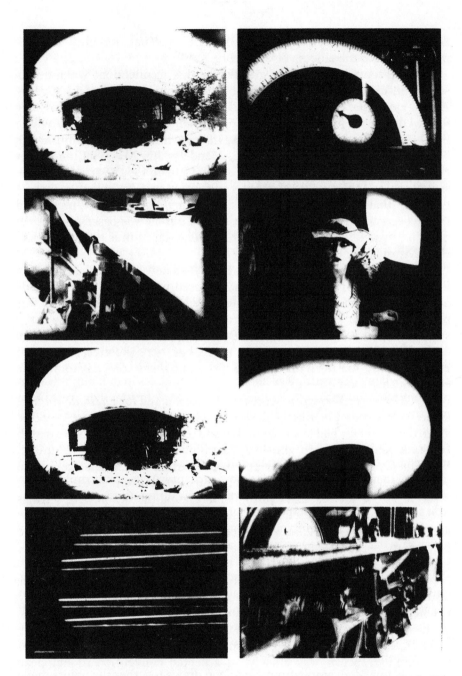

Figures 1–8. Frame stills from a rapid montage sequence in La roue *for which Honegger wrote* Pacific 231.

exactly what she is saying. Yet the effect is a very marked one, shifting the acting style away from the exaggeratedly gestural toward the naturalistic.

Gance occasionally used scripted dialogues even in some of his very early films, but it is in *J'accuse,* made during the later stages of the Great War and released in 1919, that a written text becomes particularly prominent. The central character, Jean Diaz, is a poet who at various moments declaims one of his compositions. We don't know what this film originally looked like since only a re-cut and shortened version dating from 1922 seems to have survived. In it, Diaz is clearly speaking the lines of the poem, but we see only fragments of his declamation. The complete text appears in the intertitles.[20] The same thing happens in *La roue* when, in an imagined sequence, Elie uses a poem (written, like the one in *J'accuse,* by Gance) to declare his love for Norma. Again, the complete version of the film is lost, and in the prints that survive, the text of the poem is usually given in the intertitles. But it is clear that voice was already an important element of film production, that actors spoke scripted lines even though these might never be heard, or indeed seen, in the cinema, except perhaps at special screenings about which we have very little information.

There is one film, however, that is so well documented that we can establish exactly how sound—music, dialogue, and declamation—was used during filming and performance: the 1927 *Napoleon.* But first a note of caution: when critics enthused about Gance's success in dubbing voices on to silent footage for the 1971 *Bonaparte et la Révolution,* they were often referring without realising it to sound sequences filmed with the original actors for the 1935 sonorised version. Even so, it is clear that speech was of paramount importance in the silent version, and one of the advantages of the 1935 re-edit is that it includes dialogue sequences that were cut from the silent distribution prints to make way for intertitles. One example from the closing stages of the film demonstrates how different it was when it was first screened at the Paris Opera in April 1927. After arriving at the Albenga encampment and restoring order, Bonaparte harangues the Army of Italy promising the spoils of war, honour, and glory. Even in the restored print, there are only fragments of the speech interrupted by titles. But at the Opera, these lines were declaimed by an actor. The speech was present in its entirety in the image and in the theatre, producing a completely different engagement from the one we now experience. And as the army marched off in the final triptychs, the rhythm of the images exactly matched that of "Auprès de ma blonde," sung by the soldiers within the film and by the chorus in the theatre.

A further example from *Napoleon* draws together the points made so far about music and voice. The sequence is a purely fictional representation of how the Marseillaise came to be adopted by the Parisian Revolutionaries. Like other montage sequences, it begins quite slowly. We are at a political meeting in 1792 at the former Cordeliers monastery. While

Robespierre, Marat, and Danton are in dispute about principles and tactics, a massive crowd waits in the church for the meeting to begin. A man begins to distribute a song, which is of course Rouget de l'Isle's *Chant du départ*, soon to be known as *La Marseillaise*. Danton's secretary, Camille Desmoulins, reads a copy, realises the song's potential importance for the Revolution and persuades Danton to look at it. Abandoning the speech he was going to make, Danton takes Rouget de l'Isle up into the pulpit to teach the song to the crowd. It is greeted by an outburst of cheers and applause and, as the enthusiasm mounts, the rhythm of the cutting gradually increases, culminating in a montage of single frame close-ups of people singing and the superimpression of an animated tableau of the Marseillaise copied from Rude's sculpture on the Arc de Triomphe.

It's a remarkable sequence in that its rhythmic patterns are precisely structured on music, with a climax that corresponds in the acceleration of the cutting to the musical crescendo and prolonged final chord. It was also a laborious process with an effect Gance was particularly proud of. Just to edit ninety–four shots into fifteen seconds of accelerated montage had, he claimed in *Autour de Napoléon*,[21] involved two weeks of intensive work—in addition to the time spent shooting dozens of close-ups of individual singers in the studio. But it depended for its effect on an exact synchrony of image and sound, and to achieve this, the conductor was provided with a mechanism for controlling the speed of projection, an interesting example of sound given priority over the image. The need for such precise synchrony always caused problems, and the attempt was probably abandoned by provincial cinema musical directors just as it was by Gance in the 1935 sound version and by Carl Davis in the Thames presentation of Kevin Brownlow's reconstruction on Channel 4. And yet that synchrony is an essential part of the experience. The 1971 *Bonaparte et la Révolution* clearly demonstrates that, despite a soundtrack that is frequently excessive. The effect of live sound was, according to contemporary critics, electrifying.

What makes this sequence particularly useful for the study of sound in silent cinema is that there are very detailed accounts of how it was filmed and performed. For the shooting, Gance had recruited workers on strike from a neighbouring car factory to supplement the usual supply of extras. To establish the mood, he went up into the pulpit and announced: "I am going to try out a new technique. It's quite complex and I'm going to have to ask you to make a special effort that you'll be able to manage if you apply yourselves to it heart and soul. I want you to sing the Marseillaise twelve times in a continuous crescendo." The result, according to one of Gance's assistants, was a resounding cheer, a unique phenomenon in studio filming.[22] Gance had also taken other precautions to ensure the desired result. In addition to the permanent ensemble of musicians, he had hired drummers and trumpet players. He also had the opera singer Koubitsky (playing

Danton) to lead the singing along with another singer, Maryse Damia (the animated Marseillaise in the superimpressions). When it was all over, there was more spontaneous cheering and, as one witness said, if Gance had ordered his Thousand to storm the National Assembly, they would have obeyed without question.[23]

Music and voice are so clearly integrated here into the production process that the sequence would have been inconceivable without them. Rhythmical montage transformed it radically, but its impact derives initially from a lack of simulation. Verismilitude in this instance means a cast completely caught up in the fiction it is acting out.

Since the sound was of course not recorded, it is important to note how the silent images were "interpreted" in performance. At the Opera premiere, there was a brass band as well as an orchestra, plus a chorus whose professionalism must have jarred with the images of Sans-culottes struggling to learn the notes of their future national anthem. In addition, there was Koubitsky up on the stage, synchronising with his own image in the film (provincial cinemas also used soloists for this sequence). This may seem to be in complete contradiction to the attempt to achieve verisimilitude within the image, but it was in fact an interpellation of the audience, casting them in the same role as the revolutionary strikers, inviting them to share in their enthusiasm. At the Opera premiere, the distinguished audience just cheered, but less pretentious spectators did join in the singing. The elaborate press book prepared by Jean Arroy for distribution to cinema managers didn't just specify how the music should be played and the need for a chorus, it also included the words of the Marseillaise so that they could be distributed to the audience. And it spelled out which verses of other revolutionary songs should be sung at other moments.

Ultimately it was for the audience to recreate the film's atmosphere through its own participation, and this is frequently what happened. To quote just one example from the numerous letters preserved in the Gance archive describing a screening of *Napoleon* in a small provincial town in the Vaucluse. "When at the Assembly Rouget de l'Isle sings the Marseillaise for the first time and the orchestra played our national anthem with great vigour, many people rose to their feet and sang . . . and the old men wept."[24] The actual sound might not literally correspond to what it had been in the studio, but the image necessitated a similar sound and a similar response.

In effect, this sequence, through its combination of image and live sound operates a dramatic shift in patterns of identification. We do not look toward Danton or Bonaparte as sources of knowledge (although there are looks of approval within the image to guide us). We are positioned with regard to an experience, a supposedly historical one recreated in the studio and then actualised. Like the extras, we are called on to enter into that experience.

This, it seems to me, is something specific to the sound of silent cinema. In the sonorised version the impact is quite different. It's still exciting, and there is Henri Verdun's vibrant score. But we are also more distanced. Because the film *contains* the sound and the image, all the dynamism is up there on the screen and doesn't ultimately concern us directly. In the silent version the sound is present, provoking a response to *it*, and through it a different relation to the image, a participation, an engagement with the film. The cheering and applause is as much the audience celebrating its own experience as an appreciation of visual effects. *Napoleon* and the Marseillaise sequence may indeed be exceptions, but only to the extent that they exemplify what silent cinema, in contrast to the early talkies, aspired to be through an equation of production and performance.

This emphasis on participation in a performance and on celebration suggests a need for the careful examination of the ideological effects of the sound silents. Although we might be tempted to view the experimentation with sound in the Marseillaise sequence as radical in terms of accepted film practices, for example, through its changing of the relationship between spectator and spectacle, it is politically closer to the reactionary in its privileging of feeling and intuition. It may challenge received conventions of realism, but in its attempt to produce a collective enthusiasm it seeks to construct a unified spectator and a united audience summoned to respond dynamically and uncritically, to collapse identity into the experience of the actual. That, in 1927, could be seen as an endorsement of authoritarianism, as indeed it was by Moussinac and Vuillermoz who, despite divergent political positions (Moussinac was a Marxist, Vuillermoz an establishment critic), both condemned the film's proto-fascist tendencies even though they admired its innovations. The most ardent defenders of *Napoleon* were in fact members of the patriotic right who not surprisingly argued that politics was an irrelevance for the evaluation of art. This, however, is only a single example and one which is relatively easy to document and contextualise. Although the excitement, cheers, and applause that greeted the fusion of sound and image in *La roue* may suggest that the effect on the audience was similar, a great deal of empirical research will have to be done for a more extensive study of ideological effectivity to be possible.

Returning, then, to the empirical, I want to end with some remarks on the use of sound during the final moments of the silent era, taking as example the screenplay of *Sainte-Hélène*,[25] written by Gance in the winter of 1927–1928.

Sainte-Hélène was originally intended to be the last episode in a cycle of six films covering the whole of Napoleon's career, but it was given priority because of the difficulty of financing the intervening films. In the event, Gance was unable to obtain sufficient backing in France even for a single sequel, and the script was sold to a German producer who passed it to Lupu Pick to adapt and direct.

The important point about Gance's original screenplay is the complex and extremely detailed way the use of sound was mapped out at the drafting stage. Sound, in what was still to be a "silent" film was not an afterthought or an adjunct, it is expressly designated in the script as an integral part of the production.

Much attention is paid to sound effects, cannon fire, thunder, ocean waves. And once again there was to be an exact matching of sound and image. For one sequence, Gance specifies that the movement and dynamic theme have to be the Scherzo before the final Allegro in Beethoven's Fifth. And for the death scene, he notes even more specifically: "The rhythm and theme of the heroic march at the end of the Ninth Symphony, on the screen and in the orchestra pit. A wave of power and joy that sings. Suddenly an absolute silence for the ear and the eye." Then there is a curious reference to a *"speaker"* who quotes a long text by Chateaubriand about Napoleon's funeral that the images must precisely match. And, in the final moments, a play on silence, the sound of the waves, and the climactic music—Beethoven, Berlioz, and Revolutionary songs. What we have, then, is an idea of sound that is quite distinct from that which was already being used in the early talkies. Sound determines but does not restrict. The image also "sings."

To sum up, I want to argue that sound in the silent cinema has to be attended to much more carefully than it usually has been. Music was more than just a convenient analogy, and research of the kind pioneered by Noel Burch has to be extended and filled out. The numerous well-documented studies of cinema's attempts to incorporate recorded sound may be valuable contributions to the history of film technology, but they tend to invite teleological modes of analysis, as if the story of early cinema was one of a gradual progression toward *The Jazz Singer* and its more sophisticated successors. Sound functioned *differently* during the silent era. It supplied a set of credentials and a guarantee of respectability. It provided a theoretical basis for techniques such as rhythmical montage. Essentially it produced effects in the cinema that recorded sound could not, a sense of immediacy and participation. Live sound actualised the image and, merging with it, emphasised the presentness of the performance and of the audience. It is from that play of interpellation and positioning—the placing of the spectator within an immediate experience—that "silent" cinema derived much of its potency.[26]

NOTES

1. Most recently at the "Putting Narrative in Place" weekend school, Derby, 10–12 December 1982. See also Noel Burch, "How We Got into Pictures: Notes Accompanying *Correction Please*," *Afterimage* 8–9 (1981), 24–38.

2. For details, see Brian Coe, *The History of Movie Photography* (London: Ash and Grant, 1981), p. 95.

3. Until 1907, they were all directed by Alice Guy. See Alice Guy, *Mémoires d'une pionnière du cinéma* (Paris: Denoël/Gonthier, 1976).

4. Elie Faure, *Oeuvres complètes, III*, ed. Yves Lévy (Paris: Pauvert, 1964), pp. 1060–1 (letter dated 13 May 1926).

5. *Cinéma-Ciné-pour-tous* (15 December 1923), 9–10.

6. *Comoedia* (31 December 1922), 4.

7. *Cahiers du cinéma* 202 (1968), 13.

8. Cinémathèque française.

9. *Cahiers du cinéma* 202 (1968), 14.

10. On this issue, see David Bordwell, "The Musical Analogy," *Yale French Studies* 60 (1980), 141–56.

11. Notably in "Le cinéma de demain," *Conférencia* 23 (1928), 197–209.

12. Abel Gance, *Prisme* (Paris: Gallimard, 1930), pp. 175–6.

13. Gance to Henri Langlois, 23 November 1975 (Centre national de la cinématographie).

14. Roger Lion, "Un grand artiste française: Abel Gance," *Filma* (15 May 1920), 5–8.

15. Gance to René Jeanne, 14 October 1920 (Cinémathèque française).

16. Henri Fescourt, *La foi et les montagnes* (Paris: Paul Montel, 1959), pp. 245–6.

17. Emile Vuillermoz, *Comoedia* (31 December 1922), 4.

18. Letters of Gance and Honegger, December 1927 (Cinémathèque française).

19. Leéon Moussinac, *L'humanité* (1 May 1927).

20. And in Léon Moussinac's literary adaptation of the screenplay, *La Lampe merveilleuse*, Paris, 1922.

21. A film about the making of *Napoleon*, released in 1928.

22. Jean Arroy, *En tournant "Napoléon" avec Abel Gance* (Paris: La renaissance du livre, 1927).

23. Emile Vuillermoz, "La machine à explorer le temps," *L'impartial français* (19 March 1926).

24. René Bonnaventure to Gance, September 1929 (Institut des hautes études cinématographieques).

25. Centre national de la cinématographie.

26. An earlier version of this article was presented at the SEFT Sound Cinema weekend, Triangle Arts Centre, Birmingham, 29–30 October 1983.

Mikhail Yampolsky

Kuleshov's Experiments and the New Anthropology of the Actor

Kuleshov's theoretical legacy is usually divided into two parts: one is devoted to the problems of montage and is rightly considered to be the more valuable and original; the second is concerned with the elaboration of the problem of the cinema actor and, in particular, of the theory of the *naturshchik* [model actor] and of rehearsal method. The books that Kuleshov wrote are organised along these lines. Both *The Art of Cinema* [Iskusstvo kino, 1929] and *The Practice of Film Direction* [Praktika kinorezhissury, 1935] begin with a statement of montage theory and then move on to an exposition of the problematic of the actor. This model has been adopted in most histories of cinema that contain an account of Kuleshov's theoretical views. Because of this, the correlation between montage theory and the anthropology of acting appears, as a rule, to be highly ephemeral. However, there is every reason to believe that the theory of montage derives genetically from the new conception of the anthropology of the actor and is based completely on it. The expositional structure adopted by Kuleshov and his popularisers masks to a considerable extent not just the profound unity of Kuleshov's film theory but also its true sense.

I

Kuleshov's conception of the actor is not distinguished by any great originality but is borrowed almost entirely from theatre theory of the 1910s and

From Richard Taylor and Ian Christie, eds., *Inside the Film Factory* (London: Routledge, 1991). This essay was translated by Richard Taylor and first appeared in a shorter version in French as "Les expériences de Kuleshov et la nouvelle anthropologie de l'acteur," *Iris* 4.1 (1986). Reprinted by permission of the author and Routledge. One illustration had to be replaced; the second had to be omitted.

the beginning of the 1920s. There was at that time in Russia an active reaction against the method of Stanislavsky's Moscow Art Theatre. The principle of the transformation and embodiment of the actor in the character was being actively elaborated at the beginning of the 1910s: the major influences on it were the views of two theorists, the Frenchman F. A. Delsarte and the Swiss J. Dalcroze. The teaching of Delsarte figures among the teachings of physiognomy, which were very popular in the nineteenth century and which owed much, for instance, to the old works of G. G. Engel. He had elaborated a highly pedantic lexicon of gestures, each of which, according to the author, had a direct correlation with the psychological state of man. The originality of Delsarte's teaching consisted to a large extent in the accentuation of the rhythmic side of mime and gesture that is predictable in a system created by a professional musician. Dalcroze created a system of rhythmic gymnastics that was extremely popular in the 1910s and on which he based an original aesthetic theory. Delsarte's ideas began to penetrate Russia at the very beginning of the twentieth century. Yuri A. Ozarovsky lectured on his teaching as early as 1903,[1] but it achieved real popularity around 1910–1913 when the former director of the Imperial Theatres, Prince Sergei Volkonsky, became its propagandist. He published a series of articles on Delsarte and Dalcroze in the periodical *Apollon* and then published, under that periodical's imprint, several books giving a detailed exposition of the new acting system. Since the Volkonsky–Delsarte–Dalcroze system had a fundamental significance for film theory at the beginning of the 1920s, and in particular for Kuleshov, we must familiarise ourselves briefly with at least those elements that were later used by filmmakers.

The Volkonsky system can conventionally be divided into two parts: the theoretical system of Dalcroze and the technological system of Delsarte, synthesised into a single whole. In 1912 Volkonsky published his translation of the book by Dalcroze's disciple, Jean d'Udine, that had gone into his system organically and represented a kind of philosophical reworking of the teaching of the Geneva rhythmologist (d'Udine relied mainly on Le Dantec, Bergson et al.). D'Udine was an ardent propagandist of the idea of synaesthesia, and he compared man to a dynamo (in one of the first manifestations of the machine ethic in aesthetics) through which the rhythmic synaesthetic inductive impulses pass. Human emotion is expressed in external movement and, what is more, that movement can "inductively" provoke in man the emotion that gave rise to the movement. He maintained that "for every emotion, of whatever kind, there is a corresponding body movement of some sort: it is through that movement that the complex synaesthetic transfer that accompanies any work of art is accomplished."[2] To ensure its artistic effectivity, every movement has to be rhythmicised, and music is the synaesthetic equivalent of body movement: "the ability to express feelings through musical combinations con-sists in nothing other than finding sound movements whose subtle rhythm corresponds to the body movement of someone experiencing enjoyment or suffering."[3] It is from this that d'Udine derives the idea of the mimetic character of music, "imitating" the internal rhythms that accompany the phenomena that exist in life. Rhythmicised body movements must, accord-ing to d'Udine, be "segmentary"—that is, they must be fixed in certain poses: "The manifestation of real artistic quality . . . requires that the rhythms, whether felt or imagined, be crystallised in an immutable form,"[4] he declared, making an analogy between human expressive movement and the musical notation that records a melody. D'Udine promoted music to the position of the metalanguage of art: "This would allow us," he wrote, "to apply my plastic definition of melody, which is that all melody is a series of consecutive propositions, to the whole field of aesthetics and in the end that would allow us to say in more general terms: *every work of art is a series of consecutive propositions.*"[5] D'Udine concluded his work with this characteristic definition of art: art is "*the transmission of an emotion by means of stylised natural rhythm.*"[6]

In his articles "Man as Material for Art. Music. Body. Dance" and "Man and Rhythm. The System and School of Jacque-Dalcroze" (1912), Volkonsky refines some of the theses of the Swiss theorist: "The first condition for creation in art is the adoption of a different rhythm, whether in the voice, in the movements of the body or in the soul's emotions."[7] Furthermore, this different rhythm must be assimilated by the actor to the point where it becomes an unconscious automatism: "Consciousness only plays its proper role when it is transformed into unconsciousness, that is when everything that has been acquired through consciousness is trans-formed into the mechanical impossibility of doing otherwise."[8] Volkonsky's actor is distinguished from Gordon Craig's "supermarionette" precisely because his rhythmicised movements are driven to unconscious-ness by inner, conscious impulses and not by simple mechanical submis-sion to the director's will.

The Delsartian, "technological" part of the system is essentially orientated toward the search for a precise record of gesture, its segmentation like musical notation, and the exposure of the psychological content of each gesture. Delsarte, with his mania for the classification of the lexicography of mime, was even more categorical than d'Udine in his insistence on the extreme segmentation of gestures: "Delsarte considered the independence of the limbs from one another to be the essential condition for expressive-ness: any interference by another limb weakens the impression."[9] To achieve a geometrically precise record of gestures Delsarte proposed to describe and produce them in three directions—width, height, and depth: "Each man is like the centre of his own universe. His 'centrality' can develop dynamically in three principal directions, which correspond to the three 'independent' directions in which the space of the universe is measured."[10] Furthermore man can, as it were, stretch out from the centre and enter an eccentric state that expresses the manifestation of will or gather himself in toward the centre (a concentric state), expressing the dominant of thought, of reason. Tranquillity, according to Delsarte, relates to the sphere of feeling. Volkonsky, following his teacher, describes all human movements according to the categories "normal," "eccentric," and "concentric." In *Expressive Man*, Volkonsky provides a very detailed analysis of the sense of all sorts of "segmentary" human movements in three directions (he calls this section of his system "semiotics"), but the main content of his work is the elaboration of the "laws of combination" of individual movements. He proclaims four principles of combination: (1) simultaneity; (2) succession; (3) opposition (total and partial); and (4) parallelism. Gesture acquires significance only in relation to its starting point, the centre, but a combination of gestures acquires meaning only through the radial directions of movement (which is why Delsarte's three "axes" are so important to him). Their opposition in radial directions is the fundamental expressive principle of the organisation of a "phrase" chain. Volkonsky provides a long list of examples of these oppositions, for example, "between the head, radiating along a perpendicular either away from or towards the body, and the hands, radiating from the elbows in the direction of breadth," and so on.[11] Volkonsky proposes that actors' movements should be constructed according to the principle of the succession of different combinations of gestures and asserts that "only such a strict observation of the law of succession, stripped of the confusion that inevitably accompanies simultaneity, is a real organic *development* of movement"[12] constructed according to natural laws, the laws of mechanics: "Just as the law of gravity is indisputable, so too are the laws of body movement and, consequently, also the laws of expressiveness; but, once laws are indisputable, their non-observance produces a lie. Study, master, observe the *law*, if you want your art to be true."[13] It was on this basis that the original ethic of the new anthropology of the actor was constructed. The laws of movement were equated to the laws of nature (mechanics) and contrasted to the voluntarism of traditional artistic creation, in the same way as truth was contrasted to lie and nature to art. The following declaration by Volkonsky had a major significance for the aesthetics of the 1920s:

> Man is a machine; yes, this machine is set in motion by feeling and 'oiled' by feeling but, since it is a machine, it obeys the general laws of mechanics. But you must remember this: if you make something mechanical without feeling (or sense), you will produce a caricature of life; whereas, if you produce a feeling with false mechanics, nothing will happen—you will achieve the absence of life.[14]

This combination, which seems strange to us now, of mechanics and "feeling" differentiates Volkonsky's ideas sharply from later Constructivism. We see before us the fruit of a meandering movement of thought that derived from the old physiognomy of pantomime and ballet but already anticipated the next step toward the machine ethic of the 1920s.

II

The new anthropology of the actor spread through Russia with unusual speed. A large number of centres for Dalcrozian rhythmic gymnastics [eurhythmics] were set up, and Volkonsky even started to publish a specialised periodical *Rhythmic Gymnastics Courses* [Listki kursov ritmicheskoi gimnastiki] (1913–1914). In St Petersburg, D. M. Musina-Ozarovskaya set up a "School for Stage Expressiveness" and then the "One Art" society, which set itself the aim of promoting a future synthesis of the arts on the basis of Delsarte's system. Representatives of the Petersburg artistic elite joined the society. Yuri A. Ozarovsky published a Delsartian journal called *Voice and Speech* [Golos i rech']. But the principal propagandist was Volkonsky, who gave hundreds of lectures about his system. The spread of the new anthropology was facilitated by the flowering of the Russian ballet, the tours of Isadora Duncan, etc. The ballet seemed for some time to be the principal expression of the new anthropological model of the actor and, more broadly, of man.

It was through theatre that the ideas of Volkonsky and his associates penetrated film circles. The first traces of their influence can be found around 1916. By 1918–1919, among filmmakers there was already an entire group of followers of Delsarte and Dalcroze. By coincidence there were among them a number of filmmakers who actively supported Soviet power and, as a result, occupied key posts in cinema immediately after the October Revolution. Among them we should name first of all the famous director and actor of pre-Revolutionary cinema, Vladimir Gardin, who in 1918 was head of the fiction film section of the All-Russian Photographic and Cinematographic Section (VFKO) of the Russian Soviet Federated Socialist Republic (RSFSR) People's Commissariat of Enlightenment (Narkompros). His associate was his old friend Vasili Ilyin, a painter, an actor, and likewise a supporter of Volkonsky's system. Gardin had been interested in the training of the new actor in 1916 and had at that time planned with Ilyin the establishment of a "Studio of Cinema Art." In his diary entry for 15 December 1916, Gardin noted, "Today Vasili Sergeyevich Ilyin is coming again to continue our never-ending discussion about the studio, the new army of film-makers who will conquer the world."[15] He characterised his attitude toward cinema at that time in the following way: "I have not withdrawn from cinema, but I have been dreaming of a studio and not of productions . . . I am interested above all in research into working methods."[16]

Because of the war, the studio never started work. After the Revolution and after holding the leading position in VFKO, Gardin achieved the improbable, the opening of the First State Cinema School, which he headed. Initially Gardin's plan had a Cyclopean character: it was his intention to open ten schools, each with a thousand students, and to create on the basis of these a new "army" of filmmakers[17] and, although this was not made clear, perhaps also a new anthropological type of man. There is little doubt that the existence of the school owed much to Gardin's enthusiasm for Volkonsky's new anthropology. It is enough to look at the complement of teachers. First Sergei Volkonsky was invited to teach there and take charge of the courses on the "system of expressive man." Many years later Gardin recalled Volkonsky's courses from 1919–1920: "The students had their hands and feet entangled in concentric, normal-eccentric and concentro-concentric positions."[18] Then there was Ilyin, of whom Kuleshov wrote in his memoirs, "Ilyin was an enthusiastic admirer of the Delsarte school and applied its teachings to our work at every opportunity. In addition, he developed and perfected it himself. We were extremely pleased with Ilyin's research."[19] Elsewhere Kuleshov affirmed that it was in fact Ilyin who introduced him to the Delsarte system.[20] One of the other teachers was Nikolai Foregger, creator of the machine dances that were to become famous in the 1920s and were so obviously linked to the "new anthropology." At one time the school was headed by Valentin Turkin, who shared the general interest in Volkonsky's system. The school maintained particularly close contacts with the Experimental Heroic Theatre directed by Boris Ferdinandov, who had created the Dalcrozian theory of "metro-rhythm." For a while Kuleshov's Workshop even took shelter in the building of this theatre. The appearance within the film school's walls of Kuleshov, who had been Gardin's protégé since 1918 (when Gardin had invited him to take charge of the newsreel and re-editing section of VFKO), was to be expected. Kuleshov professed a Delsartism that was even more orthodox than that of the other teachers.

The foundations of future Soviet film theory were being laid around the film school and in its midst. We might apparently even be justified in talking about a specific GTK-GIK film theory.[21] Before we define the main body of ideas of this collective theory, we must answer the question: why has the history of film thought ignored this important theoretical complex? We can cite a whole range of reasons. There is no written record of the ideas expressed by many of the participants in the collective. Gardin, for example, never published his theoretical findings, which became known only in 1949 after their detailed exposition in his *Memoirs*. We know practically nothing about Ilyin's ideas. By 1922–1923 there was in addition a noticeable distance emerging between Kuleshov, who had adopted the positions of LEF [*Levyi front iskusstv* (Left Front of the Arts)], and his former associates (above all Gardin), who had maintained closer links with the pre-Revolutionary artistic tradition. And we must not forget personal quarrels. At the beginning of the 1920s, there was a break between Kuleshov and Ilyin, which in Kuleshov's later memoirs was attributed to Ilyin's scholastic Delsartism,[22] although in this conflict we must obviously not exclude personal motives. The break with Turkin followed in 1925 after the publication of his book *The Cinema Actor* [Kino-akter], which contained scarcely veiled attacks on Kuleshov. Thus, at the very moment when Kuleshov's theory was beginning to achieve widespread popularity—1925—the collective of the film school was disintegrating and the traces of its former unity were being lost in later polemics and personal conflicts.

Gardin was the central figure in the history of the film school in its first stage. He had come to the notion of the need to create a new type of actor for cinema as early as 1913 while working on the film *The Keys to Happiness*. He invited the nonprofessional Alexander Volkov to play one of the leading roles, and Volkov astonished him with the veracity of his acting. Gardin was later to call Volkov "the first model actor [naturshchik] in cinema."[23] It was then that he came to the idea of the prime importance for cinema of physiognomy and physiognomic characterology, and he divided actors into three groups: the emotional type, the rational-technical type, and the technical type. Simultaneously he began to use his rudimentary knowledge of physiology and reflexology in his work with actors. By 1916, as is evident from his diary, Gardin's film theory had been fully formed. His orientation toward the model actor was already evident: indeed in 1916 Gardin was already using the term widely (possibly for the first time in the history of Russian film theory). Gardin divided each action into four "physiological" stages and based the actor's work on the transitions from one "segmentary phase" to another. On 18 May 1916, he wrote in his diary:

> Today the shooting was difficult. In the schemata that I definitively adopted for absolutely every draft *close-up montage combination* (and also for the temporal calculations of the mechanics of spiritual life), I am beginning to assemble the individual signs that characterise each element in the four-part formula that I took as the basis for all schemata:
> 1. Sensation (impression) is the external or internal stimulant.
> 2. Perception is the orientation.
> 3. Comprehension is the brake.
> 4. Appellation is the (sound) reaction—the word.[24]

The desire to divide action into such minute physiological phases (and the enormous role that he attributed to the eye in this process of movement) led Gardin toward the widespread use of close-ups, that is, the cutting off of the actor by the frame of the shot, which was partly analogous to Delsarte's "independence of the limbs from one another." The desire to set out the elements of action according to a precise four-part formula created the necessity for properly thought-out "close-up montage combinations." Hence the requirements of the new anthropology of the actor encouraged in Gardin's mind the idea of montage. Gardin himself recognised perfectly the significance of these theoretical studies: "That is how my first thoughts arose on the possibilities of montage combinations and on the conversion of acting to the expressive movement of the parts of the actor's body and to the condition of objects symbolising the actions of man," he wrote.[25] This formulation is interesting because we can still detect in it an indissoluble link between the idea of montage and the body of the actor: the "possibilities of montage combinations" are directly linked to the "conversion of acting to the expressive movement of the parts of the actor's body." Montage was thus understood as a cinematographic form of organisation of the actor's behaviour.

Gardin was simultaneously taken by the idea of founding a film school where he intended to conduct a "basic course" on "man's behaviour in front of the camera lens." He declared: "One day a new man, unspoiled by theatre, will appear in cinema. He is the one with whom and on whom it will be possible to experiment."[26] Thus by 1916 Gardin had already worked out an approach to the cinema actor as "model actor" and as material for montage treatment. By 1919 Gardin's ideas had acquired a more and more openly expressed Delsartian character. Parallel with this came a further elaboration of montage category. Even before Kuleshov arrived at the film school, Gardin was giving a special lecture on montage and at that time he defined cinema as "a rhythmic alternation of film fragments whose composition . . . was united into a film on the basis of a montage calculation, which was one of the most important calculations in the direction of a film."[27] Gardin wrote:

> Starting from this definition, I tried to establish the creative tasks in directing a work, above all to teach a sense of the rhythm of the film being made. . . . Rhythm is an endless theme. Movement and the endlessly varying alternation of acceleration and slow motion in accordance with certain calculations are the form of rhythm and the recording of them will be the technique and the sense included in the word "cinematography."[28]

Hence montage was also understood as the rhythmological key, given that the film was, in the spirit of Dalcroze and Volkonsky, proclaimed to be a "recording" of rhythm.

In practice Gardin's promised experiments with the model actor took the form of a series of exercises with "velvet screens." With the aid of these screens, he formed a window whose shape recalled the frame of a film shot. Into the window he put the face of the actor who had to work out precise mimic reflex reactions to stimuli. In this process, most attention was devoted to the movement of the eyes, which were recorded in complex schemata. As a result, Gardin elaborated "1,245 compositions which could be used to arrange the head of the person being filmed in the frame."[29] These compositions were partly copied from Delsarte's schemata. These experiments with frames transferred the whole emphasis on to close-up and the miming of the actor. The rhythmic montage aspect was here almost absent, remaining principally in the field of theory. The methodology of the velvet screens was later vehemently criticised by Kuleshov. But it is obvious that this very methodology is the direct consequence of the path taken by Gardin, a return to the sources of his film theory, the close-ups of 1916 with the most scrupulous recording of the "reactive phases." But to a certain extent it is also Volkonsky's "montage"; at any rate it is very reminiscent of the experiments that the latter conducted in his lectures. Thus, one account of his lectures reported as early as 1913 (the year when Gardin made his first film):

> S. M. Volkonsky showed nine faces on the screen with corresponding expressions, from the normal-normal (serene calm) to the eccentric-eccentric (ecstasy). These nine typical expressions incorporated nine typical glances. . . . Combined with the nine expressions that depended on the brows and eyelids, these nine glances produced 81 typical expressions for the eyes.[30]

The similarity to Gardin's experiments with the screens is striking: 1,245 compositions are, of course, the product of a gigantic detailed study of Volkonsky's 81 eye expressions. Let us note in passing that Volkonsky's faces were demonstrated on the screen and that Gardin's velvet screens corresponded to this pseudocinema.

After Gardin, the film school was headed for a short time by F. Shipulinsky, and his place was then taken by Valentin Turkin. His positions in the field of theory had a more radical character. Turkin's theoretical evolution is more difficult to reconstruct than Gardin's, but it is similar in part. In 1918 Turkin was one of the leading figures on the Moscow newspaper *Kino-gazeta*. There he published an article which was fundamental for that time, "Simulators and Models," in which he used Gardin's term in extremely declarative form:

> The first truth that I should like to proclaim is that on the screen the actor is equal to the model actor and valuable because he can, when he has thrown off the rags of stage theatricality, condescend, descend to the level of that picturesque theatricality of life that is characteristic of the beggar at the church door [etc., etc.].[31]

The pages of *Kino-gazeta* carried two other articles that were to have considerable significance later: the article "The Screen and Rhythm" by

Anna Lee (the pen-name of Anna Zaitseva-Selivanova, the future wife of Pudovkin) and Kuleshov's article "The Art of Cinema," which contained Kuleshov's first reflections on montage. Turkin, as the "leader" of the newspaper, was the "godfather" of both. The two articles are almost the first Dalcrozian declarations in film theory. Anna Lee begins her piece with an almost word-for-word repetition of Volkonsky:

> It is necessary for our intuition, our taste, our heart, our intellect—for everything, everything to merge, to vibrate and to blend harmoniously with the tasks of the artist. This is only possible when the symbols, the signs through which he wants us to read his artistic intentions are rhythmically realised. . . . It is only when he is armed with a knowledge of rhythm, especially screen rhythm, that the actor, like a singer who has mastered the musical sol-fa, will be able to do battle with any element of chance, "for no two things are more hostile to one another than art and chance" (Volkonsky).[32]

Anna Lee sensed the need to find a cinematographic equivalent to the rhythm of the actor, but she did not contemplate montage. Her solution looked extremely naive:

> The actor performs and simultaneously the camera (cameraman) operates, like a metronome establishing a certain tempo. The unit of speed of the performing actor does not correspond to the unit of speed of the camera in operation and this causes arrhythmia. . . . But, if we add to this a third rhythm, that of the projector and the theatre, the result will be rhythmic inarticulacy.[33]

Anna Lee proposes to find a "coefficient of movement," a "general constant," an "amalgamating unit" that would help to synchronise the three rhythms. Anna Lee's line of thought is very interesting: the new anthropology of the actor urgently requires the discovery of a rhythmic law of cinema, and it is to be found in the natural "metronome" of cinema, the cranking of the camera, the potential "rhythmiciser" of the choreography of cinema. It is no accident that the article states: "The grotesque results of dancing [on the screen], even when performed by professionals, confirm and underline the absence of rhythm from the screen."[34]

Kuleshov's article was written before Anna Lee's piece. But it contains a direct response to "The Screen and Rhythm." In this article, the problem of montage and rhythm was still in the background. It is evident that they did not completely preoccupy Kuleshov because the major part of the article (like his 1917 articles in *Vestnik kinematografii*) was devoted to the problems of the art of set decoration. There was none the less a passage that appeared to be extremely close to Gardin's views at that time:

Each individual work of art has its own basic method to express the idea of art. Very few film-makers (apart from the Americans) have realised that in cinema this method of expressing an artistic idea is provided by the rhythmical succession of individual still frames or short sequences conveying movement—that is what is technically known as montage.[35]

This first definition of montage in Kuleshov's work is still pure Gardin and imbued with the spirit of Dalcroze–Volkonsky. The basis of cinema is rhythm (as in Anna Lee), but its realisation is in montage. Lee's article apparently had a powerful effect on Kuleshov and played a particular role in his theoretical evolution. In 1920 in his theoretical "summing up," "The Banner of Cinema," he openly argued against "The Screen and Rhythm," beginning the exposition of his own theory with precisely the question of dance. Without naming Anna Lee, he sets out, with some misrepresentation, her position on the discrepancy between the camera and the choreography of cinema and then argues:

> Let us suppose that dance turned out on screen as well as when it was performed during the shooting, what would we have achieved by this? We should have achieved a situation in which the art of dance could be precisely reproduced on a strip of film. But in that case cinema would have been no more than living photography of dance and on screen we should have achieved the reproduction of the art of *ballet* but there would be no cinema art in it at all.[36]

This polemic explains the origin of one of Kuleshov's experiments, "the dance." But it is equally evident that it also follows the broad outlines of film theory at that time, from the rhythmic anthropology of man to rhythmic montage as its cinematographic quintessence. In this sense, Kuleshov was not very original. Gardin was thinking along the same lines, and Turkin was evolving in the same direction. In 1918 he was fighting for the model actor. And there is nothing more natural than that in 1922 he should be one of the principal propagandists of rhythmic montage.

We shall cite a lengthy quotation from Turkin that expresses his 1922 views:

> The basic element in the form of cinema art is montage. . . . Experience [perezhivanie], mood, the expression of movements of the soul are false means for the actor to make an impression on the audience. The principal means of making an impression in cinema is montage. Montage is the combination of separate moments of action according to the principle of the strongest impression. Action unfolds in space and lasts in time. Art consists in the construction of space and the composition of movement (action) in time. The composition of movement (action) in time is its distribution in a definite rhythmic schema. Action on screen is composed

of the alternation of fragments and the movement of a man, a horse, a car, an aeroplane in individual fragments. Each movement of the fragments (between and within the fragments) must be constructed rhythmically (or metro-rhythmically, if we accept the new phraseology). The rhythmic construction of cinema action is montage.[37]

Everything in this statement is very characteristic of the type of thinking associated with the film school group. Everything begins with the actor, then passes to rhythm and concludes with the assertion that the rhythmic construction of a film is montage.

Turkin's position is, of course, close to Kuleshov's position in 1918. But we should not assume that this is the result of a straightforward borrowing. In 1918 Kuleshov was saying the same thing as Gardin. In 1922 Turkin is repeating both of them. What we have here is not so much the product of the individual creativity of each one of them as the fundamental principle of what we have already called "the 'film school' film theory."

III

Gardin had met Kuleshov in Moscow in 1918. "In the space of 10 minutes, he managed to utter the word *montage* 20 times,"[38] Gardin recalled. Kuleshov's enthusiasm for montage probably predetermined his assignment to the news-reel section and to his later work on re-editing films. In the process of re-editing, Kuleshov discovered his famous "effect" with Mosjoukine's face. In the summer of 1919 he set out with Eduard Tisse, later Eisenstein's cameraman, for the Eastern Front, where he filmed a newsreel. He returned from the front in October 1919. Gardin's film school had begun work in September 1919. The work of the film school interested Kuleshov a great deal, and he was always visiting it "as a guest." In 1920 he got what he had no doubt wanted very badly: he was appointed to the staff of the school as a teacher. This happened approximately at the end of March or the beginning of April 1920, and Kuleshov immediately joined in as one of the most active members of the collective. For the whole of April he worked with Gardin and his wife Olga Preobrazhenskaya on a "sketch of film rehearsals on an agitational theme in three reels and 86 scenes with an apotheosis."[39] The sketch was based on Gardin's velvet screens and was shown on 1 May. At that moment, Kuleshov was a long way from opposition to Gardin and was actively assimilating the new anthropology of the actor. At that time he was apparently mastering Volkonsky's teaching, with which he had come into contact at the school, and studying Delsarte and Dalcroze.

Kuleshov arrived at the school as a "specialist in montage" with a whole series of relatively vague notions about it that gradually took shape into a system with an active orientation toward the new anthropology. The year 1920 was marked by a strengthening of his theoretical work. It was then that he wrote his programmatic text, "The Banner of Cinema." But the differences in principle between his theoretical position and Gardin's soon became apparent. They are recorded in the article "What Must Be Done in Film Schools." The starting point for Kuleshov's argument here was Delsarte's system:

> Nature has made man so that every emotion he experiences is accompanied by a specific sign in his body and face. . . . Consequently the teacher must show the pupil the law of nature that corresponds to the particular task. . . . For theatre actors these laws have been discovered by Delsarte. It would not be a bad idea to re-examine them and extract from them anything that might prove useful to the film-maker.[40]

Kuleshov did not incline toward Delsartian semiotics, unlike Gardin, who had stuck with the search for a mimic alphabet of signs, but toward Volkonsky's "laws of combination" in which the sense derived from oppositions, contrasts, parallelisms, etc. It was in this context that he subjected the system of velvet frames to a critique, but with one reservation: "Basically, of course, this idea is fine but the significance of close-up for the film-maker lies solely in montage and it can have no independent value for him."[41] He went on to set out his own methodology, demonstrating the error of Gardin's ways:

1. An incorrect exercise. In the first frame, you show a man with a look of hatred: in the second, another man whose look answers the first—triumph, etc.
2. A correct exercise, which has to be performed several times. The first frame is as in the previous instance, for the second time you see the man's look of hatred in the frame, and in the following frame a hand holding a letter. The content of the scene has changed.[42]

It is not difficult to see that Kuleshov was proposing to reconstruct his own experiment with Mosjoukine in the velvet frames. But the most interesting thing in the article was the fact that the Mosjoukine experiment, which was not directly mentioned, was inextricably linked to the body of the actor understood as the universal model for montage: "If we mask the actor and force him to strike a sad pose, the mask will express sadness: but if the actor strikes a joyful pose, it will look to us as if the mask is joyful too."[43] Kuleshov was already rethinking the Delsarte–Volkonsky system as a source of pure montage: segments of the human body are like signs opposed to one another, and they make sense in precisely that opposition. The description of the man in the mask is a direct transposition on to the actor's body of the "Kuleshov effect," in which Mosjoukine's masklike face changed its expression within various montage juxtapositions.

Thus, Kuleshov had fully mastered the main complex of ideas of the "film school theory" but was fighting to reorientate it in principle toward montage, toward the cinematographisation of Delsarte on the basis of the principles of montage. The conclusion to the article left no doubt whatsoever on this score:

> All kinds of art have one essence and we must look for that essence in rhythm. But *rhythm* in art is expressed and achieved in various ways: in theatre through the actor's gesture and voice, in cinema through montage. Consequently the arts differ from one another in their specific methods of mastering their material, their means of achieving rhythm. . . . In using the arguments that have just been set out, we want to remind you once again of the importance of Delsarte in the model actor's *pose*. For now it is more obvious that the working methods of other arts can also be applied to cinema but that this *must* be done in a cinematographic way: that is, we take the law of an idea that is common to all the arts and look for means that are *characteristic of cinema* to exploit that idea.[44]

An eloquent argument: for Kuleshov montage was a specifically cinematographic analogue of the Delsartian pose. They had a common aim: rhythm.

By 1921 there was an urgent need to subject Kuleshov's ideas to experimental verification (cf. Gardin's tendency to experiment with the model actor). In March 1921, after receiving 90 metres of film, Kuleshov shot six montage experiments. Here is a list of them taken from Kuleshov's application to the Photographic and Cinematographic Section of the Artistic Sector of the Moscow Regional Political Education Committee:

1. a dance, filmed from one place—10 metres
2. a dance, filmed using montage—10 metres
3. the dependence of the model actor's experience on the causes of that experience:
   (a) 14 metres
   (b) 20 metres
4. the arbitrary combination of various scenes of action into a single composition—13 metres [the "creative geography" experiment]
5. the arbitrary combination of the parts of different people's bodies and the creation through montage of the desired model actor—12 metres [the "created man" experiment]
6. the uniform movement of the eyes of a model actor—2 metres.[45]

Of these six experiments the history of cinema has preserved the memory of only two: the "created man" and "creative geography"—the others are practically never mentioned. But if we look at the whole programme of experiments in its entirety, we can easily see that the sixth experiment fell within the Dalcroze–Volkonsky orbit. The third experiment recalled the Mosjoukine experiment but was partly reformulated in the categories of reflexology. The first, second, fourth, and fifth experiments are closely linked to one another. First we have the non-montage image of a dance (not specifically cinematographic); then we are offered three different types of the dismemberment and combination of objects. The dance is composed of fragments that have been filmed with a single model, while the fourth and fifth experiments assemble the body of a man or the "body" of the world from fragments of various objects. The Delsartian idea of dismemberment and combination is here clearly evident.

Judging by the frequency of the references in the texts and its place in the list, the "dance" experiment was the most important to Kuleshov, although in later analyses it has been completely overshadowed. The significance of this experiment does not depend merely on the retrospective polemic with the article by Anna Lee, to which we have referred. The dance was essentially the only subject that clearly raised the problem of rhythm. Rhythm had been postulated as the principal aim of montage, but neither the Mosjoukine experiment nor the "created man" was a complete response to this aim.

It is also essential to remember that in the 1920s, even more than in the 1910s, the tendency to transform choreography into a metamodel for the performing arts was being reinforced. It was Tairov who made a significant contribution to choreographic rhythmology, and Meyerhold's biomechanics is genetically linked to it. But for Kuleshov, it was the theory and practice of Boris Ferdinandov's Experimental Heroic Theatre, with which he maintained very close links, that were of major importance. It is, of course, no accident that after the break with the film school, the "Kuleshov collective" moved into the building occupied by the Experimental Heroic Theatre. In his memoirs, Kuleshov wrote enthusiastically about Ferdinandov, clearly counting him among his "teachers."[46]

Among Moscow theatres at the beginning of the 1920s, there was none that was as clearly orientated toward choreography as the Experimental Heroic Theatre. V. Tikhonovich, who took Ferdinandov's ideas to the verge of absurdity, wrote:

> The "anarchy" that reigned in the drama theatre was linked to the fact that in drama people do not dance, but walk, stand, sit, lie, etc., they do not sing, but speak, shout, cry, laugh, are silent, etc. . . . It has to be said that the dramatic theatre has simply *fallen behind* opera and ballet in its own artistic development. . . . But, say the Old Believers, we shall more or less

eradicate the clear boundaries between drama, ballet and opera. Even better, this is a *compliment* to the Ferdinandov system: it seems to lead us towards a *synthetic* theatre, a theatre of gesture and dance merged into a single whole, of merged speech and song, a theatre which provides obvious opportunities for the future.[47]

Ferdinandov created the system of metro-rhythm that was popular in the 1920s. His starting point was the fact that theatre was a wholly dynamic art. The organisation of the dynamics of artistic form had to take on a metro-rhythmic form that was subject to the basic laws of mechanics. Ferdinandov tried to reduce all stage movements to metres that were close to those of music and poetry. He distinguished two-beat and three-beat measures of movement. The metric organisation of stage movement set Ferdinandov the problem of recording movement: "The resolution of the bases of theatrical recording," he wrote, "is a problem for regular theatre: we are also working on it in our theatrical laboratory."[48] He also paid a considerable tribute to reflexology. But it is particularly interesting for us that Ferdinandov spoke systematically of montage:

> Theatre is the art of the human body, consisting of three basic elements: the acoustic (sound-voice), the mimic (movement proper) and the psychological (sensation, reflex, deed, feeling—in a word, emotion)—plus montage which surrounds the man-actor in his main work.[49]

Although for Ferdinandov montage was in many ways an external element, it was also subject to his metro-rhythm: "The same laws of metro-rhythm, tempo, accord, theatrical harmony and counterpoint also guide the construction of theatrical montage . . . and its combination with the actor's basic work."[50] Thus a kind of choreography was promoted to the position of an organisational principle in relation to montage as well. Furthermore the montage principle was also introduced into the actual work of the actor. Ferdinandov's theatre was called "normative" or "analytical" theatre precisely because it postulated the necessity for the montage segmentation of movements: "You can construct a stage work on a succession of elementary movements, using the movement of only one organ of the body at each moment in time,"[51] wrote the theatre enthusiast Nikolai Lvov. This "successive" and analytical plastic art was described by Ferdinandov's opponent Ippolit Sokolov as a collection of "typically Jewish artificial little gestures bordering on caricature . . . an insupportable uniformity of conventional and schematic movements."[52] In many ways, theatre was being constructed as an analogue of the system of "notation" of rhythmicised movements.

Kuleshov's move away from Gardin's methodology was clearly stimulated by the influence of Ferdinandov's metro-rhythm, based essentially on Volkonsky's system, which it had significantly modernised. "In

normative theatre people work unconsciously with primitive cinematographic technique,"[53] Kuleshov wrote in 1922. But in the "Work Plan for
the Experimental Cinema Laboratory," compiled in 1923, we find:
"Work in time. The preparatory concept of metre and rhythm. Exercises.
Notes and notation. Exercises."[54] These are already Ferdinandov's
themes. As early as 1914, S. Volkonsky had called for the use of cinema
for the purpose of quasi-choreographic teaching, in conservatoires, for
instance, "as the most powerful teaching instrument; it will be a mirror
reflecting the way in which we should and should not move."[55] By the
1920s, cinema was already beginning to prove equal to choreographic
notation. At that time, the press put forward the idea of using cinema to
record dance: "It is very probable that a precise record of dance is not
possible. . . . The failures that have characterised research in this field
compel us to abandon the notion of developing a system to record dance
and turn all our hopes to cinema."[56]

Turkin fully shared the idea of cinema as transfigured choreography
and the inclination toward Ferdinandov's system. In his 1925 book *The
Cinema Actor*, this problem is given prominence:

> The developed technique of montage has enriched the transmission of
> dance on the screen. Dance has begun to be composed of dismembered
> moments of movement, filmed from various distances and various angles
> and alternating in a proper and measured order. Its compositional element
> has become the movement-fragment (i.e., a fragment of cinema film on
> which the dancer's movement has been recorded: because dance on screen
> is as much the "dance" of man in individual fragments of film as the
> alternation, the "dance" of the actual fragments of film).[57]

Cinema, as we shall see, was to be simultaneously an analytical record of
dance and rhythmicised montage choreography. Turkin went on:

> The question of dance has a special significance for contemporary cinema
> and, in particular, for the mastery of film acting. The search for strict artistic
> form in cinema is moving towards the measured construction of the actor's
> movement on the screen and of the rhythmic montage of the film, i.e.
> towards the creation from the movement on the screen of a kind of "dance."
> . . . Film drama is trying to immerse itself in the culture of dance, in rhythm,
> so that it actually becomes "dance," a sort of contemporary, realistic or, if
> you prefer, analytical or biomechanical ballet.[58]

(This is comparable to the ideas expressed in Fernand Léger's *Le
Ballet mécanique* [France, 1924].)

That is why on 8 March 1921, Kuleshov filmed a dance by the
ballerina Zinaida Tarkhovskaya in the first and most important of his series
of projected montage experiments (see figure 9). Later, in Alexander

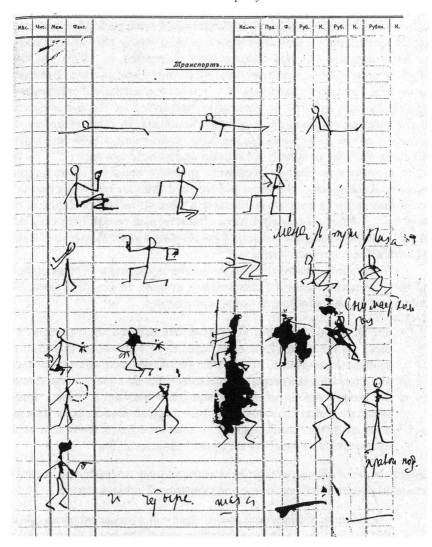

Figure 9. "Action score" by Kuleshov for a 1921 "film without a film."

Belenson's book *Cinema Today* [*Kino segodnya*, 1925], Kuleshov quite unambiguously indicated the link between montage and choreographic notation:

> Each gesture has its duration and that duration can be recorded by a sign that can be studied and reproduced. The alternation of accented and unaccented notes will create a temporal metre, which determines the metric system and the temporal character (just as in montage).[59]

Thus even in 1925, the "dance" experiment preserved the importance of a "symbol of faith" as the supreme expression of the link between montage and the new anthropology. Montage was now the expression of the new conception of man and derived literally from the human body, as a record of its movement, as the mechanical expression of its natural rhythm, as the embodiment of the concept of the body analytically dismembered. Montage was now induced by body rhythm, by the body's new being, in the broadest sense of the word. Man's body was the raw material for theatre. The "body" of the world, transformed into the "body" of the film stock, was the raw material for cinema. The analogies now were almost absolute and immutable.

The later development of cinema revealed the repetitive character of the metro-rhythmic element in montage. In Kuleshov's later analyses, metro-rhythm passes into the shadows and the semantics of montage is promoted to the forefront. By 1929 Kuleshov was already concentrating exclusively on his experiments with "creative geography" and "created man," and furthermore he traced these experiments back to *Engineer Prite's Project* [*Proekt inzhenera Praita,* 1918].[60] The link with the anthropology of the 1910s was also camouflaged by Kuleshov's move closer to Constructivism. In 1922 he was one of the leading theorists of *Kino-Fot*, the journal headed by Alexei Gan, the theorist of Constructivism. This *rapprochement* was based on the machine cult. Volkonsky had already made the connection between the regularity of the movements of the human body, its automation, and the machine. But in the 1920s, these ideas were developed in a much more radical way. In this respect, the polemic conducted by Ippolit Sokolov against the Dalcrozians was particularly characteristic:

> The actor on the stage must first of all become an automaton, a mechanism, a machine. . . . Henceforth painters, doctors, artists, engineers must study the human body, not from the point of view of anatomy or physiology, but *from the point of view of the study of machines.* The new Taylorised man has his own new physiology. Classical man, with his Hellenic gait and gesticulation, is a beast and savage in comparison with the new Taylorised man.[61]

This was a clear attack on Dalcroze–Volkonsky and their cult of antiquity. Sokolov went on to the heart of the matter: "The training for the aesthetic gesture is the rhythmicisation of movement. The rhythmicised gesture must be constructed on psycho-physiological and technical rhythm and not on purely musical rhythm."[62] The machine cult attempted to disavow its sources, to renounce the musical-choreographic model. Henceforth the model actor was to be understood in a purely mechanical sense. Oskar Bir set American film actors up as an ideal when he said, "They are not actors at all but organs of movement."[63] Cinema was once again described as an organism with, in its structure, the same constitution as the actor: "Cinema is first of all a machine. . . . What it shows on the screen is the definitive mechanisation of life."[64] Alexei Gan applied these ideas to the Kuleshov Workshop:

> Why? Because, as an element of cinema's raw material, disorganised nature, whether static or in motion, lies on the screen and produces absolutely unnatural images.[65]

As we can see, Gan's ethic repeated Volkonsky's almost word for word, although it is true that he only repeated what corresponded to the mechanistic laws of nature. But the sudden move toward the declarative machine cult concealed the continuity of ideas. Kuleshov responded actively to Constructivist slogans. In an unsigned article, "The History of the State Institute of Cinematography," published in *Kino-Fot* and probably written by Kuleshov, Gardin was given a "dressing-down" for distancing himself from the "left-wing tendency," and the orientation toward the "mechanisation of human movements" was proclaimed.[66] The short period of *rapprochement* with the Constructivists played an important role in the later evaluation of Kuleshov's work and in his break with preceding tradition. But Kuleshov was too closely linked to the ideas of the new anthropology, which had their roots in the 1910s. It is precisely this that doubtless explains in part the unexpected move by Kuleshov and his entire collective (Pudovkin, Barnet, Komarov, and others) to Mezhrabpomfilm, the most traditional film studio in the 1920s, which preserved the best traditions of the pre-Revolutionary Russian cinema. The names of Delsarte and Dalcroze can be found in Kuleshov texts over a period of many years, and this has puzzled researchers. By the end of the 1920s, they were already being perceived as strange anachronisms. It is symptomatic that as late as 1924 an orthodox figure such as Alexander Voznesensky, who belonged entirely to the pre-Revolutionary Russian cinema, persistently recommended the methods of Dalcroze and Delsarte as a means of achieving the maximum "incarnation" [vzhivanie] in the character,[67] prolonging in his own way the Gardin line of film theory.

In the later Kuleshov texts (after 1929), which have until recently served as the basis for the evaluation of this film theory, montage and the anthropological ideas of the 1910s diverge, giving the impression of a strange eclecticism. The metro-rhythmic approach and the new anthropology differed in their methods of teaching the actor and of rehearsal, but their direct link with the montage experiments of 1921 was lost.

Nevertheless, the idea of the actor moving along axes, which was subsequently to provoke such censure, is no more than a fusion of Volkonsky's concepts on the directions of the movement of the body and Ferdinandov's inclination toward recording the movement of the actor. They make complete sense only in the context of the principle of the identity between montage and the movement of the body, of their mutual rhythmic resonance. The methodology of the training of the model actor, which was experienced in Kuleshov as a period of intensive research in the field of the "synthetic" theory of cinema, rudimentarily preserved within itself the anthropological principle of montage.

The history of Kuleshov's theoretical research reminds us once again of the fact that for thousands of years the human body has served as a model for the universe, from the theory of macrocosm and microcosm to the physiognomic teachings of the eighteenth and nineteenth centuries. This traditional metamodel has evolved from the intact body of the Middle Ages to the dismembered corpse of the nineteenth century. The idea of montage as the specific basis of a new art, cinema, is an important link in the long history of this evolution.

NOTES

Transliteration from the Cyrillic to the Latin alphabet is a perennial problem for writers on Russian subjects. Richard Taylor has opted for a dual system: in the text he has transliterated in a way that renders Russian names and terms more accesible to the nonspecialist, whereas in the scholarly apparatus he has adhered to a more accurate system for the specialist.

1. Y. A. Ozarovskii, "Sushchnost mimicheskogo ucheniya Del'sarta" [The Essence of Delsarte's Teaching on Mime], *Golos i rech'* [Voice and Speech] 1 (January 1913), 5.

2. J. d'Udine [Zh. D'Udin], *Iskusstvo i zhest* [Art and Gesture] (St Petersburg: 1912), p. 73.

3. Ibid., p. 95.

4. Ibid., p. 22.

5. Ibid., p. 100.

6. Ibid., p. 220.

7. S. Volkonskii, *Chelovek na stsene* [Man on Stage] (St Petersburg: 1912), p. 150.

8. Ibid., p. 127.

9. S. Volkonskii, *Vyrazitel'nyi chelovek. Stsenicheskoe vospitanie zhesta (po Del'sartu)* [Expressive Man. Stage Gesture Training (after Delsarte)] (St Petersburg: 1913), p. 79.

10. Cited in S. Volkonskii, *Otkliki teatra* [Theatre's Responses] (Petrograd: 1914), p. 123.

11. Ibid., p. 152.

12. Ibid., p. 169.

13. Ibid., p. 178.

14. Volkonskii, *Vyrazitel'nyi chelovek*, p. 132.

15. V. R. Gardin, *Vospominaniya* [Memoirs], vol. 1: *1912–21* (Moscow: 1949), p. 143.

16. Ibid., p. 139.

17. Ibid., p. 170.

18. Ibid., p. 178.

19. L. V. Kuleshov and A. S. Khokhlova, *50 let v kino* [50 Years in Cinema] (Moscow: 1975), p. 74.

20. See E. Gromov, *L. V. Kuleshov* (Moscow: 1984), p. 103.

21. The Film School became GTK in 1925–1930 and then GIK in 1930–1934; since then it has been called VGIK.

22. Kuleshov and Khokhlova, *50 let v kino*, pp. 74–75.

23. Gardin, *Vospominaniya*, p. 52.

24. Ibid., p. 134.

25. Ibid., p. 120.

26. Ibid., p. 138.

27. Ibid., p. 192.

28. Ibid.

29. Ibid., p. 203.

30. *Golos i rech'* 3 (March 1913), 26.

31. V. Turkin "Litsedei i naturshchiki" [Simulators and Models], *Kino-gazeta* 29 (July 1918).

32. A Lee, "Ekran i ritm" [The Screen and Rhythm], *Kino-gazeta* 29 (July 1918).

33. Ibid.

34. Ibid.

35 L. V. Kuleshov, "Iskusstvo svetotvorchestva" [The Art of Cinema] (*svetotvorchestvo*, literally "light creation," was one of the early Russian words for cinema), *Kino-gazeta* 12 (March 1918), translated in Richard Taylor and Ian Christie, eds., *The Film Factory: Russian and Soviet Cinema in Documents, 1896–1939* (Cambridge, Mass.: Harvard University Press, 1988), pp. 45–46, hereafter cited as *FF.*

36. L. V. Kuleshov, "Znamya kinematografii" [The Banner of Cinema], first published in *L. V. Kuleshov, Stat'i Materialy* [L. V. Kuleshov, Articles, Materials], (Moscow: 1979), p. 90, hereafter cited as *LVK.*

37. Strzhigotskii (pseudonym of V. Turkin), "Spor o printsipakh ili bor'ba za stil?" [An Argument about Principles or a Battle for Style?], *Kino* (Moscow) 1 (20 October 1922), 11.

38. Gardin, *Vospominaniya,* p. 174.

39. Ibid., p. 195.

40. L. V. Kuleshov, "Chto nado delat' v kinematograficheskikh shkolakh" [What Must Be Done in Film Schools], probably written in 1921 and first published in LVK, p. 158.

41. Ibid.

42. Ibid., p. 159.

43. Ibid., p. 160.

44. Ibid.

45. Ibid., p. 134.

46. Kuleshov and Khokhlova, *50 let v kino,* pp. 68–69.

47. V. T. [V. Tikhonovich], "Zakonomernyi teatr" [Regulated Theatre], *Vestnik iskusstv* [Herald of the Arts] 1 (1922), 12–13.

48. B. Ferdinandov, "Teatr segodnya" [Theatre Today], in *O teatre* [On Theatre] (Tver: 1922), p. 47.

49. Ibid., p. 44.

50. Ibid., p. 46.

51. N. L'vov, "Analiticheskii teatr" [Analytical Theatre], *Vestnik iskusstv* 2 (1922), 5–6.

52. I. Sokolov, "Metro-ritm Ferdinandova" [Ferdinandov's Metro-Rhythm], *Vestnik iskusstv* 3/4 (1922), 15.

53. L. V. Kuleshov, "Kinematograf kak fiksatsiya teatral'nogo deistviya" [Cinema as the Fixing of Theatrical Action], *Ermitazh* 13 (8–13 August 1922), 15; reprinted in *LVK,* p. 116; translated in *FF,* pp. 66–67.

54. "Plan rabot eksperimental'noi kinolaboratorii na 1923/24 god," first published in *LVK,* p. 199.

55. Volkonskii, *Otkliki teatra,* p. 188.

56. N. M., "Ballet i kinematografiya" [Ballet and Cinematography], *Ekran* 22 (21–28 February 1922), 4.

57. V. Turkin, *Kino-akter* [The Cinema Actor] (Moscow: 1925), pp. 9–10.

58. Ibid., p. 10.

59. A. Belenson, *Kino segodnya. Ocherki sovetskogo kino-iskusstva (Kuleshov–Vertov–Eizenshtein)* [Cinema Today. Essays in Soviet Cinema Art (Kuleshov–Vertov–Eisenstein)] (Moscow: 1925), p. 23.

60. L. V. Kuleshov, *Iskusstvo kino* [The Art of Cinema] (Moscow: 1929), pp. 24–27; translated in R. Levaco, ed., *Kuleshov on Film* (Berkeley: University of California Press, 1974), p. 51.

61. I. Sokolov, "Industrializatsiya zhesta" [The Industrialisation of Gesture], *Ermitazh* 10 (July 1922), 6.

62. Ibid., p. 7.

63. O. Bir, "Chelovek i mashina. Kino i teatr" [Man and Machine, Cinema and Theatre], *Vestnik iskusstv* 3–4 (1922), 14.

64. Ibid.

65. A. Gan, "Kino-tekhnikum" [The Cine-Technicum], *Ermitazh* 10 (July 1922), 11.

66. "Istoriya gosudarstvennogo Instituta Kinematografii," *Kino-Fot* 3 (19–25 September 1922), 8–9.

67. A. Voznesenskii, *Iskusstvo ekrana. Rukovodstvo dlya kino-aktërov i rezhissërov* [The Art of the Screen. A Guide for Film Actors and Directors] (Kiev: 1924) pp. 121–2.

The Periodicity and
Nationality of
Silent Cinema

Tom Gunning

"Now You See It, Now You Don't": The Temporality of the Cinema of Attractions

The revision of early film history that began in the late 1970s was only partly a process of correcting the scholarship of previous generations of scholars (who had not had easy access to film archives) through more careful film analysis and a thorough winnowing of secondary material, such as trade journals, film catalogs, and business records. The possibility of seeing and analyzing a large number of films from the period before World War I (made possible by such events as the FIAF Conference at Brighton, England, in 1978, which gathered together hundreds of rarely seen prints) certainly inspired the transformation. But the new discoveries also created and were guided by new schema through which the history of early cinema was (re)constructed. Inspired in a central way by certain insights of Noel Burch, other scholars and I began to envision early film as less a seed bed for later styles than a place of rupture, a period that showed more dissimilarity than continuity with later film style.

This sense of rupture and difference contrasted with previous assumptions about the beginnings of film style and practice. Although the history of early cinema had never been thoroughly theorized, I believe one can isolate three assumptions that underpinned what I will call the continuity model. This model sees early cinema as a preparatory period for later film styles and practices, the infancy of an art form. The first assumption appeared earliest historically and remained the least theorized because it was seen as a natural assumption. We could call this the evolutionary assumption, and it motivates the structure of early film histories such as those of Terry Ramsaye and Lewis Jacobs. This assumption sees cinema before WWI as primitive, an early stage in which later potentials are sketched out but imperfectly realized. Following a biological and teleological logic, this assumes that the later styles of cinema are a sort of natural

From *The Velvet Light Trap* 32 (1993). Reprinted by permission of the author and University of Texas Press.

norm that early cinema envisioned but was not yet capable of realizing because of technological and economic immaturity and a natural need for a period of development guided by a method of trial and error. This assumption sees film history as a linear evolutionary process in which the earliest stage is by definition a period of less development.

A second assumption can be seen as growing out of the evolutionary assumption, giving it more specificity and defining the goals of the development of film art with more precision. I will call this the cinematic assumption. The work of classical film historians Lewis Jacobs, Georges Sadoul, and Jean Mitry all show its influence. In this assumption, the development of film came from a discovery and exploration of its true cinematic essence. This development usually takes the dramatic form of a liberation of film from a false homology that restricted it to the technological reproduction of theater. In this assumption, editing usually plays the key role, but other inherently "cinematic" devices of camera mobility and freedom of shooting angle also help define a uniquely cinematic essence. Within this scenario, early cinema makes the initial error of simple reproduction and theatricality and then dramatically discovers its own nature.

The third assumption is perhaps the most subtle and was the last to be articulated, appearing in the semiological writing of Christian Metz. Metz reworked the assumption of a natural cinematic essence by highlighting the narrative function, declaring that cinema only truly appeared when it discovered the mission of telling stories: "The very nature of the cinema rendered such an evolution if not certain at least probable."[1] Mitry had already formulated the cinematic assumption by seeing early cinema as a struggle between theatricality and narrativity,[2] and Metz extends this formulation into what we could call the narrative assumption. All three assumptions can function together to form a tightly knit understanding of the continuity of early cinema with its later development. The telling of stories supplies the goal of the evolutionary assumption (cinema must evolve as a better and more efficient teller of stories) as well as a motive for its differentiation from theater (since silent cinema was mute, it had to compensate with other regimes of signifiers to carry narrative information and therefore developed its own language).

When André Gaudreault and I introduced the term *cinema of attractions* in the early 1980s, we were trying to undo the purchase these assumptions had on conceptualizing early film history.[3] Of course, these assumptions are not simply illusions to be dispelled; they do contain schema that have been important for certain periods of film history. In particular, my own work on the early films of D. W. Griffith reexamined the narrative assumption and found that the function of storytelling was determinate for stylistic transformations in Griffith's Biograph films.[4] But my historical work also questioned Metz's theoretical assumption of a natural match between cinematic form and the mission of narrative. The dedication of film form to a narrative task that rules Griffith's early work was hardly the outcome of a previous evolution or gradual discovery of film's essential nature. Griffith and his contemporaries (and some immediate predecessors) were engaged in a redefinition rather than a discovery of film—a redefinition shaped by an economic reorganization attempting to regulate the film industry in the wake of the enormous expansion of nickelodeon exhibition. It was at this point in history and within this intersection of economic and social forces that film "discovered" its narrative vocation.

However, cinema before 1908 (or so) presents a different landscape. Here the assumption of narrative primacy becomes more of a barrier to understanding than a useful hypothesis. While storytelling is not totally foreign to cinema before the nickelodeon boom (1905–1909), a number of apparent stylistic anomalies and an often radically different mode of exhibition lead us in another direction. Rather than early approximations of the later practices of the style of classical film narration, aspects of early cinema are best understood if a purpose other than storytelling is factored in.

Cinema as an attraction is that other purpose. By its reference to the curiosity-arousing devices of the fairground, the term denoted early cinema's fascination with novelty and its foregrounding of the act of display. Viewed from this perspective, early cinema did not simply seek to neutrally record previously existing acts or events. Rather, even the seemingly stylistically neutral film consisting of a single shot without camera tricks involved a cinematic gesture of presenting for view, of displaying. The objects of this display varied among current events (parades, funerals, sporting events); scenes of everyday life (street scenes, children playing, laborers at work); arranged scenes (slapstick gags, a highlight from a well-known play, a romantic tableau); vaudeville performances (juggling, acrobatics, dances); or even camera tricks (Méliès-like magic transformations). But all such events were absorbed by a cinematic gesture of presentation, and it was this technological means of representation that constituted the initial fascination of cinema.

My emphasis on display rather than storytelling should not be taken as a monolithic definition of early cinema, a term that forms a binary opposition with the narrative form of classical cinema. Rather, films that precede the classical paradigm are complex texts that occasionally interrelate attractions with narrative projects. My point is not that there are no narrative films before the nickelodeon era but rather that attractions most frequently provide the dominant for film during this period and often jockey for prominence until 1908 or so (and even occasionally later). The desire to display may interact with the desire to tell a story, and part of the challenge of early film analysis lies in tracing the interaction of attractions and narrative organization. The ambivalence that Noel Burch found in the work of Edwin Porter may be partly explained by this interaction, with the famous close-up of the outlaw firing the pistol at the camera in *The Great Train Robbery* functioning as a fairly autonomous attraction while most of the film strives for a sort of linear narrative.[5] In classical cinema, narrative integration functions as a dominant, but attractions still play a role (moments of spectacle, performance, or visual pyrotechnics) with their subordination to narrative functions varying from film to film. Similarly, I do not want to identify narrativity exclusively with the classical paradigm. There are many ways of telling a story in film, and some of them (particularly in cinema before the 1920s or, obviously, in avant-garde work) are clearly nonclassical. In some genres (musicals, crazy comedies), the attractions actually threaten to mutiny. By describing narrative as a dominant[6] in the classical film, I wish to indicate a potentially dynamic relation to nonnarrative material. Attractions are not abolished by the classical paradigm, they simply find their place within it.

I propose attractions, therefore, as a key element of the structure of early film rather than as a single-tracked definition of filmmaking before 1908 (although it may, particularly in the earliest period, function as a defining element). It can only be defined with precision through contrast, however, and I want to further specify some of the ways attractions differ from the cinema of narrative integration that comes after it, as well as from most forms of cinema based on a narrative dominant.

As a new way of approaching early cinema, attractions foreground the role of the spectator. Cinematic attractions can be defined as formal devices within early film texts. However, they can only be thoroughly understood if these devices are conceived as addressing spectators in a specific manner. This unique spectatorial address defines the cinema of attractions and its difference from the classically constructed spectatorial address of later narrative cinema. While I am not sure that the metapsychology of the spectator devised in the seventies is truly adequate to the complexity of even the classical style of narrative (let alone a revision which recognizes the continued role of attractions within classical Hollywood cinema), certain basic contrasts are apparent.

Narrative invokes the spectator's interest (and even desire, in a psychoanalytical model) by posing an enigma. The enigma demands a solution and, as Roland Barthes and the Russian Formalists have shown, the art of narrative consists in delaying the resolution of that enigma, so that its final unfolding can be delivered as a pleasure long anticipated and well earned. Further, in classical narrative cinema this pursuit of an enigma takes place within a detailed diegesis, a fictional world of places and characters in which the action of the narrative dwells. From a spectatorial point of view, the classical diegesis depends not only on certain basic elements of coherence and stability but also on the lack of acknowledgment of the spectator. As the psychoanalytically shaped theory of Metz claims, this is a world that allows itself to be seen but that also refuses to acknowledge its complicity with a spectator. In the classical diegesis, the spectator is rarely acknowledged, an attitude exemplified by the stricture against the actor's look or gestures at the camera/spectator. As Metz says, the classical spectator becomes modeled on the voyeur, who watches in secret, without the scene he watches acknowledging his presence.[7]

Attractions pose a very different relation to the spectator. The attraction does not hide behind the pretense of an unacknowledged spectator (in this respect it recalls Thelma Ritter's line as Stella in Hitchcock's *Rear Window*—"I'm not shy, I've been looked at before"). As I have stated elsewhere, the attraction invokes an exhibitionist rather than a voyeuristic regime.[8] The attraction directly addresses the spectator, acknowledging the viewer's presence and seeking to quickly satisfy a curiosity. This encounter can even take on an aggressive aspect, as the attraction confronts audiences and even tries to shock them (the onrushing locomotive that seems to threaten the audience is early cinema's most enduring example).[9]

The metapsychology of attractions is undoubtedly extremely complex, but its roots could be traced to what St. Augustine called *curiositas* and early Christianity condemned as the "lust of the eye."[10] We could list a number of inherently "attractive" themes in early cinema: a fascination with visual experiences that seem to fold back on the very pleasure of looking (colors, forms of motions—the very phenomenon of motion itself in cinema's earliest projections); an interest in novelty (ranging from actual current events to physical freaks and oddities); an often sexualized fascination with socially taboo subject matter dealing with the body (female nudity or revealing clothing, decay, and death); a peculiarly modern obsession with violent and aggressive sensations (such as speed or the threat of injury). All of these are topoi of an aesthetic of attractions, whether of the cinema, the sensational press, or the fairground. Attractions' fundamental hold on spectators depends on arousing and satisfying visual curiosity through a direct and acknowledged act of display, rather than following a narrative enigma within a diegetic site into which the spectator peers invisibly.

Rather than a desire for an (almost) endlessly delayed fulfillment and a cognitive involvement in pursuing an enigma, early cinema, therefore, *attracts* in a different manner. It arouses a curiosity that is satisfied by surprise rather than narrative suspense. This different temporal configuration determines its unique spectatorial address as much as its acknowledgment of the spectator's gaze, and it is the explosive, surprising, and even disorienting temporality of attractions that I want to explore in the rest of this essay.

First let's consider the temporality of narrative. Beyond stylistic devices of temporal manipulation (those devices that we can describe as the plot or *Sjuzhet*),[11] any narrative implies a development in time. In addition to the base of simple temporal progression and change, this implies what Paul Ricoeur has called a configuration of time, time assuming a sort of shape through the interacting logic of events.[12] As Ricoeur argues, it is through this configuration that events become a story and narrative moves beyond the simply chronological. Time in narrative, therefore, is never just linear progression (one damn thing after another), it is also the gathering of successive moments into a pattern, a trajectory, a sense. Attractions, on the other hand, work with time in a very different manner. They basically do not build up incidents into the configuration with which a story makes its individual moments cohere. In effect, attractions have one basic temporality, that of the alternation of presence/absence that is embodied in the act of display. In this intense form of present tense, the attraction is displayed with the immediacy of a "Here it is! Look at it."

While this temporality is most apparent in the many one-shot films, it also determines the temporal structure of films that include more than one shot, such as the early multishot films of Méliès. The odd temporality of Méliès has been noted by John Frazer:

> The causal narrative links in Méliès films are relatively insignificant compared to the discreet events. We experience his films as rapidly juxtaposed jolts of activity. We focus on successions of pictorial surprises which run roughshod over the conventional niceties of linear plotting. Méliès' films are a collage of immediate experiences which coincidentally require the passage of time to become complete.[13]

Frazer here contrasts two types of temporality: the linear progression of plotting and causality, and the staccato jolts of surprise that characterize Méliès films. While the simple linear model may do a disservice to the possible complexities of narrative structure, Frazer's invocation of jagged rhythm catches the irruption of a different, nonconfigured temporality, that of the attraction.

The temporality of the attraction, therefore, is greatly limited in comparison to narrative, albeit possessing its own intensity. Rather than a development that links the past with the present in such a way as to define a specific anticipation of the future (as an unfolding narrative does), the attraction seems limited to a sudden burst of presence. Restricted to the presentation of a view or a central action, the cinema of attractions tends naturally toward brevity rather than extension. Such restricted focus on a simple action is beautifully indicated by an Edison catalog description of its famous one-shot film *The Kiss:* "They get ready to kiss, begin to kiss, and kiss in a way that brings down the house."[14]

This does not necessarily mean that the act of display was always restricted to the surprise burst of the instant or could not play with its temporality. Certain attractions—most obviously extended landscape panoramas or the railway journeys of the Hale's tours sort—take longer to unfold without creating the patterning expectations that narrative implies. The Biograph 1904 film within the New York subway constantly renews its sense of revelation as the change of light and shadow. The passing structures of subway supports, the appearance of stations, and turns in the track make the film frame a location of seemingly endless visual patterns.[15]

Likewise the very moment of display can be manipulated into a scenario of suspense unique to the aesthetic of attractions. Founded on the moment of revelation, the cinema of attractions frequently redoubles its effect of appearance by framing the attraction with a variety of gestures of display. The most common of these are the literal gestures of the magician in magic films who through a sweep of the hand or a slight bow directs the audience's attention to the transformation that then takes place. This gesture sets up a hierarchy between the magician as displayer and the transformation as the event displayed. Beyond enframing (and therefore calling attention to) the act of display, it also performs the important temporal role of announcing the event to come, focusing not only the attention but the anticipation of the audience.

The temporality of the attraction itself, then, is limited to the pure present tense of its appearance, but the announcing gesture creates a temporal frame of expectation and even suspense. It differs from diegetic suspense, of course, in being concerned less with *how* an event will develop than with *when* an event will occur. Early showman exhibitors were keenly aware that such focused anticipation played an important role in putting an attraction over. Since this temporality need not refer to diegetic unfoldings, the framing gesture could occur outside the actual film, embodied in the way the film was presented. The exhibitor's role as a showman presenting an attraction embodies the essential gesture of the cinema of attractions and could be dramatically intensified through temporal manipulation. For instance, Albert Smith recalled his early days as a traveling exhibitor at the turn of the century with his partner, John Stuart Blackton, and the startling effect of Blackton's lectures that accompanied their films. To emphasize the novel illusion of motion, the first frame of their most popular film, *The Black Diamond Express*, a shot of a locomotive barreling toward the camera, was projected first as a frozen image. Over this curiosity-provoking suspended moment, Blackton would intone: "Ladies and Gentlemen, you are now gazing upon a photograph of the famous Black Diamond Express. In just a moment, a cataclysmic moment, my friends, a moment without equal in the history of our times, you will see this train take life in a marvelous and most astounding manner. It will rush toward you, belching smoke and fire from its monstrous iron throat."[16]

The act of display on which the cinema of attractions is founded presents itself as a *temporal irruption* rather than a temporal development. While every attraction would have a temporal unfolding of its own and some (a complex acrobatic act, for instance, or an action with a clear trajectory, such as an onrushing train) might cause viewers to develop expectations while watching them, these temporal developments would be secondary to the sudden appearance and then disappearance of the view itself. In this sense Méliès' transformations become emblematic examples of the cinema of attractions, endlessly replaying the effect of surprise and appearance, as would a series of brief actualities of the Lumière sort, appearing one after another.

The suspense created by Blackton in the delay of the moving image of the locomotive may have similar effects on suspense within a narrative, such as the sharpening of expectation and even the growing anxiety as an event is announced but withheld. But it is not absorbed into a diegetic world of cause and effect, it has no relation to the fate of characters or the course of events. Rather, it simply redoubles the basic effect of an attraction, cathecting curiosity through delay and creating a satisfying discharge by unleashing the suspended rush of time. Not all gestures of display need to be so violent or shocking, but the shock effect highlights the attraction's disjunctive temporality. Such disjunction could also be used to an erotic effect, as the scopophilia implied by this mode becomes thematized. Edison's *What Happened on Twenty Third Street, New York City* provides a complex example.

This film from 1901 seems to transform itself from a street scene actuality to an erotic scene in the course of its single shot. Shot on the eponymous New York City street, our original attention is, as in so many early actualities, diffused across the shot, solicited by many little events, none of which seem to have any narrative purpose. Rather, we are simply absorbed in the act of viewing, responding to the display of a moment of big city life. As the shot progresses, a couple emerges from the background of street life detail, soliciting our attention as they move toward the camera. As they near the foreground, an air current from a sidewalk grate lifts the woman's dress, and the film ends after the couple reacts to this moment of disclosure and moves on through the frame. Certainly this transformation from a decentered view to a gag centered on specific characters and a moment of erotic display possesses some temporal development. In fact, Judith Mayne in *The Woman at the Keyhole* sees it as moving toward a narrativization of the display of the female body.[17]

I would not dispute Mayne's insightful reading or deny the presence of a sort of temporal development in this film, which shows how difficult it might be to find moments even in early cinema that are totally bereft of narrative development. Particularly when dealing with a film in which the issues of gender (and the relations of power and exploitation they imply) are so clearly inscribed, it is difficult to articulate such relations outside of a narrative framework. However, I would emphasize that while the film can be viewed as a proto-narrative, it is still largely under the sway of a cinema of attractions. The act of display is both climax and resolution here and does not lead to a series of incidents or the creation of characters with discernible traits. While the similar lifting of Marilyn Monroe's skirts in *The Seven*

Year Itch also provides a moment of spectacle, it simultaneously creates character traits that explain later narrative actions.

The film's title also sheds light on the structure of attractions. Its precision of location seemed to me simply documentary overkill until Brooks MacNamara explained its significance. Twenty-third Street near the Flatiron Building drew crowds of male loiterers during the turn of the century not only for the sight of New York's famous skyscraper but for less exulted visual pleasures as well. Known as the windiest corner in New York City, it was also known among the lascivious as a place where women's dresses were frequently lifted by the breeze.[18] The immediate cause of such indecent exposure (in an era where a glimpse of stocking was worth an afternoon of idleness) in this film is a hot air grate (described in the Edison Company publicity as coming from one of the large newspaper offices on the block).[19] To local audiences, at least, the title instead of connoting dull documentary precision would set up an atmosphere of titillation. Such playing with expectations recalls the structure of Blackton's locomotive show: announcement of what is to come, a delay in its revelation, followed by a diminuendo as the display ends and the attraction moves out of the frame.

A similar interaction between narrative structure and the specific temporality of attractions is found in Biograph's 1904 film *Pull Down the Curtain Susie*. Another one-shot film, *Susie* uses a multileveled set of an urban street front with residential windows to stage its drama of revelation. At the opening of the film, a man and a woman walk into the frame together. The shot is framed to focus on a second-story window so that only the heads and busts of the couple are included at the bottom of the frame as they walk (presumably on the street in front of the building). The woman gives the man a kiss, and they exit left. The woman reappears framed in the window of the set as the man reenters the street below. As the man watches excitedly, the woman begins to undress, taking off her skirt and blouse. She starts to remove her shift, then suddenly yanks down the curtain. The man throws up his arms in frustration and the film ends.

Susie unfolds a drama of sexual exhibition with an intradiegetic voyeur. While our involvement with the attraction is certainly mediated by the character of the man who shares our expectation and frustration (assuming, of course, the patriarchal ideology and sexual attitudes the film implies), and the disrobing entails some temporal development, the film nonetheless basically restricts itself to a demonstration of the simple temporality of the attraction: now you see it, now you don't. The climax here (as well as the event announced by the film's suggestive title) comes more from the disappearance of the view than its revelation. The basic structures of attractions, then, revolve around either the act of display and the anticipations that can be heightened by delaying or announcing it (or both) and its inevitable disappearance (which can be gradual or sudden and dramatic). Therefore attractions do show a sort of temporal structure, but the structure consists more of framing a momentary appearance than an actual development and transformation in time. The attraction can appear or disappear and generally needs to do both. While present on the screen, it may in fact change, but insofar as these changes begin to entail further development, we move out of the structure of attractions and into a narrative configuration.

But this does not necessarily mean that the cinema of attractions was restricted to single-shot films. A Méliès transformation film provides the most obvious model for the longer film of attractions with its succession of magical appearances, transformations, and disappearances. One may string a series of attractions together as a Magic film or a Lumière program might. The construction of such suites of attractions displays a highly paratactic structure with no attraction preparing the way for the next, but a simple rule of succession functioning. However, as with the vaudeville show, which would exemplify this variety format, a number of nonnarrative logics might determine the arrangement of attractions.

This was a consideration not only in the production of a film but in the arrangement of a program of films. As Charles Musser has shown, the distinction between film and program was a vague one in this period in which the showman exhibitor asserted as much control over the final form of the film projected as the production company that issued the individual bits of celluloid with which he worked.[20] One basic consideration of such showmen was whether to opt for a basic thematic consistency (for instance, assembling films dealing with similar topics, such as military actualities) or going for its opposite and maximizing variety (following an actuality film with a gag film or trick film). Another structure of attractions relevant for both an exhibitor's program and an actual multishot film involved orchestrating the intensity, elaborateness, and emotional tone of the attractions. The obvious example of this (evident in many trick films) would be ending the film with a particularly spectacular attraction or with a gag. Or, alternatively, attractions could be crossbred with narrative forms, but with attractions still dominating, so that narrative situations simply provided a more naturalized way to move from one attraction to the next. This is clearly evident in Méliès's or Pathé's early extended trick films in which a well-known fairy tale might provide a logical connection between a series of tricks and spectacular effects, the famous "pretext" of a story line on which Méliès would hang his attractions.[21]

This capacity of an attraction to create a temporal disjunction through an excess of astonishment and display rather than the temporal unfolding essential to narrative explains one of the most interesting interactions between narrative form and the aesthetic of attractions, the apotheosis ending. This ending, which entered cinema from the spectacle theater and pantomime, provided a sort of grand finale in which principal members of the cast reappear and strike poses in a timeless allegorical space that sums up the action of the piece. The apotheosis is also the occasion for scenic effects through elaborate sets or stage machinery, as well as the positioning of the performers (often in the form of a procession, or an architectural arrangement of figures, with actual characters often supplemented by a large number of extras precisely for their spectacular effect). Such endings are frequent in the *ferrique* films of Méliès and Pathé, and examples can be found in Méliès's *The Kingdom of the Fairies* and *The Impossible Voyage*, Porter's *Jack and the Beanstalk*, and Pathé's *Le Chat botté*, *La Poule aux oeufs d'or*, and *Aladin du lampe merveilleuse*. Occasionally they also appear in more realistically but still spectacularly conceived dramas, such as Pathé's *Policeman's Tour of the World*, which ends a tale of a worldwide pursuit with an allegorical image of detective and thief shaking hands over an image of the globe, while extras parade by in native costumes of the various countries through which the course of the pursuit ran.[22] What is striking about these apotheosis endings is the way more complex narrative films make use of their "show-stopping" nature to produce a nonnarrative form of closure. Although often integrating the narrative outcome of the action (Jack with the giant's treasure, Azurine and Belazor's connubial bliss and assembled offspring, the rapprochement between thief and detective), they effectively halt the narrative flow through an excess of spectacle, shifting spectator interest from what will happen next to an enjoyment of the spectacle presented to them. In other words, a change in spectatorial registers and temporality takes place with the nondevelopmental time of a crowning attraction closing off the narrative and guaranteeing spectator satisfaction on two levels: the resolution of narrative action and the satiation of visual pleasure.

The apotheosis ending demonstrates once again that in spite of (indeed because of) the structural differences between the temporality and visual pleasure offered by attractions and those structured by narrative, the two ways of addressing spectators can frequently interrelate within the same text. Rather than a developing configuration of narrative, the attraction offers a jolt of pure presence, soliciting surprise, astonishment, or pure curiosity instead of following the enigmas on which narrative depends. However, this burst of presence can itself be structured by playing with or delaying its act of presentation and disappearance. Further, it can interact with narrative structures either by dominating them or by submitting to their dominance and assuming circumscribed roles within a narrative logic.

If we consider the sorts of attractions I have examined here in order to investigate their temporality, certain insights into the metapsychology of the spectator of early cinema suggest themselves. The sudden flash (or equally sudden curtailing) of an erotic spectacle, the burst into motion of a terroristic locomotive, or the rhythm of appearance, transformation, and sudden disappearance that rules a magic film all invoke a spectator whose delight comes from the unpredictability of the instant, a succession of excitements and frustrations whose order cannot be predicted by narrative logic and whose pleasures are never sure of being prolonged. Each instant offers the possibility of a radical alteration or termination. As one perceptive reader of an earlier draft of this essay pointed out, the title of this essay, a familiar phrase from midway ballyhoo and magic shows, implies precisely this discontinuous succession of instants: *now* you see it, *now* you don't. In contrast, narrative temporality moves from *now* to *then*, with causality as a frequent means of vectorizing temporal progression. My title phrase stresses both the spectator awareness of the act of seeing and the punctual succession of instants, while narrative temporality moves through a logic of character motivation ("First she . . . , *then* she . . . ").

Relating the temporality of early film to a metapsychology of the spectator, a well-known (and frequently cited) game of "now you see it, now you don't" occurs. How does the cinema of attraction's pattern of presence/absence, its rhythm of appearance and disappearance, relate to the game little Hans played of "fort/da" ("gone/there"), so profoundly analyzed by his grandfather Sigmund Freud as a way of mastering the trauma of his mother's absence? Recall the scenario: little Hans deals with his separation from his mother by playing with a string attached to a wooden spool. His game consists of casting the spool away from him ("fort") and then retrieving it by its string ("da"). The rhythm of presence and absence demonstrates Hans's control of his spool toy in contrast to his inability to control his departing and returning mother.[23]

Elsewhere I have related Hans's game of disappearance and reappearance to the editing structures of early chase films, as the spectator learns to construct a broader geography from individual shots by recognizing that although the chasing party disappears in one shot, he or she will reappear in the following one.[24] To my mind, then, Freud's grandson's game figures a narrative trajectory, a game of anticipation and prediction, stringing the spectator along. As Freud observed, Hans has mastered a disturbing experience of separation in which he was a passive participant (unable to control his mother's actions) by refiguring it in a symbolic game in which he plays an active role.

If the classical spectator enjoys apparent mastery of the narrative thread of a film (able to anticipate future action through her knowledge of the cues and schema of narrative space and action), the viewer of the cinema of attractions plays a very different game of presence/absence, one strongly lacking predictability or a sense of mastery. In this sense we can see the relevance of Lynne Kirby's description of the early film spectator as a victim of hysteria.[25] The cinema of attractions truly invokes the temporality of surprise, shock, and trauma, the sudden rupture of stability by the irruption of transformation or the curtailing of erotic promise. Like the devotees of thrill rides at Coney Island, the spectator of early film could experience the thrill of intense and suddenly changing sensations.

This strongly discontinuous experience of time may be seen as an ideal form of early cinema's difference from later classical narrative. Certainly not all early attractions sought to shock their spectators. But rather than a purely passive recording of theatrical acts of slices of life, we see that the act of display in early film also carried at least the possibility of an experience of a time of pure instance. It was partly this temporality that explains the enthusiasm the early avant-garde had for the aesthetic of attractions, whether in variety theater, the fairground, the circus, or early cinema. The gesture of display figured a time that seemed to escape from a linear or successive configuration of time. The potential shock of the cinema of attractions provided a popular form of an alternative temporality based not on the mimesis of memory or other psychological states but on an intense interaction between an astonished spectator and the cinematic smack of the instant, the flicker of presence and absence.

NOTES

The author would like to thank Lucy Fischer for her comments on an earlier draft of this essay.

1. Christian Metz, *Film Language: A Semiotics of the Cinema* (New York: Oxford University Press, 1974), pp. 44–45.

2. Jean Mitry, *Histoire du cinéma*, vol. 1 (1895–1914) (Paris: Editions Universitaires, 1967), p. 370.

3. André Gaudreault and Tom Gunning, "Le Cinéma des premier temps: Un défi a histoire du film?" in J. Aumont, A. Gaudreault, and M. Marie, eds., *Histoire du cinéma: Nouvelles approches* (Paris: Publications de la Sorbonne, 1989), pp. 49–63 (first presented at Cerisy Colloquium in 1985). See also Tom Gunning, "The Cinema of Attractions: Early Cinema, Its Spectator and the Avant Garde," in Thomas Elsaesser, ed., *Early Cinema: Space Frame Narrative* (London: BFI, 1990), pp. 56–62.

4. See Tom Gunning, *D. W. Griffith and the Origins of American Narrative Film* (Champaign: University of Illinois Press, 1991).

5. Noel Burch, "Porter or Ambivalence," *Screen* 19 (Winter 1978–79), 91–105.

6. The concept of the dominant comes from the Russian Formalists. For good summaries, see Victor Erlich, *Russian Formalism: History and Doctrine* (New Haven, Conn.: Yale University Press, 1981), pp. 212, 233; Peter Steiner, *Russian Formalism: A Metapoetics* (Ithaca, N.Y.: Cornell University Press 1984), pp. 76–77, 104–111. Kristin Thompson has used the concept in a number of fruitful ways in film analysis in *Breaking the Glass Armor: Neoformalist Film Analysis* (Princeton, N.J.: Princeton University Press, 1988), pp. 43–45, 89–131.

7. Christian Metz, *The Imaginary Signifier: Psychoanalysis and the Cinema* (Bloomington: Indiana University Press, 1975), pp. 61–66, 91–97.

8. Gunning, "The Cinema of Attractions," p. 57.

9. For a fuller discussion of the relation of the cinema of attractions to the experience of shock touched on here, see Tom Gunning, "An Aesthetic of Astonishment: Early Cinema and the [In]Credulous Spectator," *Art and Text* 34 (Spring 1989), 31–45.

10. St. Augustine, *The Confessions* (New York: New American Library, 1963), pp. 245–7.

11. The concept of the *Sjuzhet* (sometimes translated as "plot") also comes from the Russian Formalists. See Boris Tomashevsky, "Thematics," in Lee T. Lemon and Marion J. Reis, eds., *Russian Formalist Criticism: Four Essays* (Lincoln: University of Nebraska Press, 1965), pp. 66–78. David Bordwell applies the concept to film with clarity and precision in *Narration in the Fiction Film* (Madison: University of Wisconsin Press, 1985), pp. 50–57.

12. See Paul Ricoeur, *Time and Narrative*, vol. 1 (Chicago: University of Chicago Press, 1984), pp. 66–77. I want to thank Vicente Benet of the Universitat Jaume, Castello, Spain, for pointing out to me the relevance of this concept to early film.

13. John Fraser, *Artificially Arranged Scenes: The Films of George Méliès* (Boston: G. K. Hall, 1979), p. 124.

14. *Edison Film Catalogue* in Charles Musser, ed., *Motion Picture Catalogs by American Producers and Distributors. 1894–1908: A Microfilm Edition* (Frederick, Md.: University Publications of America, 1985).

15. The unfolding of a landscape may imply a different spectator reception than the shock of display found in many typical films of the cinema of attractions. However, as constantly changing views they still possess the essential nonnarrative emphasis on display that defines the cinema of attractions. Further, early catalogs for films taken from trains also stressed the experience of speed and sudden changes in terrain and other experiences of shock and surprise. I thank Janet Staiger for her comments on this issue at a presentation of a shorter version of this paper at the 1991 SCS Conference at USC.

16. Albert E. Smith with Phil A. Koury, *Two Reels and a Crank* (New York: Garland Publishing, 1985), p. 39.

17. Judith Mayne, *The Woman at the Keyhole: Feminism and Woman's Cinema* (Bloomington: Indiana University Press, 1990), pp. 162–4.

18. This information can be found in print in the WPA 1939 *Guide to New York City*. Policemen assigned to scatter such loiterers coined the later familiar catch phrase "Twenty Three Skidoo." My intense thanks to Brooks MacNamara for the information and the source and to Ben Singer for further confirmation.

19. Musser, *Motion Picture Catalogs*, p. 86.

20. Musser makes this point in a number of his writings; see *The Emergence of Cinema*, vol. 1 of *History of the American Cinema* (New York: Charles Scribner's & Sons, 1990), pp. 179–81, 258–61.

21. Georges Méliès, "Importance du scenario," in Georges Sadoul, *Georges Méliès* (Paris: Segher, 1961), p. 118.

22. An insightful discussion of this final shot can be found in Phil Rosen, "Disjunction and Ideology in a Preclassical Film: *A Policeman's Tour of the World.*" *Wide Angle* 12:3 (1990), 20–37.

23. Little Hans's game is described and analyzed in Sigmund Freud, *Beyond the Pleasure Principle*, vol. 18 of *The Standard Edition of the Complete Psychological Works of Sigmund Freud* (London: Hogarth Press, 1955), pp. 14–17.

24. Tom Gunning, "D. W. Griffith and the Narrator-System: Narrative Structure and Industry Organization in Biograph Films, 1908–1909," Ph.D. dissertation, New York University, 1986, 114–5.

25. Lynne Kirby, "Male Hysteria and Early Cinema," *Camera Obscura* 17 (May 1988), 113–131.

Charles Musser

Pre-Classical American Cinema: Its Changing Modes of Film Production

Recent historians have demonstrated that pre-1907 early cinema was both radically different from, and much more complex than, the descriptions offered by their predecessors. The work around *Life of an American Fireman* as well as more general examinations of early cinema's system of representation are well known.[1] Although less attention has been given to the question of production, much of my own work has emphasized the crucial creative role of the exhibitor, his responsibility for editing, and what we would now call postproduction. Thus cinema included sophisticated evening-length programs as early as 1897, with the exhibitor, not the film producer, responsible for their final authorship. Surviving one-shot films often served only as building blocks for much more complex programs. Many of these responsibilities were then assumed by the producer in the first years of the new century, creating a fundamental reorganization of production.[2]

Despite the extensive nature of this historiography, a key area has been left virtually untouched and unquestioned. This involves the organization of production within the filmmaking process itself. Many scholars, including myself, had virtually accepted the framework of our predecessors. This is understandable. Because information about actual filmmaking before 1910 is extremely fragmentary, we lacked ready evidence to challenge the conclusions of previous historians as well as our own preconceptions. My own work, for example, often tended to treat Edwin Porter as the "compleat filmmaker" who was involved in and controlled all aspects of film production.[3] This perspective roughly conformed to the typology of film production offered by Janet Staiger in *The Classical Hollywood Cinema*. Staiger's exemplary model clarified and systematized the implicit

This is a slightly expanded version of an essay that originally appeared in *Persistence of Vision* 9 (1991). Copyright by the City University of New York on behalf of the Film Faculty of the City University of New York. Reprinted by permission of the author and copyright holder.

paradigms employed in much writing about pre-1915 cinema.[4] Thus cinema before 1907 was dominated by what Staiger appropriately calls the cameraman system of production. As she describes it, the cameramen would typically "select the subject matter and stage it as necessary by manipulating setting, lighting, and people; they would select options from available technological and photographic possibilities (type of camera, raw stock, and lens, framing and movement of camera, etc.), photograph the scene, develop and edit it."[5] This was the framework from which I and others started.

In my own research and that of Tom Gunning, contradictory information gradually emerged.[6] Gunning, for example, unearthed a *Photoplay* magazine article in which Florence Lawrence reminisced about her first appearance in motion pictures. This film, *Daniel Boone, or Pioneer Days* (1906–1907), was "codirected" by Wallace McCutcheon and Edwin Porter. Shortly thereafter, I located a set of payroll books at the Edison National Historic Site which established that both Porter and McCutcheon were then receiving identical salaries—$40 per week. This period of what Lawrence termed "joint direction" went from May 1905 to May 1907 when McCutcheon left and was replaced by J. Searle Dawley. The apparently conflicting claims of authorship involving Porter and Dawley for such films as *Rescued from an Eagle's Nest* (1908) are easily resolved if we apply the notion of collaborative or joint authorship to these films.

Continued research in the pre-1907 period revealed more and more collaborative pairings. At Vitagraph, co-owner J. Stuart Blackton played the burglar in *Burglar on the Roof* (1898) and other early comedies while his partner Albert E. Smith ran the camera. Albert E. Smith then appeared in *The Vanishing Lady* (1898) and other magic films of the same period as Blackton turned the crank. Since these partners were engaged in a collaborative undertaking on every level, this method of production might be called the "collaborative system." Its model was the more general one of business partnership and involved an underlying equality between the principals.[7] The collaborative system did not always function within the ideal circumstances of absolute equality for multiple reasons. Collaborators were not always evenly talented, and often one of the collaborators had more power or authority. Nevertheless, the horizontal relations of equality rather than the vertical ones of hierarchy dominated.

Extensive research indicates that the collaborative system of production dominated American cinema until 1907 or 1908, particularly in the case of fiction filmmaking. To lay this out in systematic detail would not only duplicate work done elsewhere but limit the amount of attention this article can pay to the new typology it proposes. Let us briefly consider, however, a few key examples. Significantly, Edison and his colleagues employed collaborative methods during the process of developing their modern motion picture system. Rather than argue whether it was Thomas

A. Edison or William Kennedy Laurie Dickson who really invented the kinetograph and kinetoscope, we need to see them as working together. Moreover, this team, which formulated general principles and established priorities for research, overlapped with another team dealing with the actual hands-on mucking about that typified the Edison lab.[8] This second team of W. K. L. Dickson and William Heise, with assistance from other employees at the laboratory, made and operated the actual equipment. Their ultimate success was documented by a film (late summer/early fall 1892) showing the two collaborators shaking hands before the camera, congratulating each other. The battle over credit, as if the invention of a motion picture system could and should be credited to one person, has preempted and thus obscured the more fundamental one involving the organization of invention-oriented work.

Film historians have tended to ignore Edison's pre-kinetograph career, but Edison consistently relied on partnerships as an approach to the problem of both business and invention, particularly prior to his move to the West Orange laboratory in 1888. Partnership was inscribed within the very names of his many earlier business operations: Edison & Murray, Edison & Unger, and Edison & Harrington.[9] Although the Edison Manufacturing Company, which operated the motion picture business resulting from the kinetograph inventions, was owned solely by the renowned inventor, collaboration continued to be the organizing basis for making films. The move from experimental to commercial production involved few changes in the organization of film production. In 1894–1895, W. K. L. Dickson, a man familiar with the theater, worked with the performers for the many brief scenes taken by the new motion picture camera while Heise typically operated that camera. This collaborative pairing continued until Dickson's departure in April 1895. Although Heise then worked alone, the resulting level of productivity was extremely low. By August, Alfred Clark from Raff & Gammon had joined Heise, bringing new ideas and renewed energy to the production process. Such duos typified production at Edison whether it was James White working with William Heise in 1896–1897 or White touring the world, shooting travel films with Frederick W. Blechyenden in 1897–1898.

The extensive nature of this collaborative system became apparent with the recent location of a second volume of Edison payroll books, from the period between 1896 and 1906. This revealed that the Edison Manufacturing Company hired a George S. Fleming in January 1901, just as the new Edison studio on Twenty-First Street in New York City was opening. Fleming was an actor and scenic designer. Porter, who had been improving Edison motion picture equipment, joined him as cameraman, and the two worked together. What we see here is a pairing of men with complementary skills. Working together, Fleming constructed the sets and directed the actors while Porter shot the scenes, developed the film, and edited the results. Yet much of the actual filmmaking—the choosing of subjects and planning of actual scenes—was done by both men. Porter proved to be the more accomplished of the two. Although Fleming was initially paid $20 per week to Porter's $15, Porter's salary was soon increased to the same level. In April 1903, Fleming left and was replaced by William Martinetti, also a scenic designer and man of the theater, who likewise made Porter's identical salary of $20 per week. McCutcheon and Dawley were thus part of a pattern in Porter's filmmaking career, which dated back to his entrance into serious film production and continued until he retired from filmmaking in 1915.[10]

Outside of the Edison Manufacturing Company and its licensees, the collaborative system flourished as well. At the American Mutoscope & Biograph Company, Frank Marion and Wallace McCutcheon worked closely together from at least 1900 (according to the 1900 census the two men and their families were then living together) until McCutcheon joined Edison in May 1905. Under their guidance, one-reel "feature" production became Biograph's commercial keystone in the summer of 1904. Paley & Steiner was another partnership, which produced the popular Crescent films in 1904–1905. The collaborative method of production was still largely in effect at Essanay in mid-1908 when Lawrence Lee, actor and playwright, worked with Gilbert P. Hamilton, a veteran cinematographer. According to one journalist, "Responsibility for making the picture rests entirely with Hamilton, but Lee must produce the material to be photographed."[11] Although Lee headed the actual troupe of actors and production personnel, he often had to defer to Hamilton's judgment.

> Lee picks what is to him the ideal spots for his scenes and then consults Hamilton, whose practiced eye will tell him at once if the lighting, color, etc. will produce a suitable picture. Often the photographer vetoes absolutely the dramatist's suggestion. Then Lee must start again, rearrange his pawns in the moving picture game and change his system to coincide with the limitations of the camera.[12]

In the United States at least, fiction filmmaking—whether short comedy skits, magic films, or longer story films—was typically conducted by collaborative teams. For actualities, the situation involved greater variation. At least into 1898, collaborative teams usually worked on all kinds of films, even simple actuality pictures, partially because American equipment was bulky and complicated to operate. Although cameramen were increasingly likely to work alone (or with an assistant) when taking actualities, the collaborative model was never entirely abandoned. Edwin Porter and James B. Smith worked together on a group of actualities in April and May 1903. In some respects, we can see the solitary cameraman as a collapse of the collaborative system, made possible by better, more "user-friendly" equipment.

Perhaps the best example of early widespread use of a "cameraman system" was in France where a single cameraman could easily operate the lightweight Lumière cinématographe. The solitary still photographer was the Lumières' model for the motion picture cameraman. Although the Lumières and their cameramen did produce a number of simple improvised skits, their heavy emphasis on actualities made the cameraman system possible even as the cameraman system reinforced their proclivity for nonfiction film. Representational methods, as determined by subject type, and production methods were complementary.

In the United States, the cameraman model was employed in numerous situations, as cameramen such as A. C. Abadie (Edison), G. W. Bitzer (Biograph), and William Paley crisscrossed the country taking actualities. Yet when solitary cameramen were employed for travel films and industrials, they frequently worked with or for a client, recreating a working relationship that bore a strong resemblance to the collaborative system of production. Often cameramen would work alone on some films and collaboratively on others, shifting easily from one method of filmmaking to the other. Thus, the collaborative method and the cameraman method functioned within a coherent system of early film production: they outline crucial parameters within which virtually all filmmaking occurred prior to 1907–1908.

Extensive research into the period before 1909 also reveals that motion picture companies often had multiple production units and so incorporated organizational elements that involved hierarchy. After taking some early films themselves, the Lumière brothers soon had numerous cameramen filming throughout the world. From June 1897 and into 1907, the Biograph Company had two or more camera units operating, usually in different parts of the country—or the world. The Edison Manufacturing Company had two units in operation by mid-1897 and three by March 1898: often collaborative teams, these units were coordinated to some degree out of the Edison company's offices. However, American companies generally had only one studio with a single stage for fiction films. There they based one production unit, typically consisting of a small group of personnel, while smaller units, sometimes only the solitary cameraman, traveled to different locations usually to make nonfiction films. Thus a "mixed-mode" (i.e., fiction and actuality), multiunit system was an important aspect of film production virtually from the outset.

To summarize, film production before 1907 was more complex than is generally recognized because

1. The most important film companies typically had more than one production unit operating at any given time and so relied on a multiunit system of production. This already involved a certain measure of planning and coordination by a level of management that was not directly involved in the filmmaking itself.

2. A collaborative method of production was commonly used, particularly for making fiction films, in the United States prior to 1908–1909. This usually involved the uniting of complementary skills—those of theatrical and filmic expertise. Although theoretically involving an association of equals, this horizontal organization of labor could be limited or modified by hierarchical consideration.

Although the organization of production might therefore be fairly elaborate, these companies found it difficult to have multiple units simultaneously pursuing fiction filmmaking on a sustained basis. When in 1897 the Biograph group expanded by constructing a second studio in distant England, the resulting production was headed by two owner-managers, who promptly set up their own separate sister organization. Vitagraph had two units making fiction films in 1905–1906, but they operated as largely autonomous entities under the respective sponsorship of cameramen-partners J. Stuart Blackton and Albert E. Smith. More generally, when companies formed multiple units to make fiction films, it led to the breakdown of early cinema's system of production.

The Breakdown of the Collaborative System and the Rise of a Central Producer System

If a close examination of U.S. filmmaking practices before 1908 yields an unexpectedly complicated picture, we should not be surprised if the transition to new and more familiar organizational forms of film production was likewise somewhat different than conventional wisdom has suggested. The system of production that early film had developed in the first decade began to break down rapidly after 1907–1908. Before considering this thoroughly, let us first review Janet Staiger's helpful typology of film production and the historical development it posits. Staiger offers five distinctly different and successive systems of production that ensued after the cameraman system fell from dominance. At least three of these are immediately relevant for this discussion.

1. the director system, dominant from 1907 to 1909
2. the director-unit system, which developed as the manufacturers increased output after 1909
3. the "central producer" system, which became dominant around 1914[13]

Staiger acknowledges that companies practiced many variations of these systems, but efficiency as well as commercial needs and the possibilities of adapting previous methods to new contingencies encouraged the development of certain stable working methods.

My research, however, indicates that American production gradually underwent only one fundamental transformation during this period. Occurring primarily in the area of fiction filmmaking, it involved a shift from a mode of production dominated by collaboration to the central producer system as outlined by Staiger. This shift proceeded awkwardly and unevenly. It involved hesitations and often resistance by those working within the old system. Although the collaborative system of production has continued to operate in many filmmaking situations to this day, a sharp break is evident within the emerging Hollywood industry between 1907 and 1909. This transformation in production methods thus parallels the shift in representation and narrative form that I have discussed elsewhere.[14]

The development of the central producer system reflects a more general transformation of American business practices that have been examined by Alfred Chandler, Jr., and others. Chandler sees a fundamental shift from traditional forms of management typically involving partnerships to new ones consistent with the basic hierarchical structure of the modern business enterprise.[15] Staiger's model is also consonant with Chandler's analysis, moving from the traditional craft model of the cameraman system to the complex multiunit production of the central producer system, involving greater division of labor and hierarchy. To better understand the ways in which the alternative model I am proposing can claim greater historical validity, we might briefly consider Staiger's view of the director and director-unit system.

Staiger has argued that the shift to a director system reflected the shift from actuality film production to fiction film production, which occurred around 1907. This causal explanation relies overmuch on some of Robert C. Allen's earlier speculation, which has not proved entirely valid. While actuality filmmaking was all but eliminated from the repertoire of leading production companies in 1907, it had been marginalized several years earlier. Fiction filmmaking had become the dominant type of production by the second half of 1904. From mid-1904 through 1907, 85 percent of the film prints sold by the Edison Company were of fictional or at least acted subjects (including some staged materials with documentary elements).[16] If anything, the increased importance of fiction filmmaking *strengthened* the collaborative nature of early film production. Porter had not really had a regular collaborator between the departure of George S. Fleming in 1903 and McCutcheon's arrival in 1905, Will S. Rising and G. M. Anderson assuming such roles only with some irregularity. Although Paley had worked with stage director Henry C. Vincent on *The Passion Play of Oberammergau* (1898), in 1904 he joined forces with William Steiner in a collaborative venture making numerous fiction films for Paley & Steiner. Nonetheless, as Staiger suggests, the increase in fiction film production also encouraged a greater division of labor. At the Edison Company, this division of labor included not only Porter and his collaborator but William Martinetti, who continued as the art director and scenic designer, and William J. Gilroy, who was hired full-time as a general assistant responsible for props and costumes.

It was the increasing rate of film production, a response to the nickelodeon boom, that broke down or at least marginalized early cinema's collaborative mode of production. This increase forced new management structures that more clearly favored vertical rather than horizontal methods of organization. Modern tools of management were implemented that assured clearer hierarchy and greater accountability.

In the United States, this reorganization may have first appeared at Vitagraph, significantly the largest and most successful domestic film producer. Even though Vitagraph then had three separate production units making fiction films between October 1906 and early 1907, the process of reorganization had not yet begun. These three units were headed by cameramen J. Stuart Blackton, Albert E. Smith, and James Bernard French, the latter Vitagraph's senior and most trusted employee (and its first hired projectionist). Working with each unit was an "artist and general assistant" responsible for the "posing and arranging of scenes."[17] Among these were William V. Ranous and George E. Stevens. Clearly, it would be inaccurate to consider these stage directors/managers as "film directors" in the somewhat later sense of the word. They worked with cameramen who were also the producers and/or company owners. These stage directors had a highly circumscribed area of authority. Each production unit was largely autonomous, functioning independently under the protection of a key figure. Moreover, almost everyone had multiple responsibilities. French was in charge of the projection department that hired operators (out-of-work operators often served as extras in these films).[18] Although a stage manager, Stevens was occasionally responsible for shooting exterior scenes as well. Lack of specialization and broad expertise thus characterized production at Vitagraph, the most successful American producer, into early 1907.

When Albert Smith left for Europe to establish Vitagraph's European branch offices at the beginning of 1907, his departure encouraged the reorganization of production along new lines. French assumed responsibility for managing the increasingly large studio. Blackton remained as producer to oversee all three units, each headed by a director. Less experienced cameramen, perhaps including operators who had taken local views for Vitagraph's by-now-disbanded traveling exhibition companies, were hired to work under these directors. The cameramen, however, reported not only to the newly created film directors but also to the head of production (i.e., Blackton) and the studio manager. As producer and owner, Blackton, not the director, was in the position of immediate authority over department heads. In the process, a new vertically organized structure, fundamentally different from the previous one that was predominantly horizontal, began to emerge.

The emphasis should perhaps be on "began," since this new multi-unit, hierarchical structure was not immediately institutionalized. When Albert E. Smith's attention was freed from pressing business issues, he resumed his place behind the camera and, in the fall of 1907, photographed *Francesca di Rimini*, "conceded by experts to be one of the best pieces of motion picture photography ever made."[19] When George E. Stevens defected to Edison, he was not immediately replaced. Nor were others. Early in February 1908, Blackton and William V. Ranous were heading the sole unit then operating at Vitagraph. "I took *five* pictures this week (5)—that's the record so far," Blackton boasted to Smith. "Am doubling in brass these days—Upstairs set, focus and grind the crank—then downstairs and join the negative." In this same letter, Blackton noted that this was a period of "troubles," which perhaps helps to explain this otherwise puzzling contraction.[20] (Since employees had multiple skills, those who had been attached to the now disbanded units could have been assigned different tasks.) As filmmaking at Vitagraph became more ambitious and the company's business more complex, the multiunit organization was reestablished on a firmer basis. By July 1909, when Vitagraph hired Maurice G. W. St. Loup as a director, the multiunit system was well in place as several directors once again worked under Blackton's supervision.[21]

A similar shift from collaboration to hierarchy and the central producer system occurred at Edison in 1908–1909. In June 1908, Edison organized a second studio-based production unit for fiction films. Dawley, who had been Porter's collaborator for the previous year, was assigned to work with a new cameraman, Fred Armitage. Significantly Dawley and Armitage received the same salaries ($40 per week), indicative of the continuing reliance on a collaborative system. While Porter now operated the first unit alone, he also supervised the second unit. Porter may have had sole responsibility for this first unit in theory, but in practice he continued to rely on his old collaborator. Dawley's memoirs suggest that he was torn by conflicting demands between the two units.[22]

By January 1909, the continuing nonhierarchal organization of production at Edison had clearly proved unsatisfactory. Senior executives limited Porter's responsibilities to that of studio head with two units operating under him. Dawley was given a raise to $45, so he was making more than his cameraman, Armitage. H. C. Matthews was hired to work as a director for $40 per week while his cameraman associate, Henry Cronjager, made only $25. These salary inequities suggest that the director was gaining greater responsibility and authority. Although Porter had been assigned the role of a "central producer," he did not function well in this hierarchic situation. The Edison veteran was quickly replaced by Horace G. Plimpton, who did.

Edison increased its number of employees not only because it had added new units of production but because, like Vitagraph and Biograph, it was developing a stock company of actors.[23] The Edison stock company gained its first two members in the second half of 1908 and was firmly in place by 1909. Emerging out of the informal association of actors with the company, the stock company helped to regularize production still further. Putting actors on a regular payroll (previously, they had only been paid for the days they worked) meant that the efficient use of their labor was important. Management became much more important as a result.

There were many pressures on film companies that encouraged them to move toward a central producer system. The ability to save on salaries through assigning work previously done by highly paid personnel to people in lower pay categories may have been an inducement, as Staiger maintains. However, some detailed division of labor and the use of inexpensive labor categories had been typical before 1907, even from the industry's outset. Since directors, featured actors, art directors, and even cameramen received higher salaries as the industry developed, there was certainly a greater range of salaries, but the average salary level appears to have increased. In any case, such savings were not nearly as crucial as the gains in accountability and efficiency through specialization, the regularization of production, and vertical organization.

The process of reorganization certainly favored the increased authority of the director for numerous reasons. In particular, the areas of directorial responsibility were expanding in 1908–1909. The development of an actors' stock company, issues of casting and performance, the difficulty of telling a clear, logical story in front of the camera, all emerged as key issues in the film industry at this time. For these, the director more than the cameraman was central. Likewise, the reconceptualization of cinema as a form of theater rather than a type of magic lantern performance focused attention on the profilmic elements and on the director. But if the director emerged as a key figure in 1908–1909, he nonetheless remained firmly under the control of producers such as Horace Plimpton and J. Stuart Blackton.

Are the director and director-unit systems then phantoms, or are they somehow subsumed under the central producer system? Both, in fact, seem to be true—a conclusion that obviously needs to be substantiated and clarified. The "director system" never really existed in the United States, although its structure resembles one possible structural arrangement under the central producer system. Staiger has suggested that with the onset of the director system, the function of director and cameraman were differentiated, with the director assuming a dominant role. This might seem logical except that, as we have already seen, such separation had been the very basis for numerous filmmaking partnerships from the outset of motion picture production. Although the director did come to dominate this working relationship after 1907, *he remained under the producer.* The terms *director* and *producer* were not synonymous, as Staiger suggests, even if there were specific companies in which a single individual assumed both roles.[24] Let us return to this in a moment, using Griffith as an example.

The director-unit system, in which "no one seemed to care about cost," is likewise a mirage—the bogey man of management's imagination.[25] By mid-1909 the Edison Manufacturing Company was costing out each film and ranking each director by production cost per negative foot. Edison continued this policy until the company was sold in 1918.[26] As studio managers, Plimpton and then L. C. McChesney maintained substantial control over individual productions. Again, the cameramen did not simply work for the directors but had their own hierarchy within the camera department (F. S. Armitage was department head) and also reported directly to Plimpton. By 1908–1909, tentatively completed pictures were screened by a committee that included Thomas Edison and other executives (among them Plimpton) who decided what changes, if any, should be made before release. It was then Plimpton's job to implement these changes. Plimpton dealt with purchasing literary works for adaptation and typically assigned them to directors (although the directors often did the actual adaptation). The scenario department also screened and purchased scenarios submitted by freelance writers. Plimpton thus truly acted as a studio head or mini-mogul.

Inevitably the degree of control by the producer over the director fluctuated from production company to production company, within production companies from director to director and with any given director from film to film. In many instances during the 1910s, directors did enjoy substantial autonomy. This was particularly evident, as Staiger points out, when a unit of actors and production personnel was working in some distant locale, far from the studio office. The central producer recognized that costs would be higher and control reduced during such sojourns, but the benefits were thought to outweigh the drawbacks.

More generally, the issue of management's control is raised when any multiunit system is involved—whether it be before 1907 or after. Thus, Edison and Biograph in the late 1890s and early 1900s would frequently send their various cameramen off to perform tasks that involved great autonomy. Yet at other times, a producer such as James White or Wallace McCutcheon would accompany one or more crews and supervise the filming quite closely. At Edison, it is clear that Porter's collaborative teams enjoyed considerable autonomy in some areas and some instances but not in others. After 1909, the parameters ranged from almost complete dominance of producer over director to virtual autonomy by the director (assuming the latter stayed within certain guidelines): these are two extremes of the producer-director relationship in the central producer system.

A production entity such as the one headed by Thomas Ince for the New York Motion Picture Company epitomized at least one extreme of the central producer system. There, Ince developed the detailed continuity script that greatly circumscribed the creative authority of those actually making the film. Staiger reports that a typical injunction appearing on these scripts read, "it is earnestly requested by Mr. Ince that no change of any nature be made in the scenario either by elimination of any scenes or the addition of any scenes or changing any of the action as described, or titles, without first consulting him."[27] Yet Ince's sister operation, Mack Sennett's Keystone Company, also implemented a central producer system but allowed its directors much wider autonomy. If there was an overall trend toward greater centralization, greater division of labor, and as Staiger points out, more detailed and thorough preplanning (propelled in many instances by the shift to feature production), the practices of many directors and companies contradicted any hard and fast generalizations.

The diversity of possible relationships within the central producer system is important to note since on paper it can appear to implement a rigid, hierarchic chain of command. In practice this system could be extremely flexible, at least when it came to a handful of key positions. Relationships shifted to reflect the relative skills, talents, and power of these production personnel. Thus, situations existed in which the producer did the bidding of the director or director and producer deferred to the star actor. On the other hand, producers could also be the stars and take as much credit and authority for themselves as possible—as the approaches of Thomas Ince and Cecil B. DeMille make clear.

The very flexibility of the central producer system within a general framework involving division of labor and accountability allows new insight into the "director system." Here tendencies to generalize from Griffith's unique situation have misled many historians. Griffith's role at Biograph represented an interesting and somewhat unusual variation of the central producer system, not some distinct interim category. This uniqueness was a conjunction of at least two factors at Biograph. First, the lengthy and highly successful McCutcheon/Marion collaboration did not involve the familiar pairing of cameraman with theatrical expert. McCutcheon occasionally operated the camera but most of these Biograph films employed another cameraman who was not one of the collaborators but comparatively subservient to them. The subordination of the cameraman (either Bitzer or Marvin) to Griffith conformed more readily to pre-existing practices at Biograph than at other studios.[28] Second, Biograph had been in a period of protracted crisis when Griffith took over. Although not all historians may agree, I believe his accomplished output in 1908 did much to rescue Biograph from commercial disaster. This gave him unusual leverage in the company. He soon served not only as a director but as the company's producer. He thus took control of the editing process, which remained barred to directors at Edison and other companies. (At Edison, for example, editing was first done by the cameraman until 1910; thereafter the film editor generally reported to the producer.) Biograph was an unusual case in that the collaborative system broke down, and the director emerged as the key figure within a production unit even though the company had not yet set up multiple units of production.

In 1908–1909, D. W. Griffith's ability to work efficiently meant that he could produce and direct two reels of film per week—as much as several production units at Edison. (Biograph, however, had typically been a more efficient studio than Edison in terms of quantity of films or finished negative produced.) By 1910 Griffith was producing and directing some Biograph films while supervising the direction of others. Biograph thus concentrated positions and responsibilities in one person, Griffith. This was highly unusual, yet reflected Biograph's special place in the industry. It sold more prints of its pictures domestically than any other company inside the Motion Picture Patents Company. Griffith was one of the first producer-directors and so gained a high degree of control over the production process and the pictures he made. This, in combination with his innovative approaches, explains why auteurist criticism works so well with Griffith in comparison with his contemporaries directing at most other studios.

The central producer system underwent important changes and developments during the 1910s along lines discussed by Staiger. There was further division and reorganization of work responsibilities. Nevertheless, the 1907–1909 period was the fulcrum, the breakpoint between (1) the filmmaking process built around traditional forms of organization, of partnership, that was consonant with structures of small-scale capitalism and (2) production based on modern corporate structures and industrial capitalism. Within these two structures, there was room for much variation. After 1909 smaller companies, such as the Independent Moving Picture Company (IMP) or American Film Company, often operated only a single production unit with a director working under, or with, a producer—unless, of course, these two functions were combined. These may or may not have been preludes to the formation of multiunit organizations. Multiple or single units were not characteristic of any period even though they involved different issues of organization and management.[29]

Film Manufacturing: Film Production and the Factory

The present article illuminates the ways in which pre-1907–1908 film production was distinctly organized and the manner in which it was subsequently transformed. The process corresponds to the fundamental transformation in representation occurring at the same time. The film as a self-sufficient narrative text became dominant. The rigorous liner progression of time as the film unfolds from shot to shot, plus the regular use of intertitles, helped to ensure minimal levels of narrative coherence. In 1908 the Edison licensees also introduced a formal, regular release schedule for their films. It was at this point that cinema finally conformed to the definition of mass communication offered by Everette Dennis and Melvin L. DeFleur.[30] During this brief but crucial period of transformation, cinema became a form of mass communication/mass entertainment and finally involved a kind of mass production.

In many respects, Bordwell, Staiger, and Thompson's *The Classical Hollywood Cinema* addresses the issue of mass production by posing a riddle or raising a paradox that it does not fully answer or resolve. The paradox is this: Hollywood is a form of mass production and employs the factory system[31] but

> In filmmaking mass production never reached the assembly-line degree of rigidity that it did in other industries. Rather it remained a manufacturing division of labor with craftsmen collectively and serially producing a commodity.[32]

Here Staiger echoes and somewhat qualifies a truism regarding American production—the studio as factory and assembly line. As Robert Kolker began his book on post-1960 auteur directors,

> When the studios, as independent corporate bodies, fell apart in the late fifties and early sixties, assembly-line production ended. Previously each of the major studios was a self-contained filmmaking factory with its own labor pool of producers, directors, writers, payers, and technicians, turning out many films during the years of peak production. This self-containment and mass production created mediocrity to be sure, as well as an arrogance that comes with security of product and market.[33]

In his discussion of Warner Bros., Rudy Behlmer remarked that the studio system "was essentially a factory-like method of turning out product to distributors. . . . Basically, it was not much different from the manufacturing of automobiles. But there was one difference: despite attempts at standardization, no picture could be *exactly* the same as another one on the assembly line."[34] Even an astute cultural historian such as David James has seen Hollywood as "in virtual imitation of the paradigm of modern industry, the Ford production line."[35] These assertions seem less dependent on careful investigations and analyses of filmmaking processes (and their comparison to the automobile assembly line) and more indebted to comments made by such alienated artists and intellectuals as the Hollywood writers of the 1930s.[36] They doubtlessly reflect political critiques, notably George Lukács's concept of reification in which the factory becomes the model for all social relations and "the fate of the atomized, fragmented, reduced worker becomes the typical human fate."[37] Max Horkheimer and Theodor

W. Adorno systematically applied these ideas to the culture industry when the studio system was at its height. The culture industry, they argued, offers "a constant reproduction of the same thing."[38] They find "the assembly-line character of the culture industry" in "the synthetic, planned method of turning out its products (factory-like not only in the studio but, more or less, in the compilation of cheap biographies, pseudodocumentary novels, and hit songs)."[39] If all films are endless repetitions of the same thing, with a few modest variables such the number of stars or story type, then producing movies might indeed be seen as functionally equivalent to the assembly line. Such a metaphoric critique of the motion picture industry has often been taken too literally. The equation of the film studio with a factory needs to be reexamined on the most concrete of levels.

If mass production ended with the demise of the studio system, Staiger and others have suggested that the shift from pre-1907 methods of filmmaking to subsequent organizational models explains how filmmaking became a form of mass production. Although the corporate system of organization (hierarchy and the dominance of the central producer system) and cinema as mass entertainment happened at roughly the same time and are interconnected, they are not one and the same nor does one immediately follow from the other. We need to look outside the narrow process of film production for a more adequate explanation of our instinctual feeling that cinema, indeed, had become a form of mass production. An elision is embedded in these references to the assembly line, a confusion between filmmaking in its narrow sense and cinema in its largest sense (film production, exhibition, and reception). A close analysis of the organization and restructuring of labor and production responsibilities before 1909 can provide insight into how cinema became a form of mass production in ways not *directly* dependent on the reorganization of filmmaking units.

Our understanding of cinema is inadequate if we look too narrowly at the filmmaking process itself, at what was then referred to as negative film production—preproduction, filming, and postproduction—that is everything up through the making of the finished negative. Making film prints was another crucial aspect of the process of film production. Moreover, the final product "consumed" was not the film itself but the screening or show. Keeping this in mind, we might again ask: how is the cinema a form of mass entertainment and mass production? and in what ways is it analogous to other forms of production such as the manufacturing of cars? Since companies in the period we are considering had names such as the Edison Manufacturing Company and the Essanay Film Manufacturing Company, where did this manufacturing occur? Who and where were the functional equivalents of the workers on the assembly line?

From its outset, the motion picture industry performed a substantial amount of manufacturing in two areas: the production of film prints and the production and assembly of projectors, kinetoscopes, and mutoscopes.[40] The process of filmmaking, of creating the film negative, what might be considered the template for the final film, was only one aspect of their business, and in some respects it was initially the easiest and least time-consuming. Perforating raw stock (typically still done by the production companies through the early 1900s), printing, and developing were time-consuming, labor-intensive jobs; perforating 200 feet of film stock took one hour until 1902 when the time was reduced to twenty minutes; printing 200 feet of positive film on continuous printers took twenty minutes until that date—at which point step printers were introduced and the time reduced to six or seven minutes.[41] However, it only took three and a half minutes to actually run the raw stock through the camera! Needless to say, developing was done by hand. At the turn of the century, a film company would manufacture twenty to thirty prints of a reasonably popular subject. Truly the "manufacturing" of film prints took many more person-hours than the filmmaking process. Today, making film prints is highly mechanized and involves comparatively little labor. Perhaps because of cinema's traditional "film-as-art" bias, we often do not even think of print manufacturing as part of film production. If we were to compare the film industry to the auto industry, the making of a complete film (up until the negative cutting) is similar to the making of a prototype for a car. Once the prototype is made, the corporation can make as many copies as it desires. However quickly and routinely a film is made, filmmaking itself (that is, negative film production) does not involve mass production or factorylike assembly. Rather, if *cinema* involves mass production, it occurs at a later stage, after the creative filmmaking process is completed.

We must ask: how was cinema's organization of manufacture similar to or different from the auto industry? In the film industry, the delivery of the product from negative to the consumer involved two quite separate processes: first, the manufacturing of the film prints, and second, their projection in theaters. We might, then, think of cinema as unusual because film manufacturing does not involve the manufacturing of a final product but of another template. Projection can be seen as the final manufacture of the motion picture product. Exhibition is not normally conceived of as a process of manufacture, and certainly it does not happen within a conventional factory setting. The theaters where light is repeatedly projected through these templates are more analogous to stores (and nickelodeons were, of course, typically converted storefronts). They are even more like fast-food restaurants or popcorn machines, in that the final stage of production is performed where the sales are being made.

At the turn of the century, cinema was hardly a form of mass production or mass communication. Rather than standardized entertainment, each exhibitor offered his or her own distinctive program. Cinema may have involved some standardized elements, but there was a tremendous variation across programs even when they were on the same basic subject, such as the Spanish-American War or President William McKinley's funeral. This began to change with the shift in editorial control from exhibitor to production company, a process occurring most dramatically between 1899 and 1903–1904. This shift was a crucial event in the history of motion pictures. Before that date, the exhibitor typically selected short, one-shot films and organized them either into a narrative or a variety show (or some combination of the two). Until 1903–1904, screen titles were still projected using slides. Much of the process of "postproduction" was thus done in the projection booth, where the operators (later called projectionists) had to make the physical cuts—the alternation between titles on slides and the moving pictures on film.

Once production companies were producing titles on film and incorporating these into their prints, a fundamental reorganization of labor had been achieved. The edits were made by the production company, not the operator, and conceived by the filmmaker, not the exhibitor or showman. The film company thus edited short shots into a "picture" that functioned as a prototype.[42] Multiple copies were then made off the negatives (templates) and then assembled to conform to the prototype by a staff of mostly female workers (figure 10). They performed their tasks in a way not unlike the assembly of a car, a watch, or other technological product.[43] This reorganization of work centralized key elements of creativity within the production company. Editorial decisions were made by the production company rather than the exhibitor. Although there were limits to this standardization of mass production of projected images in the silent era, as both Richard Koszarski and Miriam Hansen remind us, we cannot overemphasize the fundamental shift that had taken place.[44] It simplified the role of the projectionists who soon (in the nickelodeons appearing after 1905) spent their days mechanically turning the crank of the projector. Thus if we are to consider "the degradation of work in the twentieth century"— the subtitle for Harry Braverman's book *Labor and Monopoly Capital*—film historians should look to the film laboratories, their finishing rooms, and the projection booths. Here, they will find cinema's version of the assembly-line workers. The projection booth was its own individualized sweatshop—dangerous, unhealthy, with almost unbearable working conditions and low pay. The results gave many people pleasure, and these theater-factories may have been at times a place where working-class patrons could reconstitute their own cultural sphere, but the nickelodeons also produced a regimentation of work that was alienated labor in every sense. If we are looking for the *systematic* dehumanization of workers in the motion picture industry, it is to such workers that we should turn first, rather than to those involved in the filmmaking process.

Cinema became a form of mass production not because of the way that a picture was made, as Staiger has suggested, but because multiple prints could be struck and assembled, rapidly circulated, and repeatedly

Figure 10. Women checking and assembling film prints (ca. 1909). Courtesy of the Museum of Modern Art/Film Stills Archive.

shown.[45] Calling the film studio a factory or referring to films as "sausages" is to indulge in metaphorical activity with an underlying critical purpose. Such an approach is valid for a number of reasons. It underlines the constraints on creative filmmaking, which Hollywood has too often favored; it underscores the extent to which the producers were interested in profits rather than the film as a cultural product; and it draws attention to the ways in which film companies were often run according to a military regimen. Such criticisms, however, have fostered glib analysis, of which I, too, have been guilty.[46] It equates two different kinds of standardization— standardized Hollywood fare with factorylike standardization of production. Hollywood filmmaking involves division of labor and hierarchy. It can involve exploitation of workers in low-level positions through long hours, limited tasks, and poor pay. But it does not involve detailed division of labor in the way discussed by Braverman or Marx.

Within the modern editing department, where I worked for most of a dozen years, there are boring tasks such as reconstituting trims and doing log sheets. Yet all editors were once assistant editors and apprentices and at one time or another performed these tasks. And it is not at all unusual for assistants to make assemblies or even cut a scene or two. In many ways, assistants are responsible for the actual running of the editing room and so gradually gain the knowledge needed to one day become editors. The organization of work seems very close to a ceramics studio where the apprentice mixes glazes and wedges clay while the master makes the pots. Here, too, the apprentice, typically, will be assigned the easier pot-throwing tasks and will gradually develop the skills necessary to becoming a master potter. Both are fundamentally different from the factorylike process of manufacture that involves detailed division of labor, the production and assembly of interchangeable parts, the separation of planning from execution.[47]

The dividing line between planning and execution in cinema is a strong one. On one hand, there are those who are involved in the process of making the film prototype; on the other, there are those who produce and project its copies. At least until the institutionalization of film schools, there were innumerable examples of apprentice editors and production assistants who worked their way up to become directors or producers, never mind editors or assistant directors. After 1908 there were very few examples of projectionists who became editors or cameramen, not to mention filmmakers.

In examining the process whereby Hollywood divided labor, we must consider the history of those specific practices. Editing in the 1890s was quite different from editing in 1906 and different again from editing in the 1920s. As editing became a more and more elaborate and complex practice, the film industry needed professionals who could concentrate their attention on this aspect of filmmaking. The characteristics of a detailed division of labor do not explain this development. Staiger examines the industry through Harry Braverman, who

> argues that the central difference between the modes is that in a detailed division of labor the conception and execution of the work is divided: management does all of the former and laborers do only the latter. As the work is complicated and the tasks are segmented further, the individual worker becomes more and more specialized and loses understanding of the entire process.[48]

Film editors remain involved in both the conception and execution of the editing. If the script for a film is *like* a blueprint, it is not *the equivalent* of a blueprint. An editor works from the rushes with the script only as a guide. Scenes are dropped or rearranged. Characters are emphasized or sometimes even left "on the cutting room floor." One cannot leave off a fender and have a finished car, or remove a floor from a building once it is built. If one wants a different fender or a different lobby, one makes a new blueprint and reworks from that. The editor and cinematographer are like actors working with a script. Although some directors see actors as living mannequins and editors as just a pair of hands, other directors see themselves involved in a series of collaborations with actors, cinematographers, editors and so forth. Here again, there exists a wide range of possible working relationships.

Although working in the former situation may make an editor think that he or she is working on an assembly line, this is more a question of management style than structural organization of work.

Although filmmaking has generally required the larger and larger mobilization and coordination of artists, crafts people, and artisans, the process whereby the resulting prototype is turned into mass entertainment has taken less and less skill, fewer and fewer people. A striking contrast between the cinema and the auto industry is that cinema's post-prototype manufacturing process began to be automatized at an unusually early stage. With sophisticated printers, the elaborate assembly of prints ended with the coming of sound. And today, most projectionists no longer have to change reels during a screening; one person can show several films simultaneously in a multiplex theater.

The thrust of this essay has been to show the ways in which early filmmaking practices were more complex than has generally been recognized. Its collaborative, comparatively nonhierarchic system of organization was not a simpler version of later film production but fundamentally different.[49] The post-1908 introduction of hierarchy and division of labor did not reduce most workers engaged in filmmaking to mindless drones, but it did circumscribe the parameters within which they made decisions and the quality of their interpersonal interactions. It is not surprising, therefore, that the collaborative system of filmmaking flourished in the 1920s as an alternate approach to dominant filmmaking practices. If avant-garde filmmakers of the 1920s revived many representational techniques of pre-1908 cinema, giving them a new meaning, they also chose to work collaboratively. *Manhatta* was made by Paul Strand and Charles Sheeler, *Entr'acte* by Francis Picabia and René Clair, and *Ballet mécanique* by Dudley Murphy and Ferdinand Léger. They constructed alternatives not only to classical cinema's system of representation but to its system of production. For many of the same reasons, collaborative approaches to film production have persevered to this day, particularly in areas of independent documentary filmmaking.

NOTES

This essay is based on a paper originally presented at the 1989 Society for Cinema Studies Conference in Iowa City. It was completed while on an NEH fellowship. Thanks to Tom Gunning and Richard Allen for their assistance on revisions.

1. Noël Burch, "Porter and Ambivalence," *Screen* 19 (Winter 1978–79), 91–105; Charles Musser, "The Early Cinema of Edwin S. Porter," *Cinema Journal* 19:1 (Fall 1979), 1–38; André Gaudreault, "Detours in Film Narrative: The Developing of Cross-Cutting," *Cinema Journal* 19:1 (Fall 1979), 39–59, translated by Charles Musser and Martin Sopocy; Tom Gunning, "The Cinema of Attraction," *Wide Angle* 8:3–4 (1986), 63–70. The literature on this subject has become extensive, including Miriam Hansen, "Adventures of Goldilocks: Spectatorship, Consumerism, and Public Life," *Camera Obscura* 21 (1990), 51–71; and Judith

105

Pre-Classical American Cinema

Mayne, *The Woman at the Keyhole: Feminism and Women's Cinema* (Bloomington: Indiana University Press, 1990).

2. Charles Musser, *The Emergence of Cinema: The American Screen to 1907* (New York: Scribners, 1990); Musser, *Before the Nickelodeon: Edwin S. Porter and the Edison Manufacturing Company* (Berkeley: University of California Press, 1991).

3. For instance, Musser, "The Early Cinema of Edwin S. Porter."

4. As Staiger points out, hers is the first attempt to provide a systematic typology of this kind (David Bordwell, Kristin Thompson, and Janet Staiger, *The Classical Hollywood Cinema* [New York: Columbia University Press, 1985]).

5. Ibid., p. 116.

6. Tom Gunning discusses the appearance of several director-cameraman teams in the pre-1907 cinema (Gunning, "D.W. Griffith and the Narrator System," [Ph.D dissertation, New York University, 1986], pp. 93–95).

7. Partnership was still an exceedingly common method of doing business in the 1890s, and some names of these pairings, such as Raff & Gammon, figure prominently in cinema's early history.

8. Andre Millard, *Edison and the Business of Innovation* (Baltimore: John Hopkins University Press, 1990).

9. Matthew Josephson, *Edison* (New York: McGraw-Hill, 1959).

10. Porter's final collaborator at Famous Players in 1914–1915 was Hugh Ford, who figured prominently in the American theater, having been the stage producer for Israel Sangwill's *The Melting Pot* (1909). See Israel Sangwill, *The Melting Pot* (New York: Macmillan Company, 1909), p. vii.

11. "Essanay Staff," *Film Index* (6 June 1908), 6. Identified in this article as J. R. Hamilton, the cameraman gives his first name, middle initial, and brief career biography in Gilbert P. Hamilton, affidavit, *Motion Picture Patents Company v Carl Laemmle and Independent Moving Pictures Company*, No 7-151, *Affidavits Used in Opposition to Motion for Preliminary Injunction*, 419.

12. *Film Index* (6 June 1908), 6. This account, in fact, suggests some ways in which the collaborative system was breaking down and would be replaced by an organization of work relying on the film director and much greater hierarchy. With two Essanay units then in operation, someone had to head the unit and be accountable to the home office. Hamilton was the logical choice. With increased responsibility came greater authority.

13. Bordwell et al., *Classical Hollywood Cinema*, p. 93.

14. Charles Musser, "The Nickelodeon Era Begins: Establishing the Framework for Hollywood's Mode of Representation," *Framework* 22/23 (Autumn 1983), 4–11; reprinted in Thomas Elsaesser, ed., *Early Cinema: Space, Frame, Narrative* (London: British Film Institute, 1990), 256–74.

15. Alfred D. Chandler, Jr., *The Visible Hand: The Managerial Revolution in American Business* (Cambridge, Mass.: Belknap Press of Harvard University Press, 1977).

16. Bordwell et al., *Classical Hollywood Cinema*, pp. 115–6; Robert C. Allen, "Film History: The Narrow Discourse," in *Film: Historical-Theoretical Speculations: The 1977 Film Studies Annual* (part 2), (Pleasantville, NY:Redgrave, 1977), pp. 13–15; Charles Musser, "Another Look at the 'Chaser Theory,'" *Studies in Visual Communication* 10:4 (Fall 1984), 37–41. Robert C. Allen backs off from his earlier position in "Looking at 'Another look at the 'Chaser Period,'" *Studies in Visual Communication* 10:4 (Fall 1984), 47.

17. George E. Stevens, unfiled deposition, April 1907, Edison National Historical Site, West Orange, New Jersey; G. M. Anderson had been another such stage director at Vitagraph in 1905 through early 1906, when he left to work for Harry Davis.

18. Max Hollander, "Recollection of an Old-Timer," *The Motion Picture Projectionist* (October 1927), 9–10. Richard Koszarski kindly brought this article to my attention.

19. Albert E. Smith, deposition, 25 March 1911, in *Motion Picture Patents Company v Carl Laemmle and Independent Moving Pictures Company of America*, No 7-151, U.S.

District Court, District of New York, filed 27 March 1911, *Complainant's Papers on Motion for Preliminary Injunction*, 85.

20. J. Stuart Blackton to Albert E. Smith, 15 February 1908, Albert E. Smith Collection, UCLA. These films were each approximately half a reel (500 feet) long. After the sharp recession of October 1907, the next half year was a period of economic retrenchment. It was also a period of commercial uncertainty within the industry that ultimately led to the formation of the Association of Edison Licensees in early 1908.

21. Maurice G. Winterbert St. Loup, affidavit, 14 April 1911, *Motion Picture Patents Company v Carl Laemmle and Independent Moving Pictures Company*, No. 7-151, *Affidavits Used in Opposition to Motion for Preliminary Injunction*, 373. "Making Motion Pictures," *New York Dramatic Mirror* (1 May 1909), 37. Currently available documentation about Vitagraph in the 1907–1909 period is fragmentary and contradictory; it does not illuminate the process of transformation with much precision or clarity. A careful review of such evidence indicates that the shift from a collaborative model to a hierarchical one was more difficult and protracted at Vitagraph than I have previously suggested in both *The Emergence of Cinema* and *Before the Nickelodeon*.

22. J. Searle Dawley, unpublished memoirs, J. Searle Dawley Collection, Academy of Motion Picture Arts and Sciences, Los Angeles.

23. The increasing level of production likewise encouraged Vitagraph to establish a stock company of actors. By 1907 many leading players and stars of later films were working for the studio in some capacity. Leo Delaney, who appeared in *Foul Play* (1906) and *The Wrong Flat* (June 1907), continued to appear in Vitagraph productions into the 1910s. William J. Shea, who later appeared with John Bunny in such comedies as *Davy Jones in the South Seas* (January 1910), had a role in *Amateur Night* (April 1907). Florence Turner teamed up with Florence Lawrence in *Athletic American Girls* (July) and *Bargain Fiend; or Shopping a la Mode* (July). Basic elements of the studio system were beginning to emerge in the second half of 1907.

24. Staiger discusses the "director system" in Bordwell et al., *Classical Hollywood Cinema*, pp. 117–20.

25. Ibid., p. 135.

26. Edison Manufacturing Company, accounting documents, in "Motion Pictures" files for 1909–1918, Edison National Historic Site, West Orange, N.J.

27. Janet Staiger, "Dividing Labor for Production Control: Thomas Ince and the Rise of the Studio System," *Cinema Journal* 18:2 (Spring 1979), 16–25.

28. And from early 1897 to 1903, Biograph's outdoor studio placed the cameraman in a protective shack that removed him from the stage area and any possibility of participating in actual direction of the actors.

29. The American situation needs be contrasted to European practices, particularly in France, as Richard Abel has begun to do in his excellent new book, *The Ciné Goes to Town: French Cinema 1896–1914*. (Berkeley: University of California Press, 1994), pp. 22, 467. There he looked at four production companies and indicated that they utilized the following production methods: Lumières—cameraman system; Gaumont—collaborative system (pre-1908); Méliès—collaborative system favoring the director; and Pathé—the "director-unit system" (1905–1907). More generally, Abel points toward some key differences between the organization of production in France versus the United States. In France, writer-directors such as Zecca and Méliès dominated the production process, and the position of the cameraman was significantly weaker than in the United States (Abel, *The Ciné Goes to Town*, pp. 9–23). Did cameramen serve as less well-known collaborators for filmmakers in these instances, or were they directly beholden and responsible to the writer-directors-producers who thought of themselves as authors (auteurs) and recognized as such? If the latter, Staiger's discussion of a "director system" may well be applicable to the French situation in a way that is not appropriate for the American. Such a director-dominated system would then have occurred much earlier in France, paralleling and having much in common with the collaborative system in the United States.

The case of Pathé in 1905–1907, when a number of directors were working under the supervision of Ferdinand Zecca, is likewise an interesting one. Zecca may not have had as much control over the different production units as many subsequent producers, but I have tended to assume that Pathé probably provided the first example of the central producer system anywhere. Admittedly arguments of any kind tend to be speculative since there is currently a paucity of relevant information, but the size of the company's output and the resulting need for coordination would seem to have provided powerful inducements for an effective head of production. Moreover, Zecca's move from heading a single Pathé production unit in 1900 to overseeing a multiunit organization by 1905 parallels even as it precedes the kind of shift I am tracing in this article.

The case of Pathé might be contrasted to that at Gaumont where more information is available. Artistic director Alice Guy initially collaborated with cameraman Anatole Thiberville. From a single unit headed first by Guy and then Louis Feuillade, Gaumont shifted to a multiunit system in 1908. Crafton, reports that Feuillade, as "chef du service artistique des théâtres et de la prise du vue," supervised production and acted as an intermediary between Léon Gaumont and the filmmaking staff. Within this group, directors "were not governed by the division of labor established in later studios"; key personnel often collaborated together, sometimes codirecting with a director occasionally even assuming the role of cameraman (Donald Crafton, *Emile Cohl, Caricature, and Film* [Princeton, N.J.: Princeton University Press, 1990], pp. 115–20). In at least some instances, cameramen and directors were paid the same salaries. Here there was a central producer system, but the hierarchical chain of command was modified by continued collaboration within and among loosely defined production units.

30. Melvin L. DeFleur and Everette Dennis, *Understanding Mass Communication* (Boston: Houghton Mifflin, 1981), p. 11.

31. Bordwell et al., *Classical Hollywood Cinema*, p. 95.

32. Ibid., p. 93.

33. Robert Phillip Kolker, *A Cinema of Loneliness* (New York: Oxford University Press, 1981), p. 3.

34. Rudy Behlmer, ed., *Inside Warner Bros. 1935–1951)* (New York: Viking, 1985), p. xiii.

35. David E. James, *Allegories of Cinema: American Film in the Sixties* (Princeton, N.J.: Princeton University Press, 1989), p. 8.

36. Richard Fine, *West of Eden, Writers in Hollywood, 1928–1940* (Washington, D.C.; Smithsonian Institution Press, 1993).

37. Andrew Arto and Eike Gebhardt, eds., *The Essential Frankfurt School Reader* (New York: Continuum, 1982), p. 196.

38. Max Horkheimer and Theodor W. Adorno, *Dialectic of Enlightenment* (New York: Herder & Herder, 1972), p. 134.

39. Ibid., p. 163.

40. Both the Edison Manufacturing Company and the American Mutoscope & Biograph Company were structured as large corporate entities.

41. "How Moving Pictures Are Made in Pittsburgh for Amusement, Practical and Scientific Purposes," *Pittsburgh Post*, 9 December 1906, 4G.

42. This might be done either on a workprint or cutting copy or in the form of a finished negative.

43. Whether the assembly of each print was accomplished by a single worker or serially by several workers is not clear and in this instance would appear relatively unimportant.

44. Richard Koszarski, *An Evening's Entertainment* (New York: Scribner's 1990), pp. 53, 59–60; Miriam Hansen, *Babel and Babylon: Spectatorship in American Silent Film* (Cambridge, Mass.: Harvard University Press, 1991). Two things need to be said: first, while the overall entertainment in a movie theater may have retained many nonstandardized elements in the nickelodeon era (vaudeville, illustrated songs, musical accompaniment) from the

showman's perspective, this was not the case from the perspective of the film company, second, the editing or shortening of feature films in late 1910s and the 1920s, discussed by Koszarski, did not take place during the nickelodeon era and ended with the coming of sound. In any case, this re-editing was different from the fundamentally creative organization of narrative performed by exhibitors at the turn of the century.

45. Bordwell et al., *Classical Hollywood Cinema*, pp. 119–20.

46. In the documentary film *Before the Nickelodeon* (1982), I am guilty of such characterization when discussing the one-reel films Porter and his actors made with comparative rapidity.

47. However, something resembling the detailed division of labor has often been utilized in sound cutting. Particularly in Hollywood during the 1930s, there were assistant sound editors who spent years cutting in the sounds of shoe taps as Fred Astaire and Ginger Rogers danced about the stage. Although James Foly eliminated those nightmares (along with their jobs), equally narrow and repetitive tasks are sometimes inflicted on sound editors to this day.

48. Bordwell et al., *Classical Hollywood Cinema*, p. 92; Harry Braverman, *Labor and Monopoly Capital: The Degradation of Work in the Twentieth Century* (New York: Monthly Review Press, 1974), pp. 72–75.

49. Even early filmmaking commonly occurred within the large-scale multiunit corporatelike entities, with the making of film prototypes the responsibility of only one department. Already in 1894 the Edison Manufacturing Company had a unit that made the film prints and another that manufactured kinetoscopes. Another division made batteries, some of which were used to operate exhibition machines. In addition there was a separate unit responsible for marketing. After 1901, these units were often in distinct, geographically separate areas: negative production was located in New York and print production in New Jersey. This was also true for Biograph, which manufactured few projectors but many mutoscopes. Even in the 1890s, the film industry was composed to a significant degree of large-scale business entities. Within other departments of these corporations, the division of labor and hierarchy was significantly more developed. Even when these organizational tools were subsequently applied to filmmaking, film companies generally recognized that efficiency and low unit costs were important but not in themselves the key to profitability.

Richard Abel

Booming the Film Business: The Historical Specificity of Early French Cinema

At a recent Society for Cinema Studies Conference panel on the "History and Historiography of National Cinemas," Alan Williams got me to accept the somewhat foolhardy task of addressing a deceptively simple question.[1] How can one justify doing work on a particular national cinema—why is it that we assume that French cinema is a viable epistemological category? Williams knew that this question would be especially troublesome given my current project, a history of the first twenty years of French cinema, from 1895 to the beginning of the Great War in 1914. But it troubled him as well and should trouble anyone doing research on a so-called national cinema or, even more broadly, a national culture. Now that I have had some time to reflect on the question further, I want to extend my preliminary conference remarks into a more considered argument.

Certain lines of inquiry seem out of bounds from the start. One obviously cannot resort to the argument that, once the American cinema consolidated its hegemonic position during the Great War, alternative national cinemas—such as the French cinema of the 1920s—could be said to emerge in resistance to it.[2] Nor can one argue that the early French cinema constituted anything like a "monolithic category"—that is, that it was completely distinct or sharply differentiated from, say, the early American cinema.[3] All sorts of practices precluded any such distinction. The cheap cost of producing short story films and the initial lack of legal protection meant that a popular film such as Biograph's chase film, *Personal* (1904), could be replicated (whether duped or reshot) in slightly different versions from country to country as well as from company to company— see, for instance, Edison's *How a French Nobleman Gets a Wife . . .* (1904) and Pathé's *Dix Femmes pour un mari* (1905). Techniques also spread rapidly from one company or country to another—as in the use of dissolves

From *French Cultural Studies* 1:1 (1990). Reprinted by permission of the author and Alpha Academic, England.

to link shot-scenes in early French, British, and American films. Even production companies were not always exclusively tied to their national point of origin. The cameramen that Lumière dispatched throughout the world, between 1895 and 1897, screened *actualité* films on or near the site of their making (although it was a Frenchman operating a French camera-projector who almost always put on these "colonial shows") before shipping them back to France. And the largest British film company, Urban Trading, established in London in 1903, saw its interests soon shift to its Paris branch office; within three years, that office had turned into the independent French production company, Eclipse.

How, then, can one claim that early French cinema is a relatively distinct category of national cinema? To my mind, the best line of argument is to demonstrate its historical specificity as a cultural practice. First of all, early French cinema can be situated economically within the historical context of imperialism, which defined Europe as well as the United States in the late nineteenth century. Here I use the term *imperialism* in the sense that, following Eric Hobsbawm, the world economy of capitalism had become an aggregate of more or less solid blocs or rival national economies that, fuelled by the search for profitable investments as well as markets for products, embarked on a binge of global expansion or colonial conquest.[4] Between 1880 and 1914, in fact, most of the world outside Europe and the United States was partitioned into territories under the economic and political domination of a half-dozen states. This space of colonial expansion, along with that constructed by the more direct trading rivalry between national economies, provided a field of exploitation for Pathé when the company became the first to move into mass production in 1903–1904, as a partial consequence of which it assumed a position of dominance as the world's largest film producer and distributor.[5] Perhaps in imitation of the hugely successful French automobile industry, Pathé quickly set up a network of film distribution agencies around the world, to some extent following Lumière's earlier routes of dissemination.[6] The first Pathé agencies spread out through the "First World" of developed nations, and client states such as Russia which absorbed nearly a quarter of France's export capital investment: Moscow (February 1904), New York (August 1904), Brussels (October 1904), Berlin (March 1905), St. Petersburg (December 1905), Milan (May 1906), London (July 1906), Odessa (July 1906).[7] Within another year, Pathé offices were opening up and monopolizing central Europe as well as the colonized areas of India, Southeast Asia, Central and South America, and Africa. And in the colonies in particular, the French cinema, as exemplified by Pathé's products, served a useful purpose as propaganda—French comic films and their disarming power of laughter, wrote a Colonel Marchand, "are obviously a weapon of conquest in Africa and many other places as well."[8]

In this period of expansion, however, certain tendencies in the French national economy set limits on the policies and practices of whole industries as well as individual companies within France itself. Large-scale industrialization, for instance, with its attendant principles of economic concentration in "trusts" and scientific management, came rather slowly to France—partly because the larger French banks tended *not* to invest in industrial enterprises and because the Third Republic governments consistently discouraged such concentration as a violation of the ideal of a "balanced economy."[9] In 1896, for instance, while 84% of industrial firms had just one to four employees, only 1% had more than fifty.[10] Typically, an industry was comprised of middle-sized or even small-scale companies, none of which felt any compunction to corner the market and eliminate its competitors.[11] Given the character of the French economy, the rapidity of Pathé's growth was unusual—by 1906, there were over 1,200 employees in its cinema division alone[12]—yet it was supported, generally, by a steady, substantial rise in overall French industrial productivity beginning around 1905 and, specifically, by a 1906 law mandating that employers give their employees one day off a week.[13] Even more unusual, however, was its attempt to establish a monopoly within the French cinema industry by restructuring and extending its proliferating operations. Simply put, Charles Pathé divided his company into more or less separate sectors of film production, distribution, and exhibition—the company already was manufacturing and marketing cameras and projectors as well as doing its own film processing—to the point where control could be exercised over every stage of the business, from production to consumption.[14] In late 1906, for instance, Pathé began constructing a circuit of permanent cinemas, which, in less than three years, had reached 200 across France.[15] Then, in the autumn of 1907, the company established the first of six regional distribution offices for renting (rather than selling) its weekly programmes of film releases and primarily to its own cinemas.[16] This monopolistic strategy of restructured vertical integration would prove only partially successful, however; and within several years, the cinema industry assumed the more characteristic profile of a French industry—with a half-dozen different firms competing in each of the sectors involving the production, distribution, and exhibition of films as well as the manufacture of cinema equipment.

One of the reasons for Pathé's difficulties, of course, lay outside France, and specifically in the United States, where the nickelodeons and vaudeville houses soon formed an exhibition market at least ten times greater than that in France itself and where Pathé films constituted up to one-third of the total films screened.[17] By late 1909, for instance, according to *Ciné-Journal,* for every five film prints distributed in France, forty were reserved for the rest of Europe and elsewhere, while 150 were shipped to the United States.[18] This meant that Pathé, and the French cinema industry generally, was increasingly vulnerable to developments that would strengthen the American cinema industry and fuel its expansion. When Edison, for instance, launched its own plans to monopolize that industry, Pathé agreed (partly because of the continuing threat of Edison's film patents suits)[19] to become a member of the Film Service Association (in January 1908) and its successor, the Motion Picture Patents Company or MPPC (in December 1908).[20] At first, the move seemed advantageous because it excluded most other foreign competitors from the American market, protected Pathé's one-third share of that market, and probably shored up the company's own monopoly strategy in France. But these advantages quickly evaporated as "independent" producers and distributors emerged to seriously erode the MPPC position. And Pathé's own position was further compromised in 1909 by Eastman Kodak's decision to cut off all deliveries of film negative, when the French company determined to construct its own facility for the manufacture of negative,[21] and also by the establishment of a National Board of Censorship, which seems to have been especially insistent on "cleaning up" American cinemas by refusing to approve Pathé films.[22] By 1910–1911, Pathé's share of the American market was dropping considerably, and its days of dominating the world cinema market were numbered.

A second, also quite general argument for viewing early French cinema as a relatively distinct category would place it within the related historical context of nationalism in Europe, specifically in the emergence of the French Third Republic between 1871 and 1914, when France essentially redefined itself as a nation-state through a particular set of social institutions.[23] French historians now agree that "the real cement which kept the republican majority together" during this period "was the common desire to secularize the State and social life."[24] The principal means to that end was a new secular system of education, which wrested control of schooling from the Catholic Church. Here, the state primary schools were particularly important, after attendance was made compulsory in 1882, for they ensured that a new generation—especially those making up Léon Gambetta's "new strata" of petit-bourgeoisie, white-collar workers, and civil servants—was taught how to be good subjects and citizens of the Republic, and they "strengthened" *la patrie* by "affirming a single, united conception of the national community," not least of all through an imposed common language.[25] Yet the free primary schools remained distinct from the *lycées* and *collèges*, which required fees for admission; and the latter continued to serve as one of the principal signs of social membership in the bourgeoisie.[26]

Almost as crucial in "cementing" the Third Republic, however, was the loosely related network of new mass cultural practices that steadily "colonized everyday life" during this period.[27] Among them were cheap daily newspapers such as *Le Petit Journal* and *Le Petit Parisien*, which rose to mass circulation levels by radiating out along the railway lines from Paris far into the provinces, illustrated magazines such as *L'Illustration* and *Lectures pour tous*, and the monthly catalogues issuing from *grands magasins* such as the Bon Marché, which had transformed the display and distribution of consumer goods into a spectacle of extravagant proportions.[28] These were more than complemented by urban spectacle entertainments of all kinds from street fairs and wax museums to automobile shows and world expositions, with the most consistently popular being the melodrama theaters and café-concerts—the latter then transformed into what Jules Claretie called the "democratized theatre" of the music halls, with their richly varied programmes and showy interiors—which, in turn, would give way to the cinema.[29] Unlike the secular school system, this new mass culture—along with city parks, railway stations, and public transport—seemed to break down or blur class as well as gender distinctions. Some observers such as Charles d'Avenal, for instance, were enthusiastic about the Paris métro (which opened in 1900), where "duchesses and millionaires [could now] rub shoulders with cooks and clerks."[30] Others, however, saw in what sociologist Gabriel Tarde called this "era of various publics," which seemed so transitory and fluctuating, an erasure of hierarchical boundaries that could prove dangerous. Yet if mass culture opened up the possibility of unexpected, undesirable change, such threats usually were overridden by the way the standardized spectacle produced by the mass-culture "image factories" tended to reinforce representations of established behaviour and encourage everyone, of whatever class, to participate in the bourgeois rites of consumption.

Indeed, the new mass culture in France shaped the subject matter of the early cinema in distinctive ways. The variety format of the spectacles, generally, determined Pathé's film production, which comprised a dozen already marketable categories or genres as early as 1902, when the company began its initial move to dominate the *fête foraine* cinemas. And particular genres assumed a privileged significance. Both Pathé and Méliès, for instance, produced expensive fantasy adaptations, from *Cendrillon* (1899) to *Aladdin* (1907), for adults as well as children, because popular nineteenth-century fantasy pantomimes were continually being revived in French theaters and music halls.[31] Pathé produced historical films, such as *Épopée napoléonienne* (1903), modelled on the French theater's "realizations" of famous historical paintings as well as on recent illustrated school textbooks. And both genres made the *tableau vivant* style of spectacular display especially characteristic of the French cinema of attractions. In the transition to a narrative cinema, moreover, Pathé's so-called dramatic and realist films played a crucial role by drawing on the melodrama theater (as well as fiction) for their subjects and strategies of representation and narration. As in *A Father's Honor* (1905), these "scenes of domestic life" focused on threats to the patriarchal family (perhaps the principal site of legitimation for the French social order) by telling stories of the threatened loss of a father or child—and less often, at least initially, the mother—through twists of fate or coincidence involving either an accident or an *apache* crime. And the traumatic loss of a child was particularly relevant in France, given the country's increasingly accepted one-child-family ideal (especially among white-collar workers) and hence its uniquely low birthrate at the turn of the century. Furthermore, these films began to deploy changes in framing—through camera movement, cut-ins, and patterns of alternation—for the purposes of narrative clarity and rhetorical intensification. And these discursive features, in turn, could be seen as symptoms, to appropriate Peter Brooks's language, of a melodramatic pressure exerted "upon the surface of things" in order to extract a so-called moral truth.[32]

Finally, there is a third argument for claiming the historical specificity of early French cinema as a relatively distinct national cinema. This, perhaps the most intriguing, comes from considering how, in responding to various economic, social, and cultural pressures, the French state, through its law courts and ministries, defined the early cinema as an institution and practice. What is interesting here is that French law followed a paradoxical course with reference to the cinema up through World War I. That is, two quite different definitions emerged as the French film industry achieved a relative degree of economic importance, around 1905–1906. One definition involved the question of whether a film could be conceived, not only as a commodity, but as an intellectual property and, if so, who had the legal right to its exploitation. The other involved the question of whether the State had the legal right to exercise control over the exhibition of films and, if so, which branch or level of the State. Yet the consequences of the court cases and ministry directives that framed these two definitions turned out to be complementary for the development of early French cinema, both as an industry and an art form.

In defining the cinema as an intellectual property, French law initially followed a course similar to the one it had taken during the previous half century when, to use Bernard Edelman's phrase, it was "surprised" by the technical innovation of photography.[33] In the 1840s, for instance, photography was viewed as no more than the product of a mechanical and chemical operation. Twenty years later, however, once photography had become a major commercial industry, French law discovered a "soul in the machine"—that is, that the photograph indeed did bear the "imprint of personality," making it the artistic product of the creative mind or imagination. With the cinema, the reversal took far less time, and the first steps dealt only with *actualité* films. Up until 1905, French law considered film to be merely the work of a machine, incapable of intelligence or interpretation—a position that a Pau court, in November 1904, used to reject the claim of a local banker that he could be the author of a short documentary on the miracles at Lourdes.[34] In February 1905, however, a Paris court took the opposite position in a case involving the famous Sorbonne surgeon.

Dr. Doyen, and the cameraman-inventor, Parnaland, the latter of whom was selling as his own the teaching-aid films he had made for Doyen of his surgical operations several years before.[35] Here, the court ruled that, because he had "first arranged his subject . . . and planned the setting," Doyen was the principal author of these films, which were indeed worthy of legal protection. Within the framework provided by education, surgeon and filmmaker became analogous, not only as teachers, but as artists. Being famous and living in Paris, rather than in the provinces, did seem to have its rewards. Within another month, a court in Narbonne extended this ruling into the public domain by granting the owner of the *fête foraine* cinema "Aérogyne" the right to record and exhibit a film showing the townspeople leaving the Saint-Just cathedral.[36] Anyone had the right, this court implied, to record and represent on film whatever was in or occurring within the public domain as common property.

After 1905, as short fiction films replaced *actualités* as the principal component of cinema programmes, which now began to compete with those of the urban music halls and melodrama theaters, French law had to confront the conflicting claims resulting from that competition. Here, rather than extend the precedent set in the Doyen case, the courts initially sought to protect literary authors against unauthorized film versions of *their* work as intellectual property. A linked series of cases, in Paris, between 1906 and 1908, established that, if a film closely resembled an original literary work (which was complicated by early film's inability to record dialogue), it constituted a form of that work's publication and performance—and so involved an author's permission and right to royalty fees.[37] Had Urban Trading, for instance, not used *Les Deux Gosses* for the title of a 1906 film and had it also varied the conception of that film's story, it would have escaped Pierre Decourcelle's suit against the company for violating his rights to one of his more popular plays.[38] These court decisions had the effect of extending legal protection to fictional films, but primarily to authorized adaptations. A film's status as intellectual property depended, consequently, on the prior legal status of the literary work from which it derived. Moreover, while granting a kind of author's rights to film, these decisions also assumed, as in publishing, the primary right of the company whose capital produced the film. This position—which granted protection to the film property under the rubric of author's rights rather than copyright (as in the United States)—was then confirmed, in November 1908, by the commission responsible for revising the 1886 Berlin Convention on the international protection of scientific, literary, and artistic production.[39] And it was complemented by the French Interior Ministry's refusal to accept films within the protection afforded by legal deposits at the Bibliothèque nationale, partly because nitrate filmstock was so inflammable.[40] Instead, especially after 1907, film scenarios were accepted there (some accompanied by a short strip of several film frames), which again tied the film to a prior verbal text.[41] Yet, as Maugras and Guégan argued at the time, the deposit of a scenario did not offer a production company complete protection for a film as an intellectual property in and of itself.[42]

In defining the cinema as a public spectacle attraction, French law followed a very different course. Throughout the nineteenth century, the French distinguished between two categories of spectacle—the so-called legitimate theater, which was under the direct control of the French state, and the *spectacle de curiosité,* which was under the control of "municipal officials," whether mayors or provincial prefects.[43] At least as early as 1901, the cinema was classed among the *spectacles de curiosité* (along with the *fêtes foraines,* then its principal venue of exhibition)—evidence for which comes from the Paris prefect's decision to suppress the final tableau of a criminal's execution in Pathé's *Histoire d'un crime* (1901).[44] In June 1906, a new Finance Law passed by the National Assembly cut funding for the national censors' staff and effectively removed the theater from any censorship restrictions whatsoever.[45] This created a sharp disparity between the legal status of the cinema and the theater as public spectacles, precisely at the moment when the French film industry was undergoing a rapid expansion. That disparity then deepened, in January 1909, when the Interior Ministry circulated a directive reminding local mayors and prefects that they had the power to ban the screening of films—especially those, whether *actualité* or fiction, which represented criminal executions.[46] His rationale was simple: "There must be an absolute ban on all spectacles of this kind—spectacles liable to provoke demonstrations which disturb the public order and the public space."[47] Although not immediately controversial, within another three years this directive would lead to several court cases and a public debate over film censorship, once a bloc of mayors and prefects in southeastern France decided to prohibit the exhibition of certain crime fiction films produced by the leading French film companies.[48]

Now, both of these definitions viewed the early French cinema, whether positively or negatively, in relation to the theater. On the one hand, the French courts and ministries pushed the industry toward a close association with the theater in terms of production, granting films protection according to their literary source, most of which turned out to be plays—for adaptations of novels often derived from already existing theatrical adaptations.[49] On the other hand, they separated the cinema from the theater, in terms of exhibition, subjecting its actual performance to much greater censorship restrictions. This had the effect, I would argue, of provoking a series of efforts within the industry that, while asserting the cinema's autonomy as a mass cultural practice, would grant it a legal status commensurate with that of the theater, its "high culture" rival. In 1907, Edmond Benoît-Lévy, a Paris lawyer, educator, and editor of the first trade journal devoted to the cinema, *Phono-Ciné-Gazette,* laid out the position underlying these industry efforts quite clearly. "Film does not constitute an ordinary sort of merchandise," Benoît-Lévy, asserted, "but a literary and artistic property."[50] "It is a literary and artistic property in a double sense," he added, "for a film consists of an idea and its application simultaneously. Invention makes it a non-written literary property, and photography makes it incontestably an artistic property."[51] Or, as Maugras and Guégan put it a year later, a film possesses the two elements required of any work of art: production, the creation of mental work or the imagination, and execution, the skill of professional craftsmanship or artistry.[52] The sum total of the efforts this discourse supported might best be described as a strategy of legitimation for the cinema as a cultural practice in France. Yet that strategy also coincided with and served to legitimate, in turn, Pathé's strategy of expansion within the French film industry. For each of Pathé's moves—in production, distribution, and exhibition—was inextricably bound up with specific efforts to redefine the cinema's legal status. And the ground for each one was prepared for by *Phono-Ciné-Gazette* and its editor, Edmond Benoît-Lévy.

From 1906 to 1908, Benoît-Lévy, who seems to have been a model Third Republic entrepreneur cum civic leader at the turn of the century, dedicated himself almost exclusively to promoting the cinema as the fulfilment of the long-cherished dream of a *théâtre populaire* and to convincing people that the twentieth century would indeed be the century of the cinema.[53] The initial front on which he moved was exhibition, in an attempt to re-situate the cinema as a legitimate theatrical enterprise. In May 1906, for instance, he had the Société populaire des beaux arts sponsor a special *fête cinématographique* at the Trocadéro Theatre in Paris, whose 3-hour programme was comprised of 17 recent Pathé films.[54] So successful was the May 13 programme—4,000 people apparently attended, many of them from the bourgeois clientele that supported the legitimate theater—that a second programme was scheduled 2 weeks later, with a dozen additional new Pathé films.[55] The following year, also in Paris, on May 11, *Phono-Ciné-Gazette* organized another *grande fête* in the Salle Elysées-Montmartre at the smaller Théâtre Trianon (2,000 people attended), this time with a programme of recent films from Gaumont, Raleigh & Robert, Vitagraph, Méliès, and Pathé.[56] By then, however, in a business arrangement with Benoît-Lévy, Pathé had embarked on a long-range project of constructing a circuit of permanent urban cinemas throughout France.[57] The first in Paris, the 300-seat Omnia-Pathé (its façade a *mélange* of Métro entrance and Oriental palace) opened on 15 December 1906, right next to the Théâtre des Variétés and across from the Musée Grévin.[58] By the summer of 1907, there were at least fifty new or converted cinemas throughout the city, many of them in the shopping and entertainment districts; and Pathé posters extolled the Omnia-Pathé for appealing to everyone in the family, and especially women, as well as every social class, including the bourgeois élite.[59]

Benoît-Lévy was also involved in Pathé's transformation of the film distribution system in France—from direct sales to restrictive rental contracts. His articles in *Phono-Ciné-Gazette,* beginning in July 1907, provided a quasi-legal basis for this move, claiming that a company such as Pathé had the right, analogous to that of a publisher or theatrical producer, to forbid anyone from presenting its films without permission and payment. Furthermore, as a top executive or board member, he had a hand in four of the six regional affiliates Pathé set up, in the summer and fall of 1907, to distribute the company's film product.[60] Benoît-Lévy was even more personally involved, however, at least initially, in the move to associate the cinema more closely with the theater in terms of production. Here, his principal contribution may well have been to avert a "war" that threatened to break out, in early 1907, between French playwrights and the film industry,[61] whose traces are evident in the court cases establishing author's rights to film properties. Specifically, that spring, Benoît-Lévy negotiated with the Société des auteurs dramatiques to make a film version of Michel Carré's popular pantomime, *L'Enfant prodigue.*[62] Recorded at the Gaumont studio, in May 1907, this early feature-length film (1,600 metres) was projected through the summer months at the Théâtre des Variétés and then in selected theaters throughout France but met with a mixed response (at the time, Carré knew very little about filmmaking).[63] Less successful than anticipated, *L'Enfant prodigue* did, however, offer a model for future relations between the two culture industries—both in its contractual arrangements for royalty fees and its employment of "serious" theater actors.[64] Although Pathé apparently refused to be a party to this particular venture, the company drew on Benoît-Lévy's project in instituting more permanent theatrical enterprises the following year. In February 1908, it provided financial backing—in the form of studio equipment and distribution agreements—to the new production company called Film d'Art, which engaged directors and actors from the prestigious Comédie Française in Paris.[65] And, in June 1908—with the lure of production money, a brand new studio, and exclusive distribution rights—Pathé persuaded Pierre Decourcelle, who had some influence in the Société des gens de lettres (SGL), to form another production affiliate, SCAGL, which then enjoyed the right to adapt any work by SGL authors.[66]

Despite the efforts of Benoît-Lévy, Pathé and others, the French film industry's strategy of legitimation did not immediately succeed in redefining the legal status of the cinema. Not until the late 1920s and 1930s would the French courts and State ministries fully recognize film as an intellectual property in and of itself and wrest censorship control from municipal officials—and then simply by transferring that control to the State.[67] Their efforts did succeed, however, in transforming the social status of the cinema and, thereby, securing the industry's sustained economic growth. The new urban cinemas, modelled closely on the music halls and legitimate theaters, for instance, appealed especially to the rapidly increasing white-collar and civil servant strata of the lower bourgeoisie "all too eager," in Lenard Berlanstein's words, "to build their lives around their leisurely pastimes."[68] And, by 1910, prestigious Pathé cinemas such as the Omnia-Pathé and the Cirque d'hiver, whose programmes featured Film d'Art and SCAGL productions, would be credited with attracting and holding a regular bourgeois clientele.[69] Finally, the consequences of the industry's strategy were just as significant on the critical discourse surrounding the cinema, particularly on that discourse which, after 1908, sought to claim its status as an art form. Two points are particularly salient here, and they can serve as a conclusion.

First of all, the industry's strategy of legitimation encouraged many of the earliest French writers who took the cinema seriously to equate the cinema with the theater or, at least, to put particular emphasis on their interrelations. In his review of Film d'Art's initial production, *L'Assassinat du Duc de Guise* (1908), for instance, Adolphe Brisson, perhaps the most widely respected theater critic of the time, simply assumed that the cinema was "a new form of theater" and then began to tease out its potential aesthetic.[70] For Brisson, both cinema and theater privileged the actor's performance; but, in the cinema, the actor's gestures and movements were primary rather than, as in the theater, subordinated to or dependent on words and vocal intonation. Furthermore, those gestures had to be precise, natural (drawn directly from life), and flexible enough to suit the dramatic situation rather than, as in pantomime, be drawn from a fixed lexicon of conventional signs. Most writers following Brisson shared his view that the cinema was a new form of theater—especially of the melodrama, whose affective mode of representation insisted on expressing what verbal language left unsaid. By 1910, in the pages of *Ciné-Journal*, the most important of the new French trade journals, editor Georges Dureau and scriptwriter Georges Fagot were arguing over which production company, Film d'Art or SCAGL, as representative of the best the cinema had to offer, consistently came closest to achieving the high standards of theatrical art.[71] That what might be called the theater analogy, at the level of both commercial enterprise and critical discourse, became so prominent in French cinema, perhaps more so than in any other national cinema, owes a good deal, I would argue, to the historical specificity of certain French legal definitions. And the battle to break that analogy would be fought not once—by Émile Vuillermoz, Louis Delluc, and others during and after the Great War—but over and over again in French writings on the cinema.[72]

The second point also concerns the long-term ramifications of the French cinema's legal status. For most writers accepted as well the idea, sanctioned by the industry and French law, that the dramatist or scriptwriter was, as in the theater, the real author of the film. "The cinema actor must collaborate with the author of the scenario," wrote Dureau, in 1911, "he is the body for which the scriptwriter is the soul."[73] This was such a "universal" position that it was not until just before the war that filmmakers such as Léonce Perret and Georges Lacroix at Gaumont began to protest in letters to the press against the lack of attention accorded their work.[74] That protest took a different course after the war, yet the legal assumption of authors' rights still provided a crucial context for Louis Delluc, Léon Moussinac, and others as proponents of the earliest version of what would later become familiar as the *auteur* theory. In order for filmmakers to become the "true authors" of their films, Delluc argued, they had not only to direct a film's production but also to compose its scenario.[75] In addition, he and his colleagues sought to distinguish the film artist or *cinéaste* who composed original scenarios from the more common *metteur-en-scéne* of adaptations[76]; and they did so by continuing to adhere to the principle of French law by which a literary or artistic property was viewed as the product of a single individual. In other words, their advocacy of a *politique des auteurs* constituted a kind of aesthetic resistance that sought to reverse the interpretive trajectory their initial legal premise had taken. For they were intent, after all, on reasserting the individual as the creative subject of film. What these writers faced, however, were historically specific conditions quite different from those earlier confronting Benoît-Lévy, conditions within which both the French film industry and the French state, now that the prewar strategy of legitimation had served its purpose, were inexorably bent on securing the collective space of that subject, not for an "author" but for capital.

NOTES

1. Shorter versions of this essay were presented at the Society for Cinema Studies Conference, Iowa City, Iowa, 15 April 1989, and at the American Historical Association Conference, San Francisco, 28 December 1989.

2. See, for instance, Richard Abel, *French Cinema: The First Wave, 1915–1929* (Princeton, N.J.: Princeton University Press, 1984), pp. 243, 290–4; and Sandy Flitterman-Lewis, *To Desire Differently: Feminism and the French Cinema* (Urbana: University of Illinois Press, 1990), 23–27.

3. The term *monolithic category* comes from an excelleht paper by Philip Rosen, "Making a Nation in Sembene's *Ceddo*," Society for Cinema Studies Conference, Bozeman, Montana, 30 June 1988.

4. Eric Hobsbawm, *The Age of Empire, 1875–1914* (New York: Pantheon, 1987), pp. 34–83. See also Jean-Marie Mayeur and Madeleine Rebérioux, *The Third Republic from its Origins to the Great War, 1871–1914*, trans. J. R. Foster (Cambridge: Cambridge University Press, 1984), pp. 94–100, 271–8.

5. The best early source of information on Pathé-Frères is R. Binet and G. Hausser, *Les Sociétés de cinématographe* (Paris: La France Economique et Financière, 1908), pp. 14–29. It was no idle boast to say that Pathé films were seen by 300 million people around the world—Edmond Benoît-Lévy, "Causerie sur le cinématographe," *Phono-Ciné-Gazette* 63 (1 November 1907), 382.

6. France exported more automobiles than did any other country before 1914—see François Caron, *An Economic History of Modern France*, trans. Barbara Bray (New York: Columbia University Press, 1979), pp. 107–8. Between 1899 and 1903, the value of the

industry's exports rose from 2 million to 51 million francs—Eugen Weber, *France: Fin-de-Siècle* (Cambridge, Mass.: Harvard University Press, 1986), p. 207.

7. "Informations financières: Pathé-Frères," *Phono-Ciné-Gazette* 78 (15 June 1908), 631.

8. "Lettre du Colonel Marchand," *Le Film* 2 (7 March 1914)—reprinted in Marcel L'Herbier, ed., *Intelligence du cinématographe* (Paris: Coréa, 1946), p. 93.

9. Mayeur and Rebérioux, *The Third Republic*, pp. 268–9; Richard F. Kuisel, *Capitalism and the State in Modern France* (Cambridge: Cambridge University Press, 1981), pp. 12, 15.

10. Mayeur and Rebérioux, *The Third Republic*, p. 50. In 1906, about 50 percent of French workers still labored in firms with less than five employees—Mayeur and Rebérioux, *The Third Republic*, p. 268.

11. Caron, *An Economic History*, pp. 163–71. See, also, Gordon Wright, *France in Modern Times*, 3rd ed. (New York: Norton, 1981), p. 279; and Michael B. Miller, *The Bon Marché: Bourgeois Culture and the Department Store, 1869–1920* (Princeton, N.J.: Princeton University Press, 1981), p. 12.

12. *Films Pathé-Frères* (Paris, 1907), p. 4.

13. Caron, *An Economic History*, p. 27; and Charles Rearick, *Pleasures of the Belle Epoque: Entertainment and Festivity in Turn-of-the-Century France* (Berkeley: University of California Press, 1985), p. 30.

14. Some of the groundwork for this monopoly strategy was laid by François Valleiry, in "Le Cinématographiste de la Ville de Paris," *Phono-Ciné-Gazette* 42 (15 December 1906), 471–2; and by Francis Mair, in "Le Cinématographe et les compagnies d'assurances," *Phono-Ciné-Gazette* 42 (15 December 1906), 472–3.

15. See, for instance, "Ciné-Nouvelles," *Phono-Ciné-Gazette* 42 (15 December 1906), 474; François Valleiry, "Les Cinémas de Paris," *Phono-Ciné-Gazette* 53 (1 June 1907), 210; Georges Sadoul, *Histoire générale du cinéma, II: L'Epoque Pathé, 1903–1909* (Paris: Denoël, 1948), p. 345; and Emmanuelle Toulet, "Le Spectacle cinématographique à Paris de 1895 à 1914," Thèse à l'Ecole de Chartes (Sorbonne, 1982), pp. 558–9.

16. Francis Mair, "A la compagnie Pathé: la nouvelle situation," *Phono-Ciné-Gazette* 56 (15 July 1907), 270; "Informations financières," *Phono-Ciné-Gazette* 68 (15 January 1908), 469; and the Pathé-Frères ad in *Phono-Ciné-Gazette* 74 (15 April 1908), 564.

17. See, for instance, "Editorial: What Does It Mean?," *Moving Picture World* 1:34 (26 October 1907), 536; "Notes from Manufacturers: Pathé," *Moving Picture World* 7:3 (16 July 1910), 165; "Kinematography in the United States," *Moving Picture World* 21:2 (11 July 1914), 176; and Frank L. Dyer's testimony in *United States v M.P.P.C.*, vol. 3 (1914), 1504. I am grateful to Nancy Rosenbloom for providing me with a photocopy of the Dyer testimony.

18. Georges Dureau, "Le Point de vue national," *Ciné-Journal* 73 (10 January 1910), 3–4.

19. See, for instance, J. A. Berst's testimony in *United States v M.P.P.C.*, vol. 3 (1914), 1768–9. I am grateful to Charles Musser for providing me with a photocopy of the Berst testimony.

20. For a good historical overview of the Film Service Association and the Motion Picture Patents Company, see Kristin Thompson, *Exporting Entertainment: America in the World Film Market* (London: British Film Institute, 1985), pp. 10–27.

21. A specific source here is William Selig's letter of 4 November 1909, reporting on his August to September visit to the major film production companies in France—Box 26 of Kleine Optical, Manuscript Division, Library of Congress. I am grateful to Nancy Rosenbloom for a photocopy of this 10-page letter.

22. This tentative conclusion comes from a perusal of H. N. Marvin's testimony in *United States v M.P.P.C.*, vol. 1 (1914), 222, as well as selected notes and documents from the Edison Papers Library, all of which Nancy Rosenbloom provided to me in photocopy.

23. See, for instance, Hobsbawn, *The Age of Empire*, pp. 142–64; and Weber, *France: Fin-de-Siècle*, pp. 239–40.

24. Mayeur and Rebérioux, *The Third Republic*, p. 84.

25. Ibid., pp. 69–70, 86. See, also, Eugen Weber, *Peasants into Frenchmen: The Modernization of Rural France, 1870–1914* (Stanford, Calif.: Stanford University Press, 1976), pp. 303–38.

26. Mayeur and Rebérioux, *The Third Republic*, pp. 109–19; and Hobsbawn, *The Age of Empire*, pp. 174–9.

27. The metaphor of cement to describe social cohesion comes from Emile Durkheim, *Les Règles de la méthode sociologique* (Paris: Alcan, 1895). See, also, T. J. Clark, *The Painting of Modern Life: Paris in the Art of Manet and His Followers* (Princeton, N.J.: Princeton University Press, 1984), pp. 9, 202–4; and Hobsbawn, *The Age of Empire*, pp. 105–6.

28. The primary source for the history of the French press is Claude Bellanger, Jacques Godechot, Pierre Guiral, and Fernand Terrou, *Histoire générale de la presse française, III: De 1871 à 1940* (Paris: Presses universitaires de France, 1972). See, also, Weber, *Peasants into Frenchmen*, pp. 195–220, 452–70; Rosalind Williams, *Dream Worlds: Mass Consumption in Late Nineteenth-Century France* (Berkeley: University of California Press, 1982), pp. 11–12, 66–70; Miller, *The Bon Marché*, pp. 165–89; Mayeur and Rebérioux, *The Third Republic*, pp. 116–7; and Hobsbawn, *The Age of Empire*, p. 89.

29. Rearick, *Pleasures of the Belle Epoque*, pp. 83–84.

30. Georges d'Avenal, *Les Mécanismes de la vie moderne*, I (Paris: Flammarion, 1902)—quoted in Weber, *France, Fin-de-Siècle*, p. 71. For an analysis of d'Avenal's writings, see Williams, *Dream Worlds*, pp. 94–106.

31. See, for instance, John Frazer, *Artificially Arranged Scenes: The Films of Georges Méliès* (Boston: G. K. Hall, 1979), pp. 1–21. The elaborate seasonal and holiday displays mounted by the grand magasins may also have provided an incentive for these féerie films—see Miller, *The Bon Marché*, p. 176.

32. Peter Brooks, *The Melodramatic Imagination: Balzac, James, Melodrama and the Mode of Excess* (New Haven, Conn.: Yale University Press, 1976), pp. 2, 15. Both Tom Gunning and Maureen Turim express a similar idea in different contexts—see Tom Gunning, "What I Saw from the Rear Window of the Hôtel des Folies-Dramatiques, or the Story Point of View Films Told," in André Gaudreault, ed., *Ce que je vois de mon ciné . . .* (Paris: Méridiens-Klincksieck, 1988), p. 41; and Maureen Turim, "French Melodrama: Theory of a Specific History," *Theater Journal* 39 (October 1987), 312.

33. The following brief survey of French law dealing with photography comes from Bernard Edelman, *Ownership of the Image: Elements of a Marxist Theory of Law*, trans. Elizabeth Kingdom (London: Routledge & Kegan Paul, 1979), pp. 45–46, 49–51.

34. E. Maugras and M. Guégan, *Le Cinématographe devant le droit* (Paris: V. Giard et E. Brière, 1908), pp. 100–5. Paul Leglise, *Le Politique du cinéma français: le cinéma et la IIIe République* (Paris: Lherminier, 1970), p. 15.

35. Maugras and Guégan, *Le Cinématographe devant le droit*, pp. 105–10. Leglise, *Le Politique du cinéma français*, pp. 15–17. Edelman, *Ownership of the Image*, p. 47.

36. "Une Grave Décision," *Phono-Ciné-Gazette* 14 (15 October 1905), 225–7. "Chronique judiciaire," *Phono-Ciné-Gazette* 23 (1 March 1906), 94. Leglise, *Le Politique du cinéma français*, p. 17.

37. See, for instance, Fernand Divoire, "Le Cinématographe et les auteurs," *Phono-Ciné-Gazette* 44 (15 January 1907), 32–33; "Ciné-Nouvelles," *Phono-Ciné-Gazette* 52 (15 May 1907), 190; "Les Auteurs et le cinématographe," *Phono-Ciné-Gazette* 81 (1 August 1908), 679; "Procès des auteurs contre le cinématographe," *Phono-Ciné-Gazette* 84 (15 September 1908), 726–7; Leglise, *La Politique du cinéma français*, pp. 19–21.

38. Maugras and Guégan, *Le Cinématographe devant le droit*, pp. 115–8.

39. "Propriété littéraire," *Phono-Ciné-Gazette* 79 (1 July 1908), 645; H. B., "La Conférence de Berlin et le cinématographe," *Ciné-Journal* 15 (26 November 1908), 3; Maugras and Guégan, *Le Cinématographe devant le droit*, pp. 127–39; Leglise, *Le Politique du cinéma français*, p. 23.

40. Leglise, *Le Politique du cinéma français*, pp. 21–22.

41. For a description of these deposits, see Emmanuelle Toulet, "Une année de l'édition cinématographique Pathé: 1909," in Pierre Guibbert, ed., *Les Premiers Ans du cinéma français* (Perpignan: Institut Jean Vigo, 1985), pp. 133–4.

42. Maugras and Guégan, *Le Cinématographe devant le droit*, pp. 51–52.

43. Neville March Hunnings, *Film Censors and the Law* (London: George Allen & Unwin, 1967), pp. 332–3; Leglise, *Le Politique du cinéma français*, p. 29.

44. René Jeanne and Charles Ford, *Histoire encyclopédie du cinéma, I: Le Cinéma français, 1895–1929* (Paris: Robert Laffont, 1947), p. 78.

45. Hunnings, *Film Censors and the Law*, p. 332; Leglise, *Le Politique du cinéma français*, p. 27.

46. René Jeanne and Charles Ford, *Le Cinéma et la presse, 1895–1960* (Paris: Armand Colin, 1961), pp. 188–90; Hunnings, *Film Censors and the Law*, p. 333; Leglise, *Le Politique du cinéma français*, pp. 29–30.

47. Edelman, *Ownership of the Image*, 48.

48. Hunnings, *Film Censors and the Law*, pp. 334–5; Leglise, *Le Politique du cinéma français*, pp. 30–31; and Richard Abel, *French Film Theory and Criticism, 1907–1929: A History/Anthology* (Princeton, N.J.: Princeton University Press, 1988), pp. 12–13.

49. See, for instance, Rick Altman, "Dickens, Griffith, and Film Theory Today," *The South Atlantic Quarterly* 88 (Spring 1989), 321–59.

50. Francis Mair, "A la compagnie Pathé: la nouvelle situation," *Phono-Ciné-Gazette* 56 (15 July 1907), 270. Benoît-Lévy often wrote under the pseudonym of Francis Mair.

51. Edmond Benoît-Lévy, "Le Droit d'auteur cinématographique," *Phono-Ciné-Gazette* 62 (15 October 1907), 365.

52. Maugras and Guégan, *Le Cinématographe devant le droit*, pp. 25–28.

53. François Valleiry, "Les Cinématographes de Paris," *Phono-Ciné-Gazette* 49 (1 April 1907), 131. Benoît-Lévy apparently also wrote under the pseudonym of François Valleiry. He had founded the Société populaire des beaux arts (1894), for instance, and was an active member of the Ligue d'enseignement (the organization most responsible for initiating the secular education system in France).

54. François Valleiry, "Notre festival phono-cinématographique au Trocadéro," *Phono-Ciné-Gazette* 27 (1 May 1906), 105–6; "Programme de la fête cinématographique, et phonographique," *Phono-Ciné-Gazette* 28 (15 May 1906), 191.

55. François Valleiry, "La Première Fête cinématographique," *Phono-Ciné-Gazette* 29 (1 June 1906), 210–11; and Francis Mair, "La Deuxième Soirée du Trocadéro," *Phono-Ciné-Gazette* 30 (15 June 1906), 229–30.

56. "Ciné-Nouvelles: Grand Fête du Phono-Ciné," *Phono-Ciné-Gazette* 51 (1 May 1907), 172; and Charles Delac, "Grand Fête du Phono-Ciné," *Phono-Ciné-Gazette* 52 (15 May 1907), 185. Benoît-Lévy also briefly set up what he called a "ciné-club" in the spring of 1907—see "Le Ciné-Club," *Phono-Ciné-Gazette* 50 (15 April 1907), 145.

57. Benoît-Lévy's associates in the company he formed, in early November 1906, included Charles Dussaud, Maurice Guégan, and E. Maugras—see "Société pour Exploiter le Cinématographe Pathé-Frères," *Phono-Ciné-Gazette* 46 (15 February, 1907), 74; and "Documents financières," *Phono-Ciné-Gazette* 54 (15 June 1907), 230.

58. "Ciné-Nouvelles," *Phono-Ciné-Gazette* 41 (1 December 1906), 453; "Ciné-Nouvelles," *Phono-Ciné-Gazette* 42 (15 December 1906), 474.

59. See, for instance, the Théâtre Cinématographe Pathé ad reproduced in *Phono-Ciné-Gazette* 41 (1 December 1906), 456; François Valleiry, "Les Cinémas de Paris," *Phono-Ciné-Gazette* 53 (1 June 1907), 210; and "Ciné-Nouvelles," *Phono-Ciné-Gazette* 55 (1 July 1907), 253.

60. See, for instance, "Informations financières," *Phono-Ciné-Gazette* 58 (15 August 1907), 304–5; "Informations financières," *Phono-Ciné-Gazette* 68 (15 January 1908), 469; and the Pathé-Frères ad in *Phono-Ciné-Gazette* 74 (15 April 1908), 564.

61. See, for instance, "Cinéma et Théâtre," *Phono-Ciné-Gazette* 44 (15 January 1907), 32; and Fernand Divoire, "Le Cinématographe et les auteurs," *Phono-Ciné-Gazette* 44 (15 January 1907), 32–33.

62. "Les Auteurs cinématographiques," *Phono-Ciné-Gazette* 83 (1 September 1908), 709.

63. "Ciné-Nouvelles," *Phono-Ciné-Gazette* 52 (15 May 1907), 190; "Ciné-Nouvelles," *Phono-Ciné-Gazette* 53 (1 June 1907), 211; François Valleiry, "Théâtre des Variétés," *Phono-Ciné-Gazette* 56 (15 July 1907), 270–1; and "Ciné-Nouvelles," *Phono-Ciné-Gazette* 59 (1 September 1907), 321.

64. See, especially, François Valleiry, "Droits d'auteur," *Phono-Ciné-Gazette* 54 (15 June 1907), 230; and Valleiry, "Théâtre des Variétés," 270–1.

65. Covielle, "L'Illustre Cinéma," *Le Matin*—reprinted in *Phono-Ciné-Gazette* 71 (1 March 1908), 514–5; "Informations financières," *Phono-Ciné-Gazette* 75 (1 May 1908), 583; "Revue financière: Société Film d'Art," *Argus-Phono-Cinéma* 72 (16 May 1908), 11; and Binet and Hausser, *Les Sociétés de cinématographe*, pp. 66–67.

66. See, for instance, "Informations financières," *Phono-Ciné-Gazette* 78 (15 June 1908), 631; and "Informations financières," *Phono-Ciné-Gazette* 81 (1 August 1908), 680.

67. See, for instance, Hunnings, *Film Censors and the Law*, pp. 344–7; and Edelman, *Ownership of the Image*, pp. 53–59.

68. Lenard R. Berlanstein, *The Working People of Paris, 1871–1914*, (Baltimore: Johns Hopkins University Press, 1984), p. 122. I develop this argument more fully in "The 'Blank Screen of Reception' in Early French Cinema," in *Iris* 11 (1990), 26–47.

69. See, for instance, "Music Halls," *Comoedia* (3 June 1910), 4.

70. Adolphe Brisson, "Chronique théâtrale: *L'Assassinat du Duc de Guise*," *Le Temps* (2 November 1908)—reprinted in English translation in Abel, *French Film Theory and Criticism, 1907–1929*, pp. 50–53.

71. Georges Dureau, "Film d'Art et films d'art," *Ciné-Journal* 94 (11 June 1910), 3–4; and Georges Fagot, "La S.C.A.G.L.," *Ciné-Journal* 95 (18 June 1910), 23.

72. For an extended version of this argument, see Abel, *French Film Theory and Criticism, 1907–1939. A History/Anthology* (Princeton, N.J.: Princeton University Press, 1988).

73. Georges Dureau, "L'Art du théâtre et celui du cinématographe ne sont pas régies par les mêmes règles," *Ciné-Journal* 169 (18 November 1911), 3–4.

74. Léonce Perret, "Lettre," *Ciné-Journal* 246 (10 May 1913), 17; and E.-G. Lacroix, "Propos d'un metteur-en-scène," *Le Journal* (17 February 1914), 7.

75. See, for instance, Louis Delluc, "Cinéma," *Paris-Midi* (2 February 1919), 2, and (12 May 1919), 2.

76. See, for instance, Léon Moussinac, "Cinématographie," *Mercure de France* (1 November 1921), 784–6; and Louis Delluc, "Prologue," *Drames du cinéma* (Paris: Editions du monde nouveau, 1923), pp. ii–iii—both reprinted in English translation in Abel, *French Film Theory and Criticism, 1907–1929*, pp. 249–50, 285–6 (respectively).

Heide Schlüpmann

Cinema as Anti-Theater: Actresses and Female Audiences in Wilhelminian Germany

Cinema in Germany, as in other countries, developed both out of show business and out of the realm of technical-scientific invention, as seen in the collaboration among the photographic, optical, and manufacturing industries. Domestic producers, such as the Skladanowsky brothers and Oskar Messter, were soon joined by other firms, including branches of foreign companies.[1] Nevertheless, in comparison with other countries such as England, France, the United States, and even Scandinavia, film production in Germany was relatively limited. Thus it would seem productive to focus attention on how films were exhibited and received rather than how they were produced. In contrast to the relatively small number of films being made, the development of movie theaters kept pace with that in foreign countries. Consequently, German cinema began primarily as a consumer for the international market, not as a supplier.

In the domestic market, production began to be allied inseparably with exhibition. By 1910, there was a decisive upswing in the number of German films made, accompanied by an intersection of cinema and the world of show business.[2] Paul Davidson is a typical representative of this period, linking the network of production and exhibition to the existing institution of theater. In 1906 he founded AKT (Allgemeine Kinematographische Theatergesellschaft) and, in 1909–10, built his first Union-Theater in Berlin. From this base he established one of the most significant production firms of the prewar period, Projektions AG Union (PAGU).[3] Davidson's success was founded on that of Asta Nielsen, the star of PAGU, and one of the most renowned silent film actresses of the 1910s.

It was not until this period, between 1909 and 1914, that the German cinema developed its distinctive contours in the short feature.

From a special issue, devoted to early cinema audiences, of *Iris* 11 (Summer 1990). Reprinted by permission of the author and the Institute of Cinema and Culture, University of Iowa. Translated by Ellen Risholm.

These films differ from the better-known German silent films of the 1920s and represent a transition from the early kind of cinema, for which Tom Gunning created the notion of "cinema of attractions," to the later well-known narrative cinema. The specific aesthetics and the social meaning of this cinema have been handed down to us in two ways: through the extant films—which are very few—and through the literature resulting from the campaign against the cinema of that time. These writings include both reform debates and concepts of film aesthetics. In Germany these two types of "production," industrial-technical and cultural-journalistic, for the most part remained separate. This differs from the United States, where there was a wide spectrum of reform movements supported by liberal journalists such as Ida Tarbell, Louis Reeves Harrison, and W. Stephen Bush, who eventually became actively involved in film production.[4] Even Jane Addams, who in the beginning fought for strong censorship, later participated in a melo-drama production, *Votes for Women* (1913). The emancipatory movements in Germany were not at all involved in the film controversy in the press, but one cannot fail to notice the influence of the conservative reform movement on film production. With the exception of the *Autorenfilme*,[5] which originated elsewhere, this exchange did not take place in the area of film production. It was the civil and cultural framework of the state that became the site of exchange, responding to the new medium's status as a hybrid of business and culture.

What were the subjects of Wilhelminian cinema between 1909 and 1914? And of film journalism? The beginnings of the feature film—at that time called *Kinodramen*, cine-dramas—included most of the genres that had developed in international cinema. These were mainly social dramas, crime stories, and *Sensationsfilme*.[6] (Comedies were usually distinguished from the dramas in the current usage.) As far as can be detected from the surviving films, such films were usually set in bourgeois and city milieux. Depiction of the lives of workers and rural types is less common. These movies preserve public life through a combination of documentation and staging. The shots of streets, plazas, cafés, amusement parks, factories, and modes of transportation capture the façade of a city milieu in a moment of transition. This is the case in social dramas such as *Heimgefunden, Von Stufe zu Stufe, Lebensbeichte einer Probiermamsell* (ca. 1910), but especially in a number of *Kriminalfilme*, such as *Die Abenteuer eines Journalisten, Das Recht auf das Dasein*, and *Der geheimnisvolle Klub* (all three, 1913). These productions, however, also pointed in the direction of narrative fiction and thematized the nonpublic, that is, private and intimate places. Some examples are *Grausame Ehe* (ca. 1910), *Ich will keine Stiefmutter* (ca. 1910), *Die Vernunft des Herzens* (1910), *Vergebens* (1911), *Madeleine* (1912), *Hochspannung* (1913), *Die Czernowska* (1913), *Die Fächermalerin* (1913), and *Pauline* (1914).

Many of the narrated stories exploited the "unstaged" reality of the inside of a factory, bank, or workshop. Others presented the studio-built facsimiles of "Gründerzeit" apartments, the conservatory of a bourgeois villa, or a petit bourgeois kitchen. Occasionally they dealt with the plight of a woman on her own or the problems of a bourgeois social climber. Usually, though, they were about the intimate atmosphere surrounding marriage and prostitution. These films also portrayed normally hidden elements, such as the world of crime, and peripheral nonbourgeois characters, such as the circus artist and the Bohemian.

Meanwhile, the writings of the reformers addressed the immoral, unnatural, noncultural, and un-German aspects of cinema. They condemned the depiction of sexuality and crime, the stimulation of the senses, and the excitation of the "nerves." They opposed the presence of women on the screen and in the theater, and naturally they demanded the protection of children. They gave expression to fears of moral and social revolution, as well as anarchy. Although the reformers conjured up a nightmare of film production in the hands of the Social Democrats, what they actually feared was the disruption of dominant cultural and moral values, and, in the final analysis, their own identity.

If one looks at both sides of Wilhelminian cinema, it becomes apparent that the issue is less one of class difference than differences and contradictions within the bourgeoisie. During the transition to a bourgeois institution, early German film production acquired its own character by developing an oppositional "bourgeois" form, despite considerable resistance on the part of the cultural bourgeoisie. This separate form found partial support only among some members of the oppositional intelligentsia in the cities. On the contrary, the main impetus of film journalism was to outline a restorative cinema institution that would affirm the state. Censorship certainly had the potential to influence production. However, the mechanisms for wielding this influence had not quite yet evolved.[7]

Cinema, in the transition to a bourgeois institution of mass culture, was marked by the resolving of contradictions within the bourgeoisie. In *Screening Out the Past,* Lary May demonstrated how the American cinema reform movement was not primarily concerned with protecting middle-class ideology against a threatening new form of amusement associated with the new mass of immigrants. Rather, the reform movement's concentration on cinema sprang from the necessity to come to grips with a contradiction inherent in modern bourgeois society. The traditional democratic order defined by the supremacy of the male bourgeois was endangered by the blurring of class differences in consumer culture and the disruption of the family attributed to women joining the work force. If the American "progressives" advocated a restoration of Victorian values, it implied more than the preservation of a mainly middle-class order. It implied the restitution of the family as the source of disciplinary order for society. According to May,

> Not only did modern industrialism unleash conflict and exploitation, but the breakdown in class divisions within amusements and the great increase

in consumption of goods and services that followed seemed to threaten the old democratic culture. In response, Progressives tried to unify all groups around vice and civic reform, in order to restore the good family as the controlling force over society. More than searching for order, these people tried to recreate the sexual order of the past, and make it relevant to the modern era.[8]

It was soon realized that this new phenomenon of a consumer culture not only threatened Victorian values but also held the potential for its salvation. Cinema was recruited to solve the social problem of "rescuing the family."

In the same sense, "rescuing the family" can be read as a motto for the German reform movement but not for pre-World War I film production. The disparity between the reformers and the producers reflected the special social and political position of the German bourgeoisie, which found itself in a schizophrenic situation. There had been a tremendous economic boom in the face of monumental political inefficacy, and bourgeois-industrial power was couched within a feudal-agrarian government.[9] Relinquishing political power to the advantage of the aristocracy was, on the one hand, Bismarck's project, and on the other, the basis of an alliance against the workers' movement. Because the opposition between economic power and political inefficacy was in the end in the interest of the bourgeoisie, cultural practice did not aim to remove this barrier but rather strove to cover it up. No longer the advance guard of bourgeois emancipation, the educated bourgeoisie placed itself firmly on the side of the state and supported a notion of culture that excluded business and technology. The dichotomy between business and politics is mirrored in that between film production and the cultural politics of film.

The Cultural Politics of Film

The exclusion of business and technology from "culture" had a tradition in Germany. As Fritz K. Ringer pointed out in *The Decline of German Mandarins*, the conception of German culture and education, which developed in opposition to practical knowledge and civilization, was closely tied to the key role that scholars, the "mandarins," played in the "transformation of an essentially feudal state into a heavily bureaucratic monarchy."[10] Education was the bourgeois' means of attaining administrative positions that were otherwise reserved for the nobility. Concomitantly, this advancement was supported by the development of political theories that demanded legality and legitimacy in government. Although the doctrine of legality made the position of scholars within the governmental system indispensable and strengthened the constitutional freedom of all citizens, the doctrine of legitimacy committed the state to "culture," which meant that it had to secure the position of a cultural elite that need not demonstrate "usefulness."[11]

As Ringer argued, the bourgeois conception of culture has always been elitist, but there was still some room for emancipatory elements. These were lost sight of in the nineteenth century:

> The mandarins' ties to the rest of the middle class were loosened, and their obligation to the status quo increased. A moment arrived at which their leadership was threatened more from below than from above, and from that point on, they gave an even greater emphasis to the defensive and vaguely conservative side of their philosophy. By around 1890, at any rate, many German academics had come to assume the stance of Platonic philosopher-statesmen preparing to meet the onslaught of the mechanics.[12]

In particular, the unusually abrupt onset of industrialization in Germany led to an intensification of the opposition between culture and civilization, once again cutting off the cultural realm from the material realm of business and technology.

Although culture resists utilitarianism, its more-or-less hidden "functionalizing" takes place in the service of the state. Culture transforms itself from a realm that the state guarantees to a free space that only survives insofar as culture conversely guarantees the existence of the feudal state in the face of the socialist threat. It is this utilitarianism behind the "bearers of culture" that relates to cinema without exposing the bourgeois notion of culture. As new technology, the medium was acceptable to the reformers from the beginning as simply a means of national education and for the distribution of culture because it could only strengthen their position.[13] But as "the movies," cinema was the enemy; not only did it withdraw the new medium from the control of the educated bourgeoisie, it also withdrew the people from the reformers' control.

Cinema lifted the barriers between industry and technology, and culture. In film's transition from a technical, scientific, and research medium to a form of entertainment, it invaded the bourgeois refuge of culture. As long as the filmmaker did not move beyond the scope of the already delineated "lower" culture, he posed no threat. But the proliferation of projection venues and the appropriation of the bourgeois form of the stage play were proving to be major irritations.

The reformers' shift from a rejection of cinema to the preliminary drafts of a feature film aesthetics evinces an increasing understanding of how the cinema, which threatened the elitist position of the educated bourgeoisie, could restore and preserve the status quo. Lawyers and jurists were the first to give expression to this utilitarian thinking. They were interested in the promotion of an industry that had importance for the state. The only problem was how to bring this undesirable cultural expression under control. The responsibility for this task fell to teachers and scholars.

Progressive intellectuals, at least those not subscribing to popular affirmative conservatism, were the only ones contemplating a reform of culture and art through technology. They were more likely to sympathize with the Social Democrats, and in any case they did not fear the workers' movement. This view was expressed by a tradition of liberal journalism that, although less influential, arose in concert with the reformist press. The development of the *Autorenfilme* also reflects this liberal social position. In the final analysis, though, the question surrounding cinema is not about culture but about the public sphere.

This distinction was barely understood by liberal intellectuals and even less so by the various emancipatory activists, such as the socialists and the women's and homosexual movements. Otherwise they would not have ignored this new medium. Only the reformers' plans for a restorative cinema reveal an inkling of what it was all about. "Rescuing the family" played a crucial role in the counteremancipatory solution for the crisis in the bourgeois public sphere.

A Clash of "Spheres"

Because of the enormous economic development at the end of the nineteenth century, the bourgeois identity was threatened from within and without: from the inside by a generally accepted dependence on the feudal state, and from the outside through the masses' demands for participation in the public sphere. This tension highlights the discrepancy between economics and politics.

Although the bourgeoisie averted the outside threat by renouncing a claim to political self-consciousness, the internal threat was not so easily elided. Acceptance of the feudal state consequently destroyed the public sphere's participation in the realm of literature and culture. Culture changed from a public force into a private "possession." The crisis in the cultural sphere was inseparable from the political opposition against feudal order; both revealed the public's dependence on restoring a feudal-patriarchal role for the bourgeois in the home.

Robbed of his political public sphere, the bourgeois was relegated to the intimate sphere of the family as the last bastion of his identity. But even this foundation was shaken by the economic crises that led to women's increased presence in the work force. Because the feudal system had positioned women's domestic function as "natural," any disruption in this social order was a challenge. The changes in the cultural public sphere upset this belief in nature just when it was most needed and most fervently clung to as a social rationale. Regaining political force would have meant recognizing the feudal structure underlying this definition of nature, thus prompting a decision either to identify with feudalism or to change this basic presumption. The women's movement tried to start with the latter. But within the bourgeoisie as a whole, the decision was made to embrace the feudal structure and insist on maintaining family order. Moreover, accepting their loss of political power, culture became, for the bourgeois, a vehicle for pretending that he still had at least some power as a "private man." Politically identified with feudalism, culture became an emblem of the bourgeois' economic status.

Instead of striving for a public sphere that would not exclude women and the working class, the patriarchal order of the family, although shaken in reality, was publicly promoted as a form of culture, reconciling bourgeois self-consciousness with feudal power.[14]

The attempt to erect the family model on the foundation of a mass-cultural public sphere signifies more than the ideological affirmation of the bourgeois lifestyle. It signals the subjugation of mass culture to the dominant power relations without this power having to become visible.

However, film production and exhibition in Wilhelminian Germany evolved independently of the educated bourgeoisie. Cinema was based on those bourgeois forces that were excluded from "culture"; technology, business, artistry, spectacle, and entertainment. Also among these marginal bourgeois forces were women and the "little people," such as workers and office employees, who constituted the audience. The cinema foregrounded economy and technology as "material" forces in the cultural sphere but also fostered material interest in aesthetic pleasure. In the cinema, the "cultural asset," which had already been reduced to mass-produced commodities such as cheap romances and icons of kitsch, was not placed under supervision but placed on exhibit. And in the cinema, international modernism triumphed over the nationalism of the dominant culture, physical acting styles triumphed over interiority, and the cinema included women as social and cultural beings.

The cinema took on the characteristics of an oppositional public sphere because it had to assert itself in the face of a dominant "false" public realm represented by the reformers. This oppositional public sphere found its power not directly in another class but rather in the fact that the bourgeois forces, which had never come into their own, found for the first time an entrepreneurial basis. Theaters fought the cinema as their most powerful competitor. But it was more than just an economic rivalry. It reflected the lowered status of the bourgeois theater while it seized the unfulfilled claims of the bourgeois public sphere. Just as the theater once offered the possibility of a gradual emancipation from the feudal order, the cinema now offered similar potential for emancipating bourgeois society from the inevitable tendency to institute feudal-patriarchal structures—tendencies sustained by the Bismarck state but especially inherent in the family.

The Film Actress and the Female Audience

Looking back on the history of cinema, the appropriation of theatrical forms has been portrayed as no more than a process of conforming to bourgeois norms. If this were so, then the reformers would not have reacted so strongly to the "cine-drama." The phenomenon of "bourgeoisification" is more subtle. One way of looking at early cinema that does not see it merely as a stage in the development of the subsequently established cinema is to examine the aesthetics of the nonnarrative, nonvoyeuristic film. Another way is to direct attention to the early narrative film.

Most of the early German nondocumentary films, according to Gerhard Lamprecht's catalogue, were either short theatrical scenes (the so-called *Tonbilder*) or dramatic re-creations of "real events" out of the past or present, the "komische" *szenen* or *Kolportage*—for example, *Die Flucht und Verfolgung des Raubmörders Rudolf Henning über die Dächer von Berlin* (1905). Films of this variety that still exist include *Der Hauptmann von Köpenick* and *Wie Bauer Klaus von seiner Krankheit geheilt wurde* (both 1906). From the year 1909, there are some representative comedies, *Don Juan heiratet, Klebolon klebt alles,* and two films dealing with motherhood and sexuality, *Mutterliebe* and *Wem gehört das Kind?*. In 1910 there were two films with similar subjects, *Ich will keine Stiefmutter* and *Die Vernunft des Herzens,* a story of a married woman with a lover and her girlfriend who protects them from the husband. In 1910, both Henny Porten and Asta Nielsen started their careers as heroines of melodramas and social dramas, Porten in Messter's *Tonbilder* and Nielsen in the Danish Cinema. The appearance of such themes as marriage, motherhood, and love indicate the intrusion of women in the public sphere of cinema. Both the subjects and the way the films treat the subjects show that film production was beginning to take a female audience into consideration. The content refers to real problems of women, but the way of telling the story tends to repress forms of display that, because they appealed to scopophilia, were not suitable for women. Yet the issue was more fundamental than just a question of erotic pleasure. There is a prejudice articulated by Jean Paul, "Only the man, but not the woman, looks at himself."[15] The development that started in these short narrative films does not follow the path of continuing conformity to bourgeois norms. The introduction of stories provokes an examination of the male norm, and female reality and gender difference in the cinema asserts itself and finds expression in a separate cine-drama aesthetics. Its form, far from being an imperfect prototype of the later feature film, must be freed from preconceptions and viewed in its singularity and difference. The cine-drama did not come "from above"; it arose as an act of film production against subjugation under the established culture and in so doing forced itself on and shocked the bourgeois world.

This encroachment was not the only shocking aspect of a dramatic art based on the medium of technological reproduction and exhibition. Most important, cinema exposed the rights of a female audience. Much of the reform debate appears to be a repetition of the discussions surrounding theater in the eighteenth century. Studies by Klaus Laermann and by Ursula Geitner have discussed the contradictions of the classical bourgeois theater as manifested in the ambivalent representation of the feminine on stage and in the status of the actress.[16]

Theater, the first bourgeois public sphere, competed with the representational public sphere of the nobility.

> To begin with, the German bourgeoisie could not fight for a political public sphere in direct and open conflict with the aristocracy. Rather, it made use of a technique of indirect "self-empowerment." In a roundabout way through the media of, above all, literature and theater, it created a cultural public sphere for itself, whereby it attained a modest degree of social power.[17]

The theater, where the bourgeois was confronted with himself in the actor, played an important role in the formation of a new self-consciousness. This identification with the actor allowed the bourgeois spectator to ignore the feudal order, and he took his life into his own hands by exercising choice. The actor's changing roles introduced a panorama of possibilities that could be selected or rejected. So as the place of self-thematization, the theater sharpened the faculty of judgment.

At the same time, the theater was not held by all in high esteem. The position of actresses in bourgeois society was especially precarious. They generally were not admitted into the circles of high culture and remained identified with show business. Although the actress was something of a "public person," it was in an undesirable sense for the bourgeoisie. Eighteenth-century emancipation of the individual identified humanity as male and led to the exclusion of the other half of the middle class from the public sphere. Woman was aligned with naturalness and so was deemed incapable of self-reflection or decision making. The theater then opened up a space for female self-assertion that was too radical for the bourgeoisie to tolerate. Laermann writes:

> Since the eighteenth century it became possible in Germany to present people as men *and* women in the flesh, to show how they interact as women *and* men, moving beyond the scope of the obvious. And for precisely this

reason, it could and should help the bourgeoisie to better understand themselves as people. However, even the open depiction of gender difference as well as the possibility of bringing this to the stage seemed to be somewhat scandalous to them. The degree of open representation attained by the actors made the bourgeoisie uneasy and they were plainly unable to overcome their ambivalent opinion of them. This is above all apparent in their attitude towards actresses.[18]

Since Rousseau, the attitude toward the actress had been tied closely to the definition of woman as true nature. The actress, who practiced appearances and presented herself publicly, stood in fundamental contradiction to this domestic concept of woman. But attitudes toward actresses were also determined by the contradictions that had come to exist between bourgeois society and the theater. Both gender difference and defining one's own intimate sphere were implicated in the notion of self-thematization. However, this could not be left entirely to the cultural public sphere, particularly since women also participated there. So it was relegated to the private discourse of the scholars and scientists.[19]

In the public sphere of the theater, it was possible to question gender dominance imposed by the fissure between the public sphere and the private sphere of family and domestic intimacy. The domestication of this potential began with the actress as both a person and as a female role in the drama. As a result of economic changes toward the end of the nineteenth century, the cultural revision of this separation of public sphere and family was overdue. Film seized on this unfulfilled potential of the theater as an opportunity to build its own cultural public realm, a self-thematization that included the intimate sphere, gender difference, and the role of the woman. The cine-drama touches on the past thought to have been overcome in the "Gründerzeit" theater, often called "the bulwark against bad reality."[20]

Two early tendencies in German film production played an important role in the development of cine-drama's form: the documentation of public events, which now can be seen as male self-depiction in the medium of technical reproduction (the film as mirror), and the confrontation with female depictions that did not fit into the prevailing order of the family. Film craftsmen and exhibitors created a public sensation with these "documentary" films, but after the first decade of German film they could not claim their own cultural public sphere. The profilmic mise-en-scène, as well as film techniques such as tinting and toning, dissolves, and special effects, were in general devoted to the tradition of a cinema of attractions. Presenting such spectacles as conflagrations, the magical appearance of angels, tricks, and tableaux, as well as subjects such as exquisite objects, scenes with poetic ambiance, touching and breathtaking performances, the earliest films appealed to both the male and female desire to see. But this changed with the display of women and men as erotic objects, achieved only with the appearance of recognized actors and actresses in their films after about 1909. Although retaining ties to the exhibitors' trade, the actor brought to film a different cultural self-understanding and above all the capacity to give a voice to those technicians and exhibitors who heretofore had been excluded from culture. Film forced them to accomplish this by new means and not by traditional dramatic devices. These technical innovations opened up possibilities that the theater had never realized but possibilities that were different for actors and for actresses.

Initially the film actor found himself reduced to *Schaustellung*, exhibiting his body. But this did allow him to thematize the problems of the body and to present physical appearance itself as a role and to play out gender difference. This exhibitionist tendency on the part of actors is especially evident in early comedies, for example, Josef Giampietro in *Don Juan heiratet* or Hans Junckermann in *Wo ist Coletti?*

The film actress, though, found herself relegated to her own history, social experiences, and capabilities. Equality in front of the camera signaled emancipation for the actress who, in the theater, had to act out her social role as naturalized, that is, without artifice, because the exhibition of her body had always been the basis of her profession. At the same time her powers of imagination and dramatic interpretation were in demand to satisfy the desires of an audience that the film industry was coming to rely on: women.

The female audience became the impetus for the narration of stories in the cinema and for the introduction of stars, above all actresses. While the bourgeois theatergoer was reacting with public disapproval, his wife was already spending her free time in the cinema. Women's curiosity offered the economic basis on which the cultural representation of the hero in conflict with the interests of women could be realized in the context of the cine-drama. The cinema was often the only source of pleasure that women could enjoy outside of the home. It was more than mere entertainment; women spectators brought to cinema the right "to see themselves"—their wishes and opportunities, but also to see their everyday life and milieu— which was unrealized by theater.

The reformers addressed the "cine-drama" as soon as stage plays began entering the cinema, and they denounced the medium as nothing less than a takeover of theater's public sphere. Economic interests played a role in this takeover, but the fact that film succeeded as an oppositional cultural public sphere must be attributed to the interests of the technicians, exhibitors, actors and actresses, and decisively, the female audience. It was no accident that the appropriation of the drama form by the cinema at first resulted in the development of films that reflected the presence of women. Corresponding to the contradictory meanings inherent in the concept of a female audience, dramatic adaptations took two forms, the melodrama and the social drama.

Cine-melodrama's development respected the distinction between low and high art by falling back on a form of folk theater that succeeded by conforming to the dominant cultural order. The introduction of the melodrama into cinema only completed the tendency in theater to have the woman appear as male projection. Thus, for example, Henny Porten in *Tragödie eines Streiks* had to portray motherhood as a human principle that could only be damaged by class struggle. Instead of opening the eyes of women, the melodrama presented the perfect illusion of allowing women to see themselves on the screen. But in the second form, the social drama, the actress stands in for the gaze of a female spectator, affecting the aesthetic structure of the films by introducing an opposition to the dominant cultural public sphere. The female spectator participates in the conspiracy of female pleasure against patriarchal order, as in *Die Vernunft des Herzen*, observing the husband through the keyhole, or she might follow her curiosity and look into the world of a mistress in *Vergebens*, or she might follow the opposition of a model against male images of womanhood as in *Die Sänden der Väter* (1912) and in the end identify with the act of destroying the painter's work.

One should not confuse the social drama with the American "social problem film." The German social drama was not characterized primarily by its social content, and there were few specific references to social problems such as union organization, sexual politics, or the women's movement. It was more closely related to the Danish *Sittendrama*, the drama of morals, a mixture of optical attraction and thematization of domestic female life. It was primarily form and not content that determined the specificity of the social drama. This form, distinct from the stage-drama, accommodated women's interests in self-thematization and in the thematization of the private and the intimate. In this capacity, film superseded the stage drama as the better form for constituting the happenings of everyday life and establishing a sense of the present. Only by being stripped of its power and having its semantic content laid bare could the drama become effective in the film's "social drama."

Exhibition practice and the technology of mechanical reproduction, and not dramatic adaptation, were the constitutive moments for the appearance of feminine and intimate life in the cinema. The camera mediated woman's look into "her worlds," both the traditional domestic world and the modern public world into which she was preparing to enter. And the hidden world of love affairs and prostitution was also included.

Gender difference in the audience was reflected in the performance of the actress. She cultivated erotic attraction for the male gaze; for the female audience, however, she placed herself on show in her social role. The dual self-depiction of the actress is the decisive moment in the social drama.

As Ursula Geitner points out, the actress has always been the "modern" woman, laying claim to a public, self-determined existence and adopting an experimental relationship to the world:

The actresses distance themselves from their natural, caste-like status assigned them at birth conquering other terrain and combining experiences, knowledge and expectations into new roles. They are then comparable to those male individuals who have learned to matter-of-factly make use of the advantages of a modern society no longer organized by class.[21]

While they were on stage, actresses had to hide their own specific modernity behind images of women that were created by men. Film, on the other hand, gave actresses the chance to emancipate themselves from these images through self-portrayal. Neither a dramatist nor a director determined their performance in front of the camera. In her memoirs, Asta Nielsen related the custom of the director to pass around only a rough outline of the story with notations such as "Asta's big scene." It was left to the actress to improvise the performance.[22] She had no other obligation beyond being aware of the new needs of her female audience. The film actresses celebrated their self-depiction at the moment of the "entrance of woman into the modern." However, this exemplary performance, dependent on the reflexivity inherent in acting, was just one component. The other was the continuing representation of an existence that had been forced on the actress, which was not at all modern and autonomous but archaic and dependent.

The social position of the majority of actresses in Wilhelminian Germany was desolate.[23] Despotic contracts, low fees, and the obligation to provide their own costumes—unlike their male colleagues—kept them as a group on the brink of prostitution. Finding a lover belonged to the image of an independent life which had always drawn women to the theater, but more often than not, it was material need and not choice that made becoming a mistress or a courtesan the more likely prospect. And, after all, it pleased the male theatergoers as well as the critics to regard the actress as being sexually available. In the cinema, by bringing her social situation to light at the same time that she was exhibiting her body, the actress obstructed the spectator's one-sided mental image of erotic availability without giving up the right to sexuality.

Displaying herself in her modernity was not yet synonymous with the embodiment of modern women figures. But instead of being fixed in the beautiful appearances of expressive nature, the actress could finally transform herself and work against the prejudice that, as a woman, only feelings and not action were proper to her and that she must not act out those feelings but rather embody them. Moreover, she could battle the prejudice that showing herself in public was equivalent to prostituting herself.[24] Apart from the audience's "mandate" for a new characterization, the technical properties of the new medium also made possible innovations in the film actress's performance. The camera's mobility acted in concert with her art of dramatic transformation; the separation of the image from the body emphasized that passionate acting in front of the spectator is not truth but merely appearance. Despite objections that film increases the illusion of witnessing reality, the recording properties of the camera actually document precisely the difference between performance and reality in the social dramas. By capturing both equally, it distinguishes performance theatricality from reality.

Presenting erotic stimuli in the social drama was not hindered by an internal censorship, moral cloak, or pedagogical intention, as was the case in the melodrama. But no doubt it was tied to the display of the archaic, asocial—certainly not modern—position of woman in society. This depiction affronted the spectator's mental image at the same time that it afforded female spectators a kind of mirror in which they could see their imprisonment within patriarchal structures.

Aspects of modernity and eroticism in the actress's self-depiction in front of the camera can also be found in other cine-dramas such as the crime film and the *Sensationsfilm*. But the dissection of social reality is a defining feature of the social drama. To demonstrate the actress as a modern woman imprisoned within patriarchal structures necessitated a visualization of a reality that was beyond the reality conveyed by her physical presence in front of the camera. This recorded documentation is not sufficient to depict the reality of the power structure. On stage, the actress always appeared in a framework that obscured the underlying social structure. While the social drama in film incorporates elements of the theater drama, by shifting the view from that of the male audience to that of the actress, the film audience could visualize in her representation the oppression of the female sex. These elements of theater drama become recorded signs of patriarchal power within the documented reality—that is, the performance between actor and actress—but also in the recording of the display of erotic attraction.

Asta Nielsen is probably the exemplary actress of early cinema who is generally known to have determined the course of her films. Her autonomy, even sovereignty, and the explorative unfolding of the acting possibilities of film, was only possible because of the structure of the cine-drama and the social drama, which actresses in general helped define. Although Nielsen was praised for the development of a unique filmic language, many other actresses of the period also contributed. Some of them we do not know by name, and even those we know—Lissi Nebuschka, Wanda Treumann, and Fern Andra, for example—are more familiar than their films. For others we are fortunate in having surviving visual proof of virtuosity: Hanni Weisse, Manny Ziener, Käte Wittenberg, Dorrit Wiexler, Senta Eichstaedt, Ilse Bois, and Margarete Hübler. Their performances involved an imparting of the self, giving a voice to a female presence in early cinema narratives, a voice notably absent in those adaptations of melodramas that perpetuated the stage image of woman as prescribed by the dramatic sources. Henny

Porten was a star who fit in well with the conventions of the melodramatic scene. In her almost static appearance, which hid her corporeality under a corset and matronly clothes, and in her theatrical gestures, the specific dynamic of female performance was virtually suffocated.

The limits of the social drama are encountered in the taboo surrounding the male body. If the actor were to display his body for the interested gaze of the other sex as the actress does, female subjectivity would not only compete with the man's, but patriarchal power within the "dramatic" performance would be abolished, bringing the social drama to an end.

Early cinema did not transcend social drama in its emancipatory drive. But it focused as much as possible on woman's subjectivity and on modernity as potentials for role play and exploration of the gaze. The cinema of 1912–1913 did, however, initiate a redistribution of the power of authorship in cinema, thus reinforcing the subject position of the male actor. But it was not until the consolidation of the German film industry during World War I and the awareness of the military and the government of cinema's importance as a bourgeois counter-public sphere, with its discussion of sexual difference and the position of women, that this development almost came to an end.

NOTES

1. These included the British-owned Deutsche Bioskop (1897), Deutsche Mutoskop und Biograph-Gesellschaft (1899, the American Mutoscope and Biograph subsidiary), as well as newly founded companies such as Duskes (around 1906).

2. According to Heinrich Fraenkel, the number of firms quadrupled in the years 1910–1914 from 24 to 104. H. Fraenkel, *Unsterblicher Film. Die große Chronik von der Laterna Magica bis zum Tonfilm* (Munich: Kindler Verlag, 1956), p. 183.

3. All dates from F. von Zglinicki, *Der Weg des Films—Die Geschichte der Kinematographie und ihrer Vorläufer*, 2nd ed. (Hildesheim: Olms Presse, 1979).

4. K. Sloan, *The Loud Silents: Origins of the Social Problem Film* Urbana: University of Illinois Press, p. 11.

5. The term *Autorenfilme*, "author's films," refers to films adapted from theatrical works by established authors, somewhat analogous to the French Film d'Art genre.

6. *Sensationsfilme* was a term often used by the producers, promising a movie with plenty of sensations, especially circus attractions, but also horror effects, danger, and life-and-death thrills.

7. The founding of Universum Film A. G. under Ludendorff during World War I set up the basic parameters for the realization of this project, which fully manifested itself only at the end of the Weimar Republic and the beginning of fascism. Goebbels carried out the institutional as well as aesthetic reorganization of cinema, completely fulfilling the demands of the reformers and placing cinema under state supervision.

8. L. May, *Screening Out the Past: The Birth of Mass Culture and the Motion Picture Industry* (Chicago: University of Chicago Press, 1983), p. 46.

9. "Around 1880," Arthur Rosenberg writes, "the political backbone of the German bourgeoisie was broken." About the unsuccessful democratization before the World War I, he says: "The political advocacy for the parliamentarization of Germany did not so much

mean the transfer of power from the Kaiser to the Reichstag, but rather from the aristocracy to the bourgeoisie." A. Rosenberg, *Die Enstehung und Geschichte der Weimarer Republik* (Frankfurt a. M.: Athenäum, 1928/1988), p. 45.

10. F. K. Ringer, *The Decline of the German Mandarins* (Cambridge: Harvard University Press, 1989), p. 7.

11. "It argues that the state derives its legitimacy not from divine right, for that would stress the prince's whim, nor from the interests of the subjects, for that would suggest a voting procedure, but exclusively from its services to the intellectual and spiritual life of the nation. It clearly follows that government must give material aid to the cultural and educational program of the elite and that it must do so without demanding an immediate practical return." Ringer, *The German Mandarins*, p. 11.

12. Ringer, *The German Mandarins*, pp. 123–4.

13. Arthur Rosenberg establishes a direct connection between the inadequate political will of the work force and the deficits of a political education that the work force directly or indirectly could only receive from the bourgeoisie. This is evident in the example of England: "A similar tradition of the German bourgeoisie was missing . . . In the German Kaiserreich the worker certainly learned writing and reading, technical skills, discipline and organization—in grade school, in the army, and in the factory. But he never acquired a political conception of the world. He had no idea how the political, economic and social revolution which he longed for would come about. Nor did he know which path would lead out of the sad present into a better future. The educational endeavors of the social democratic party, as successful as they might have been for the individual, could not fill this gap." Rosenberg, *Die Entstehung und Geschichte der Weimarer Republik*, p. 48.

14. This is also partially represented in the woman's newly assigned role of personal hygiene. Karin Hausen points out that this not only deals with the production of ideology but also with the changes in the everyday life of women. "Up to the beginning of the 20th century, the high esteem of education, which made one capable of more than superficial conversation, and the high esteem of readiness to give attention to the husband's and children's needs moves more and more into the foreground." K. Hausen, "Eine Ulme für den schwankenden Efeu," in U. Frevert, ed., *Bürgerinnen und Bürger, Geschlechterverhältnisse im 19. Jahrhundert* (Göttingen: Vandenhseck & Ruprecht, 1988), p. 94. She also pulls together the rising age of marriage with women's increasing educational efforts.

15. Jean Paul [Johann Paul Friedrich Richter], in E. Berend, ed., *Levana oder Erziehlehre (Sämtliche Werke, Historisch-Kritische Ausgabe)*, 1st ed., vol. 12 (Weimar, 1937), quoted in U. Geitner, *Schauspielerinnen: Der theatralische Eintritt der Frau in die Moderne* (Bielefeld: Haux, 1988), p. 274.

16. K. Laermann, "Die riskante Person in der moralischen Anstalt. Zur Darstellung der Schauspielerin in deutschen Theaterzeitschriften des späten 18. Jahrhunderts," in R. Möhrmann, ed., *Die Schauspielerin, Zur Kulturgeschichte der weiblichen Bühnenkunst* (Frankfurt a. M.: Insel Verlag, 1989), pp. 127–53.

17. Ibid., p. 131.

18. Ibid., p. 133.

19. C. Honegger, *Die Codierung der Geschlechter in der Moderne, Kulturelle Umbrüche und die Wissenschaft vom Menschen 1750–1850* (unpublished manuscript), Frankfurt a. M. She shows how the definition of femininity was scientificized and removed from public thematization and self-thematization by women writers. The "science of woman" was carried out in the framework of an anthropology that aspired to universal science before it turned into gynecology in the nineteenth century.

20. A. Meyhöfer, *Das Motiv des Schauspielers in der Literatur der Jahrhundertwende* (Köln and Wien: Bohlau, 1989), p. 277. She pursues the tremendous importance of theater in the *Gründerzeit*, which she sees in connection with the political-social developments: "Towards the end of the 19th century, the liberal bourgeoisie had to make the best of being driven out of the parliaments and the fading of its enlightened ideals of freedom and

individuality. The theater became a bulwark against an untenable reality, and the feeling of no future."

21. Geitner, *Schauspielerinnen*, p. 272.

22. A. Nielsen, *Den tiende Muse* (Copenhagen: Guldendal, 1946).

23. Cf. T. Kellen, *Die Not der Schauspielerinnen. Studie über die wirtschaftliche Lage und die moralische Stellung der Bühnenkünstlerinnen* (Leipzig, 1902); M. Giesing, *Ibsens Nora und die wahre Emanzipation der Frau, Zum Frauenbild im wilhelminischen Theater* (Frankfurt a. M., Bern, N.Y., 1984); M. Möhrmann, "Die Herren zahlen die Kostüme. Mädchen vom Theater am Rande der Prostitution," in Möhrmann, ed., *Die Schauspielerin*, pp. 261–80.

24. Klaus Laermann points out the contradictions that accompanied the appearance of the actress. Ursula Geitner stresses how an actor-oriented theory of sentimentality developed as a solution to these contradictions: "The conception of sentimental-natural expression tries to master the problem of dramatic art in its own way: the actress becomes the sentimentalist, the portrayer of her nature. When Friedrich Theophilus Thilo introduced his title-heroine 'Emilie Sommer' as actress in his trivial letter novel that appeared in 1780–82, neither its publication nor the dramatic art required of the actress on the stage allowed Emilie's *nature* to be faulted. With Emilie, Thilo's novel staged, in complete opposition to Diderot's 'paradox of the actor,' the paradoxical play about an actress who does not act" ("Die riskante Person," p. 270).

Theorizing a Cultural
History of Silent Cinema

Rick Altman

Dickens, Griffith, and
Film Theory Today

Thus Sergei Eisenstein opens his classic essay on "Dickens, Griffith, and the Film Today":

> The kettle began it . . .

> Thus Dickens opens his *Cricket on the Hearth:*

> The kettle began it . . .

> What could be further from films! Trains, cowboys, chases. . . . And *The Cricket on the Hearth?* "The kettle began it!" But, strange as it may seem, movies also were boiling in that kettle. From here, from Dickens, from the Victorian novel, stem the first shoots of American film esthetic, forever linked with the name of David Wark Griffith.[1]

Item: *The Cricket on the Hearth,* Charles Dickens, 1845. Theatrical adaptations: Albert Smith, 1845, in three parts; Edward Stirling, 1845, in two acts; W. T. Townsend, early 1846, in three chirps (!); Ben Webster, early 1846, four versions (straight play, pantomime, burlesque, and extravaganza); Dion Boucicault, 1862, three acts entitled *Dot, A Fairy Tale of Home;* the Pinkerton translation, in 1900, of Goldmark's German three-act opera; H. Jackson, 1906, a burlesque called *What Women Will Do;* N. Lambelet, 1906, a drama; W. T. Shore, 1908, an adaptation simply named *Dot.* Griffith is known to have based his version on the Albert Smith adaptation.[2]

Eisenstein again, later in the same essay:

> When Griffith proposed to his employers the novelty of a parallel "cut-back" for his first version of *Enoch Arden (After Many Years,* 1908), this is the discussion that took place, as recorded by Linda Arvidson Griffith in her reminiscences of Biograph days:

> When Mr. Griffith suggested a scene showing Annie Lee waiting for her husband's return to be followed by a scene of Enoch cast away on a

desert island, it was altogether too distracting. "How can you tell a story jumping about like that? The people won't know what it's about."

"Well," said Mr. Griffith, "doesn't Dickens write that way?

"Yes, but that's Dickens; that's novel writing; that's different."

"Oh, not so much, these are picture stories; not so different."

But, to speak quite frankly, all astonishment on this subject and the apparent unexpectedness of such statements can be ascribed only to our— ignorance of Dickens.[3]

Item: *Enoch Arden.* Alfred Lord Tennyson, 1864. First theatrical adaptation: Arthur Mathison, 1869, Booth's Theatre, New York. Felix A. Vincent's manuscript promptbook indicates a pictorial, episodic construction with crosscutting between simultaneous lines of action. In the third act, as Annie Lee waits for Enoch to return, she opens the Bible, asking, "Enoch, where art thou?" Choosing a random passage to guide her, she reads, "Under a palm tree." Suddenly the flats are drawn and Annie disappears, revealing a firelit tropical vision scene, with Enoch sitting under a palm tree. The fourth act then follows Enoch, while the fifth cuts back to Annie. Subsequent stage adaptation: Newton Beers, 1889, expanded to seven acts and thirty episodes. "A complete denial," according to A. Nicholas Vardac, "of the manner of the well-made play." Act 5: "The ghostly walls of England, a line of gruesome, shadowy cliffs, rising abruptly from the sea. . . . Afterward comes the return of Annie to her cottage, where she invokes heaven to give her some token of Enoch's fate. . . . [T]he wondrous vision of the Isle of Palms is disclosed; the humble cottage disappears, and a transformation unfolds itself to the audience. Opening with the tropical night, scene follows scene, light gradually growing, until a glorious burst of sunlight reveals Enoch under a palm tree, upon which beams the blazing light of day."[4]

Few articles in the history of cinema theory have had the lasting impact of Eisenstein's treatise on "Dickens, Griffith, and the Film Today." Although the Soviet filmmaker and theoretician was hardly the first to connect American cinema to the nineteenth-century novel, his essay now serves as the locus classicus of an important strain of criticism stressing direct ties between film and the novel.[5] Eisenstein clearly knew that the ties were not as direct as he made them seem. Indeed, there are passages later in the essay that fully recognize the importance of theatrical texts in setting the pattern for cinema. Still, what is consistently remembered from Eisenstein's juxtaposition of the British novelist and the American film-maker is a clear statement of influence: Griffith learned important aspects of his craft by paying close attention to the technique of Dickens. What Eisenstein claimed in a limited context, others have raised to the level of general pronouncement: a fundamental continuity connects the narrative technique of the nineteenth-century realist novel and the dominant style of Hollywood cinema.

By and large, critics have ignored the influence of theatrical adaptations. Eisenstein provides information on the stage source of Griffith's *Cricket on the Hearth*, yet he never attributes any importance to the existence of a theatrical intermediary. Many other critics follow precisely the same logic; they identify the dramatic version from which the film author directly borrowed but assume that little is to be gained by comparing the film to an ephemeral and undistinguished stage adaptation.[6] More often, critics blithely postulate a direct connection between a film and the novel from which it is ostensibly drawn, when even minimal research clearly identifies a dramatic adaptation as an important direct source for the film. This approach is especially visible in the numerous checklists that cite well-known novels and the films apparently made from them, or well-known films and the novels that seemingly serve as their models.[7]

It is easy enough to demonstrate the debt that early cinema owes to theatrical adaptations. Robert M. Henderson identifies many of Griffith's Biograph films as coming from novelistic originals, as do Richard Schickel, Elaine Mancini, and most other critics.[8] *Ramona* (1910), for example, is said to derive from Helen Hunt Jackson's celebrated novel of the same name, but what of Virginia Calhoun's successful 1905 stage adaptation, in which Griffith himself had played the part of Alessandro?[9] Two of Griffith's Biograph films, *Pippa Passes* (1909) and *The Wanderer* (1913), are regularly traced to Browning's narrative poem, "Pippa Passes, yet this poem was regularly produced in a stage version. On 13 November 1906, for example, the *New York Times* singled out Henry B. Walthall for "a word of mention for intelligent acting" in an otherwise long and gloomy production of "Pippa Passes" at the Majestic. This is the same Henry B. Walthall who came to Biograph just two months before Griffith's version of *Pippa Passes* and who starred in *The Wanderer*. Cinema histories generally identify the Apocrypha as the source for Griffith's *Judith of Bethulia*.[10] Yet Blanche Sweet notes that a copy of Thomas Bailey Aldrich's 1904 theatrical adaptation (a play well known to Griffith through Nance O'Neil's production) was present on the set during filming.[11]

Griffith is not alone in his dependence on stage versions of well-known novels. In 1917, a "tie-in" edition of Frank Norris's novel *The Pit* reinforced spectators' impressions that the film was directly adapted from the novel. Yet the film's director, William A. Brady, had produced Channing Pollock's 1904 dramatic adaptation of Norris's novel, while the star of the film, Wilton Lackaye, played the role of Jadwin, as he had done on stage in 1904.[12] Newspaper advertisements in 1932 proudly announced "Ernest Hemingway's A FAREWELL TO ARMS, a Paramount Picture adapted from the novel of the same name," yet Paramount hired Lawrence Stallings to write the script, based on his 1930 stage production. Stallings may have been paid just as much as Hemingway for the rights to his adaptation, but the resulting film has nonetheless always been presented as a direct adaptation of the Hemingway novel.[13]

The last half of the nineteenth century and the first quarter of the twentieth were so fertile in theatrical adaptations that it is not safe to bet against the existence of an adaptation of any novel, however unlikely. In fact, at one point in his famous essay on "Theater and Cinema" André Bazin assumes with a great deal of assurance that no theatrical adaptation has ever been made out of *Madame Bovary* or *The Brothers Karamazov*.[14] Bazin's assurance piqued my curiosity.

Item: *Madame Bovary*. Gustave Flaubert, 1857. Theatrical adaptation: William Busnach, 1906. *The Brothers Karamazov*. Fyodor Dostoyevski, 1879–1880. Theatrical adaptation: anonymously published in volume 2 of the *Moscow Art Theatre Series of Russian Plays* (1923).[15]

Take any list of silent films apparently derived from novels, submit it to a few hours of research in a serious library, and you will have little trouble discovering that a very high proportion of the novels were turned into extremely popular stage shows in the years preceding the film. Yet, systematically, it is the novel that gets the attention, the novel that is mentioned in the ad, the novel that draws the screen credit. For by the turn of the century, novels were clearly a drawing card, cinema's tenuous connection to culture.[16] There is, then, a community of interest between early filmmakers and today's critics: both prefer to stress the printed word and its cultural status rather than the ephemeral popular spectacle. To critique the ideological investment apparent in preference for the novel is not, however, my purpose here.

Frankly, what difference does it make whether Vitagraph's 1911 version of *The Tale of Two Cities* derives directly from Dickens's novel or from one of the dozen or so dramatic adaptations that had held the stage continually for the half-century since the novel's publication? Not simply to contribute yet another footnote to film history but to question a certain tendency of today's cinema theory—that is what interests me. To put it bluntly, just what has Eisenstein's insistence on connecting Griffith to Dickens rather than to theatrical adaptations cost today's film theory?[17] What difference does it make to our theoretical practice that generations of film producers and scholars have repressed film's debt to popular melodrama in favor of the more durable, more culturally acceptable novel or well-made play? Or, to formulate the question in a more provocative and productive way, of what current tendencies and stresses within film theory is the neglect of cinema's debt to melodramatic stage adaptations symptomatic?

———

How classical was classical narrative? Eisenstein's essay on "Dickens, Griffith, and the Film Today," written during the war and published in English in 1949, inaugurated a long period of careful attention to filmic adaptations of well-known novels. Under the structuralist influence of the late 1960s, however, and especially after the publication of Roland Barthes's *S/Z* in 1970, a new approach to novel/film relationships prevailed. Abandoning the specific analyses by which earlier critics had attempted to establish localized novelistic contributions to the cinema, the new theorists sought instead to discover a broad set of traits shared by the realist novel and the dominant mode of commercial cinema. Already in 1953, Barthes's *Le degré zéro de l'écriture* had set up Balzac as the official representative of a mythically pure "straight" narration.[18] In the same period, André Bazin publicly recognized in Hollywood cinema all the maturity of a classical art.[19] With *S/Z* the term *classical* was finally fully stripped of its traditional historical reference to seventeenth-century French literature and associated with a specific type of narration exemplified by Balzac. "Classical," says Barthes at the outset of *S/Z*, "is the term we use to designate the readerly text." Throughout the early 1970s the importance of Barthes's terminology was reinforced by a series of paired terms that appeared to parallel his classical/modernist opposition. Barthes himself contributed the readerly/writerly (*lisible/scriptible*) distinction, as well as the related opposition between pleasure and bliss (*plaisir/jouissance*). Structuralist critics of film and literature alike repeatedly referred to Benveniste's distinction between story and discourse (*histoire/discours*).[20] Film theorists often opposed Hollywood cinema to alternative cinema or countercinema.[21]

Conceived from the start as part of a binary opposition, the notion of classical narrative necessarily involved concentration on a narrow range of targeted features, with a consequent leveling of all but certain key differences among texts. With the Balzacian model as a guide, theorists of the past two decades have built a coherent but limited model of classical narrative. With few exceptions they have stressed omniscient narration, linear presentation, character-centered causality, and psychological motivation. In addition, film theorists have pointed out the importance of invisible editing, verisimilitude of space, and various devices designed to assure continuity.

At the heart of every evocation of classical narrative lies a textbook assumption about the meaning of the term *classical*. For Bazin the term implies maturity, ripeness, harmony, perfect balance, and ideal form. For Barthes it refers to a text whose integrity and order provide assurance and comfort for the reader.[22] In David Bordwell's use, *classical* means harmony, unity, tradition, rule-governed craftsmanship, standardization, and control.[23] All three critics, it seems quite clear, ultimately owe their definition of the classical in large part to the neoclassical French literary theorists of the seventeenth century. Borrowing from Boileau and his contemporaries not only a general sense of harmony and order but also numerous specific tenets (the central importance of the unity of action, concentration on human psychology, preference for mimetic forms), critics have found in a broadly shared notion of classicism a ready-made theory. But is that theory built strongly enough to carry the weight of the novel and cinema as well?

Was classicism classical? The century of Corneille and Racine apparently provides an important model for the concept of classical narrative. According to the familiar account, French writers of the second quarter of the seventeenth century, under the tutelage of Malherbe and the Académie Française, and with the guidance of Aristotelian principles, subordinated their creative genius to a series of rules for proper literary production, resulting in works of a more ordered and pleasurable nature. During the latter half of the century, these rational rules came to be second nature to a growing group of writers, including Molière, Racine, Boileau, La Fontaine, La Rochefoucauld, La Fayette, and La Bruyère, all gathered around the Sun King, Louis XIV.[24] The good taste of these writers permitted them to reflect through the harmony of their writings the social stability of the era as well as the overall unity of the court and its regal master.

Today this traditional view of French classicism no longer counts many supporters. Inspired by the methods of the Annales School, historians have increasingly challenged the assumptions of social unity that once appeared to undergird classical doctrine. Little by little, literary scholars have revised their model of classical unity. Before World War II, Thierry Maulnier provided perhaps the strongest challenge to the traditional static conception of classicism. Where other critics stress the delicacy and order of Racine's language, Maulnier points instead to the strong opposition between the refined dignity of Racine's language and the savage emotions that it often expresses. Maulnier reveals Racine's tendency to stretch a civilized, finely crafted surface over the chaotic energy of a smoldering volcano.[25]

Maulnier's reading echoes the intriguing formula of French novelist André Gide: "A classical work is strong and beautiful only through its ability to tame its own romanticism."[26] Whereas dictionary definitions always define classicism as opposed to romanticism, Gide recognizes that the classic always *includes* the romantic. Classicism for Gide is thus not a stable style but a constant effort to corral, tame, and harness the chaotic forces that give classicism its particular power. "The more rebellious the thing mastered," says Gide, "the more beautiful the work."[27] Gide invites us to read the order of classicism as the result of tension. For him, the renowned balance characteristic of classical works is not the permanently secure balance of a symmetrical drawing, but the unstable equilibrium of a ballet dancer on point, straining her muscles to the utmost in order to appear motionless and calm.

Following the tension-based model proposed by Gide, postwar criticism has systematically reconsidered French classical authors and the classicism that they constitute. The first to undergo massive reevaluation was Racine. During the years when an apparently unproblematic notion of "classical" narrative was being elaborated, the very foundations of the term were being undermined from multiple directions. Lucien Goldmann's Marxist reading of Racine dwells on the turmoil and impossible quandaries built into the tragic genre. Charles Mauron's psychoanalytic approach reveals Racine's personal obsessions operating beneath and through the surface activities of his characters. Philip Butler was the first of many to discover Racine's predilection for baroque traits, however well he might control them in his writing. Roland Barthes gave a strong impetus to this new reading of classical texts by applying the insights of Freud's late works to Racine.[28] Over the last quarter century, this reevaluation of the orderliness and harmony of classicism has continued without abatement.

For our purposes, a simple lesson is to be learned here. The understanding of literary structure that grounds familiar notions of classicism is by no means a current one. Recent critics have not claimed that earlier researchers were wrong to stress the rule-governed craftsmanship, the standardization, the control, or the harmony of those texts thought of as classical. They have instead insisted on a more complex, more dynamic, multilevel understanding of the style and texts in question.

How classical is the classical novel? Discussions of narrative continuity from novel to film commonly privilege two novelists, Charles Dickens and Honoré de Balzac: Dickens because his are the novels that have most often been adapted into film (with or without theatrical intermediaries), and Balzac because he is regularly taken as the locus classicus of the type of omniscient narration adopted by Hollywood. Apparently representing the source—or at least a historically important example—of Hollywood's approach to narrative, Dickens and Balzac need to be carefully analyzed if we are to understand the role they play in our understanding of classical narrative. This is, of course, not the place for full-scale analysis of two such prolific authors. A rapid survey of some basic concerns may nevertheless be helpful.

The works of Charles Dickens play an intriguing role in arguments about the relationship between the novel and cinema. Of all highly respected nineteenth-century novelists, the most closely allied to popular sensibility and the melodrama is surely Charles Dickens. Among novelists his is an ambiguous name, for it invokes not only the respect for realism due a Stendhal, an Eliot, or a Hardy, but also the more popular infatuation with less respected and apparently more ephemeral writers of episodic fiction like Eugène Sue and Alexandre Dumas. In short, Dickens sits astride two opposed nineteenth-century conceptions of novel writing: one has become, through the influence of such figures as Flaubert and James, a central tradition of our high culture; the other has had difficulty surviving. Much popular fiction of the last century is as hard to locate today as the popular melodramas of the same period. Dickens retains his importance because he is a pivotal figure—accepted by scholars of the novel, yet shot through with the themes and structures of the popular serial.

Because of Dickens's connection of these two apparently separate traditions, attempts to base a model of narrative development on Dickens must be taken as fundamentally suspect. Typically, Dickens is invoked by film theorists because of his use of episodic structures, his tendency toward overstated, oversimplified emotions, and his contributions to the technique of crosscutting. In other words, he is mentioned because of his connections with popular melodrama. Yet the conclusions drawn from his presence in an argument are rapidly applied to the classical novel, to that aspect of Dickens least associated with the examples actually adduced. Because of this ambiguity, Dickens has served a spuriously pivotal function in discussions about the relationship between the cinema and the novel.

The similar position held by Balzac in French literature and narrative theory reveals more clearly the stakes of the argument. Typed by Barthes in the 1950s as the perfect "classic" in opposition to which the "modern" might be better defined, Balzac continued to serve this rhetorical function for French structuralist critics and their American followers. It was during this period that the notion of "Hollywood classical narrative" took on the status of received idea. Not just "Hollywood narrative" but "classical narrative," for the whole point was to establish important continuities between cinematic practice and the traditions of the nineteenth-century novel.

During the 1970s, however, Balzac scholarship underwent a minor revolution. While popularizing the notion of classical narrative, Barthes's *S/Z* provided a reading of *Sarrasine* that revealed the potential modernity of the Balzacian text. Many other critics, in reaction to the typing of Balzac as a "straight" or "transparent" narrator, went out of their way to demonstrate the eminently discursive nature of Balzac's narration. Within the classic novelist, the seeds of modernity could be seen sprouting.

At the same time, Balzac's debt to the Gothic novel, the serial romance, and popular melodrama was being recalled by Peter Brooks in his influential treatise, *The Melodramatic Imagination*. "Melodrama," affirms Brooks, "is hence part of the semiotic precondition of the novel for Balzac— part of what allows the 'Balzacian novel' to come into being. We can best understand this novel when we perceive that its fictional representations repose on a necessary theatrical substratum—necessary, because a certain type of meaning could not be generated without it."[29] Until recently, only the popular serial novelists of the nineteenth century seemed directly indebted to the melodramatic stage. We now more easily see that not only Sue and Dumas depend on melodrama for their inspiration and style but Balzac, Hugo, Dostoyevski, Zola, and James as well.

The role of melodrama in an apparently classical narrative will be clarified by the example of one of Balzac's most durably popular novels, *Le père Goriot.* According to the now familiar definition, classical narrative induces the reader to follow a linear chain of psychologically based causes leading from an initial question or problem to a final solution. From this standpoint, *Le père Goriot* is the most classic of novels, for it assures continuity, linearity, and psychological causality by focusing the narrative on the social and moral growth of young Eugène de Rastignac. Following the protagonist almost exclusively from beginning to end, the narrator invites us to pay primary attention to Rastignac and to his twin roles of detective and student of life. With Rastignac we discover the activities, nefarious and charitable, of his fellow boarders at the Pension Vauquer; with Rastignac we also learn about the social mores and moral dilemmas that attend life in the modern world.

Viewed in this manner, *Le père Goriot* stands as the very model of the classical novel. From the picaresque episodes of a *Lazarillo de Tormes* to the historical novels of Mérimée or Scott, from the Bildungsroman of a Marivaux or a Goethe to the nascent modernism of Flaubert, from the *roman d'analyse* of a Madame de La Fayette to the point-of-view experiments of a Henry James, the pattern remains the same. Continuity is assured by consistent following of a single character along with whom we discover the surrounding world. In contrast to the melodrama's characteristic dual-focus concentration on two separate centers of interest, I have called this type of narration "single-focus."[30] While the protagonist's body continues to serve the familiar adventure functions assigned to it by romance, the protagonist's mind here takes on a newly expanded role. Opinions and attitudes usurp the position once reserved for decisions and actions. Sleuthing replaces dueling as the key to success.

Note that this pattern systematically requires a dual vision of the world. Watching the protagonist watch the world, we simultaneously view the protagonist and the world. The protagonist of the single-focus novel provides only one possible interpretation of the world. Although it is commonly called into being by the protagonist's vision of ratiocination, the world retains its independent existence and thus its mystery and fascination. In *Le père Goriot*, the independence of the world around Rastignac is demonstrated by the rhetorical effect of his two neighbors: Vautrin, the Mephistophelean ex-convict whose get-rich-quick schemes simultaneously horrify and intrigue his young charge Eugène, and Goriot, the realist Lear, the spaghetti-making saint who would pair Rastignac with one of his money-hungry daughters.

Although Balzac carefully assured the continuity and rationality of his novel by sticking to Rastignac and his vision, his readers were not fooled. They immediately recognized that Rastignac is not alone at the center of the novel. In fact, the stage play made from the novel returns Vautrin and Goriot to the directly and melodramatically opposed positions that they have retained in the popular memory of the novel.[31]

It is important to note just how differently Rastignac is treated as a character from Goriot and Vautrin. While Rastignac is the consummate classical novel character, tying scene to scene through his well-developed psychology, ever-changing throughout the course of the novel, Goriot and Vautrin seem drawn from another world, held in ritual bondage to their roles like the blocking characters in New Comedy or, more to the point, like the antagonists of melodrama. Although Balzac psychologizes them schematically, they appear to be beyond psychology; they call instead for a mythic definition. They represent two static models of paternity, as Balzac termed them, one for Good and the other for Evil.

Balzac's novels stage a "double-tiered drama," according to Peter Brooks, "where what is represented on the public social stage is only a figuration of what lies behind, in the domain of true power and significance."[32] The domain of true power and significance in *Le père Goriot* is clearly that occupied by the timeless divinities of charity and theft, of senseless Good and intriguing Evil. In order to understand what is going on in *Goriot* we cannot remain at the levels of the character and plot that assure the novel's classical nature. We must instead view the novel as the chance passing of a historical, time-bound, psychologized character through the latest incarnation of the eternal realm of stereotypes and changeless values. Balzac's novel is not a melodrama, it is a classical novel, yet embedded melodrama is essential to its meaning, as generations of readers attest by all but forgetting Rastignac while vividly recalling Goriot and Vautrin. In order to make sense of *Le père Goriot*, we need to pay close attention to the unpsychologized stable monuments constituted by Goriot and Vautrin as well as to the young man whose itinerary is responsible for the text's unfolding.

The classical novel, I would suggest, works this way as a matter of course. Although the protagonist's trajectory may be what holds the novel together, assuring its "classical" nature, the novel's internal dialectic is completed by the presence of an unpsychologized, dual-focus tradition that the protagonist continually confronts. Quixote wants to be Amadís, the Consalve of Madame de La Fayette's *Zaïde* is living in a world of Alexandrian romances, Robinson Crusoe sets out in search of an adventure romance life, Emma Bovary would recreate the world according to the version promulgated by the popular press, while Hollywood's psychologized characters live with a supporting cast drawn from Griffith. I do not mean here simply to repeat the claims of René Girard, who taught us about the role of literary and historical figures in the triangular mediation of desire.[33] The point is not simply that the conduct of novelistic protagonists is mediated by previous literary or mythic figures but that the novel as an overtly single-focus form has a strong capacity for absorbing and displaying—in the background, as it were—the stable values and unpsychologized characters of previous dual-focus traditions.

We have learned from Bakhtin the importance of considering the novel not as a fixed form but as a process. In developing his notions of "novelization," "heteroglossia," and "hybridization," however, Bakhtin would appear to have given too little attention to the relationship among the various strains together present in a single work.[34] While this is hardly the place to expound at length on possible modifications of Bakhtin's intriguing theories, it seems clear that an understanding of the novel requires not only a model that makes room for the presence of multiple genres and modes, but also a theory of the relationship among those diverse components: we must understand the "classical" version of the novel, from *Quixote* to Proust, in terms of the relationship between the classical single-focus surface, where values are degraded and decisions are partial, and the embedded dual-focus realm of permanence and power.

In short, the classical novel is classical *and more*. Without understanding the "more" we have little chance of avoiding systematic impoverishment of the classical novel. As the example of *Le père Goriot* suggests, it is possible for a novel to display all the characteristics of classical narrative and yet not to operate through them alone. If we are to develop a model of classical narrative that is not only descriptive but also systematic, we must look past current accounts.

Was the nineteenth-century theater well made? The split between "classical novels" and "popular serials" in nineteenth-century fiction is mirrored and heightened by an even more evident split in nineteenth-century theater. On the one side stands the so-called well-made play, championed by Sarcey, Sardou, Scribe, and other students of theater history. Corresponding fairly closely to the efforts of an Austen or a Flaubert, the well-made play held out for Aristotelian principles, with particular emphasis on the importance of unity of action, in an era when the popular stage was consistently held by melodramas built according to principles of crosscutting and episodic construction like those borrowed by Griffith from the stage versions of *The Cricket on the Hearth, Enoch Arden, Ramona, Judith of Bethulia*, and *The Clansman*.

Two basic principles regarding the relationship of the novel to the nineteenth- and early twentieth-century popular stage deserve mention here. First, dramatists tended to choose their material from existing texts whose melodramatic proclivities were quite obvious. Thus Balzac, Dumas, Dickens, Hugo, and Zola remain their subjects of choice. Second, whatever the source of material, the stage adaptation tends to imprint the popular theater's own stamp on the original. I have already mentioned that Balzac's *Le père Goriot*, which so carefully concentrates not directly on the mythic figures of Vautrin and Goriot but on the young sleuth who uncovers their stories, was rapidly made into a melodrama featuring the very characters shunned by the novel's classical single-focus technique. Any of Zola's novels could easily have provided the subject for a well-made play. *L'assommoir,* for example, might well have been given a stage version respecting Aristotelian principles, with Gervaise serving as *fil conducteur.* Instead, *L'assommoir* was turned into a sensationalistic melodrama, with emphasis on Coupeau and his delirium tremens.[35] The opposition between well-made play and popular melodrama thus heightens the difference between two prose fiction traditions, each stressing separate and opposed aspects of the available narrative material.

What makes it possible to move back and forth with such ease between single- and dual-focus versions of the same story, between classical and melodramatic versions of the same tale? The case of *L'assommoir* is instructive. Anyone who has read Zola's famous *Ebauche,* his working notes for the novel, is struck by their judgmental and sensationalistic character. The *Ebauche* begins with the notes taken by Zola during his long period of research on the living conditions of the Parisian lower classes. Especially influential in Zola's thinking at this early point in his preparation was Denis Poulot's *Le sublime ou le travailleur comme il est en 1870 et ce qu'il peut être,* from which Zola borrowed many details and secondary characters for the completed novel. More to the point here, however, is the categorization of workers established by Poulot and borrowed by Zola. Constantly contrasted to the *sublime* or bad worker is *l'ouvrier vrai,* whom Zola's notes describe in these terms:

> The true worker, three hundred days of work a year, no debts, savings at home or in the bank, loves his wife and children and takes them out regularly; teaches his children, buys books, owns a clock or a watch; never drinks and doesn't work on Sunday; offers an arm to his wife (the *sublime* never does). Stays at the same job, works hard and fast, looks after himself, stays clean, and thinks clearly.[36]

When Zola reached the point of composing his novel, he retained Poulot's judgmental division, styling Lantier as the archetypal bad worker and Coupeau as his good counterpart, until Coupeau too falls prey to Lantier's bad influence and is replaced as archetypal good worker by the mythically pure Goujet. As in *Le père Goriot,* however, *L'assommoir* is held together not by the melodramatic opposition of good worker to bad but by the rise and fall of a character as yet unmarked as good or evil. Gervaise serves as our introduction to the world of the Parisian worker in order that the continuity, linearity, and psychological causality of classical narrative might be respected. As Zola advanced in his writing, however, he was constantly tempted to bring the melodramatic possibilities of his plot back to the foreground. According to his first sketch for the novel's ending, for example, Lantier was to take on Goujet in an apocalyptic battle. Gervaise would find Lantier in bed with Virginie and break a bottle of sulfuric acid over their naked bodies. Lantier, maddened by pain, would then drag Gervaise by her hair into the courtyard in front of her industrious but selfish in-laws. At that point Goujet would appear and engage Lantier in a formidable duel, lit by the setting sun.[37] That this scene never appears in the novel is a mark, one is tempted to say, of Zola's good taste; in any case, it clearly indicates that Zola's commitment to a classical mode of narration precluded overt construction of a novel along melodramatic lines. Yet Zola does not entirely suppress his melodramatic material. While it does not serve as an organizing principle, it remains constantly present, ever available as part of Gervaise's and the reader's experience. And available as well to the many stage adapters of Zola's novels. Indeed, melodramatic adaptations of nineteenth-century novels are so prevalent because the novels themselves contain a melodramatic substratum ready to erupt through its classical covering. Like Balzac, Dickens, Hugo, Dostoyevski, and James, Zola consistently turns melodramatic material into classical narrative by drawing a psychological veil over it, by taking the static elements of the melodramatic spectacle and stretching them out in linear fashion like so many links in a chain.

It is not, however, the melodramatic adaptations of novels that have been stressed by critics. Peter Brooks, whose *Melodramatic Imagination* is directly interested in the relationship between the nineteenth-century novel and melodrama, always deals with Pixerécourt and original melodramas rather than with the melodramatic adaptations drawn from novels. This is hardly surprising, however, given the near impossibility of locating texts for these popular plays. Even clear references to adaptations are hard to find; often the existence of a stage version of a popular novel must be inferred from a chance comment or discovered by careful reading of the contemporary press. Certainly, the unsure copyright status of all but authorized adaptations, along with the low critical esteem accorded them, contributes to the invisibility of the adaptation as cultural phenomenon.[38]

Most accounts of Hollywood classical narrative jump directly from nineteenth-century novels to the cinema. Only David Bordwell and Kristin Thompson have remained systematically attentive to the nineteenth-century stage as a contributing element to classical Hollywood cinema. While Bordwell stresses the influence of the well-made play in stamping out coincidence as a central form of causality, Thompson invokes the well-made play as a major source for thorough motivation and the resulting continuity of action. Thompson is especially clear in setting up a progression stretching from the novel through original well-made plays and the increasingly popular short story form to Hollywood classical narrative.[39] Like other students of cinema, however, Bordwell and Thompson pay little attention to the possible contribution of melodramatic material to the classical paradigm. This repression of popular theater has the effect of denying Hollywood cinema its fundamental connection to popular traditions and to their characteristic forms of spectacle and narrative. By eschewing the more popular serial forms and theatrical adaptations, critics abandon the opportunity to understand what is going on beneath and within the classical aspects of Hollywood narrative.

Where does this leave film theory today? I cannot fully develop here a theory of Hollywood classical narrative's popular unconscious—a theory, in short, of its dual-focus foundations. But I can suggest a few of the important concerns that a focus on popular narrative and theatrical adaptations might bring back to our notion of Hollywood classical narrative, along with the major theoretical problems implied by the symptomatic shunning of Hollywood's consistently melodramatic underpinnings. The important point is not that critics should literally pay more attention to stage intermediaries (although they probably should); by and large such stage intermediaries become rare after the early 1930s. At stake is not just a blueprint for research but an understanding of the theoretical concerns underlying the notion of classical narrative. The absence of attention to stage intermediaries is not itself the problem; it is a symptom of the real problem.

To be sure, Hollywood classical narrative is not overtly episodic. In keeping with the familiar Aristotelian strictures of the well-made play, Hollywood cinema is goal-driven, its hermeneutic moves through character-based causality toward a logical conclusion. At the same time, however—and the simultaneity of the two processes is what I want to stress here—Hollywood perpetuates the menu-driven concerns of popular theater. Spectacle is needed, as are variety and strong emotions. How can these be obtained in a form that precludes overt episodicity? With no difficulty. Decide which spectacles are needed, then make it seem that they are there for internally motivated reasons.

To be sure, Hollywood classical narrative disguises its dualisms. Unlike the Dickens of *Oliver Twist*, the Eugène Sue of *Les mystères de Paris*, and the Dion Boucicault of *Arrah-na-Pogue*, Hollywood prefers to embed its oppositions, to hide them during all but the most crucial scenes. Yet the narrative operates as it does in order to work these dualisms to the surface. Hollywood's typical linear progression, character-based causality, and continuity editing style serve as mise-en-scène of a fundamentally dualistic relationship whose presence is a precondition for Hollywood cinema, as it is for the novels of Balzac, Dickens, and Zola. The ability to foreground dualisms is, of course, the very stock-in-trade of popular theater. Constantly preferring the metaphoric to the metonymic, in Jakobson's sense of the terms, popular forms of entertainment typically operate according to familiar dual-focus patterns. Hollywood may smooth out the bumps of melodramatic theater, but no amount of smoothing can entirely dissimulate the bulge.

To be sure, Hollywood classical narrative ties its realism and its causality to character psychology. Without the possibility of development, the Hollywood character would be diminished indeed. Yet how many of Hollywood's greatest stars borrow from the nineteenth-century stage their virtual identification with a particular type of role? And how many Hollywood actors are consistently cast according to their tendency to fit into a preexisting category rather than their ability to adapt to a new one? By and large, Hollywood's character categories were set by the popular stage of the last century; the activities of individual characters must appear free in order for the film's inner motivation to operate properly, yet from the outside we easily see just how ritually bound these activities are.

For historical reasons, the notion of classical narrative has evolved in such a way as to privilege Dickens the classical novelist while repressing Dickens the source of popular melodramas. Classical narrative has thus evolved into a term designating a particular *style* more or less continuous from Balzac to Bogdanovich. Symptomatically separated from the ephemeral spectacles of the popular stage, the notion of classical narrative has never been allowed to grow into a dynamic, multilevel *system* in which coexisting contradictory forces must regularly clash. What we have is a complex description of Hollywood's most successful modes of secondary elaboration. What we need is a new look at the other Dickens, a recognition of Hollywood's debt to popular drama, and an opportunity to discover the primary operations of Hollywood's narrative work.

[....]

NOTES

1. Sergei Eisenstein, "Dickens, Griffith, and the Film Today," in Jay Leyda, ed., *Film Form*, (New York: Harcourt Brace, 1949), p. 195.

2. From F. Dubrez Fawcett, *Dickens the Dramatist: On Stage, Screen and Radio* (London: Allen, 1952), 244–5.

3. Eisenstein, "Film Today," pp. 200–1.

4. From A. Nicholas Vardac, *Stage to Screen: Theatrical Method from Garrick to Griffith* (Cambridge, Mass.: Harvard University Press, 1949), pp. 70–72.

5. See, for example, George Bluestone, *Novels into Film* (Berkeley, Calif.: University of California Press, 1968); Marie-Claire Ropars-Wuilleumier, *De la littérature au cinéma: Genèse d'une écriture* (Paris, 1970); and Keith Cohen, *Film and Fiction: The Dynamics of Exchange* (New Haven, Conn.: Yale University Press, 1979).

6. For examples of this strategy, see Noel Carroll, "Becky Sharp Takes Over," and Janice Welsch, "The Horrific and the Tragic [on Mamoulian's *Dr. Jekyll and Mr. Hyde*]," in Michael Klein and Gillian Parker, eds., *The English Novel and the Movies* (New York: Frederick Ungar, 1981), pp. 108, 165.

7. Among the most complete (outside of the absence of theatrical intermediaries) are Klein and Parker, *The English Novel and the Movies*, and Gerald Peary and Roger Shatzkin, eds., *The Classic American Novel and the Movies* (New York: Frederick Ungar, 1977).

8. See Robert M. Henderson, *D. W. Griffith: The Years at Biograph* (New York: Noonday, 1970); Richard Schickel, *D. W. Griffith: An American Life* (New York: Simon and Schuster, 1985); Elaine Mancini, "D. W. Griffith et les romanciers de son temps: Le com-

Rick Altman

mentaire social," in Jean Mottet, ed., *David Wark Griffith: Colloque international*, (Paris, 1984), pp. 195–208; and Cooper C. Graham, Steven Higgins, Elaine Mancini, and Joao Luiz Vieira, *D. W. Griffith and the Biograph Company* (Metuchen, N.J.: Scarecrow, 1985).

9. Henderson, *Years at Biograph*, pp. 27, 101, 240. Henderson's willingness to conflate novelistic and theatrical versions is exemplified by the following sentence: "The next to last film of the first California season was an ambitious adaptation of Helen Hunt Jackson's *Ramona*, the same story in which Griffith had appeared as an actor" (p. 101). The use of the term *story* to bridge the gap (and erase the differences) between novel and play is a characteristic move.

10. See, for example, David A. Cook, *A History of Narrative Film* (New York: Norton, 1981), p. 73.

11. Henderson, *Years at Biograph*, p. 152. Schickel, *An American Life*, claims that Griffith's film was directly based on the Aldrich play (pp. 190–3). The complexity of determining exact sources for Griffith's feature films is perhaps best revealed in Sarah Kozloff's analysis of novel, serialization, play, novelization, and film sources for *Way Down East*, in "*Way Down East* and *Tess of the D'Urbervilles*," *Literature/Film Quarterly* 13:1 (1985), pp. 35–41.

12. Warren French, *Frank Norris* (New York: Twayne, 1962), p. 32.

13. For a complete treatment of the practical and theoretical problems involved in reading *A Farewell to Arms* as an adaptation of Hemingway's novel, see Robert Arnold, Nicholas Peter Humy, and Ana M. Lopez, "Rereading Adaptation: *A Farewell to Arms*," *IRIS* 1:1 (1983), 101–14. For other examples, see A. Nicholas Vardac, *Stage to Screen*, especially pp. 59ff., 63–64, 69ff., 76, 79, 83, and 220ff.; and John L. Fell, *Film and the Narrative Tradition* (Norman, Okla.: University of Oklahoma Press, 1974), especially pp. 17, 21, 24, 30 (although Chap. 4 of Fell's book, on the novel, is disappointing in its failure to recognize the potential importance of theatrical adaptations of novels with what Fell terms *filmlike pre-dispositions* [p. 54]).

14. "Strictly speaking," says Bazin, "one could make a play out of *Madame Bovary* or *The Brothers Karamazov*." While recognizing the possibility of such an adaptation, Bazin has clearly chosen what he believes are extreme examples, unlikely ever to have spawned theatrical versions (André Bazin, *What is Cinema?*, trans. Hugh Gray [Berkeley, Calif.: University of California Press, 1967], p. 83).

15. *The Brothers Karamazov*, in Oliver M. Sayler, ed., *Moscow Art Theatre Series of Russian Plays* (New York: Brentanos, 1923).

16. Early editions of *Variety* and *Moving Picture World* regularly insist on a film's novelistic paternity, recognizing a recent theatrical adaptation as a second parent only when the film borrows its title from the dramatic version rather than from the original novel (e.g., the United Artists 1926 release of Herbert Wilcox's *The Only Way*, adapted from Sir John Martin Harvey's 1899 stage version of Dickens's *Tale of Two Cities*). There is good reason for cinema to avoid mentioning its debt to the stage, especially through the 1910s, for the popular theater remained cinema's strongest competitor through the war years.

17. Eisenstein is perfectly aware that Griffith's debt is more often to stage productions than to Dickens's novels ("Film Today," pp. 199, 224, 230), yet his use of the metonymy "Dickens" to refer to "theatrical versions of Dickens" has led nearly all his readers to forget the theatrical connection and to privilege the novelistic influence.

18. Roland Barthes, *Le degré zéro de l'écriture* (Paris: Editions de Seuil, 1953), especially pp. 29ff., 49ff., where Barthes mirrors Eisenstein's identification of Dickens and Griffith with bourgeois society.

19. Bazin, *What is Cinema?*, p. 29. This essay is made up of separate texts written in 1950, 1952, and 1955.

20. Roland Barthes, *S/Z* (Paris: Editions de Seuil, 1970), p. 10, and *Le plaisir du texte* (Paris: Editions de Seuil, 1973); see also Emile Benveniste, *Eléments de linguistique générale* (Paris: Editions de Seuil, 1966), pp. 237–50.

21. See, for example, Peter Wollen, "Godard and Counter-Cinema: *Vent d'Est*," *Afterimage* 4 (Autumn 1972), 7–16. Wollen's article is built on yet another series of specific oppositions: narrative transitivity vs. narrative intransitivity, identification vs. estrangement, transparency vs. foregrounding, single diegesis vs. multiple diegesis, closure vs. aperture, pleasure vs. displeasure, and fiction vs. reality.

22. Bazin, *What is Cinema?*, p. 29; Barthes, *Plaisir du texte*, pp. 20–21, 25–26.

23. David Bordwell, Janet Staiger, and Kristin Thompson, *The Classical Hollywood Cinema: Film Style and Mode of Production to 1960* (New York: Columbia University Press, 1985), pp. 3–6.

24. For a traditional historical account of the growth of classicism, see René Bray, *La formation de la doctrine classique en France* (Paris: Librairie Nizet, 1927). A more recent view of the evolution of classical theater may be found in Jacques Schérer, *La dramaturgie classique en France* (Paris: Librairie Nizet, 1966). The best statement of received notions regarding classicism is Henri Peyre, *Qu'est-ce que le classicisme?* (Paris: Librairie Nizet, 1965).

25. See Thierry Maulnier, *Racine* (Paris: Gallimard, 1936), and *Lecture de Phèdre* (Paris: Gallimard, 1943).

26. André Gide, "Billets à Angèle," in Jules Brody, ed., *French Classicism: A Critical Miscellany* (Englewood Cliffs, N.J.: Prentice–Hall, 1966), p. 65.

27. André Gide, quoted in Peyre, *Qu'est-ce que le classicisme?*, p. 144.

28. Lucien Goldmann, *Le Dieu caché* (Paris: Gallimard, 1956); Charles Mauron, *L'inconscient dans l'oeuvre et la vie de Racine* (Aix-en-Provence: J. Corti, 1957); Philip Butler, *Classicisme et baroque dans l'oeuvre de Racine* (Paris: Nizet, 1959); and Roland Barthes, *Sur Racine* (Paris: Editions de Seuil, 1963).

29. Peter Brooks, *The Melodramatic Imagination: Balzac, Henry James, Melodrama, and the Mode of Excess* (New Haven, Conn.: Yale University Press, 1976), pp. 148–9. Thomas Elsaesser also stresses the melodramatic nature of popular nineteenth-century novels in "Tales of Sound and Fury: Observations on the Family Melodrama," in Barry Keith Grant, ed., *Film Genre Reader* (Austin, Tx.: University of Texas Press, 1986), pp. 284–5. Christine Gledhill has recently made still broader claims regarding the role of melodrama as the repressed of bourgeois modes of representation in "Dialogue," *Cinema Journal* 25:4 (1986), 44–48.

30. On single- and dual-focus narration see Rick Altman, "Medieval Narrative vs. Popular Assumptions: Revising Inadequate Typology," *Diacritics* 4 (1974), 12–19; "Two Types of Opposition and the Structure of Latin Saints' Lives," *Medievalia et Humanistica,* n.s., 6 (1975), 1–11; "Interpreting Romanesque Narrative: Conques and the *Roland,*" *Olifant* 5 (October 1977), 4–28; *The American Film Musical* (Bloomington, Ind.: Indiana University Press, 1987), especially Chap. 2.

31. On the play adapted from Balzac's novel, see Pierre Barbéris, *Le père Goriot* (Paris: Larousse, 1972). It is interesting to note that Balzac's contemporaries accused him of plagiarizing for his novel another melodrama, Etienne's *Les deux gendres*; see Pierre Citron, preface to *Le père Goriot* (Paris: Larousse, 1966), p. 13.

32. Brooks, *Melodramatic Imagination*, p. 121.

33. René Girard, *Deceit, Desire, and the Novel*, trans. Yvonne Freccero (Baltimore, Md.: John Hopkins University Press, 1965).

34. M. M. Bakhtin, *The Dialogic Imagination: Four Essays*, ed., Michael Holquist, trans. Caryl Emerson and Michael Holquist (Austin, Tx.: University of Texas Press, 1981). See especially the essays entitled "Epic and Novel" and "Discourse in the Novel."

35. It is an adaptation of *L'assommoir* that causes the father's reform in Griffith's 1909 film, *The Drunkard's Reformation*.

36. Emile Zola, *Ebauche* for *L'assommoir*, original in the Bibliothèque Nationale, Nouvelles Acquisitions Françaises 10:271, fol. 142. Reprinted in Emile Zola, *Oeuvres complètes*, vol. 8., ed. Maurice Le Blond (Paris: Bernouard, 1928).

37. Zola, *Oeuvres complètes*, p. 473.

38. See Christopher Prendergast, *Balzac: Fiction and Melodrama* (London: Holmes and Meier, 1978), for another example of careful work on Balzac's debt to melodrama that nevertheless sidesteps the question of melodramatic adaptations from novels. The most careful scholarship on the relationship between novels and theatrical adaptations is in Martin Meisel, *Realizations: Narrative, Pictorial, and Theatrical Arts in Nineteenth-Century England* (Princeton, N.J.: Princeton University Press, 1983), especially pp. 247–82.

39. Bordwell, Staiger, and Thompson, *Classical Hollywood Cinema*, pp. 13ff., 168–71.

Ben Singer

Female Power in the Serial-Queen Melodrama: The Etiology of an Anomaly

Few film genres so historically anomalous, and so pertinent to contemporary discussions of gender and spectatorship, have been as thoroughly forgotten as the serial-queen melodrama. Of the more than 60 such films made between 1912 and around 1920, comprising approximately 800 individual episodes, only *The Perils of Pauline* seems to have lingered in the recesses of popular or scholarly memory. Silent series and serials are interesting for several reasons. Considered from the perspective of industry history, the serials can be seen as a resistance to the emergence of the feature film. Considered from the perspective of genre history, the serials constitute one of the most direct cinematic descendants of the "lowbrow" sensational or "blood and thunder" melodrama that dominated popular theater and cheap literature around the turn of the century. But the serial-queen melodrama is probably most striking because of its extraordinary emphasis on female heroism.

Within a sensational action/adventure framework of the sort conventionally devoted to male heroics, the serial-queen melodrama gives narrative pre-eminence to an intrepid young heroine who exhibits a variety of traditionally "masculine" qualities: physical strength and endurance, self-reliance, courage, social authority, and freedom to explore novel experiences outside the domestic sphere. A few typical titles immediately reveal this central anomaly: *The Adventures of Dorothy Dare, A Daughter of Daring, The Exploits of Elaine, The Hazards of Helen, Ruth of the Rockies, Pearl of the Army, A Lass of the Lumberlands* (figure 11), *The Girl Spy, The Girl Detective, The Perils of Our Girl Reporters.*

My immediate concern will be simply to describe what has become an extremely obscure genre. I discuss where the serial-queen melodrama fits in relation to contemporary definitions of melodrama and then enumerate some of the tropes central to the genre's affirmation of female prowess.

From *Camera Obscura* 22 (January 1990). Reprinted by permission of the author and Indiana University Press.

Figure 11. A Lass of the Lumberlands *(1916).*

Working toward an understanding of the sources of this representation of female power, I examine the serial-queen persona in sociological terms—as a reflection of both the constraints and the radical transformations of the cultural construction of womanhood around the turn of the century—and in intertextual terms, as the extension of an already pervasive popular mythology of the New Woman. The genre is paradoxical, however, in that its portrayal of female power is sometimes accompanied by the sadistic spectacle of the woman's victimization. The genre as a whole is thus animated by an oscillation between contradictory extremes of female prowess and distress, empowerment and imperilment. My explanation of this paradox focuses on the genre's social and intertextual context.

Throughout this essay I want to indicate the importance of using a variety of methods to analyze the dynamics of both textual determination and gender address. With respect to the question of textual determination—i.e., why the serial-queen melodrama came into existence in the form it did and when it did—my analysis emphasizes sociological lines of explanation. At the same time, this essay hopes to engage present-day theoretical models of spectatorship inspired by psychoanalysis. The serial-queen melodrama deviates from the key models around which these theories of gendered spectatorship have been built. Neither a classic Mulveyan model of an inherently male-oriented cinema, nor models of the woman's film that seek to explain spectatorship in terms of the difficulty of articulating female desire, can adequately account for the genre. The films call for a separate model, one that can explain spectatorship as a function of female fantasies of mastery.

Like the problem of textual determination, the issue of gender address within the genre demands a broad and flexible explanatory field. The serial-queen melodrama clearly engaged a female audience, and it is probably safe to say that this audience was the industry's primary, deliberate target. But this address by no means excluded an appeal to both sexes based on the genre's provocative destabilization of gender norms, its social topicality and its inherent melodramatic dynamism (not to mention various possible psychoanalytic forces behind the genre's fascination with images of female power and victimization). The serial-queen melodrama's elaboration of female fantasy is extraordinary and, in certain respects, unparalleled in film history, but one must nevertheless try to do justice to the historical complexity of the genre's gender address and reception.

The Other Melodrama

Film buff lingo has dubbed the heroines of this genre *serial queens,* a term that seems relatively apposite in light of the heroine's textual centrality and characterization as powerful. Although it may invite misunderstanding in the context of recent work in cinema studies, I have anchored this term with the word *melodrama* for the sake of historical accuracy and also to press an issue of semantics that seems particularly in need of examination and clarification.

While a few historical overviews have noted its extraordinary semantic sprawl, the term *melodrama* has adopted a more-or-less fixed meaning in current cinema studies. *Melodrama* as it is used today is all but synonymous with a set of subgenres that remain close to the hearth and emphasize a register of heightened emotionalism and sentimentality: the family melodrama, the maternal melodrama, the woman's film, the weepie, the soap opera, etc. But this was not the principal usage, nor perhaps even one at all, in the early years of the film industry.

It is telling, for instance, that the word *melodrama* is never once used in a 1910 magazine article entitled "The Tear-Drenched Drama," which discusses what would seem to be the direct theatrical antecedent to Hollywood's woman's weepie. "The drama of heart-ache," Alan Dale observes, caters to "the rapacity of women for the love-woe. . . . Marriage and its many variations being the biggest factor in the feminine life, women take a breathless interest in woebegone stories that delay it, or render it impossible, or offer it as the result of terrific struggle."[1] In the author's synopsis of one such woebegone drama, *The Awakening of Helena Richie,* one finds a number of elements that would later typify the Hollywood domestic melodrama:

The heroine lived a life of unwedded marriage with a gay deceiver who, in the eyes of the world, was her brother. When the guileless people of Old Chester, Pennsylvania, were present, Helena Richie was a formal and coldly affectionate sister to the man; when they were alone she would spring into his arms and fervently tell him how much she loved him! Later on, of course, her "past" was discovered by the "strait-laced" people of the village, who had "early Victorian" ideas unlike those of Helena, who talked about "living her own life" in her own way. She had adopted a boy whom she grew to love. When her "past" was revealed, the good gentleman who had assigned the boy to her care felt it his duty to remove the lad. She was not a fit person to be entrusted with the care of children. Her lover, who had an adult daughter of his own, betrayed a marked disinclination to marry Helena. . . . At this point the tears were shed lavishly. After scenes of pointless agony, in which Helena's soul underwent all sorts of contortions and gyrations, her "awakening" took place, and when she said good-bye to the little boy, in the unhappy "big" act, of course there wasn't a dry eye in the house.[2]

By present-day generic rubrics, this story is melodrama pure and simple, an almost archetypical example. The fact that "The Tear-Drenched Drama," which is essentially an essay of genre criticism, should nowhere even mention *melodrama* suggests the enormous degree to which the term's meaning has shifted since the decades around the turn of the century.

As one quickly discerns from reading newspaper reviews and magazine essays from this period, the term's crucial, defining connotation in this period related not to pathos and heightened emotionality but rather to elements essentially antithetical to Hollywood's domestic melodramas— action, thrilling sensationalism, and physical violence. Thus, in a 1906 essay entitled "The Taint of Melodrama," a critic noted: "Ask the next person you meet casually how he defines a melodramatic story, and he will probably tell you that it is a hodge-podge of extravagant adventures, full of blood and thunder, clashing swords and hair's breadth escapes."[3]

More specifically, *melodrama* was used to identify forms of popular theater and literature built around a set of immutable "lowbrow" conventions: sensational action over naturalistic dialogue and causally linked events; themes of persecuted innocence involving an extreme polarization between good and evil in a heroine-villain-hero triad; the stereotyped characterization of villainy and moral fortitude; an unabashed dependence on narrative coincidence and *deus ex machina* resolutions. Melodrama's narrative repertory included abductions, secret passageways, mutant henchmen, and what Montrose Moses described as "trap-doors, bridges to be blown up, walls to be scaled, instruments of torture for the persecuted heroines, freight elevators to crush out the lives of the deserving characters, elevated trains to rush upon the prostrate forms of gagged and insensible girls."[4]

The middle class equated this aesthetic of calamity and astonishment with proletarian vulgarity and degeneracy. Although there were strains of melodramatic spectacle in the "legitimate" productions of Dion Boucicault and David Belasco, melodrama was for the most part culturally segregated and stigmatized as a working-class amusement. As Porter Emerson Browne comments in a 1909 essay suggestively entitled "The Mellowdrammer" (mimicking a lower-class accent):

> The melodrama is the primary form of entertainment with the Other Half. In every city of any importance it has several homes. All smell equally bad and contain much the same sort of people and exactly the same sort of piece.

The essay is full of useful advice for prospective white-collar slumming expeditions to the melodrama theater:

> When you approach the box-office, don't say, "Have you, perhaps, a good aisle-seat, somewhere in the first few rows, that is not already disposed of?" Nay! Nay! The proper way to phrase your query is: "Wotter yuh got down front, Bill? . . . Huh? . . . De sekind row? Awright, Gimme it."[5]

Browne describes melodrama's audience as gossipy shop girls with mouths full of gum, weasely young men with well-watered hair and yellow suspenders embroidered with green shamrocks, and fat immigrants with respiratory problems. Given Browne's account of the plays and their audiences, it is unlikely that many well-to-do readers were convinced to take in a melodrama, even for a lark. When members of bourgeois culture did encounter the melodrama (as might occur in towns with few theaters to choose from), one could expect postures of patrician opposition. A typical example of this sensibility was expressed by a woman who wrote to the drama critic of *The American Magazine* in 1916:

> Dear Sir: This is a plea for help from the A. V. of M., meaning the American Victims of Melodrama. Consider it an urgent request to be represented as *opposed* to this onslaught of melodramatic stuff, this reeking, bloody, villain-pursued-her . . . sort of stuff.[6]

Silent series and serials represent one of the most direct and iconographically faithful cinematic descendants of the sensational melodrama.[7] While serial-queen melodramas cover a range of sensational-melodramatic subgenres (e.g., Western, Gothic, Patriotic, and Working-girl melodramas), they all concentrate on violent, intense action—abductions, entrapments, brawls, hazardous chase sequences, and last-minute rescues—in narratively stark conflicts between a heroine or hero-heroine team and a villain and his criminal accomplices. The theme of usurpation, so central to nineteenth-century melodrama, figures prominently. The villain, generally some sort of mysterious criminal mastermind, foreign operative or unscrupulous capitalist, attempts to deceive, capture, or murder the heroine to seize a secret code, scientific formula, land deed, master key, precious jewel, or similar talisman belonging, in most cases, to the heroine's father.

A 1919 article in *Photoplay* characterizes the melodramatic dynamism of serials and remarks on their connection to lowbrow literary antecedents:

> Action, action and yet more action! Situations if they come along, yes, but never worked out! . . . A famous serial writer said recently that serials consisted of action without psychology. It might be stated more simply by calling them action without padding. Something is always happening in a serial. Often the direct motive is lacking for this action, but serial audiences do not mind. They are not analytical. They want conflict and the serial producers feed it to them in reel lengths. . . . Serials are *The Modern Dime Novels!* They supply the demand that was once filled by those blood curdling thrillers. . . . Melodrama! Of course it's melodrama.[8]

By way of illustrating this frenzy of action, I would like to describe in some detail the second episode of *A Woman in Grey,* a comparatively gothic romance/adventure made in 1919. The serial concerns a hidden fortune, whose location in the long-abandoned Amory mansion can only be discovered by matching two ancient documents. Ruth Hope, with her champion Tom Thurston, finds the Codes and does battle against the villain, J. Haviland Hunter, who is trying to steal the documents and usurp the fortune. A subplot involves the mystery of Ruth's real identity: she conceals a tell-tale mark by a peculiar bracelet that covers the back of her left hand and is securely chained to rings on each finger. The serial's fifteen episodes unfold as a back and forth game of loss and repossession of the Codes, as well as a series of crises in which the villain tries either to abduct and murder the heroine or wrench the bracelet off her hand.

"The Dagger of Death," episode two, begins with a repetition of the prior episode's cliffhanger ending. Ruth, who has been abducted by the villain, jumps out of her captor's speeding car and falls hard onto the roadside. The villain stops and chases her on foot, soon catching her and, after a struggle, hurls her over a bridge above train tracks. A train passes underneath just at that moment, and Ruth's fall is cushioned by a coal car. She leaps off the speeding locomotive and tumbles down a steep embankment. Tom, who has pursued the abductors in a thrilling car chase, arrives at her unconscious body. Ruth revives as Tom is touching her bracelet with a look of perplexed concern. Later, Ruth drives up to the Amory mansion just in time to see the villain climb through a window. The villain steals one of the Codes but runs into Tom in the second-floor foyer. While the two men engage in a turbulent brawl, Ruth scales the outside of the mansion and enters a second-floor room with her pistol drawn. The villain manages to throw Tom over a bannister and down a flight of stairs, but Ruth holds him at gunpoint, dramatically unmasks him, and takes back the Code (figure 12).

Figure 12. A Woman in Grey (1920).

But the villain overpowers Ruth, throws her through a closed second-floor window, and then clobbers Tom again with the butt of his pistol. Ruth climbs back through the window and, kneeling down to help Tom, she finds the Code that the villain has accidentally dropped. The villain returns and ransacks the place looking for the Code. Ruth barricades herself in a room, but the villain finally breaks through, grabs her, and starts wrenching off her bracelet. As the episode ends, the villain takes a long dagger off a wall mount and, with Ruth splayed prone across the top of a desk, slowly brings it toward her neck.

The contrast between the serial-queen melodrama and the Hollywood domestic melodrama could not be more marked. The serial-queen melodrama has no interest in the portraiture of emotional nuance, no investment in scenarios of female martyrdom, disillusionment, repression, anxiety, resignation, and frustration. If the family melodrama can be described as a cinema in which, as Sirk put it, "everything happens on the inside"—within a zone that is doubly "inside," concentrating on the interior spaces of the home and the heart—the serial-queen melodrama is distinct in its externalization, its insistence that everything happen on the outside. It virtually eradicates any complexity of emotional entanglement and sentiment in favor of a focus on physical action and violence. It externalizes psychology in the form of fixed, unequivocal dispositions of villainy, virtue, and valor. The serial-queen melodrama externalizes its focus of diegetic interest as well as character psychology, avoiding the private sphere in favor of an adamantly non–domestic *mise en scène* of criminal dens, submarines, lumber mills, diamond mines, munitions factories, race tracks, abandoned warehouses, gothic mansions, military frontlines, rooftops, airfields, highways, and railways. The serial-queen melodrama's refusal of domesticity, its aversion to the contained realm of family drama, is felt most strikingly in its total banishment of the figure of the mother—the very emblem of the family melodrama. While a benevolent father-figure is generally established, the heroine is always without a mother and none is ever referred to. These films depict a world in which there simply is no such social and biological entity as a mother.[9]

Action Movies for Women

We are accustomed to thinking of the violent action/adventure thriller as a male genre, just as we classify the domestic melodrama as a woman's genre. It thus comes as something of a surprise to find a body of films that deviates so significantly from this framework of gender alignment. I do not propose to classify the serial-queen melodrama strictly as a woman's genre—it certainly appealed to male spectators by virtue of its "blood and thunder" dynamism of action, its inclusion of male hero-figures and its sporadic imagery of female victimization. Moreover, male spectators might have allied themselves with the serial queen as a heroic agent. The heroine exhibits a set of culturally positive behavioral traits—such as liveliness, instrumentality, and moral fortitude—that may prompt spectatorial allegiance and identification to some degree irrespective of gender identification. Nevertheless, it seems clear that the films go out of their way to construct a textual arena for fantasies appealing particularly to female spectatorial narcissism. This aspect of the genre's address to women is revealed not only through textual analysis but also through an examination of the genre's commercial intertext.

An important indication of an address to women lies in the film industry's efforts to tap into the mass readership of women's popular fiction, particularly of the adventure and romance/adventure melodramas published in serial form in daily newspapers and women's monthly magazines. Until around 1918, elaborate and well-promoted prose versions of many serial-queen melodramas were published by installment in the women's pages of newspapers and national women's magazines, scheduled to appear in print just before the theatrical exhibition of each episode. This practice began with the very first film serial, Edison's 1912 *What Happened to Mary*, which was "fictionalized" in *The Ladies' World*, a major national women's magazine. Such collaborations became especially widespread in news-

A Brand New Idea

The Fashion Drama

A motion picture of thrills and excitement centred around a magnificent fashion display.

Perfect photography, wonderful mechanical effects, exquisite costuming and a real story that will hold the attention of men, women and children.

A one reel novelty of the highest quality; two releases each month.

A splendid fashion show and a vivid drama featuring

MINETA TIMAYO, in

"The Adventures of Dorothy Dare"

The first release, "It's Never Too Late," deals with the temptations of a salesgirl in a big store who longs for finery that surrounds her.

Written and directed by H. E. Hancock for the

INTERNATIONAL

(Release Date to be Announced Soon)

EXCHANGES

NEW YORK CITY	BOSTON	LOS ANGELES	PHILADELPHIA	PITTSBURGH
729 7th Ave.	48 Piedmont St.	912 So. Olive St.	1335 Vine St.	964 Penn Ave.
CHICAGO	ATLANTA	SAN FRANCISCO	WASHINGTON	ST. LOUIS
207 So. Wabash Ave.	146 Marietta St.	280 Golden Gate Ave.	712 11th St., N. W.	3513 Olive St.

Figure 13. Advertisement in Motion Picture News *(1916).*

papers, which had been publishing women's fiction on a daily basis since the early 1890s. In 1915, for example, six of the seven New York newspapers with a circulation over 150,000 were featuring movie-serial fictionalization tie-ins in their daily or Sunday editions, or both, and in Boston, each of the four major newspapers carried tie-ins.[10]

Another indication of the serial-queen melodrama's address to a female audience is found in a contest promoting the 1915 Reliance serial *Runaway June.* Forty-eight young women won a free trip to California on a train equipped with a special car converted into a hair and nail salon. The contest was open only to women and was publicized only in women's magazines and sewing-pattern monthlies.[11]

Further evidence of the genre's address to women is the serial-queen melodrama's promotion of "fashion interest," apparent both in the *mise en scène* of the serials and in extratextual merchandising tie-ins with fashion houses. With very few exceptions, serials placed great emphasis on luxurious fashion. Serial producers were clearly mindful of the truism expressed in a 1916 article in *Motion Picture News:* "To the feminine mind, nothing appeals so strongly as clothing, hats, or shoes—in fact finery of any kind."[12] The camera tended to linger on carefully composed views of the heroine's modish and opulent outfits—all silk frills and boas and fur. An ad for *The Adventures of Dorothy Dare* promoted the display of fashions on equal footing with narrative action, describing the series as "a motion picture of thrills and excitement centered around a magnificent fashion display . . . a splendid fashion show and a vivid drama. . . ."[13] (See figure 13). While the genre's emphasis on exquisite costuming may seem to have contradicted the characteristic portrayal of an intrepid heroine, the serial's address to female spectators actually interwove these distinct aspects of narcissistic pleasure in the form of two fantasies of recognition and power. The fantasy of feminine glamour situated the woman as the passive center of attention, the decorative and charming magnet of admiration, while the fantasy of female power situated her as the active center of the narrative, a heroic agent in a male environment. The female spectator was thus offered the best of both worlds: a representational structure that indulged conventionally "feminine" forms of vanity and exhibitionism while it refused the constraints of decorative femininity through an action-packed depiction of female prowess.

Fantasies of Emancipation and Power

The clearest and most interesting indication of the genre's address to a female audience lies in its sustained fantasy of female power. Every serial-queen melodrama, without exception, places an overt polemic about female independence and mastery at the center of its thematic design. This depiction of female power self-consciously dissolves, sometimes even completely reverses, traditional gender positions as the heroine appropriates a variety of "masculine" qualities, competencies, and privileges.

It should be stressed that the films vary considerably in their precise balance between the heroine's "masculine" assertiveness and self-reliance, on the one hand, and her "feminine" glamour, charm, and dependence on male chivalry on the other. But at the very least, the genre portrays the emancipated woman out in the masculine world, seizing new experiences and defying the ideology of feminine domesticity. The genre celebrates the pleasures and perils of a young woman's interaction with a public sphere traditionally restricted to men. As "girl spies," "girl detectives," "girl reporters," "girl telegraphers," or as effervescent heiresses with an appetite for prenuptial adventure, heroines transgress the conventional boundaries of female experience. The well-known 1914 serial *The Perils of Pauline*, for example, stresses Pauline's athletic exuberance and unyielding zeal for risky experiences. The story centers on an heiress who agrees to wed an adoring suitor on the condition that she be granted a whirlwind year of adventure before settling down. Pauline's regimen of new experiences engages her in dangerous airplane races, horse jockeying, balloon flights, automobile racing, submarine exploration, and expeditions into Chinatown criminal dens (each escapade offering the villain a new opportunity to attempt Pauline's assassination).

A number of serial-queen melodramas stop at this level, simply recounting the thrills and dangers of exploring worlds out of bounds to women. Such films tend to be the most conservative in their vision of gender positions because, while they grant their heroines vivacity and curiosity, these attributes tend to increase the heroine's vulnerability in the outside world, thus necessitating a male rescue that poses a certain ambiguity about the ultimate nature of the heroine's independence.

But many serials go far beyond this level, presenting the woman as powerful in the public sphere. The genre typically grants its heroines social power in terms of conventionally male positions of professional authority. Helen in *The Hazards of Helen* is a telegraph operator on the dangerous overnight shift. In *The Girl and the Game*, Helen Holmes is in charge of an important railroad line. Ruth Ranger, in *The Haunted Valley*, is head of an enormous dam construction project. The eponymous heroine of *Patria* (her very name a concise signifier of androgyny) owns a huge munitions factory and is commander-in-chief of a sizable private army and air force. An intertitle minces no words in telling us that Captain Donald Parr, Patria's love interest, is second in command.

Figure 14. Pearl of the Army *(1916).*

The ultimate display of female power concerns the heroine's physical prowess, quick reflexes, and coordination, especially in terms of a conventionally masculine repertory of heroic stunts (figure 14). Serial heroines brawl in fist fights with enemy thugs. It is an absolute imperative to show the heroine's facility with a pistol at several points throughout a serial, as well as her agility in stunts like leaping from a speeding train into a pursuing car or jumping off a building and through an adjacent skylight three floors below.

At its most assertive, this fantasy of female prowess gravitates toward a reversal of gender positions (figure 15). In several car chases in *The Girl and the Game,* Helen controls the wheel, while her three brawny male buddies are relegated to mere passengers. In *Pearl of the Army,* similarly, Pearl and a male ally escape artillery fire by riding double on horseback, but Pearl rides in front and controls the speeding horse while the man holds on for dear life. Later in the episode, Pearl hops in an airplane (still a real novelty in 1916) and takes off singlehandedly, leaving an assortment of less deft men on the ground. The classic positions of helplessness and chivalry are often succinctly inverted, as in "Helen's Rescue of Tom" in *A Lass of the Lumberlands.* (See figure 11.) Andromeda has become Perseus, and Perseus Andromeda.[14]

Figure 15. Pearl White in The Romance of Elaine *(1915).*

The Etiology of an Anomaly

Any attempt to account for the representation of female power in the serial-queen melodrama must begin by acknowledging the great extent to which this trope stems from a commercial strategy to engage female spectators. The film industry recognized the economic significance of women moviegoers, perhaps of young unmarried women in particular, and sought greater or more stable profit by marketing fantasies of excitement and mastery geared to them. The serial-queen melodrama stands out as a significant index of the film industry's attempt to address a female audience at a much earlier date than has been presumed. The genre indicates the studios' perception of the economic import-ance of women moviegoers from the very beginning of the film industry's commercial expansion, almost a decade before the Valentino craze of the 1920s.

But over and above this economic level, the serial-queen persona must be seen in sociological terms as the reflection of a distinct historical moment in the cultural experience of womanhood. The serial-queen melodrama's investment in images of female power implies women's disenchantment and frustration with conventional definitions of gender, while at the same time it celebrates tangible transformations in women's status after the turn of the century.

Viewed as a utopian fantasy of female empowerment, the serial-queen melodrama suggests an escapist response to the constraints of women's experience within patriarchal society. The fantasy of the "masculinized" heroine, as Karen Horney observed, "may be the expression of a wish for all those qualities and privileges which in our culture are regarded as masculine, such as strength, courage, independence, success, sexual freedom, right to choose a partner."[15] In this vein, the serial-queen melodrama drew heavily on a broader feminist discourse propelled by the woman's movement, which, mobilized around the campaign for suffrage, was extremely prominent in the 1910s. The serial-queen genre consciously tapped into the movement's polemical momentum.

A sequence in an episode of the 1918 Pathé serial *The Lightning Raider*, for example, frames the heroine's aggressivity as an overtly feminist repudiation of patriarchal chauvinism. The plucky young heroine—simply named "Lightning," like a male super-hero—is trying to intercept a bouquet of roses in which a villain has hidden a vial of deadly germs. The first place she searches happens to be the site of the yearly banquet of the Society for Anthropological Research. A group of grey-haired, bearded, and bespectacled scholars sits around a large table. (The modern viewer is struck by their visual resemblance to Freud; the fact that the keynote speaker's name clearly signifies Jewishness makes one wonder whether a direct allusion was intended.) The chairman rises and announces that "Professor Absolom will now read his paper on 'The Inferiority of the Female Brain Cavity.'" Meanwhile, with ripe irony, Lightning is treacherously climbing down the side of the building with a rope. Just as the professor reads the words "From the natural timidity of the female, I deduce...." Lightning blasts in through the balcony doors with her pistol drawn. As the men scramble in surprise and fear, Lightning literally heaves them out of her way, knocking over their chairs and spilling them onto the floor. She corrals them into a corner, where they stand trembling as she rips apart the flowers looking for the vial. She leaves with a big grin, saying something like "so long suckers."[16]

The serial-queen melodrama's mythology of female power can be seen as a response to the patriarchal ideology of femininity so clearly critiqued in this sequence. But the genre marks a crucial paradox in this respect, since it not only conveys women's frustration with the cultural constraints of femininity but also encapsulates positive changes in the social reality of women around the turn of the century. Lewis Jacobs's assessment of the genre's heroines is apt: "Their exploits paralleled, in a sense, the real rise of women to a new status in society."[17] The historical spectator undoubtedly would have recognized and understood the serial-queen as a socially reflexive stereotype, and one already familiar in a variety of adjacent entertainment forms. The serial-queen persona reflects and embodies the decisive transformations in the cultural construction of womanhood that accompanied America's shift to industrial capitalism and an urban consumer economy. The scope of these transformations was enormous: in one way or another they all involved the expansion of the woman's sphere of experience beyond the sheltered boundaries of the domestic circle.

Whereas few modes of public experience were acceptable for an unaccompanied woman in the Victorian era, the years between 1880 and 1920 generated a new conception of the woman's legitimate domain. Significantly lower fertility rates and the proliferation of labor-saving machines and commodities gave both lower- and middle-class women more freedom to pursue activities outside the household.[18] Whereas only about 10 percent of women worked in paid labor in 1880, this figure had almost doubled by 1910, or tripled if one looks only at the urban population. By 1910, over 40 percent of young, single women worked for several years before marriage, and the figure was probably over 60 percent in urban areas. The massive development of the department store made shopping a condoned activity for housewives and encouraged their presence in the public sphere, as did new music halls, amusement parks, and movie theaters.[19] An unprecedented degree of independence and mobility was reinforced by the diffusion of new means of transportation, especially the electric trolley (its miles of track increased by 245 percent in the northeast between 1890 and 1902), and the bicycle, which in the mid-1890s took on heightened social-symbolic importance as an emblem of female emancipation.[20] An astounding growth in the formation of women's social clubs, which served as a wellspring for feminist awareness and suffrage activism, provided a major new form of public experience for middle-class women. Even the emergence of electric street lights played a role in expanding the world for women. In an 1896 article on "Women Bachelors in New York," Mary Humphreys writes:

> The increase in the number of women abroad at night, with no other protector than the benign beams of the electric light, affords a new and interesting manifestation of the streets. They are found in the streetcars at hours that once would have been called unseemly; they are substantial patrons of the theater.[21]

The premise of this article, crystallized by the oxymoronic term *woman bachelor*, was that female experience in urban America could be characterized in terms of a new masculinization.

Popular culture synthesized and symbolized these transformations in the social configuration of womanhood through a cultural construct dubbed the "New Woman." For years, print media and popular entertainments were preoccupied with this buzz-image, perennially attempting to define, evaluate, caricature, and mythologize its various dimensions.

The remarkable cultural saturation of the New Woman stereotype stemmed from the clarity of its dialectic opposition to the "Cult of True Womanhood," the paradigm of femininity that dominated the nineteenth century and whose key terms, as Barbara Welter's influential essay elucidates, were "piety, purity, submissiveness, and domesticity."[22] Welter quotes a passage from *Sphere and Duties of Woman,* a typical mid-nineteenth-century handbook defining the nature of the "true woman":

> She feels herself weak and timid. She needs a protector. She is in a measure dependent. She asks for wisdom, constancy, firmness, and perseverance, and she is willing to repay it all by the surrender of the full treasure of her affections.[23]

In sharp contrast to this ideal, a 1902 magazine article gets to the core of the New Woman image:

> The energetic, independent woman of culture is frequently caricatured as the "New Woman." . . . [T]he key-note of her character is self-reliance and the power of initiation. She aims at being in direct contact with reality and forming her own judgement upon it."[24]

As America moved into modernity, an ideology of ultimate female dependence began to shift (although it would never completely yield) to a cultural image of women as capable of standing on their own. Whereas a playwright in 1825 typically likened women to "ivy fondly clinging to the tall oak's majestic side," a 1911 magazine essay entitled "The Masculization of Girls" spoke of "the Girl's strange metamorphosis from the clinging vine of yesterday to the near-oak of today."[25] Minna Thomas Antrim's essay describes the "Masculine Girl of today":

> She tells herself exultantly that she is man's (almost) brother. . . . She loves to walk, to row, to ride, to motor, to jump and run, not daintily with high heeled, silk-lined elegance, but as Man walks, jumps, rows, rides, motors, and runs.[26]

Charles Dana Gibson's parodic illustration "One of the Disadvantages of Being in Love with an Athletic Girl," published in *Life* in 1902, typifies the mass-media's insatiable interest in this new configuration of femininity, and compresses the various forms of celebration, curiosity and mild paranoia that this interest entailed. (See figure 16.)

The New Woman's trademarks—energy, self-reliance, direct contact with the extradomestic world—were clearly the terms of a revised femininity celebrated and exaggerated in the serial-queen melodrama. Any consideration of the etiology of this genre must stress the great extent to which it self-consciously drew on an already codified and pervasive popular discourse around the New Woman.

Figure 16. Charles Dana Gibson, "One of the Disadvantages of Being in Love with an Athletic Girl," Life *(1902).*

More specifically, the serial-queen melodrama developed out of several interrelated popular entertainments that had already transposed the figure of the New Woman into action-oriented narratives aimed primarily at working-class readers and theatergoers. In the last part of the nineteenth century, dime novels, story papers, popular newspapers, and popular-priced melodramas all developed subgenres built around the exploits and perils of working-girl heroines. One sees scattered instances of climactic female agency in stage melodramas as early as the mid-1860s. In Augustin Daly's *Under the Gaslight* (1867), for example (figure 17), the heroine hacks her way out of a locked woodshed and saves a man tied to the railroad tracks (directly anticipating "Helen's Rescue of Tom" shown in figure 11).[27] Displays of female heroics and stunt work took on particular importance in a wave of "Ten, Twent', Thirt'" productions between approximately 1903 and 1908. Sensational melodramas such as *Nellie, The Beautiful Cloak Model* (1906), *For a Human Life: The Great Sensational Story of a Girl Detective* (1906) and *Bertha, the Sewing Machine Girl* (1906) provided an immediate prototype for the serial-queen melodrama. Dorothy Pam's description of the 1907 melodrama *Edna, the Pretty Typewriter* could easily refer to any number of serial-queen films:

> With a combined western and urban setting, [this melodrama] has the heroine jump from the roof of a building to the top of a moving elevated

Figure 17. Under the Gaslight, *stock poster, about 1880.*

train, leap from the racing car in which she is a prisoner to the pursuing car, and escape from a vault blown open by nitro-glycerin.[28]

Similar narrative and quasi-narrative representations of dynamic New Women were also an important feature in metropolitan newspapers by the mid-1890s, corresponding to the onset of what Terry Ramseye called "the volcanic school of journalism." The popular newspaper, an entertainment form through and through, combined vibrant lithographs and sensationalistic accounts of curiosities, disasters, scandals, stunts, and accidents. Women readers were crucial to this new form of mass entertainment largely because of its dependence on revenue from department store advertising aimed at female consumers. The necessity to cater to women merged with the policy of sensationalism in two forms: columns devoted to brave or unconventional exploits by actual women, and "plucky girl reporter" features.

In the *New York World* of Monday, March 23, 1896, the lead article on the front page concerns a Jersey City housewife who battles relentlessly with a burglar and wins. The customary plethora of headlines and subheadlines that precede the actual text of the article read: "She Held a Burglar/Little Mrs. Gilligan Rolled Downstairs with Him in Her Grip/Then They Fought on the Floor/Once He Got Away by Slipping Off His Coat, but She Sprang on Him Again/Husband Came after She Had Him Safe."

The "Plucky Girl Nabs Thief" item congealed into something of a newspaper staple during this period. An item in an 1896 New York *Sunday*

Figure 18. New York World *(1896).*

World column entitled "Woman's Record during the Week" exemplifies the formula:

> It is pleasant to turn . . . to the excellent record of Mrs. Bloomer, who well deserves her name. Mrs. Bloomer is a lady of high standing in Port Jervis, N.Y. She follows the usual careful housewife's habit of looking under the bed for a man, and her vigilance was rewarded by the discovery of a man there several evenings ago. Did Mrs. Bloomer shriek and faint? She did not. She seized a revolver, dragged the man ignominiously forth, took his revolver from him, made him empty his pockets before her, and finally gave him into the willing arms of the law—all without assistance and in the coolest possible manner.[29]

A regular column comprised of such items began in the *Sunday World* in August 1895. Its most frequent heading was "The 'New Woman' in Everyday Life/ Various Interesting Manifestations of the Emancipated Female's Foibles and Freaks, and Her Curious Interests, Powers and Exploits." Along with accounts of bravery—women snaring burglars or rescuing people from fire, drowning, or angry lions (figure 18)—the most common subject in these New Woman columns related to women at work in traditionally male jobs such

Figure 19. New York World (1896).

as steamboat engineer, deputy marshal, bank president, coroner, coal miner, grist mill operator, bicycle mechanic, itinerant photographer, carpenter, marble cutter, lawyer, dentist, physician, and insurance broker.[30]

A second prominent genre emerged alongside the New Woman articles in the mid-1890s. What I call "stunt articles" recounted exploits contrived by daring women reporters. Telling of their adventures in first-person narration, a small group of "plucky girl reporters" became familiar, consistent personalities, much like serial queens. The sole objective of these women reporters was to seek out "novel and thrilling experiences" that extended the experiential sphere of women. Stunt articles vivified places and experiences that were out of reach to most women, restricted by virtue of either their danger or their indelicacy—which is to say, these articles explored for women territories culturally proper to men.

Many stunt articles focused on the intrepid pursuit of physical peril and kinesthetic excitement. Kate Swan scales the Harlem River Bridge just for the thrill of it, conquering "A Spot No Woman's Foot Ever Before Trod" (see figure 19); she kayaks through a mad whirlpool in the East River at midnight; she struggles in a bout with a champion wrestler; she works as a stoker, heaving coal into the fiery furnace of a North River ferry boat; she drives a locomotive through the B. & O. Tunnel at 75 mph, becoming the first woman ever to run an electric engine. Dorothy Dare, becoming "the first woman to take a spin through the streets of New York in a horseless carriage," drives at the dizzying speed of 30 mph; Sallie Madden shoots a perilous mountain chute on a frail railroad car.

Other articles, while involving less physical action, were nevertheless daring, and similarly took women to places lying outside their traditional sphere of experience—opium dens, mass burials, leper colonies, execution chambers, insane asylums, gambling dens, police patrols, mortuaries, flop houses, and freak shows. In perhaps the most telling stunt of all, Dorothy Dare simply dresses up in men's clothing to explore New York at liberty. The serial-queen melodrama's intertextual link to both the New Woman news features and these stunt articles is, I think, direct and self-evident. The connection is made explicitly in the resurrection of Dorothy Dare as a series heroine in International's *The Adventures of Dorothy Dare* (1916) and in titles such as Mutual's 1917 *The Perils of Our Girl Reporters.*

The serial-queen melodrama clearly extends an image already constructed in the urban mythology of popular entertainment. It is important to underscore that this discourse was rhetorically polyvalent in nature. The genre's portrayal of the New Woman, like that of its intertextual precursors, suggests a complex mixture of social reflection, utopian fantasy, and simple curiosity. First of all, as I have suggested, the genre documents and celebrates concrete sociological changes in the cultural construction of womanhood. There is a tangible link, in other words, between social facts and cultural representation. Society represents itself to itself with a certain degree of fidelity. But, as I have also argued, the genre functions on the level of female fantasy and escapism. The utopian image of female prowess and emancipation may tell us as much about the continuing cultural restrictions on female experience as it does about her new exposure to the public sphere. The genre's focus on female heroic agency may both memorialize an actual expansion of women's sphere of experience and, as vicarious fantasy, suggest the continuing constraints of conventional definitions of gender.

Finally, I think it cannot be stressed too much that the image of the New Woman captured the attention of both men and women at the turn of the century by virtue of its sheer novelty and curiosity. Beyond any coefficient of social reflection or utopian fantasy (and inseparable from either), the widespread cultural fascination with the New Woman, particularly with her disruption of normative definitions of femininity, suggests the appeal of simply playing around with gender for its own sake. Helen Holmes's extraordinary daredevil stunt work in *The Hazards of Helen*, for example, may have less to do with an earnest stake in a progressive ideology of female emancipation than with the utter novelty and curiosity value of a spectacle based on the "category mistake" of a woman taking death-defying physical risks, getting filthy, brawling with crooks in muddy riverbanks—in short, of a woman acting like a man.[31]

The Other Side of Empowerment

Female power constitutes the serial-queen melodrama's central theme, but it would be a mistake to characterize the genre as a one-dimensional exposition of Amazonian prowess. There is another representational strain that, while it does not surface in all serial-queen melodramas, plays an extremely pronounced role in those films in which it does appear. This strain involves the lurid victimization of the heroine by male villains who exploit their greater size, strength, and sadistic guile to render her powerless and terrified. All serial-queen narratives, by definition, place the heroine in positions of danger—it is a necessary part of her emancipation and "masculine" agency. But a number of serial-queen films—comprising perhaps a third of the genre—go much further and amplify an extremely graphic spectacle of female distress, helplessness, and abject terror. In films such as *The Perils of Pauline*, *The Exploits of Elaine*, *The Fatal Ring*, and *A Woman in Grey*, the heroine is systematically assaulted, bound and gagged, hurled out windows or off bridges, terrorized by instruments of torture and dismemberment, and threatened with innumerable means of assassination (figures 20 and 21). The genre thus couples an ideology of female power with an equally vivid exposition of female defenselessness and weakness.

The genre's fixation on female imperilment stems immediately and unequivocally from the basic iconographic formula of sensational melodrama in its various lowbrow stage and dime novel manifestations. At the very core of virtually all sensational melodramas, from the eighteenth century onward, one finds the persecution of a virtuous heroine by a diabolical villain. Essayists and critics writing near the turn of the century

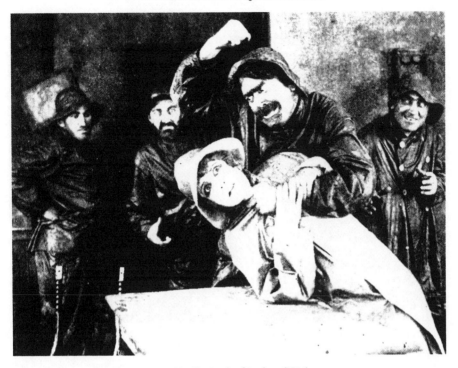

Figure 20. The Perils of Pauline *(1914).*

had no difficulty stereotyping this classic configuration of villainy and victimization[32]:

> The villain, without provocation, punched the heroine in the nose or kicked her feet from under her.
>
> *Chicago Republic*, 1903

> The villain, who has learned that he is next of kin and so will inherit millions—millions—millions in the event of the death of the girl whom he has quite given up hope of winning, tries upon the heroine and her sole defender every known, and some unknown, ways of inducing physical disintegration
>
> Porter Emerson Browne, 1909

> Just when the heroine is about to be disintegrated by the sausage machine, or reduced to longitudinal sections by the buzz-saw, or run over by the express-train as she lies bound across the rails, or blown to bits by the powder-barrel as the fuse sputters nearer and nearer, then . . . in jumps the hero.
>
> Rollin Lynde Hartt, 1909

Figure 21. The Perils of Pauline *(1914).*

You may lock the heroine in a lion's cage, throw her off of the Brooklyn Bridge, tie her to the subway tracks, and dangle her by a rope from the windy summit of the Singer tower.

Clayton Hamilton, 1911

The spectacle of abduction and violent imperilment is the most crucial element in the sensational melodrama's generic iconography (along with the corollary spectacle of escape or chivalrous intervention). This image of female victimization in the serial-queen melodrama clearly conforms to a formula already firmly codified by the serial's intertextual matrix.

Female victimization may have become such a central generic convention in sensational melodrama in the first place because of the clarity with which it could function in terms of social allegory. Thomas Elsaesser argues, for example, that the inherently melodramatic tragedies and sentimental novels of Richardson, Schiller, and Lessing hinge on "a metaphorical interpretation of class-conflict as sexual exploitation and rape" and thus express "the struggle of a morally and emotionally emancipated bourgeois consciousness against the remnants of feudalism."[33] American popular melodrama at the turn of the century continued to use crises of female victimization to stress themes of class stratification and injustice, although its contrasts and clashes were adjusted downward a notch to counterpose not a villainous aristocracy and virtuous bourgeoisie, but rather a corrupt bourgeoisie and poor-but-noble working class.

The serial-queen melodrama marks an interesting shift in this vein of social allegory, since the films almost never directly address issues of social injustice or pose the characters as symbolic stand-ins for entire socio-economic classes. The heroine and hero are invariably depicted as belonging either to a blithe upper or solidly professional middle class. Serials dispense with the stage melodrama's glorification of "only a working-girl" and completely avoid the pathos of stoic poverty sometimes attached to her victimization. (There are no sick mothers or blind sisters for the heroine to provide for.) The serial-queen melodrama also has no place for the stage melodrama's typical "blue shirt lead" (the working-man good guy) or its retinue of comic street-life characters. The benevolent wino messengers, soubrettes, bootblacks, and immigrant peddlers—ennobled by their street smarts, moral fortitude, and impudence in the face of social elitism—are entirely omitted.

The serial-queen melodrama's allegorical shift is fundamental: it translates through metaphor the social dynamics not of class, but of gender. The films chart the social instability and oppressiveness feared not by a "morally and emotionally emancipated" underclass but rather by the similarly emancipated New Woman in the public sphere. The genre captures the basically paradoxical nature of female experience at this historical threshold. With its repudiation of domesticity and its fantasy of empowerment, the serial-queen melodrama celebrates the excitement of the woman's attainment of unprecedented mobility outside the confines of the home. But, correspondingly, in its imagery of female victimization the genre also envisions the dangers of this departure. Its scenes of assault, abduction, torture, and intimated rape suggest the worst-case scenario of woman's entry into the mixed-sex, mixed-class, and mixed-ethnicity chaos of the modern urban milieu.

Popular magazines in this period began to describe a general disintegration of public civility coinciding with the greater independence of women in an urbanized America no longer protected by Victorian strictures of social decorum. Eleanor Gates's 1906 article in *The Cosmopolitan Magazine* entitled "The Girl Who Travels Alone" describes a new social problem, particularly severe in New York but existing in all the country's urban centers—the harassment of unaccompanied women in the form of relentless unwanted advances by strange men. According to Gates such harassment included rude calls in Central Park by ethnic packs, especially native-born "foreigner's sons"; "forced kissing" on the subway by college rowdies; lewd calls by wagondrivers; or ultimately even physical harm, as in the case of "Dr. S___," a young woman physician:

> As she approached a subway entrance at Forty-second Street, carrying her satchel, a man whom she had never seen before took her by the arm. What

he said was so infamous that she struck him. He struck back at her, tore her dress, and knocked her down the flight of steps. A crowd gathered, but no bystander offered aid.[34]

Gates claimed her examples, which "could be multiplied by the thousands," left out those which "would not bear publication"—probably a reference to rape. All these problems arose from the convergence of the new anonymity and heterogeneity of the modern city and, as Gates put it, "the social conditions in this country that admit the widest liberty to women."

The venerable Harvard psychologist Hugo Munsterberg, in a 1913 *New York Times* essay, encapsulated a fundamental ambivalence about the new "American position of the woman outside of the family circle":

> Her contact with men has been multiplied, her right to seek joy in every possible way has become the counterpart of her new independence, her position has become more exposed and more dangerous.[35]

Munsterberg's assessment could almost stand as a synopsis of a serial such as *The Perils of Pauline*, with which it almost precisely coincides. (*Pauline* was probably being shot while Munsterberg was writing his essay.) Like the controversial wave of "white slavery" films also appearing at this time (depicting the abduction, imprisonment, and forced prostitution of innocent women in the cities), the serial-queen genre gives shape to a pervasive social anxiety—one felt by both men and women—about the consequences of woman's emancipation and independence in the heterosocial public sphere. The serial-queen's oscillation between agency and vulnerability expresses the paradoxes and ambiguities of the woman's situation within the advent of urban modernity.

Conclusion

The serial-queen melodrama's impulses of female empowerment and imperilment can be understood, on the one hand, as allegorical reflections of a complex historical moment in the sociology and ideology of gender and, on the other, as adaptations of sensational tropes already popular and conventional in the genre's adjacent lowbrow entertainment forms. One cannot understand the serial-queen melodrama without understanding its sociological context and intertextual matrix. The serial-queen melodrama is especially valuable in indicating the inadequacy of approaches that presume that psychoanalytic interpretation can stand by itself in explaining and decoding a film's textual dynamic. The genre underscores the great degree to which social topicality and intertextual prefabrication determine textual design.

But I would like to end by stressing that historical contextualization of the sort I have attempted here does not obviate ostensibly less empirical, or at least less historically specific, approaches. Whether or not the cultural-historical lines of analysis pursued here can be considered a "sufficient" explanatory field, it is crucial to examine various types of psychoanalytic explanation both on principle—as the logical extension of historiography's recognition of the complexity and openness of historical determination—and, less idealistically, simply on the basis of the provocative congruencies one is able to map out between the serial-queen melodrama and an array of psychoanalytic phenomena.

The spectacle of misogynistic sadism is certainly a prime candidate for psychoanalytic interpretation. The serial-queen melodrama—at least one branch of this genre—could be regarded as one of the first systematic explorations and exploitations of a strain of perverse stimulus that would later shape the psycho-killer crime thriller, the Hollywood "slasher" films of the 1970s, and violent pornography—to mention only the most overt instances within a dominant cinema putatively defined by a pervasive misogynistic sadism. But much more than male sadism is at issue in the serial-queen melodrama. The genre is a particularly fascinating text for psychoanalytic exegesis because it is structurally capable of accommodating a complex interplay of disparate psychic fantasies and anxieties relating to both male and female subjectivity.

Spelled out most simply, the serial-queen melodrama provokes basic questions pertinent to psychoanalysis: what explains the female spectator's interest in a fantasy of a masculinized woman? What explains her interest in viewing female victimization? And likewise, what explains the male spectator's interest in female prowess and in victimization? Psychoanalysis offers a number of compelling hypotheses about these spectatorial phenomena and about their paradoxical combination within a psychic/textual economy. One could draw parallels between the serial-queen melodrama, as it separately engages both male and female subjectivity, and psychoanalytic theories of sadism, masochism, penis envy, phallic narcissism, the disavowal of sexual difference, and, perhaps most acutely, the fantasies and anxieties of both male and female oedipal trajectories.

I will have to defer an adequate explication of this ungainly roster to another discussion. Suffice it to say here that while the serial-queen melodrama is clearly useful as an illustration of the methodological importance of sociological and intertextual contextualization, I think it will also serve as a valuable case study pointing to the need to work from a greatly expanded and polyvalent conception of both gender address and textual determination.

NOTES

I am grateful to Tom Gunning and Lea Jacobs for their generous help on this manuscript.

1. Alan Dale, "The Tear-Drenched Drama," *Cosmopolitan Magazine* (January 1910), 199–205.

2. Ibid., p. 201.

3. Frederic Taber Cooper, "The Taint of Melodrama and Some Recent Books," *Bookman* (February 1906), 630–5.

4. Montrose J. Moses, "Concerning Melodrama," *The Book News Monthly* (July 1908), 846.

5. Porter Emerson Browne, "The Mellowdrammer," *Everybody's Magazine* (September 1909), 347–54.

6. Walter Prichard Eaton, "Is 'Melodramatic Rubbish' Increasing?" *The American Magazine* (December 1916), 34, 114, 116.

7. Series installments were narratively self-contained, each presenting a complete story in itself, yet forming part of a greater textual entity through the repetition of ingredients such as character and setting. Serials, on the other hand, entailed an overarching story that carried over from episodes to episode. Most serial episodes in the 1910s ran one or two reels in duration (a quarter to a half hour), were released weekly, and were preplanned to end after about 15 episodes. Series often had no preplanned number of episodes and would run until popularity waned. Kalem's *The Hazards of Helen*, for example, ran for 119 episodes between 1914 and 1917. I offer an overview of the history of film serials in "Serial Films 1913–1956," in G. Nowell-Smith, ed., *The Oxford History of World Cinema* (Oxford: Oxford University Press, 1995).

8. Frank Bruner, "The Modern Dime Novel," *Photoplay* (June 1919), 118.

9. By the same token, I know of no serial-queen films showing siblings of any sort, and since all heroines are unmarried (and occasionally remain so even after the last episode), there are no husbands and no conjugal tribulations of the kind central to the domestic melodrama.

10. For a detailed history of fiction tie-ins in early film, see Ben Singer, "Fiction Tie-ins and Narrative Intelligibility, 1911–1918," *Film History* 4:5 (November 1993), 489–504. The New York newspapers with a circulation over 150,000 in 1915 included the *American*, the *Globe and Commercial Advertiser*, the *Journal*, the *Mail*, the *Sun*, the *Times*, the *Tribune*, and the *World*. Only the *Times* eschewed fictionalization tie-ins. The Boston papers included the *American*, the *Globe*, the *Herald and Traveler*, and the *Post*. Circulation figures are listed in *American Newspaper Annual and Directory* (Philadelphia: Ayer, 1915). From lists published in trade journal advertisements, one can estimate that a given "film novel" might have been serialized in anywhere between 50 and 200 newspapers across the country.

11. Advertisement, *Motion Picture News* (20 March 1915), 1717.

12. C. D. Crain, "Fights for Men, Finery for Women," *Motion Picture News* (29 July 1916), 818.

13. Advertisements, *Motion Picture News* (21 October 1916), 2490. Although this ad does not indicate a specific tie-in, the film probably announced one in a title card. At the end of each episode of *The Ventures of Marguerite*, for example, an intertitle reads, "The exclusive creations worn by Miss Marguerite Courtot in this series furnished by Russek, of Fifth Avenue, New York City." Fashion tie-ins were usually promoted as a big asset. A publicity article in *Motion Picture News* for Pathé's series *Who's Guilty?* announces that "All of Miss Nilsson's gowns in the 'Who's Guilty?' series were made especially for her by Hickson, the Fifth Avenue modiste. The striking blonde beauty that is one of Miss Nilsson's chiefest charms is admirably set off by the queenly sweep of the frocks that Hickson has furnished her. There seldom are fewer than four Hickson gowns to each 'Who's Guilty?' photo-novel, but in one Miss Nilsson is seen in fourteen of the smartest costumes that Hickson could turn out." ("'Who's Guilty?' Series Will Come from Pathé

May 8," *Motion Picture News* [22 April 1916], 23.) Charles Eckert, "The Carole Lombard in Macy's Window," *Quarterly Review of Film Studies* 3:1 (1978), 1–22, compellingly describes the pervasiveness in the 1930s of the use of movies to advertise particular fashion lines. It is evident from series and serial fashion tie-ins that this practice had already been fully implemented by the mid-1910s.

14. A synopsis intertitle provided for the last episode of Mutual's *The Girl and the Game,* a 1915 railroad serial, indicates that the heroine rescues her male allies about ten times more often than they are called on to rescue her: "The story to date: Helen Holmes prevents collision of train carrying her father and Storm, saves Storm from death on burning train; recovers accidental duplicate map of railroad cut-off, averting withdrawal of financial support. By desperate leap, Helen recovers payroll from thieves. Kidnapped by Seagrue, Helen is rescued by Storm and Spike. She brings deputies to prevent death in rival camp's pitched battle. Helen rescues Storm, Rhinelander, and Spike from runaway freight car by desperate chase in automobile, ditching car to prevent collision with Limited. Rescues Spike from lynching, captures ore thieves. Saves lives of Rhinelander and Storm trapped by mine cave-in, regains money stolen by Seagrue's agents. Helen accepts Storm's proposal of marriage. After daring ride, Helen uncouples freight and prevents terrible wreck."

15. Karen Horney, *New Ways in Psychoanalysis* (New York: Norton, 1939), p. 108.

16. There is no intertitle to indicate Lightning's exact line as she leaves.

17. Lewis Jacobs, *The Rise of the American Film: A Critical History* (New York: Teachers' College Press, 1969), p. 270.

18. For information on marriage and fertility rates between 1890 and 1920, see Margaret Gibbons Wilson, *The American Woman in Transition: The Urban Influence, 1870–1920* (Westport, Conn.: Greenwood, 1979), p. 174. Concerning changes in the nature of housework, see Ruth Schwartz Cowan, "The 'Industrial Revolution' in the Home: Household Technology and Social Change in the 20th Century," *Technology and Culture* 17 (1976), pp. 1–23. Reprinted in Martha M. Trescott, ed., *Dynamos and Virgins Revisited: Women and Technological Change in History* (Metuchen, N. J.: Scarecrow 1979). Information about female participation in extradomestic work can be found in United States, Bureau of the Census, *Comparative Occupation Statistics for the United States, 1870–1940,* by Alba M. Edwards (Washington, D. C.: GPO, 1943), p. 99, and Joseph A. Hill, *Women in Gainful Occupation, 1870–1920,* U.S. Census Monographs 9 (Washington, D.C.: GPO, 1929), p. 23. Both are cited in Elyce Rotella, *From Home to Office: U.S. Women at Work, 1870–1930* (Ann Arbor, Mich.: UMI Research, 1980), tables 2.2, 2.4, and 2.8.

19. Sales by department stores escalated from a zero-point in 1889 to $161 million in 1899, $676 million in 1909, and $2,588 million in 1919. See Harold Barger, *Distribution's Place in the American Economy Since 1869* (Princeton, N.J.: Princeton University Press, 1955), pp. 148–9, cited in Wilson, *American Woman in Transition,* p. 174. Concerning involvement in public entertainments, see Kathy Peiss, *Cheap Amusements: Working Women and Leisure in Turn-of-the-Century New York* (Philadelphia: Temple University Press, 1986).

20. Miles of tracks in the North Atlantic region increased from 2,952 in 1890 to 10,175 in 1902. In the United States as a whole, coverage rose 178 percent, from 8,123 to 22,589. See United States, Department of Commerce and Labor, *Street and Electric Railways,* Bureau of the Census, Special Reports (Washington, D. C.: Department of Commerce and Labor, 1903), p. 34. A table broken down by region is reproduced in Wilson, *American Woman in Transition,* p. 27.

Throughout 1895, Sunday editions of the more popular newspapers, such as the New York *World* and *Journal,* were full of articles and illustrations concerning the appropriation of the bicycle by women. These items clearly demarcate the bicycle as a node of a social debate between the New Woman, who was enjoying a new athleticism and mobility, and conservative forces, denouncing the compromise of gentility and specifically condemning the appearance of "bloomers" as a clothing for feminine outdoor activity. See, for example,

Ida Trafford Bell, "The Mission of the Bicycle for Women: Women's Fight for Liberation," *Sunday World* (18 August 1895), 33; "Around the World on a Bicycle, Nellie Bly, Jr. Makes the Most Extraordinary Journey Ever Undertaken by a Woman," *Sunday World* (20 October 1895), 29.

21. Mary Humphreys, "Women Bachelors in New York," *Scribner's* (November 1896), 635. Quoted in Wilson, *American Woman in Transition*, p. 27.

22. Barbara Welter, "The Cult of True Womanhood: 1820–1860," *American Quarterly* 18 (1966), 151–74.

23. George Burnap, *Sphere and Duties of Woman*, 5th ed. (Baltimore, Md.: 1854), p. 47; cited in Welter, "Cult of True Womanhood," p. 159.

24. Boyd Winchester, "The New Woman," *Arena* (April 1902), 367, cited in Wilson, *American Woman in Transition*, p. 3.

25. Samuel Woodworth, *The Widow's Son; or, Which Is the Traitor?* (New York: 1825), p. 64; cited in David Grimsted, *Melodrama Unveiled: American Theater and Culture, 1800–1850* (Chicago: University of Chicago Press, 1968), p. 175. Minna Thomas Antrim, "The Masculization of Girls," *Lippincott's Monthly* (1911), 564. Echoing this theme, a film reviewer in 1911 commended the depiction of "a girl who has to fight her way instead of having it prepared for her; the kind of up-to-date heroine that American audiences admire more than the clinging vine variety," Louis Reeves Harrison, "Superior Plays: 'The Reform Candidate' (Edison)," *Moving Picture World* (September 1911), 957.

26. Antrim, "Masculization of Girls," p. 565.

27. *Under the Gaslight* is supposedly the first melodrama to have used the last-minute rescue of a character from an on-coming train. The man saved declares, "Victory! Saved! Hooray! And these are the women who ain't to have a vote!" The play is anthologized in Michael Booth, ed., *Hiss the Villain: Six English and American Melodramas* (New York: Benjamin Blom, 1964). Climaxes involving the hero's rescue by the heroine were evidently a relatively common melodramatic trope. In Joseph Arthur's *Blue Jeans* (1890), the heroine smashes through a locked door to rescue the hero from an unpleasant bifurcation by a buzz saw. In Charles Blaney's *The Factory Girl* (1903), the heroine smashes through a large window to save the hero from being decapitated by some kind of industrial guillotine.

28. Dorothy Pam, "Exploitation, Independence and Solidarity: The Changing Role of American Working Women as Reflected in the Working-Girl Melodrama 1870–1910," dissertation, New York University, 1980. *Edna, The Pretty Typewriter* was written by the preeminent "Ten, Twent,' Thirt'" playwright, Owen Davis, who also created a successful stage adaptation of the first serial-queen melodrama, *What Happened to Mary*. "Ten, Twent,' Thirt'" was a colloquialism for popular sensational stage melodrama, so-called because of its inexpensive ticket prices geared toward a working-class patronage.

29. "Woman's Record during the Week," *Sunday World* (19 April 1896), 21.

30. A variety of titles headed these columns. One that is particularly interesting in its feminist sarcasm is "Frail Woman's Achievements: New and Startling Records Made by Her during the Week—Some Extraordinary Freaks and Fashions of the Season," (12 April 1896), 31.

31. A cognitive approach to the pleasure provided by such "category mistakes" may be worthwhile. The interest generated by this kind of serial may ultimately relate to the processes of human curiosity per se. The trope of the masculinized heroine may hinge on an aspect of our cognitive make-up that makes us curious about (or, in other contexts, horrified by) disruptions of our most basic schemes of cultural categorization—in this case, the scheme of gender.

32. The first quotation is from an editorial, *Chicago Republic* (28 December 1903), 6; the second is from Porter Emerson Browne, "The Mellowdrammer," *Everybody's Magazine* (September 1909), 347–54; the third is from Rollin Lynde Hartt, *The People at Play* (Boston: Houghton Mifflin, 1909), p. 166; the fourth is from Clayton Hamilton, "Melodrama, Old and New," *Bookman* (May 1911), 309–14.

33. Thomas Elsaesser, "Tales of Sound and Fury: Observations on the Family Melodrama," *Monogram* 4 (1972), 2–15. Reprinted in Christine Gledhill, ed., *Home Is Where the Heart Is: Studies in Melodrama and the Woman's Film* (London: BFI, 1987).

34. Eleanor Gates, "The Girl Who Travels Alone: an Inquiry into a Distinctly American Problem That Has Been Created by the Social Conditions in This Country Which Admit the Widest Liberty to Women," *Cosmopolitan Magazine* (December 1906), 163–72. In the next month's issue, Gates discusses similar problems of sexual harassment as they relate specifically to working women in "Making Her Way in the World," *Cosmopolitan Magazine* (January 1907), 308–15.

35. Hugo Munsterberg, "Muensterberg [sic] Vigorously Denounces Red Light Drama," *New York Times* (14 September 1913).

Yuri Tsivian

Russia, 1913: Cinema in the Cultural Landscape

But in Petersburg streets you could hear
The new century coming near
Not a date, but The Real Thing.
(Anna Akhmatova, 1913)[1]

Due to peculiarities of the Eastern cultural calender, it was not until 1913 that Russia's *fin de siècle* was ultimately over. In 1913 several things happened that could be read as signs of the new age. Serious dramatic theatre seemed once and for all to have broken down into forms of scenic *Klein-kunst*—the cabaret and vaudeville format (called "theatre of miniatures" in Russia), which looked preposterous on the Russian stage; in the streets, one could see young people with bizarre hieroglyphs painted on their faces; the whole country was scandalized by the tango; passion for cinema was reaching epidemic proportions. On top of everything, Russian Futurist poets passed all bounds in their onslaught on "public taste," becoming the number one sensation of the year.

These events (purely coincidental from the perspective of a modern art historian) made a coherent picture for the contemporary observer. To borrow the notion used in Viktor Shklovsky's writings, we are dealing with the landscape effect: although we know landscapes are formed by objects that simply happen to be there, we cannot help reading some kind of internal necessity into the way this tree, this river, and that mountain are grouped. Apparently, the effect of compositional motivation works with cultural landscapes as well. This article deals with the way cinema was inscribed into the cultural landscape of Russia through the lens of the 1913 observer.

This essay originally appeared, in both Italian and English, in *Griffithiana* 50 (May 1994). Richard Abel has modified the English text slightly for this volume. Reprinted by permission of the author and the Cineteca del Friuli, Italy, which distributes the journal through The Johns Hopkins University Press.

Shorter Plays and Longer Pictures

On the first of January, 1914, the influential conservative newspaper *Novoye vremya* [New Times] portrayed the stage life of the past year as cinematically feverish:

> People chased after novelty for novelty's sake; the main motive was curiosity; the main attraction—the rapid succession of impressions. People looked as briefly and as quickly as possible, and chased on after tomorrow. Every new season the life of the city becomes more complex and its pulse more febrile. In this connection—or is it by mere chance?—in 1913 the number of big legitimate drama theatres in Petersburg decreased, while "theatres of miniatures" multiplied impressively. . . . Here are some of them: The Liteinyi, The Troitski, The Crooked Mirror, The Bat, The Queen of Spades, etc., etc.[2]

The disintegration of legitimate theatre came as a belated Russian response to the craze for reduced forms begun in the West in the 1890s.[3] In 1908 The Bat (the famous Chauve Souris founded by Nikita Baliev, rather than the Petersburg Bat of 1913 mentioned in the above quotation) was born out of a professional club where weekly in-joke pastiches had been staged by legitimate theatre actors just for the fun of it. Half a year later The Bat was followed by the Crooked Mirror, the Petersburg theatre of parody.

The popularity of these cabaret-style intimate theatres generated an avalanche of emulations. By 1911 the Russian version of *Kleinkunst* had trickled down from elitist to mass entertainment. Aleksandr Kugel, who masterminded the splendid Crooked Mirror, grieved in an article written in 1912: "The worst happened to theatres of miniatures: they were vulgarized. The basically aristocratic idea [behind the theatre of small forms] became, literally, the playground of the rabble."[4] As to their exact number, Kugel was not sure: "These theatres proliferate like lower organisms, like amoebas, and in the place of one theatre of miniatures which dies ten new ones emerge."[5] Indeed, about 125 cabarets and miniature theatres operated in Moscow and Saint Petersburg in 1912[6]; reportedly, there were about 240 of them in Russia when the craze reached its peak in 1913.

In 1913 two kinds of "short-form theatres" (another accepted Russian term for the new artistic activity)[7] existed, each with its own stylistic strategy. The high-brow, tongue-in-cheek *cabarets artistiques* lived on middle-class curiosity about celebrities, trendy art, and the ways of bohemia. The Moscow Bat introduced a habit promptly adopted by other elitist cabarets: touring celebrities—mainly foreigners—would be invited for a soiree during which the unsuspecting guest of honour was artfully involved in semi-improvised happenings. Thus, the famous Austrian conductor Arthur Nikisch came to The Bat only to find himself conducting a local regimental brass band using a rose for a baton.[8] A trick The Bat played on Max Linder, who came to Russia for a visit in late 1913, was worthy of Linder's own best filmic gags.

The most notorious night-time cabaret of the elitist type, The Stray Dog (Saint Petersburg, 1911–1915), brought together talked-about artistic figures of the time and those interested in seeing them live.[9] In 1913 the place was frequented both by refined Ackmeist poets (Anna Akhmatova and Osip Mandelstam were among the regulars) and provocative Futurist dandies such as the top-hatted Vladimir Mayakovsky.

More trivial theatres of miniatures offered variety-format entertainment reminiscent of French Grand Guignol and vaudeville theatres in America. Here the rule was diversity and brevity—qualities that the above-cited article in *Novoye Vremya* traced, with characteristic essentialism, to the feverish tempo of the modern city.

Although, historically, the emergence of miniatures had nothing to do with the influence of cinema on theatre format, in 1913 it must have been difficult to avoid jumping to the wrong conclusion. Theatre journals accused cinema of generating the epidemic of short forms.[10] Due to similarity of formats, in the cultural landscape of the year, cinema and the short-form theatre overlapped.

Today we realize that this overlap was no more than a temporary intersection of two autonomous trajectories, something similar to astronomic eclipses, which can only be observed at certain times from certain points. In the historical trajectory of Russian theatre, the epidemic of short forms proved to be a temporary craze. In 1926 (by then the craze was already over) Aleksandr Kugel argued that the epidemic had been necessary for the renovation of nineteenth-century playwriting and performance:

> The very idea of breaking up the complicated organism of the contemporary theatre into primal elements had something valuable and, above all, historically motivated about it. Evolution is not always synonymous with complication and often deviates from the way we expect things to evolve. Instead of evenly branching on both sides of the main stream, the evolutionary process often lends to disintegration when something has grown too heavy to grow further. The mechanical growth of theatre routine impeded its real growth. We had to do something to find the new form, to compress, to condense, to break up the theatre into its primal elements. . . . The *Klein Kunst* was to take us to the *Gross Kunst* in the end.[11]

To look at it retrospectively, the short format was but a brief episode in film history as well. As it happened, 1913 was the crucial year for the passage to feature-long pictures.[12] However, this trajectory is easier to define after the event than it was for someone moving along with it. In fact, few of the contemporaries really believed in features. Rather, the accepted opinion was that long films were not "in the nature" of cinematic narrative and that the vogue for features was bound to pass. Here is a typical statement voiced in an open letter of 1913 signed by a group of worried cinema owners:

> Longer footage impedes the diversity of the programme. A film of 2,000 or 3,000 meters often takes up the entire time of the show, and this makes us eliminate scenic and scientific pictures which causes displeasure among the patrons accustomed to the diversity of impressions one expects of electric theatres.[13]

For theatre critics, too, the idea of short forms looked unmistakably cinematic. Among other things, theatres of miniatures were accused of adopting a marketing strategy unfit for live theatre.[14] A miniature show would last for about an hour and a half, each programme consisting of diverse items: a sketch, a song, a monologue, a Grand Guignol scene, a bedroom farce, a compressed version of an operetta, etc. Then the same show was repeated three or four times an evening.

This system was believed to affect acting and directing. While brevity and diversity were seen as useful for bringing in fast and flexible acting badly needed on the Russian stage ("we want a *Mädchen für Alles,* wrote the playwright Lev Vasilevski, we want actors who can act in any genre and do not need two acts to get started"),[15] the rotation was considered detrimental: no actor was believed to be able to do the same act for four runs a day without risking turning into a mechanical shadow of the cinema.[16]

Evidently, we are dealing with formal similarities misread as influence or kinship. Narrative forms, too, seemed to have become unmistakably cinematic. Directing a play for a theatre of miniatures came down to stripping it down to essentials—the process called, in Russian theatrical lingo, "rabotat' na vymarkakh" (act by blue-pencilling).[17] A programme presented by the Petersburg Theatre of Miniatures (whose name gave rise to the generic term) in November 1911 opened with the self-reflective sketch, "How Miniatures Are Made," showing two blue-pencillers [*maraly*] shortening each other's plays until nothing of the text was left over.[18]

The result was too familiar to go unnoticed. Acting by blue-pencilling was exactly what filmmakers had been doing for about a decade before the advent of short-form theatres (and what they were trying to get rid of by progressively expanding film footage). Space allowed for narrative prescribed narrative pace. This pace was particularly striking when well-known works were adopted for films or theatre of miniatures.

Narrative affinity made cinema an ideal target for parody on the miniature stage, a genre particularly favoured by The Crooked Mirror.[19] In 1911 Nikolai Yevreinov and Aleksandr Kugel included a "cinematic" version of *Government Inspector* among ironic sketches showing five different ways Gogol's celebrated comedy might look as staged by fashionable directors. The synopsis for the "film" took less than a page; the style was modelled after Max Linder's Pathé comedies; the famous epistle informing the Town Council of the inspector's arrival was shown as a huge "letter insert" covering the whole stage.[20]

In December 1913, The Crooked Mirror staged Pushkin's novel in verse, *Yevgenii Onegin*, as if adapted for Russian film. The subtle thing about this spoof (written by Boris Geyer) was the new title chosen for the assumed screen version: *Tatyana Larina*.[21] The name of the female protagonist eponymized in place of the male hero's name is a clear sign that the penchant of female audiences for Russian film melodrama and its feminine narrative perspective, first formulated for us by Miriam Hansen,[22] was evident to the 1913 observer.

Compatible formats let cinema theatres and theatres of miniatures work like two well-meshed gears. In 1911 many of the latter dismissed orchestras and began showing films between acts.[23] The osmosis was reciprocal.[24] Cinema theatres responded by engaging live actors to fill pauses between reels. "That's where all those jobless actors wind up!" exclaimed Bentovin.[25]

Thus, concidentally, the archaic "vaudeville format" into which cinema had been born in America around fifteen years earlier, was revived in Russia in the early 1910s. At times, the shift of media occurred within one and the same play. In 1911 the Petersburg Mozaika [Mosaic] (the new name given to the Liteinyi founded in 1909 in an attempt to introduce a Russian variety of Grand Guignol theatre) came up with the horror play *Submarine Shipwreck*, in which a film sequence showing a submarine sinking was followed by the harrowing scene inside the boat with live actors groaning, swearing, and praying.[26]

In 1913 cinema and theatre came so close that they seemed to be merging. Pavel Orlenev experimented with alternating screened and live scenes in Ibsen's plays performed on the legitimate stage.[27] Songs, playlets, ballet scenes, seances of hypnotism, and what not flourished in film palaces. The alliance, however, was short-lived. As films increased in footage, they needed all the space there was for their own narratives.

The separation did not pass without regret. When in 1916 some cinema owners introduced double projectors, spectators occasionally complained about the loss of diversity. Trade papers implored: "Your patrons leave exhausted, unable to ingest the ten reels which you shove into them one by one."[28] Nonetheless, the time for miniatures was over both in the history of cinema and theatre—a temporary overlap in the moving cultural landscape of 1913.

The Duel of Top Hats

We rang for room service and the year 1913 answered: it gave Planet Earth a valiant new race of people, the heroic Futurians. The Fathers (Briusov, Baby Balmont, Merezhkovsky, Tolstoy, and the rest), with napkins draped over their arms, served us another Tsushima on a platter.

> The youn-n-n-ger generation has smashed the dish; a casual kick
> sent it flying from the hands of the panicky waiter. (Velimir Khlebnikov,
> "! Futurian")[29]

For conservative observers, 1913 was the year of sensationalist
reputations. "What events can we call typical for the year that has just
passed?" reflected *Novoye vremya* on January 1, 1914, and gave this answer:

> If we were to address the question frankly it would emerge that what
> interested most people was Willy Ferrero, Max Linder, and the Futurists: a
> *Wunderkind*, a clown, and a bunch of half-wits.[30]

I am not sure about Willy Ferrero (a 7-year-old American-born
conductor touring in Europe), but Futurism and Max Linder were positively
two major peaks in the cultural landscape framed by 1913. The fame that
befell Russian Futurists was triggered by the almanac *A Slap in the Face of
Public Taste* (released in January) and maintained, throughout the rest of
the year, by a series of public debates staged with an eye for scandal. As
much as by poems and declarations, scandals were provoked by Futurists'
public behaviour and the way they dressed. The costume Vladimir Mayakovsky flaunted in 1912 turned him into an accomplished character of
Grand Guignol[31]; later he changed it for a dandyish top hat worn in an
impossible combination with a collarless yellow blouse. To add radishes in
buttonholes and bizarre miniatures painted on their faces, "a bunch of
half-wits" was the mildest thing a paper such as *Novoye vremya* could say
about Russian Futurist poets and artists.

As to Max Linder, his stardom in Russia dated back to 1910 (figure 22).
In 1913, stimulated by Linder's visit to Saint Petersburg (in late November) and
Moscow (early December), the craze grew into madness. Conscious of the effect
produced by his live appearance, Linder referred to the present visit as a reunion
with a dear family. "Zhyvoi Maks" [the incarnate Max] was followed by hordes
of worshippers; in Moscow, a crowd of students carried him all the way from
the station to the hotel.[32]

Linder's first performance was arranged as a surprise stunt perfectly
matched to the occasion. Some time past the starting hour, the manager
came out to announce that Max Linder had been delayed and might not
arrive at all. After a minute of suspense, the lights went out and a film was
shown of Max Linder making his way to the theatre by car, on horseback,
etc. Finally, the audience saw him descend from a balloon by a guide-rope
and crash straight down through a roof. At this point,

> the screen suddenly gave way to the stage, and there he was, the real Max
> Linder, sliding down a rope from the ceiling on to the stage, accompanied
> by a shower of plaster and bits of wood, wearing a grey sports coat and a
> battered version of his famous top hat.[33]

Нашъ шаржъ.

Максъ Линдеръ.

Figure 22. Max Linder caricature by Vladimir Mayakovsky (Kine-Zhurnal 23 [1913]).

As the show went on, Linder presented *Love and Tango*, a comic sketch culminating in an elaborate tango routine performed with Maria Mitchell in an unexpectedly serious manner.[34]

Why the tango? In addition to his comic talent, Linder's fame in Russia was based on the way he dressed. There Linder passed for a model dandy, "the George Bryan Brummell of city squares."[35] To crown his visit, Max had to bring something stunning, a fad fresh from Paris. Tango was a happy choice: in 1913 the dance was yet a hearsay sensation badly in need of being taught and legitimized in Russia.

In Moscow Linder was invited to The Bat (the artistic cabaret I have mentioned earlier) in which he was given a reception inspired, in all probability, by a mirror gag in one of his films. On the stage, Linder was greeted by an actor made up as Max Linder by the virtuoso make-up artist M. Faleyev of the Moscow Art Theatre. After a glass of champagne, two more Linders showed up, until finally a quintet of Maxes were singing a song in honour of the singular guest, our unique Linder.[36] This joke looks like a gentle revenge stage actors took on their confrere boosted by the age of technical reproducibility.

Max Linder's visit was frowned on by Russian Futurist poets who feared it might prompt the press to make some undesirable parallels. The very first day he arrived in Saint Petersburg from Paris the unsuspecting Linder stole a Futurist show. In his memoirs published in 1929, the Futurist poet Benedikt Livshits remembered that day with retrospective jealousy:

> On the following day after a loud public event organized by the Futurists on the stage of the Troitski theatre (Khlebnikov was there, too, standing up to take a bow each time Burliuk mentioned his name), the very same people rushed to the Zon theatre to see the King of Screen, Max Linder.[37]

Why, of all people, was Livshits jealous of Max Linder? The fact that Linder was cheered by the same people who had appeared at the Futurist event the day before was seen as a symptom of misperception. Sharing fans with a comedian implied that the fame enjoyed by Futurist poets was of the same kind as Linder's.

The fear was not without grounds: in 1913 Futurism was mainly perceived as literary slapstick. Irrespectively of Max Linder's visit, in the cultural landscape of Russia the perception of cinema and Futurist poetry converged. Sensationalism, global ambitions, slipshod performance, and above all, the notorious "pulse of the big city" were the points of convergence. The image of the cinematic text was catalysed and distilled from what readers perceived as the vagaries of Futurist poetics; similarly, cinema contributed to the image of Futurist discourse.

Here is one example out of many. In an attempt to challenge narrative time, Futurist poets experimented with *tempus reversus*. Velimir Khlebnikov's play *The World Reversed* [sic] (*Mirskontsa*, 1912) starts from the moment when the hero runs away from his own funeral and finishes with a silent scene in his pram. In 1913 a trade journal reporter alluded to Khlebnikov's play in connection with a tiny event related to the ban on public entertainments during the week of Lent.

> A company of young people, who were clearly unable to survive for a week without the cinematograph, rented a separate room in a restaurant and

invited in a pianist and a projectionist with all his equipment. . . . Someone there had the bright idea of running one of the films backwards. It turned out to be incredibly funny: dead people came to life, the hero first drowned then hurled himself out of the water, and so on. . . . Those people were just born Futurists, they were longing for the appearance of what our old futurists call "The World Reversed" [*Mirskontsa*].[38]

Whatever absurdity the critics discovered in films was immediately labelled "futuristic"; conversely, Mayakovsky's poems were criticised for being as illiterate as cinema intertitles. Ungrammatical, asyntactic, incoherent, spasmodic, senseless—these are only some of the features that Futurists and cinema were found to have in common. Here is one of such statements (from the pen of Fyodor Otsep):

> The Futurists have neither wonder, nor belief in wonders. But if such things do not exist, then long live drunken visions, nightmares, delusions. . . . It is the same in the cinematograph: instead of ecstasy, there are hallucinations; instead of pathos, there are drunken daydreams. . . . It is as if the cinematograph and Futurism intersected.[39]

Such was the scene for the moment when Max Linder came to Russia. In the eyes of the Futurists, Linder's image of a perennially well-dressed buffoon[40] threatened to epitomize the unwelcome parallel between cinema and their own literary endeavour.[41] The Futurists' painted faces and eccentric outfits were not buffoonery for buffoonery's sake. Rather, it was their tribute to famous literary dandies of the past, such as Théophile Gautier and Oscar Wilde.[42] These implications, however, were lost on a general public whose attention the Futurists had to share with Max.

On the 21st of November, 1913, Linder was invited to the bohemia-style cabaret The Stray Dog, the one in which the Petersburg cultural elite gathered for nightly happenings.[43] As a guest of honour, Linder was admitted free of charge and cheered with an improvised nonsense rhyme sung in chorus,

> Mama—kinder,
> Bravo—Linder,
> Bravo—Maks,
> Tak-s![44]

According to the memoirs published later by the Ackmeist poet Georgi Ivanov, the visit was spoiled by reciprocal misexpectations: The Stray Dog regulars were willing to be entertained while Max Linder obviously settled for an intellectual conversation.

> Linder walked in stiffly with a strained smile on his face. Having answered the cheers with a reserved bow, he bowed again and sat down, without taking off his white kid-gloves.

"Look here! Look here! He is about to do a trick!"

But Linder had no intention to perform tricks. He looked ludicrously serious, declined wine, smiled haughtily, answered curtly. His only interest was in Rembrandt's collection in The Hermitage which he discussed with an air of scholarly pedantry.[45]

According to Benedikt Livshits, Vladimir Mayakovsky was there, too, wearing his famous top hat and yellow jacket with broad black stripes. In the strenuous atmosphere of the failed evening, the co-presence of two identical top hats imbued with entirely different meanings must have been a hilarious sight. In his memoirs, Livshits referred to this encounter as a silent duel the Futurist poet fought against his cinematic *Doppelgänger* for the soul of the Petersburg public:

> The stupendous tail-coat of the man from Paris was crossed out by the stripes of Mayakovsky's home-spun jacket, and if the duel of the two top-hats, "the top-hat as such" and the Futurian top-hat, was lost by Linder, it did not happen because of the patriotism of the Russian public who, as we know, always prefer things foreign, but because the Petersburg public, surfeited on Futurist "attractions," were asking for spicier food than that served by the irresistible Max.[46]

In January 1914, when the founding father of the Italian Futurism Filippo-Tommaso Marinetti visited Russia for a series of public lectures, Russian Futurists split into two camps: those who welcomed their Western confrere, and those who rejected Marinetti or, for that matter, any artistic connection between Futurism in Italy and Futurism in Russia. In the eyes of Khlebnikov and Livshits (both of whom associated the poetry of the future with Russia's Asian—"scythian"—roots), Marinetti appeared as another European *Doppelgänger* capable of compromising the movement and obscuring its national identity. During Marinetti's first public lecture in Petersburg, Khlebnikov distributed a stack of flyers warning against "bending the noble neck of Asia under the yoke of Europe":

> The people who wish no yoke on their neck will [step aside and] quietly watch the dark deed happening, as they did in the shameful days of Verhaeren[47] and Max Linder. People of free will stepped aside. They remember the law of hospitality, but they keep their bow drawn, and their brow is wrathful. Stranger, beware of the country you came to![48]

Three Views on the Tango

For twenty years have I been doing this with my husband, and only now I learn it's called "the tango." (A joke circulating in Russia in 1913.[49])

Фигуры танца «танго».

Позиціи ногъ кавалера и дамы въ танго.

Figure 23. The tango steps demonstrated by the Moscow dancers Elsa Kryuger and Valli (Teatr i iskusstvo 21 [1914]).

Linder's dancing lesson did not go awry. Brought to Russia in autumn 1913, tangomania instantly grew into a major landmark on its cultural scene. Disturbingly libidinous, the tango arrived here flavoured by the recent scandals it caused in the West. As journals had it, Kaiser Wilhelm II of Germany declared war on the tango; the tango had been banned in England; the queen of Italy, however, was rumoured to secretly love the dance. Everywhere in Europe the tango had become a political issue (or so Russian media alleged), demarcating rightists from leftists and the progressives from the conservatives.[50] Rather than being a mere ballroom sensation, the tango craze of 1913 arrived in Russia disguised as an ideology that, in the year to come, affected theatre and cinema and coloured intellectual discourse.

Apart from instructional booklets (figure 23) with photographic records of every step (out of sixty exotically named tango steps, twelve were considered the minimum to learn), the tango was channelled into the country through films and theatres of miniatures. Kri-Kri's slapstick version of the dance, *Kri-Kri e il tango* (Cines, 1913), must have flashed across Russian screens early in the autumn; in November the "live" Max Linder appeared in the above-mentioned farce *Love and Tango,* of which the centre piece—a seriously performed choreographic turn—was packaged into Linder's usual comic routine.[51]

Theatres of miniature turned out to be the ideal venue for tango performances, given as straight dancing acts or disguised as a vaudeville skit. A Russian one-act miniature play called *The Power of the Tango* (*Vlast' tango*), chronicled the dull family of a factory owner being caught by the whirlpool of tangomania. The playlet is set in Moscow and gives the time of action as the beginning of winter 1913.[52] Prophesied by a mysterious "T" printed on a scrap of a newspaper, the craze is triggered as an American tango dancer named Muza Grekson arrives. The whole thing ends by everybody dancing tango, including the conservative merchant and a half-paralysed grandmother.

Performed on a variety stage or in a film palace between reels, a turn of tango (with a lecturer announcing: "El Corte," "El Paseo," "The Scissors," "Media Luna") counted as a self-sufficient act. The beautiful Elza Kryuger (remembered by the Pordenone audience as the bad girl in Yevgenii Bauer's *Silent Witnesses* [1914]) was known for her superb tango performance in Artsybusheva's Theatre of Miniatures.[53] Occasionally, one could see such acts registered on film. In February 1914, The Russian Gold Series released *The Tango* directed by Iakov Protazanov—a five-minute-long piece of choreography performed by Potopchina and Kuzhietsov. Evidently, movie house instrumentalists were expected to know the music.

What made the tango so magnetic? During 1913–1914 this question had been raised more than once. Apart from various press discussions, two public sessions (called *disputy*—open debates—a widespread form of intellectual activity in Russia) were held in Saint Petersburg and Moscow with the participation of renowned literati and theatre figures.[54] The tone for the Moscow debate was set by Mikhail Bonch-Tomashevski (a noted theatre person, later a film director) who chaired the meeting and delivered a keynote address soon to be published as a separate volume called *The Book about The Tango: Art and Sexuality.*

Bonch-Tomashevski's speech touched on two points: what makes the tango so erotic; does the tango herald the new style of the twentieth century? To set off what he sees as an apparent paradox of the tango, Bonch-Tomashevski starts by contrasting it to other dances deemed dangerously immodest, primarily the French can-can and Isadora Duncan's pseudo-Hellenic ecstasy. Part and parcel of the playful nineteenth century, "the old good can-can" excited the viewer by means of whirling tempo and effusive gesture, whereas the spell of the tango is worked up by slow, almost hypnotic steps: "simple movements, smooth and reserved, punctuated by tip-toe halts—and nothing else."[55]

As to Isadora Duncan's barefoot dancing, which found its second home on Russian variety stages, its provocativeness (or so Bonch-Tomashevski's line of reasoning goes) is largely due to Duncan's semitransparent Greek tunic.[56] To be sure, Duncan's free-floating movements evoke our urban nostalgia for Hellenism—but, apart from that, what counterpart does her pastoral prophesy find in the iron-clad twentieth-century city? The modern man is defensive, Bonch-Tomashevski argues; because we know our bodies are far from the Hellenic ideal, we overdress rather than expose them to fresh kisses of the wind:

The age of secret emotions and hidden faces, the twentieth century belongs to the man with a mask. That is why, however hard we try, we are lost to happy and naive dances of the Hellenes. . . . [Our dance], the tango, requires an impeccable tail-coat for the man and a closely fit dress for his snake-like partner. . . . The tango dancer reminds one of a tightly stretched bow-string, but the arrows of ecstasy that he casts are invisible. Constrained by its mournful rhythm, the ecstasy of the tango is like fire under the ice.[57]

At this point Bonch-Tomashevski evokes the name of Sigmund Freud, a rather unexpected reference to be made in Russia in the 1910s, even in a lecture subtitled *Art and Sexuality*.[58] The tango, Bonch-Tomashevski argues, is a perfect icon of the modern age because it conveys the idea of suppressed sexuality:

The ultimate message of the new dance is attuned to modern psychology. The tango dancer is a symbol of subterranean rumblings heard beneath the surface of everyday life. But the whole point about the spell of tango is that the crust will never yield, the emotion will never reveal itself through an unruly gesture or indecent movement.[59]

This struggle of outer pressure and repressed desire, insists Bonch-Tomashevski in the forthright manner anticipating so many Freudian readings to come, is expressed in the way the tango minimizes body contact:

The tango requires motionless faces and utmost immobility of bodies. The tango is a silent scene. Not a single muscle will stir on the face of a sophisticated dancer; chastely, his gloved palm touches hers, chastely, their legs evade crossing; and only their avid eyes never lose the eyes of the partner. . . . Yes, the tango is sexual. Imperceptible motions are saturated with the electric current of feeling. . . . The tango lends its rigid mould to the sexuality of our age; and after many years this dance will serve as an evidence of the way we felt and loved in the first half of the twentieth century.[60]

Bonch-Tomashevski's psychology of tango caused notable response.[61] A most remarkable criticism came from Petersburg, from the pen of Aleksandr Kugel whom I mentioned earlier in connection with the theatre of parody, The Crooked Mirror.[62] Yes, the tango is all about sexuality, Kugel argues, and it does serve as an icon of the new century, but for different reasons than those given by Bonch-Tomashevski. Yes, the tango and the French can-can are different, but not because they manifest two different forms of sexuality. What has the can-can to do with sexuality? We admire the can-can because it is indecent, as we love Paul de Kock for his obscene stories, which we never expect to be erotic:

When the can-can dancer throws up her bent knee revealing the *dessous*, it is as if she said to us: "look how funny it is." It is buffoonery, this is *drôle*, but it is neither *suggestif* nor *troublant*. We feel nothing of the kind the great [dressmaker Charles Frederick] Worth wanted us to feel at the sight of the *dessous*.[63]

Rather than sharing Bonch-Tomashevski's idea of the suppressed desire, Kugel stresses the air of reticence protecting what he calls "the tragic sexuality of the tango." Sex is mystery, Kugel argues, and with the mystery gone, sexuality disappears. Unlike the can-can, the matchish, and other rollicking dances, the slow tango excites because it never tells the whole story. Its slowness (Kugel proceeds) is like the slow narrative of Paul Bourget's novels in which a simple encounter, manifestly sexual from the very first minute, is nevertheless presented in tantalizing, painfully slow details.

> The tango is serious, the tango is tragic—this is what Bonch-Tomashevski fails to notice, and what I believe to be the most curious thing about the dance. The tango is never performed *aus reiner Tanzlust*. . . . It tells the sad story of desire, with its painful joys and sweet torments. The tango is a dance of the neurasthenic Sex. Where are you, animal spirits of bacchanalia? The tango has no spark of youth, as there is no youth in this century. As clearly as we conceive a young person absorbed in lively cotillion, the ideal tango couple, in my mind's eye, is composed of a man about forty and a woman of thirty to thirty-five years old. The tango tells the story of experience, after-taste, resentment; it tells us about the fatality of sexual drive. The tango has no smile. The smile is banished. A smile would ruin the very character of the tango, the dance manifesting the grave submission to necessity, to the solemn rhythm of cultural rites . . . [64]

As the two views cited above indicate, the tango was boosted as an icon of the new age; because of this claim, and also because this "dance of tragic sexuality" was, as we can see now, a swan song of the *fin-de-siècle* sensibility rather than the symbol of the future, the tango presented a very likely target for Futurist attacks. An episode related to Filippo-Tommaso Marinetti's visit to Russia gives an idea of this third view on the tango. As Benedikt Livshits' book of memoirs reports, invited to the Petersburg Stray Dog cabaret (the first week of February 1914) Marinetti did his best to torpedo the dance:

> As soon as someone happened to approach the piano and take a chord or two of the tango melody (a must of the season), Marinetti would stir and break into thundering abuse, probably quoting some scathing phrases from his manifesto *Down with the Tango and Perceval!* published ten days before he came to Russia. "To possess a woman does not mean rubbing

against her, it means penetrating her body!" he shouted ferociously. Then, addressing a petrified couple having just taken a tango position: "Putting a knee between her thighs? What innocence! What will your other knee do?" Stricken by Marinetti's aphorisms, even the most inveterate tangoers froze to their chairs.[65]

Cinema in the Landscape of Culture

In our search for causality in film history we sometimes overlook the role of random combinations. Strictly speaking, it was by mere chance that the cinema boom, the tango craze, the Futurist *Sturm und Drang*, and the vogue for cabaret-format theatres came together to form the cultural landscape of Russia in 1913. But, since cultural history deals with mindscapes rather than landscapes, no strict boundary can be carved between the casual and the causal. Not only do coeval events correlate in the mind of the contemporary observer, but they also interact and interbreed in the "real" space of culture.

This is all the more true in regards to the inclusive medium of cinema. For example, when the suicidal hero of *Child of the Big City* (1914) puts a pistol to his head, Yevgenii Bauer cuts away to a laborious tango routine, a three-shot sequence that he drags out for almost two minutes, until the suspense is completely gone. Inept by narrative standards, this cut makes more sense in the context of "the tragic ritual of sex" or whatever other overtones the tango may have evoked in the contemporary viewer.

In fact, one may argue that the effect of the tango culture on the Russian film was even more pervasive. The idea occurred to me as I read Barry Salt's description of Asta Nielsen's acting: "Her movements and poses, which owe a lot to the stage dancing (though not ballet) of the period, combined with an occasional well-placed 'thinks' look towards the camera, formed a powerful instrument of expression in films made by Urban Gad from *Afgrunden* (1910) onwards."[66] Indeed, the style (and also the story) of Gad's film originates from the *apache* dance we find Asta Nielsen and her circus boyfriend performing in a music-hall sequence of *Afgrunden*. Salt's insightful remark (coming from a former professional dancer) reminds us of the transparency of intracultural boundaries in so far as the genesis of film style is concerned. Protean by definition, film form readily lends itself to the underlying structure of represented events. Thus, in a rather ingenious attempt (for a film of 1913) to mimic the POV of the dancer in *Kri-kri e il tango*, its Cines cameraman used a "merry-go-round pan" shot with the camera and two actors mounted on a kind of rotating platform so that the dancing crowd spins round while the main couple, slightly rocking, is kept permanently in frame (MCU). Although the spinning movement (used in the Kri-Kri film to emphasize the vertiginous whirl of tangomania) is more characteristic of the waltz rather than the tango, the important thing here is that the choice of filmic style is cued by a dance.

Speaking of the Russian film style, I have the impression that the tango played a larger part in its formation than occasional dancing inserts may lead us to conclude. First tested in Vladimir Gardin's and Iakov Protazanov's film *The Keys to Happiness* (which proved to be the greatest hit of 1913; no extant prints are known), its pause-pause-pause technique of acting (also called "the braking school") was originally conceived as a cinematic counterpart of Stanislavsky's method of acting on stage.[67] During the following year, this acting technique evolved into a specific melancholy mood particularly pervading Yevgenii Bauer films. Exotic as they may seem to the distant observer, Bauer's unsmiling characters, each with some past tragedy inscribed in the way they move and pause, looked perfectly in place on the cultural scene dominated by the metronome of the tango.

In November 1913, a film was made that can be seen as an ironic snapshot of the cultural landscape of the year. Conceived and performed by a group of Futurists calling themselves The Donkey's Tail, the film *Drama in the Futurist Cabaret No. 13* (no extant prints known) was, to believe the leading Futurist figure David Burliuk (who may have been one of those involved in the production), "a drastic parody of the cinematic Grand Guignol, a widespread genre in those years."[68] Set in a fictional *cabaret artistique*, the *Drama* was introduced by an expository intertitle: "The hour thirteen has struck. The Futurists are gathering for a party."[69] A Futurist poet is seen waving a sheet of paper as he recites a poem not a sound of which, of course, reaches the cinema audience; in addition, while reading the poem, the poet keeps turning his backside to the viewers.

I presume this scene was supposed to illustrate the denial of sense and sound—a cornerstone thesis of the Futurist's poetic doctrine, originally devised to motivate Futurist's "hand-written books" of poetry [*samorunnye knigi*]. According to Khlebnikov's manifesto "The Written Character As It Is" (1913), the new poetry prioritizes the visual substance of speech [*zryava*] over its "sonic skin" [*slukhava*].[70] Silent film must have looked an ideal medium to illustrate the concept of soundless poetry; on top of everything, when the sheet of paper is finally shown on a CU insert, the viewer sees zig-zags and letters scattered about in disorder. This verse is dedicated to the "rayonist" painter [*luchist*] Natalya Goncharova, the acknowledged leader of The Donkey Tail.

The next scene is called "The Futurist Tango," a solo (!) performance by the danceuse Elster (dressed in a white costume slit to the waist), now down on her knees and letting her head drop to the floor, now

Figure 24. Examples of body painting drawn by Mikhail Larionov for the Futurist manifesto "Why We Paint on Our Faces": left to right, left cheek, right cheek, breast (Argus 12 [1913]).

straightening up and throwing out her legs. As she completes the dance, Elster gets down on her knees before Goncharova and kisses her foot.

The film's climax is an *apache* dance (rather reminiscent of Asta Nielsen's in *Afgrunden*) performed on a table by a couple armed with crooked daggers. This is the "Futuredance of Death" during which one partner must kill the other, chosen by drawing lots. Eventually, the woman dancer is killed and, bare-breasted, is taken out into the cold. Violating the rite announced by an intertitle "A Futurefuneral," the killer kisses his victim before throwing her corpse into the snow and is exiled from Futurism on the grounds of sentimentality. The exile kills himself at the outer door of the cabaret, whereupon, in a scene suspiciously similar to the closing sequence of Yevgenii Bauer's *Child of the Big City* made some five months later, one by one the rest of the Futurists indifferently step over the corpse of the transgressor.

Masterminded by Natalya Goncharova and the cofounder of "rayonnism," Mikhail Larionov, the Futurist movie was marked by a patent gimmick to become much wider known than was the film itself. Its opening scene showed the Futurists busy painting on each others' faces, with Goncharova baring her breasts to be painted on, too. Originally devised for *Drama in the Futurist Cabaret No. 13*, the practice of painting on faces outgrew the film and turned into a trademark by which the Futurists were recognized at public gatherings and in the streets. This habit became so notorious that Mikhail Larionov and Ilya Zdanevich felt they had to theorize it, which they did in December 1913, in a manifesto called "Why we paint on our faces" (figure 24). Basically, the statement comes down to two points. First, painting on faces means art intruding into life: "We link contemplation with action, and throw ourselves into the crowd."[71] This explains why Futurist face paintings looked like hieroglyphs composed of shop signs, house numbers, and notation in music.

Secondly—and this is the point where traces of the cinematic origin of the practice can be discerned—the manifesto extols body painting as painting on the *moving* base. Painting on live substance heralds the new quality of transience in art, its accord with time rather than space. That is why face-painting is radically different from tattooing:

> The tattoo does not interest us. The tattoo is made once and stays forever. Our faces stay painted for an hour, and as our emotions change, we change paintings on our faces. [It is similar to] the way a picture devours [another] picture, [to] the way shop windows—our faces—flash past and intersect each other when seen through the window of a rushing car. . . . Our face is the screech of a street-car giving a warning to a hasty passer-by, our face is the tipsy sound of the great tango.[72]

An insignificant detail, an aside of film history, the practice of face-painting turned into a major element in the history of Futurism. But can we always tell significant things from less significant ones? Taken separately, Futurism, the cabaret, and the tango are but insignificant episodes in the history of literature, theatre and music; taken together, they form an inimitable cultural amalgam of 1913—the stuff Russian films were made of.

NOTES

1. Anna Akhmatova, *Beg Vremeni, Poems, 1909–1963* (Minsk, 1983), p. 174.

2. *Novoe vremya* [New times] 1:14 (January 1914), 14.

3. On the emergence of Russian "theatres of miniatures," see Laurence Senelick's excellent "Boris Geyer and Cabaretic Playwriting," in Robert Russell and Andrew Barratt, eds., *Russian Theatre in the Age of Modernism* (New York: St. Martin's Press, 1990), pp. 33–37. See also Lyudmila Tikhvinskaya, "Russkoye kabare," *Moskovskij Nabliudatel'* [The Moscow observer] 9 (1992), 35–41.

4. Homo Novus [A. Kugel], "Zametki" [Notes], *Teatr i iskusstvo* [Theatre and art] 24 (1912), 491.

5. Ibid., p. 489.

6. Tikhvinskaya, "Russkoye kabare," p. 35. The article misdates the Petersburg Bat and The Queen of Spades as founded in 1914.

7. Laurence Senelick traces the name back to the German *Kleinkunst* meaning minor art. Senelick, "Boris Guyer," p. 36.

8. Yevgenii Khokhlov, "The Next Number in Our Programme . . ." (R. Yangirov's publication), *Moskovskij Nabliudatel* [The Moscow observer] 9 (1992), 53.

9. For information on The Stray Dog cabaret, see A. E. Parnis and R. D. Timenchik, "Programmy 'Brodyachei sobaki'" ["The Programmes of the 'Stray Dog'"], *Pamyatniki kul'tury: Novye otkrytiva* [Cultural texts: New discoveries] (Leningrad, 1985), pp. 160–257; John E. Bowlt, "An Eventful Interior: Some Thoughts on the Russian and Soviet Cabaret," in Stephen C. Foster, ed., *"Event" Art and Art Events* (Ann Arbor/London: University of Michigan Press, 1988), pp. 87–97.

10. Impressionist [V. Bentovin], "Samooborona" [Self-defense]. *Teatr i iskusstvo* [Theatre and art] 40 (1911), 740.

11. A. Kugel, *Listya s Dereva* [Leaves of a tree] (Leningrad, 1926), p. 196.

12. See Ben Brewster, *"Traffic in Souls:* An Experiment in Feature-Length Narrative Construction," *Cinema Journal* 31:1 (Fall 1991), 37–57.

13. *Vestnik kinematografii* [Cinema herald] 17 (1913), 19.

14. Impressionist [V. Bentovin], "Samooborona," p. 739; Kugel', "Zametki," p. 490.

15. L. Vasilevski, "Teatry miniatyur i kinematograf" [Theatres of miniatures and cinema]. *Birzhevye Vedomosti* [Stock market herald] 13231 (4 November 1912).

16. Ibid.

17. L. Nikulin, "Letnee delo" [Summer business], *Teatral'naya gazeta* [Theatre gazette] 24 (1915), 7.

18. "Khronika" [Daily events]. *Teatr i iskusstvo* [Theatre and art] 48 (1911), 928.

19. The Crooked Mirror was in the habit of putting on parodies of the "cinematograph," mimicking paraphernalia of a cinema performance by using a droning "reader," jerky movements, flickering illumination, etc. See "Krivoe zerkalo" [The Crooked mirror], *Teatr i iskusstvo* [Theatre and art] 7 (1911), 148. For information on these parodies see Senelick, "Boris Geyer," pp. 45, 53.

20. Nikolai Yevreinov, *Dramaticheskiye Sochineniya* [Dramatic Works] Vol. III (Petrograd, 1923) [Plays for the Crooked mirror], p. 16.

21. Senelick, "Boris Geyer," p. 53.

22. Miriam Hansen, "Deadly Scenarios: Narrative Perspective and Sexual Politics in Pre-Revolutionary Russian Film," *Cinefocus* 2:2 (spring 1992), 10–19. The article was written in 1988 and published in German in 1990.

23. Impressionist, "Samooborona," p. 739.

24. In my use of the term *reciprocal osmoses* as applied to culture, I follow Robert Schmutsler's study *Art Nouveau* (New York: Abrams, 1962), p. 11.

25. Impressionist, "Samooborona," p. 739.

26. Ibid., p. 790.

27. On the more detailed history of this genre and on parallel experiments in Western cinema, see Yuri Tsivian, "Early Russian Cinema: Some Observations," in R. Taylor and I. Christie, eds., *Inside the Film Factory: New Approaches to Russian and Soviet Cinema* (London, New York, 1991), pp. 24–30.

28. Open letter addressed to the exhibitors of large cinema theatres in Moscow signed by a (assumed) spectator (*Proektor* [Projector] 3 [1916], 5–6).

29. Ronald Vroon, ed., *Collected Works of Velimir Khlebnikov*, vol. 1 (Cambridge, Mass./London: Harvard University Press, 1988), p. 260.

30. *Novoe vremya* [New times] 1:14 (January 1914), 14.

31. Benedikt Livshits, *Poluturaglazyi strelets* [One-and-a-half-eyed Archer] (Moscow, 1991, first published in 1929), pp. 101–2.

32. V. Doroshevich, "Max Linder," *Russkoye Slovo* [The Russian Word], 283 (8 December 1913), 5. For a photograph of the march see *Rampa i zhizn'* [Footlights and life] 49 (1913), 14.

33. Agasfer [A. Zinger], "Maks Linder v Peterburge," [Max Linder in St. Petersburg], *Kino-kur'er* [The Cinema Courier] 1 (1913), 15. According to M. Malthête-Méliès, Georges Méliès staged a similar act in 1905 (M. Malthête-Méliès, *Méliès l'enchanteur* [Paris: Hachette, 1973], pp. 398–9. For more information see Yuri Tsivian, "Early Russian Cinema," pp. 24–26.

34. Agasfer "Maks Linder v Peterburge,"; my spelling of the name of Linder's partner is based on reverse transliteration from Russian (for her photograph see *Ogonek* [Small light] 98 [1 December 1913], 11).

35. Livshits, *Poluturaglazyi strelets*, p. 139.

36. Khokhlov, "The Next Number," p. 53.

37. Livshits, *Poluturaglazyi strelets*, p. 139. The English translation of this book published in the United States in 1977 was not available to me at the moment of writing this article. Livshits' memoirs were twice published in Italian in 1968 and 1989.

38. Mavich [M. Vavich?], "Postnye temy" [Lenten themes], *Cine-fono* 1 (1914), 23–24.

39. F. M. "Tri kinematografa," *Cine-fono* 11 (1914), 22.

40. P. Friel, "The First Gentleman of Comedy," *Cinefocus* 1:1 (1990), 8–11.

41. This, in fact, did not happen on the scale it could have. Only occasional parallels were drawn between Linder and the Futurists in articles dealing with Linder's visit (e.g., a cartoon portraying Linder as "The Victor of the Universe" in a mocking reference to Khlebnikov's self-appointed title "The Chairman of the Globe," see *Rampa i zhizn'* [Footlights and life] 49 (1913), 14).

42. Yu. B. Demidenko, "Kostyum i stil' zhizni: Obraz russkogo khudozhnika nachala XX veka" [Costume and the style of life: Image of the Russian artist in the beginning of the 20th century], *Panorama iskusstv* [Panorama of arts], vol. 13 (Moscow, 1990), pp. 76–77.

43. For more information on this event see Parnis and Timenchik, "Programmy 'Brodyachei sobaki,'" pp. 215–6.

44. G. Ivanov, "Marinetti i Linder" [Marinetti and Linder], *Segodnia* [To-day] 95 (5 April 1931), 5. "Tak-s" in Russian is an interjection expressing puzzled reserve.

45. Ibid.

46. Livshits, *Poluturaglazyi strelets*, pp. 139–40.

47. The Belgian symbolist poet Emile Verhaeren visited Russia shortly before Linder.

48. V. Khlebnikov, *Sobranie proizvedenij v 5 tomakh* [Collected works in 5 volumes] vol. 5, (Leningrad, 1933), p. 252.

49. For this epigraph I am indebted to Grigori Zaslavski who told me the joke.

50. "Vse tantsuyut tango" [Everybody dance the tango], *Argus* 12 (1913), pp. 112–3. I found no records of the reaction of the Russian court.

51. I wonder if this was not a live version of a Max Linder film. Here is the story: surprised by the husband in a lady's room, Max who pretends to be her hair-dresser styles the lady's hair and shaves her husband. In passing, he swallows a live canary bird, topples a piano, hides in a chest to miraculously reappear in the viewing hall of the theatre (*Kine-Zhurnal* 23 [1913], 30).

52. P. Yaron and V. Delli, *Vlast' tango* [The Power of the Tango] (Moscow, 1914). The cover gives December 3 as the date the playlet had passed Theatre Censorship Board; thus, November is likely to have been the first month of the tango craze.

53. M. M. Bonch-Tomashevski's *The Book about the Tango: Art and Sexuality* (Moscow, 1914) was illustrated with a series of photographs showing Kryuger and Valli demonstrating the tango steps.

54. I am not sure about the exact date of the Petersburg debate; the Moscow debate took place on February 6 (Russian-style calendar), 1914.

55. Bonch-Tomashevski, *Book about the Tango*, pp. 24, 29.

56. On Isadora Duncan's reception in Russia, see Laura Engelstein, *The Keys to Happiness: Sex and the Search for Modernity in Fin-de-Siecle Russia* (Ithaca and London: Cornell University Press, 1992), pp. 414–20.

57. Bonch-Tomashevski, *Book about the Tango*, pp. 21, 27.

58. Freud's works began to be translated into Russian in 1911 but were not widely discussed outside of professional circles (Engelstein, *Keys to Happiness*, p. 132).

59. Bonch-Tomashevski, *Book about the Tango*, pp. 27, 33.

60. Ibid., pp. 27, 31, 41.

61. Press response to the Moscow discussion is briefly outlined in Bonch-Tomashevski's preface to his book, *Book about the Tango*, pp. 5–6.

62. Homo Novus [Aleksandr Kugel], "Zametki" [Notes], *Teatr i iskusstvo* [Theatre and art], 21 (1914), 466–9.

63. Ibid., p. 468.

64. Ibid., p. 469.

65. Livshits, *Poluturaglazyi strelets*, p. 179.

66. Barry Salt, *Film Style and Technology: History and Analysis* (London: Starword, 1983), p. 120.

67. See Sergei Volkonski's 1928 analysis of Russian acting quoted in Yuri Tsivian, "Cutting and Framing in Bauer's and Kuleshov's Films," *KINtop 1: Jahrbuch zur Erforschung des Frühen Films* (Frankfurt, 1992), p. 111.

68. "Kinematograf v mojei zhizni," [Cinema in my life] *Russkij golos* [The Russian Voice] [New-York] (3 July 1938).

69. Several reviews published in January 1914 (the month of release) served as a basis for plot reconstruction. The most reliable critical reconstruction was published in Estonian by the late Rein Kruus (to whom I am indebted for the picture showing a scene of the film); for the present article I am using Semen Ginsburg's summary (see his *Kinematografiia dorevoliutsionnoi Rossii* [Cinema of the pre-revolutionary Russia], [Moscow, 1963], p. 233) in Jerry Heil's translation (J. Heil, "Russian Futurism and the Cinema: Majakovskij's Film Work of 1913," in *Russian Literature*, vol. XIX-II [1986], pp. 178–9).

70. Here I am quoting the terms used by Aleksei Kruchenykh and Velimir Khlebnikov in "Bukva kak bukva" [The letter as the letter], a draft version of "The Written Character As It Is" [Bukva kak takovaya] (Khlebnikov, *Sobranie proizvedenij v 5 tomakh*, p. 248).

71. Mikhail Larionov and Ilya Zdanevich, *Pochemu my rask-rashivaemsya* [Why we paint on our faces], *Argus* 12 (1913), 116.

72. Ibid., p. 118. In the original text the word that I read as *tango* is spelt as *bango*, which makes no sense unless we consider it a misprint or a Futurist neologism (a less likely hypothesis since there are no other such games in this manifesto).

Intertextuality and
Reception in Silent Cinema

William Uricchio and Roberta E. Pearson[1]

Dante's Inferno and Caesar's Ghost: Intertextuality and Conditions of Reception in Early American Cinema

Introduction

The past decade has seen an increasing interest in audience reception, but scholars have concentrated their efforts on contemporary viewers/readers. These reception studies, having direct access to real readers, can encompass a potentially infinite array of data. Reception, then, remains problematic primarily at a theoretical level, with theory delimiting the evidence base. Fewer scholars have as yet taken up the daunting challenge of historical reception studies, which requires dealing with living subjects' memories of initial reception or speculating about the reception of long-silent subjects. In both cases, the restricted evidence base presents immense theoretical complexities.

In this paper, we wish to discuss the conditions of reception for two films made by the Vitagraph Company in 1908, *Francesca di Rimini* and *Julius Caesar*. Vitagraph's prominence among American film producers would have ensured that these films were widely distributed and widely seen. Vitagraph, one of the three most important of pre-Hollywood American film studios, exceeded its closest rivals, the Edison and Biograph Companies, in both film production and scale of operation.[2] An energetic and innovative publicity department helped the studio maintain its high public profile, advertising directly to film distributors and exhibitors through its in-house organ and constantly planting stories in the trade press. In an era when studio "brand" loyalty seems to have been a major determinant of film attendance, the Vitagraph name on a film most probably ensured good audience turnout.

From *Journal of Communication Inquiry* 14:2 (1990). Reprinted by permission of the authors and the School of Journalism and Mass Communication, University of Iowa.

While Vitagraph's status permits us to conclude that both *Francesca di Rimini* and *Julius Caesar* would have potentially attracted significant numbers of viewers, we have practically no evidence as to how these audiences may have "made sense" of the films. Film scholars have tended to discuss historical reception primarily through industry discourse, that is, through examining production records, publicity, and the trade press. While this usefully illuminates the producers' and industry's perceptions of audience reception and while conditions of production obviously form an important component of conditions of reception, they do not constitute the full picture. Yet going beyond producer discourse in an attempt to locate historical readers within their conditions of reception presents difficulties.

Aside from randomly preserved and often class-restricted individual utterances in letters and diaries, most available evidence both originated from and was maintained by institutional sources, which are again class-specific. Thus, while one might easily locate reviews of a nineteenth-century Shakespearean production, one cannot so easily locate individuals' reactions to this production, determine who attended or discover where the play was publicized. Greater difficulties face those interested in early twentieth-century Shakespeare films, which had a more marginalized cultural position. How, then, can one adduce broader conditions of reception, given the class-bound inflection of the nature and availability of the surviving evidence? While we are ourselves confined to institutional sources, we have nonetheless attempted to expand the evidence base to include little-used sources such as postcards, advertising, statuary, paintings and other ephemera, many of which are visual in nature. The emphasis on visual evidence, of course, seems logical, given that we are working with primarily visual texts, but perhaps more important, some of this evidence had broader cultural circulation than more traditional nonvisual sources.

Drawing on new information sources does not solve our theoretical difficulties, for we must still determine the relationship among our films (the texts), the textually related evidence (the intertexts), and broader social/cultural factors (the context), in order to adduce conditions of reception. We approach this relationship through dialectically interacting text, intertext, and context. Intertextuality serves as the activating element, linking text and context, so that, as Bennett and Woollacott point out, text, intertext and context should not be seen as separate entities.

> The process of reading is not one in which the reader and the text meet as abstractions but one in which the inter-textually organized reader meets the inter-textually organized text. The exchange is . . . 'muddied' by the cultural debris which attach to both texts and readers in the determinate conditions which regulate the specific forms of their encounter.[3]

Intertextuality constitutes an essential component of the conditions of reception. For us, intertextuality ranges from a narrow construction of directly related textual references, to a fuller construction, which includes more ephemeral, less directly related and locatable, cultural expressions. Intertextuality thus embraces everything from textual sources such as plays and paintings to culturally pervasive artifacts such as advertising and textbooks.

The interaction of textual signifying practices in conjunction with the relevant intertextual frames allows access to a plurality of interpretive stances all of which "make sense" of the text. The construction of such interpretive stances, which we term *reading positions,* necessitates discovering the cultural artifacts that people would have encountered in their daily lives and that consequently would have conditioned their viewing of specific films. What knowledge might potential viewers have brought with them to the nickelodeon? How might different intertexts have produced various readings of the same text?

The interaction of text and intertext occurs within a cultural context, the delineation of which provides essential evidence about the conditions of reception. Context embraces everything from the specifics of theatre architecture, to the economics of the film industry, to literacy rates and immigration policies. Clearly, in a paper of this length, we cannot address any of these factors in great depth and hence will focus on situating texts in a cultural context through considering the circulation of relevant intertexts among different social formations. In other words, which viewers may have been exposed to which intertexts?

Historical happenstance introduces such vagaries into the array of evidence available for particular texts that, rather than focus on one film and deal with inevitable lacunae, we have, for heuristic purposes, chosen two films that respectively best illuminate two different functionings of intertextuality. We use our two films, *Francesca di Rimini* and *Julius Caesar,* to explore the text/intertext/context interaction, focusing on text/intertext with the former and intertext/context with the latter.[4] With *Francesca,* we look closely at textual signifying practices and then present an array of intertexts that may have given rise to different reading positions for the film. With *Julius Caesar,* we try to determine what social formations might have been exposed to which intertexts and what the consequences may have been for the conditions of reception.

Significant differences between our two films make them an ideal complementary pair for our purposes. The textual bases crucially distinguish these films from each other. The Vitagraph *Francesca di Rimini* ultimately derives from a short passage in Canto V of Dante's *Divine Comedy,* subsequently retold in elaborated versions by numerous authors. Although not all editions of *Julius Caesar* are precisely alike, all circulate as "Shakespeare's *Julius Caesar*" and retain a certain uniformity, whereas the versions of the *Francesca* story circulate under the names of their various authors (Boccaccio, Leigh Hunt, George Boker, etc.) and exhibit great disparities of plot, characterization, etc. *Francesca* thus encourages a level of interrogation not necessary with *Julius Caesar*, since viewers may have had much wider ranging intertextual frames available to make sense of the text. This renders the *Francesca* text/intertext interaction in a sense more interesting than that of *Julius Caesar*.

Another crucial difference between the two films relates to the greater historical centrality of Caesar, as well as the greater centrality of Shakespeare in an English-speaking country, Shakespeare's *Julius Caesar* permeated late nineteenth- and early twentieth-century U.S. culture to a greater degree than *Francesca di Rimini* and Dante. Whereas Dante intertexts tended to circulate within fairly restricted social formations, Shakespearean intertexts penetrated into most segments of late nineteenth- and early twentieth-century American society. This greater cultural permeation renders the intertext/context interaction more interesting for *Julius Caesar* than for *Francesca di Rimini*.

Thus, this essay does *not* seek to compare and contrast *Francesca di Rimini* and *Julius Caesar* with regard to the same criteria. Rather, the disparities between the two permit us to explore two different uses of intertextual evidence to speculate about historical reception in cases in which direct markers of reception do not exist.

Francesca di Rimini

Vitagraph's *Francesca di Rimini* concerns a triangle among the hunchbacked Lanciotto, Lord of Rimini, his bride, Francesca, and his handsome brother, Paolo. Paolo serves as his brother's emissary to Francesca, who gives Paolo a locket for Lanciotto but does not see her betrothed until the wedding day. Francesca, who immediately fell in love with Paolo, recoils in horror from her finance's deformity but goes through with the ceremony. After the marriage, Lanciotto, called to the wars, leaves Francesca in Paolo's protection. The two begin a love affair, spied on by Pepe, the jester, who throughout the film has been providing a running gestural commentary on the action. Pepe brings the news to Lanciotto, who kills him in a rage. Returning home, Lanciotto discovers the truth for himself and kills Francesca and Paolo. The film ends with Lanciotto committing suicide over the lovers' bodies.

The film consists of fifteen shots.[5] Thirteen of these are in the long-shot tableau style typical of the period, while two are insert closeups of the locket. These shots appear to be motivated by Lanciotto's glance, although they do not resemble the point of view structure of the classical Hollywood cinema. The action takes place on painted theatrical sets, as well as exterior locations, both typical of the period, although the costuming and sets seem relatively elaborate.

Although *Francesca di Rimini* may, to contemporary observers, seem an obscure choice for a film, the nineteenth century, in fact, produced numerous literary and dramatic recountings of the story. In 1867, *Wilke's Spirit of the Times: The American Gentleman's Magazine* reviewed a French theatrical production of the tale, assuming widespread reader acquaintance with the eponymous heroine. " . . . of all of Dante's heroines the one most loved; of all of Dante's verses those most familiar to the world. If the English reader knows nothing else of the great Italian master, he is at least conversant with the story of Francesca" (28 September 1867).

The four theatrical versions of Francesca (by George Boker, Gabriele d'Annunzio, Marion Crawford, and Stephen Phillips), produced in 1901–1902 and all heavily reviewed in the United States, attest to the story's cultural pervasiveness. The high degree of congruence between the Boker play and the Vitagraph film points to the Vitagraph producers' familiarity with this play. These significant congruences may have caused viewers to reference the Boker play, which may thus have formed an important component not only of the conditions of production but of the conditions of reception for the film.

The jester's prominence in the Boker play relative to other versions constitutes one of the key congruences. In many versions of the story, the jester either does not appear or functions as a very minor character. By contrast, the jester in the Boker version plays a role of great narrative consequence, both commenting on the action and bearing the tale of the lovers' infidelity to Lanciotto. The role of the theatrical jester thus parallels that of the cinematic jester.

Lawrence Barrett, one of the leading American actors of the late nineteenth century, first played Boker's Lanciotto in November 1882 and revived the production several times over the next five years. A program for Barrett's 1883 production illustrates a possible direct influence upon the Vitagraph film's sets and blocking.[6] The program contains a series of seven detailed sketches, portraying key moments from each of the play's six acts. A remarkably close parallel exists in terms of locations, set design and composition, and characters' postures and blocking.

The presence and treatment of the jester together with the similarity of sets may have served to trigger associations with the Boker play and the Barrett production, the intertextual resonances producing multiple possible readings. From these, we select one example: viewer affect toward Lanciotto. The casting of Barrett, the production's major star, as Lanciotto, points to what may be seen as the centrality of the Lanciotto character. The Boker play, in contrast to some other versions, presents Lanciotto not as an evil monster, but as a complex character who, acutely aware of his physical shortcomings, resists marriage with Francesca. Reviews indicate that Barrett's performance reinforced Boker's sympathetic depiction of Lanciotto. Reviewing the Barrett production, *The New York Times* said: "The first glimpse of Lanciotto reveals him as a man bearing a burden of secret sorrows; outwardly stern, his manner [is] marked by insuavity.... Inwardly the hunchback keenly feels the degradation of his affliction." (6 January 1885, p. 5). A viewer of the Vitagraph film acquainted with the Barrett production of the Boker play may have been predisposed to sympathize with Lanciotto. The editing pattern of the insert locket shot and Lanciotto's collapse after the murders may have been seen as permitting access to Lanciotto's subjectivity, while constructing him as a sympathetic character.

While we have suggested that the producers may have deliberately referenced the Boker play, we can, of course, never determine how many of the film's viewers may have known this particular intertext. How, then, might the referencing of these intertexts have produced different readings? *New York Times* reviews of the Crawford and d'Annunzio Francescas indicate that the Lanciotto of these plays conformed to a prevalent cultural stereotype of the evil hunchback, such as that seen in *Richard III*. Of the Crawford Lanciotto, the *Times* said, "Francesca's husband is a gnomelike monstrosity, who grovels at her feet in his amorous moods and is a fiend in his pursuit of revenge" (29 June 1902). The *Times* commented about the d'Annunzio Lanciotto: "[The] crippled hunchback last night was savagely virile and bestially cunning" (12 November 1902). In these plays, both of which derived from Boccaccio's retelling, the character's evil nature is constructed not only from physical appearance but from his actions. In these versions, far from resisting marriage to Francesca, Lanciotto actively deceives her by having Paolo serve as his proxy until the wedding night. Lanciotto's malevolence in these intertexts may have predisposed viewers of the Vitagraph film who knew only the Crawford and/or d'Annunzio plays to dislike the hunchback and sympathize with his victims. These intertexts may have weighted some of the film's signifying practices (e.g., Lanciotto's obviously deformed appearance and limp), resulting in a reading of his revenge as brutal and unjustified murder.

The privilege accorded star-crossed lovers, from Lancelot and Guinevere to Romeo and Juliet, may, however, suggest an alternate reading centering on the couple that would have been available to viewers familiar with such intertexts. Nineteenth-century poems and paintings, in particular, seem to have presented a romantic interpretation of the story, focusing on the plight of the doomed lovers rather than the anguish of the betrayed husband.[7] The numerous paintings depicting the tale all center on Paolo and Francesca and show them embracing, either in life or in death, or floating through eternity. For example, Rossetti's painting "Paolo and Francesca" shows the lovers clasped in each other's arms in a medieval setting, and in Cabanel's "The Death of Paolo and Francesca," the dead Francesca lies on a couch, the dead Paolo on the floor beside her, his arm around her shoulder. In the famous, and often referenced, Dore illustration, the shrouded couple floats past Virgil and Dante.

These romantic intertexts may have served to activate certain of the Vitagraph film's signifiers in a manner that produced a reading foregrounding the lovers. Hence, the film could be seen as privileging the lovers through Francesca's shrinking in horror at her first sight of Lanciotto and Paolo's collapsing in empathetic despair. The placing of the lovers in an elaborate exterior garden setting and focusing on their interaction for three consecutive shots would also suit a romantic reading.

Other intertexts indicate that a viewer may have been inclined to condemn the illicit lovers and support Lanciotto for reasons of morality. Ouida (Louise de la Ramee, author of *Under Two Flags* and other romantic novels) asserted that Lanciotto had perfect justification for killing the immoral pair. "We cannot but absolve him. [Lanciotto] did no wrong in the eyes of the church, nor would he in this age be condemned for what he did by any tribunal."[8] In a lecture on Dante given at the New York Public Library (Hamilton Grange Branch) as part of the New York Department of Education's free public lecture series, Professor Christian Gauss of Princeton spoke of Francesca and Paolo as "those guilty of lust, blinded by passion, forever borne hither and thither by the wind in the starless sky." A writer in *The New Catholic World*, while professing to understand Dante's compassion for "a doom so piteous," still asserted: "The law is a good law, and those who break it . . . confess in the tormented air that they deserve to suffer."[9]

Some commentators on the tale of Francesca da Rimini suggested that infidelity, treachery, fratricide, and suicide were typical "Italian" behavior. Ouida took a particularly harsh view of Francesca. "He [Dante] perhaps knew that Francesca had been of that temper (one to this day frequent amongst Italian women) to which it seems preferable that the beloved one should suffer in a common doom of misfortune rather than escape to be happy elsewhere."[10] In addition to condemning Francesca, the author repeatedly advanced negative stereotypes of the Italian character. Speaking of the revelation of the lovers' liaison, she said: "The usual informer and eavesdropper, who is more general in Italy, the land of spies, than elsewhere, carried the tale of their intimacy to Lanciotto."[11] Edith Wharton also attributes the tragedy to Italian "racial traits," characterizing Lanciotto as "a stealthy, smiling assassin."[12] A viewer with this intertextual framework would perhaps derive satisfaction from having prejudices confirmed, or see all the characters as equivalently immoral.

One could construct an intertextually grounded anti-Italian reading of the film simply on the basis of Ouida, Wharton, and other such writers, but it is unlikely that any reader during this period would have had so constricted an intertextual frame. The anti-Italian intertexts themselves relate to a larger cultural issue of the period: the threat to "American values" posed by immigrants, large numbers of whom were Italian. As we said above, however, fully considering such a contextual factor as this falls beyond the scope of this paper. We wish instead briefly to consider the cultural context of Dante by looking at the circulation of intertexts. What kinds of viewers might have been likely to have had preexisting knowledge of Francesca di Rimini through what intertexts?

A veritable Dante craze existed at the turn of the century at least among a restricted segment of American society. A set of Dante postcards, "A Visit to Hell with Dante—The Italian Poet," (circa 1900) cost 50 cents for twenty–five "views,"[13] at least half a day's wages for elevator men, tailors, and grocery clerks.[14] Dante societies and courses proliferated at universities, while "enterprising publishers tried to exploit this Dante furore by issuing elegant Dante calendars."[15] The intertexts we have used to extrapolate possible readings—magazines such as *The Atlantic Monthly, The Dial*, and *Blackwood's*, newspapers such as *The New York Times*, and plays produced in New York and Philadelphia—would similarly seem to address a fairly limited segment of American society.

We continue to investigate the contextual circulation of Dante and Francesca, discovering indications that the passion for Dante to some extent transcended social barriers. While Dante enjoyed nothing approaching the broad cultural permeation of Shakespeare, absent from school curricula for example, his appeal was not limited to the purchasers of elegant calendars and relatively expensive postcards. For example, the New York City Bureau of Lectures sponsored several free annual lectures on Dante during the first decade of the century. In 1897 a correspondent to *The Dial* noted in amazement that in San Francisco "is a settlement of Italian fisherman, whose condition is apparently without an aspiration other than to have a supply of the black bread they eat and sour wine they drink; *yet these people support a society for the study of Dante.*"[16]

This evidence of broader circulation further complicates conditions of reception for *Francesca di Rimini* by hinting at a range of intertexts we have yet to uncover. The intertexts we have discovered permit us to extrapolate a rich array of historically grounded readings for a fairly restricted group of readers/viewers. Ideally, further evidence concerning Dante's circulation among a more diverse social spectrum would enable us to extrapolate a yet richer array of historically grounded readings that would cut across class boundaries. The class-specific nature of the origin and maintenance of historical evidence to which we have referred above, however, may preclude a fuller understanding of Dante's circulation, and hence of the conditions of reception for *Francesca di Rimini*. For this reason we now turn to a film, *Julius Caesar*, for which we have much more complete contextual evidence.

Julius Caesar

Although Vitagraph produced several Shakespearean adaptations, we have chosen *Julius Caesar* since contemporary comments indicate that this was the most popular and most often performed of Shakespeare's plays. The film is a compression of the Shakespearean text: the fifteen shots omit six of the play's seventeen scenes. Vitagraph's release described the film as follows:

> Scene 1—Street in Rome. Casca and Trebonius upbraid the citizens for praising Caesar. Scene 2—The Forum. A soothsayer bids Caesar "beware the ideas of March." Scene 3—Mark Antony wins the race and "thrice he offers Caesar a crown." Scene 4—Cassius tempts Brutus to join the conspiracy against Caesar. Scene 5—Brutus's garden. Meeting of the conspirators. Scene 6—Caesar's palace. Calphurnia tells Caesar of her dream and begs him not to go to the senate. The conspirators enter, laugh at his fears, urge and get his consent to go. Scene 7—Street near Capitol. The soothsayer again warns Caesar. Scene 8—The Capitol. The assassination of Caesar. Scene 9—The Forum. Brutus addresses the mob. Antony enters with Caesar's body. Scene 10—Brutus' camp near Sardis. Cassius upbraids Brutus. Scene 11—Brutus' tent-quarrel-Caesar's ghost. Scene 12—Plains of Phillipi. Armies of Mark Antony and Octavius Caesar, and Brutus and Cassius. Scene 13—The Battle. "Caesar, thou art revenged even with the sword that killeth thee." Scene 14—Brutus slays himself. "Caesar, now be still. I killed not thee with half so good a will." Scene 15—Brutus' funeral pyre. "This was the noblest Roman of them all."

We could speculate about a range of intertextually grounded readings as we did with *Francesca di Rimini*. A reader familiar with the textual exegeses of contemporary literary criticism appearing in periodicals such as *Harpers* and *The North American Review* could have drawn upon contradictory intertextual frames in his/her reading of the film—some commentators praised Brutus and others damned him, while yet others complained that Shakespeare had done Caesar a misservice in portraying him as a tyrant. Similarly, theatrical reviews would have provided a myriad conflicting interpretations of the play that may have shaped viewer readings.

But rather than duplicate the text/intertext interaction, we use *Julius Caesar* to exemplify the intertext/context interaction that the limited and mostly class-restricted available evidence for *Francesca* did not permit us to explore. The massive cultural permeation of Shakespeare allows us to investigate circulation of Shakespearean intertexts as part of the conditions of reception for the Vitagraph *Julius Caesar*. Hence, while we shall, where possible, refer to *Julius Caesar*-specific intertexts, we broaden our focus beyond this play to include the cultural circulation of Shakespearean intertexts generally. What social formations might have been exposed to which intertexts and what may the consequences have been for the conditions of reception? We will first look at widely circulating intertexts representing an approach to Shakespeare probably familiar to members of most social formations. We will then look at the variations in particular intertexts, i.e., theatrical productions, which circulated among different social formations. In other words, we discuss an approach to Shakespeare that may have conditioned reception across social formations and then two different approaches to Shakespeare which may have conditioned reception for different social formations.

Shakespearean texts and intertexts had far-reaching manifestations, encompassing everything from relatively inexpensive editions of the complete works, to inclusion in school curricula, to ephemera such as advertising cards. Yet contemporary commentary indicates that knowledge of Shakespeare, for the most part, was limited to familiarity with famous phrases, speeches and scenes. "We read about Shakspere, listen to lectures about Shakspere, talk about Shakspere, quote Shakspere; but not one in ten thousand of us can really read common passages of Shakspere intelligently."[17] Even at Shakespearean performances, stated many critics, much of the audience engaged primarily with theatrical spectacle rather than the "beauty" of Shakespeare's poetry. Shakespeare's presence, as we will see, took the form of a widely circulated "reductionist" (in a nonpejorative sense) approach to the complex urtexts.

In a piece entitled "Is Shakespeare Popular?," the editor of *The North American Review* summarized the Bard's place amongst a particular social formation in early twentieth-century culture.

> If one were to assert that Shakespeare is an unpopular author, little read, and that the average man has but a slight and intermittent taste for him, one would doubtless be met with flat contradiction. The ever-multiplying editions would be pointed to, and the fact would be cited that every household of pious intent and respectable tendencies supplies itself with Shakespeare immediately after it buys the family Bible. It is incontrovertibly true that everyone of average education has been piloted through two or three plays while in the high school; and college graduates can usually claim a bowing acquaintance with two or three plays, plus some volume of textual criticism. . . . But is this a test of popularity? The great question is, What does the tired man read when he comes home from business, and what does the worn-out mother of the family read when she has time to fold her hands and sit still? And the truthful answer is that he reads the evening paper, and she reads the advertisements in the back of the magazines to see what she would buy if only she could pay.[18]

Shakespeare seems to have functioned differently in the culture than Dante. Dante intertexts seemed to have circulated mainly amongst a highly circumscribed set of readers. In this context, knowledge of *Francesca di Rimini* may have served as part of a larger process of social distinction. Certainly many readings of Shakespeare stemming from, for example, academic discourse or Shakespearean societies, functioned in a similar manner. More strikingly, however, the wide-ranging manifestations of the "reductionist" approach suggest that Shakespeare, in this sense, functioned in the construction of a cultural consensus. This consensus valorized the Bard as cultural icon and referenced the plays but did not necessarily entail widespread and intimate familiarity with Shakespeare's texts. The apparent unanimity of this approach predicated on key phrases and key images, unified social formations that differential access to and familiarity with particular texts usually distinguished.[19]

Delineating this culturally prevalent reductionist approach through investigating the circulation of intertexts enables us to address the apparent contradiction pointed to by the editor of *The North American Review*, i.e., the widespread veneration of Shakespeare coupled with equally widespread neglect of his work. To adumbrate the incredible pervasiveness of Shakespearean images and phrases in late nineteenth- and early twentieth-century America, we first briefly discuss a selection of Shakespearean ephemera dating from the period. Then we look at one of the most important of Shakespeare's manifestations—public school curricula.

Relatively inexpensive versions of Shakespeare proliferated. *The Ariel Shakespeare* sold from $15 to $35 for a complete forty–volume set or 40 to 75 cents for individual volumes, prices depending on the quality of the binding. Whereas even relatively affluent "working-men's" families might have found the price for the entire set fairly prohibitive, they could have afforded the cheaper single volumes or had access to Shakespeare through public libraries. Most "working-men's" families did purchase newspapers,[20] some of which seem to have assumed reader familiarity with Shakespeare. For example, in 1889 *The New York World* issued a complimentary city guide. A short piece, "The National Game," listed twenty-seven Shakespearean quotes meant to "convince one that the game [baseball] is of remote origin." Among these: "A hit, a palpable hit" (*Hamlet*) and "Let me be umpire in this" (*Henry VI*).[21]

Other Shakespearean ephemera, most with a strong visual component, proliferated: stereographs; sculpture; illustrated calendars with "quotes of the month"; writing tablets, again with quotes and illustrations; and card games. Space constraints prohibit our detailing the key images and phrases found in this vast range of material. Rather, we give three examples of tradecards, illustrated advertisements distributed by manufacturers, specifically related to *Julius Caesar*. N.K. Fairbanks and Company, Lard Refiners, issued a series of tradecards (circa 1880–1890) featuring "familiar quotations" from the Bard. One shows a pig in a rendering vat. The quote under him reads, "Let me have those (sic) about me that are fat, sleek headed chaps (sic), and such as sleep o'nights."[22] A tradecard for Libby, McNeill and Libby's Cooked Corned Beef shows a plump toga-clad Caesar and Brutus conversing about a slim Cassius lurking in the background. Caesar complains, "Yon Cassius has a lean and hungry look, [. . .] would he were fatter." Brutus suggests feeding Cassius the advertiser's product. A card for Barker and Company Coal shows Brutus and Cassius in Roman military costume with the caption, "Away, slight man"—a verbatim quotation. The slight misquoting and elisions on the other cards perhaps reflect the way in which such "familiar quotations" became common parlance. The illustrations on the cards suggest one means by which visual representations of Shakespearean characters became fairly standardized. Both tradecards featuring the play's characters show them in the proper attire for the quoted scenes, the images both reflecting and reinforcing a sense of the appropriate iconography.

Exposure to cultural ephemera would have depended on a range of factors such as income, reading habits, consumption patterns, etc. Exposure to Shakespeare in public schools, for a certain age cohort, would have been far more systematic and widespread, since attendance through the eighth grade was legally mandated in most locations. The *New McGuffey Fifth Reader,* widely adopted in public schools, included "Under the Greenwood Tree" from *As You Like It* and "Antony's Oration over Caesar's Dead Body." Curricular guidelines for the public schools in New York City and the Commonwealth of Pennsylvania also demonstrate that Shakespeare, unlike Dante, formed a significant part of public education during this time period. In Pennsylvania, children memorized "Under the Greenwood Tree" in fifth grade. Charles and Mary Lamb's *Tales From Shakespeare* was recommended for inclusion in the school library. New York City mandated far more Shakespeare, beginning with the memorization of Ariel's Song "Where the Bee Sucks" in grade 2B. In grade 8B students read "This was the Noblest Roman of Them All." Eighth-grade curricula also included the reading of Lambs' *Tales from Shakespeare; The Merchant of Venice,* and *Julius Caesar.*

The above tells us that students memorized and read Shakespeare but does not tell us how they were taught or what they might have learned. Although intended for college students, the outline for study for *Julius Caesar* in the journal *Education* gives some notion of how educators taught this play. The outline for study suggests three readings of the play: the first for narrative comprehension; the second for dramatic qualities; and the third for broader cultural resonance. Included in the outline for the third reading is a list of "the most striking scenes of the drama." "Caesar and his train; the thunderstorm; the midnight meeting; Brutus and Portia; Portia on the Ides of March; the assassination; over Caesar's body; the tent scene; the parley; the ghost of Caesar appears to Brutus."[23] And what might students have learned? Not much, asserted a *Harper's Weekly* column. "Nearly everyone in the educated class who was questioned had read one or two plays, usually at school, but nearly all held mistaken ideas about what they had read, and had a most superficial knowledge of the construction of the plays, the significance of the characters, and the points of preeminent excellence."[24] A short piece in *The Atlantic Monthly*, put together from "several examination papers lately presented at an academy in Pennsylvania," confirmed this impression. "Then Caesar reached the Senate safe, but Cascada stabbed him deep and Brutus gave him the most kindest cutting, which made the tyran yell, Eat, too, Brutus?"[25]

Given the pervasive references to Shakespeare we have outlined, one would expect evidence of a flourishing theatrical Shakespearean scene in this era. A 1909–1910 survey of amusements in Manhattan, however, attests that such was not the case. Theatrical production patterns, in fact, exhibited a remarkable similarity to the late twentieth-century Broadway. The contemporary equivalents of *Cats*, *The Chocolate Soldier* and *The Dollar Princess*, both musical comedies, each ran for 240 performances in the 1909–1910 season. In the same season, no Shakespeare play performed at the high price or so–called standard theatres made the list of successful, long-running performances. Indeed, plays such as *Hamlet* and *Macbeth* ranked at the bottom of the list of the shortest-running plays, with five and four performances, respectively. Curiously enough, in that season, nine Shakespeare plays appeared on the boards of the "standard forty" of a total of 121, while nine of the sixty–four productions of the lower-priced theatre were Shakespearean, or almost twice the proportion of Shakespeare at the higher-priced venues. The standard theatres charged $2 for orchestra seats and 50 cents for gallery seats, while admissions at the lower priced theatres ranged from $1 to 20 cents for the orchestra and from 25 to 10 cents for the gallery. Not surprisingly, the survey characterizes the audience composition at the higher-priced theatres as about evenly split between leisured and business classes.[26]

Did the leisured and business class spectators attending Shakespearean performances at the high-priced theatres come with detailed knowledge of the Bard and his plays and enjoy the performances through narrative engagement? Or might they have enjoyed the performances through engagement with the spectacular element? Comments on the theatrical scene indicate that the small degree of popularity Shakespeare enjoyed stemmed from the latter rather than the former. Although contemporary journals reflect a controversy over the "correct" presentation of Shakespeare (scenery and effects versus Elizabethan purity), actual performances, for the most part, followed the nineteenth-century trend toward ever more elaborate and spectacular staging. "The sum . . . expended in the production of one play of Shakespeare on the current over-elaborate scale would cover the production of two or three pieces mounted with simplicity and a strict adherence to the requirements of the text. We are told, however, that a very small public would interest itself in Shakespeare's plays if they were robbed of scenic upholstery and spectacular display."[27] The Robert Mantell productions of *Julius Caesar* conformed to audience expectations. "The general appeal of the performance is enhanced by the pictorial quality of the settings, the various scenes being carried forward in a manner which if not strictly Shakespearean, is of value in stimulating imaginations which have grown sluggish under the conditions of modern existence." (30 April 1907), 9).

How might Shakespeare have been staged for a different social formation than the leisured and business class spectators who attended the standard theatres? During the first decade of the twentieth century in New York City, both the People's Institute, a progressive reform organization, and the Educational Alliance, an immigrant aid society, sponsored free or relatively inexpensive Shakespearean recitals and productions to which residents of the teeming slums south of Fourteenth Street flocked in the hundreds and thousands. Ben Greet, an English actor-manger who produced some of these plays, argued that a proposed Shakespeare Memorial should be located below Fourteenth Street "so as to be within easy reach of the mass of the people. For it is among 'the people,' in contradistinction from 'society,' that Shakespeare is most appreciated."[28]

The people's appreciation of Shakespeare does not seem to have depended on spectacular staging. The People's Institute's traditional Christmas week one-man recital of Shakespeare plays filled the Great Hall of the Cooper Union, which seated 1,600, to overflowing while hundreds more were turned away at the door. *The New York Evening Mail* described an audience at one of these recitals. "Their attention was close, their eyes eager, their faces full of intelligent appreciation. . . . The applause, given with appreciation quite as much for the literary passages as for the emotional dramatic climaxes, burst like waves on the shore from all parts at once" (7 January 1905).

The Ben Greet Company was famed for presenting Shakespeare in the stark Elizabethan manner. Said the actor-manager: "The plays as I have given them, do not depend upon the spectacular attraction which is so large an element in the appeal of the conventional Shakespearean production of our time, with its dependence upon richness of scenic effect and its consequent sacrifice of the poetic and dramatic integrity of the text."[29] Of course, we do not wish to imply that the workers and immigrants of the lower East Side would have rejected free or inexpensive spectacularly staged productions or not have attended the uptown productions had they the money. In the absence of these alternatives, however, one-man recitals and starkly staged productions would have constituted their primary intertextual frames for the Vitagraph *Julius Caesar*.[30]

How did this film fit with the cultural circulation of Shakespearean intertexts, that is, one of the conditions of reception, we have adumbrated? The film is consistent with the key phrase, key image approach to Shakespeare that we have discovered in much of the cultural ephemera of the period. The film contains four direct quotes and a paraphrase of some of the play's best known lines, foregrounded by the Vitagraph publicity we cited at the beginning of this section. Just as the film features key phrases, it features key scenes. Above we mentioned the college study outline that enumerated the "most striking scenes of the drama." Of the ten scenes listed, eight appear in the Vitagraph film. The scenes omitted both from this list and the film deal with Marc Antony and his co-rulers, perhaps indicating a culturally prevalent narrative simplification. Architecture and costuming accord with the images circulated on Shakespearean ephemera, such as the tradecards we have described.

While the film thus exhibits congruence with many widely circulating intertexts, we have not, in this case, adduced these congruences to extrapolate variant readings of the text but rather to illustrate the way in which the film fits the culturally prevalent "reductionist" approach to Shakespeare we have sketched out. Although we may today consider a 15-minute, 15-shot Shakespeare play absurdly abridged, contemporary viewers, Shakespearean scholars perhaps exempted, would have found the Vitagraph film perfectly consonant with their intertextual exposure to Shakespeare. In this sense, the conditions of reception for viewers from all social formations would have been equivalent.

Such would not have been the case with the film's spectacular elements. The film's staging accords with the spectacle of the standard theatre. The film's action takes place in front of sets painted to resemble Roman architecture. Stephen Bush, in *The Moving Picture World*, compared Vitagraph's "excellent" representation of the Forum to the famous painting by Gérôme (5 December 1908, 447). The on-screen depiction of off-stage action further illustrates Vitagraph's incorporation of spectacle. In the play, during act I, scene ii, Marc Antony thrice offers Caesar the crown offstage, while on stage, Brutus and Cassius listen. The film's third shot, preceded by the intertitle "Marc Antony three times offers Caesar the crown," shows Caesar seated in a grandstand, surrounded by a crowd of extras. While he watches the race that Shakespeare's Casca only describes, Antony presents the crown to him.

Had the business and leisure-class viewers accustomed to the spectacular staging of the standard theatre seen the Vitagraph production, they would have found much that was familiar. Indeed, we suspect that the producers emulated the elaborate staging and costumes of the theatre as closely as possible precisely to attract this audience, which at this time attended the theatre rather than the nickelodeon. But how might those viewers accustomed to recitals and minimal staging have responded to the spectacular elements of the Vitagraph film? While the elaborate staging may have been unfamiliar, there is no reason to believe that these viewers would not have experienced visual pleasure. They may, however, have noted the absence of the verbal text more than their uptown brethren, who were reputed to relate only to the spectacle.

William Uricchio and Roberta E. Pearson

We have used the Vitagraph *Francesca di Rimini* and *Julius Caesar* to demonstrate an intertextually derived strategy for adducing historical conditions of reception that would work for any text. As we said at the outset, we selected two films because each respectively exemplifies the text/intertext and the intertext/context interactions of this strategy. In the case of *Francesca*, we can generate an array of historically grounded readings but cannot determine which readings may have been more culturally prevalent since all pertain to a restricted social formation. In the case of *Julius Caesar*, our access to a rich array of contextual data permits grounded speculation concerning the function of culturally prevalent intertexts in the conditions of reception for a particular film, but this evidence alone does not permit the extrapolation of variant readings of the text.

This strategy for surmising historical conditions of reception relies to a much greater extent on speculation than necessary when dealing with actual living viewers or specific documents about past viewers' textual engagements. Yet if one does not use the intertextual strategy we have suggested or some other approach for surmising historical conditions of reception, one must remain as silent as those distant viewers whose voices have been forever muted by the hegemonic inflection of historical evidence.

NOTES

1. The sequence of the author's names was determined by a coin toss and is not an indication of senior authorship. The authors collaborated to such an extent that they could not themselves distinguish their individual contributions to this paper.

2. In 1908, Vitagraph turned "out more new subjects each week than any other American concern" (*New York Dramatic Mirror* [14 November 1908], 10) and exported more of these films to the European market than its competitors. Vitagraph's physical plant permitted the company to maintain its superiority. As opposed to Biograph's Fourteenth Street brownstone studio, Vitagraph's Brooklyn facilities included three operating studios by the end of 1908, with two more under construction. The studio's organizational practices reflected its preeminent status. Vitagraph quickly adapted "modern" management tactics, presaging the highly specialized division of labor of the Hollywood studio system. J. Stuart Blackton, one of the firm's founding partners, served as spokesman for the film industry during the 1908 New York City controversy about the nickelodeons.

3. T. Bennett and J. Woollacott, *Bond and Beyond: Political Career of a Popular Hero* (London: McMillan Education, 1987), 56.

4. This paper forms a part of a larger project that will appear as *Reframing Culture: The Case of the Vitagraph Quality Films* (Princeton, N.J.: Princeton University Press, 1993). We focus on 1907–1913 since the film industry during these years experienced crucial changes in film form, economic organization, and audience composition, many centering around issues of class.

5. Most extant prints do have fifteen shots, although we have located two additional shots in the Paper Print Collection at the Library of Congress that may or may not have been included in the original release print. Given the unstable nature of the film stock in this period, surviving prints often vary significantly from release prints, further complicating textual analysis.

6. Program Files, *Francesca di Rimini*, The Library for the Performing Arts at Lincoln Center, The New York Public Library.

7. See, for example, R. W. Gilder, *The New Day: A Poem in Songs and Sonnets* (New York: Scribner, Armstrong and Co., 1876); M. Gray, "Francesca di Rimini," *Littell's Living Age* 199:2582 (1893), 770; J. K. Wetherill, "Francesca to Paolo," *Atlantic Monthly* (November 1884), 594.

8. Ouida, "Great Passions of History: Francesca di Rimini," *The Cosmopolitan* 18:3 (1895), 259–70.

9. W. Barry, "Dante and the Spirit of Poetry," *New Catholic World* 494:83 (1906), 145–58.

10. Ouida, "Great Passions of History," 268.

11. Ibid., 264.

12. E. Wharton, "The Three Francescas," *The North American Review* 175:548 (1902), 17–30.

13. Album 452, The Burdick Collection, Department of Prints and Photographs, The Metropolitan Museum of Art.

14. L. B. More, *Wage Earners' Budgets: A Study of Standards and Cost of Living in New York City* (New York: Henry Holt and Co., 1907), 135.

15. A. La Piana, *Dante's American Pilgrimage* (New Haven, Conn.: Yale University Press, 1948), 148.

16. K. Greydon, "Letter to the Editor," *The Dial* 23:269 (1897), 110.

17. "Why Shakspere is Not Understood," *The World's Work* 5 (1903), 3249–51.

18. "Is Shakespeare Popular?" *The North American Review* 184:608 (1907), 334–5.

19. Obviously, space constraints preclude a fully elaborated consideration of the over-determined functions of Shakespeare in American culture. On this point, we refer the reader to E. Dunne, *Shakespeare in America* (New York: The McMillan Co., 1939) and L. W. Levine, *Highbrow/Lowbrow: The Emergence of Cultural Hierarchy in America* (Cambridge, Mass.: Harvard University Press, 1988). Space constraints also preclude addressing our differences with Levine's analysis.

20. A New York City survey of the standard of living among working men's families reported that families with incomes ranging from $1100 to $1599 spent an average of $10.33 on newspapers and books, most of which went to newspapers. Of the 318 families in the survey, roughly a fourth reported reading *The New York World*. R. C. Chapin, *The Standard of Living among Workingmen's Families in New York City* (New York: Russell Sage Foundation, 1909), 216–8.

21. *Cyclopedia of Useful Information and Complete Handbook of New York City*, (New York: New York World, 1889), 48.

22. Food, Meat, Green Boxes. Bella C. Landauer Collection, The New York Historical Society.

23. M. Kingsley, "Outline Study of Shakespeare's *Julius Caesar*," *Education* 22:4 (1901), 226–35.

24. "Is Shakespeare Read?" *Harper's Weekly* 51:2615 (1907), 151–2.

25. "A School Comment on Shakespeare's *Julius Caesar*," *The Atlantic Monthly* 96:3 (1905), 431.

26. M. Davis, *The Exploitation of Pleasure: A Study of Commercial Recreations in New York City* (New York: Russell Sage Foundation, 1909), 29–43.

27. S. Lee, "Shakespeare and the Modern Stage," *Littel's Living Age* 224:2901 (1900), 539–47.

28. B. Greet, "For the Greatest Theatre in the World," *The Worlds Work* (April 1911), 14222–9.

29. B. Greet, "Shakespeare and the Modern Theatre," *Harpers Weekly*, (4 November 1905), 1604.

30. Many of the denizens of the lower East Side may also have attended Yiddish and Italian theatre productions of Shakespeare, which would also have lacked the spectacular staging of the standard theatres and emphasized the text and the performances.

Mary Carbine

"The Finest Outside the Loop": Motion Picture Exhibition in Chicago's Black Metropolis, 1905–1928

In 1905 the first black-owned movie theater, Motts Pekin Temple, opened in the section of Chicago's South Side known as Black Metropolis. An account of the opening describes 400 "well-dressed" blacks attending an all-black show, featuring the cake walk and ragtime.[1] Advertised as the "Home of the Colored Race," the Pekin was lauded by black community members such as Ida B. Wells Barnett, who commented, "The race owes Mr. Motts a debt of gratitude for giving us a theater in which we could sit anywhere we chose without any restrictions."[2] This event reveals several key aspects of motion picture exhibition in Chicago's black community before the Depression: a specific address to a black audience on the part of the theater; the presence of live entertainment rooted in African-American culture; and race as a factor affecting access to mass entertainment. Exhibition venues such as the Pekin not only demonstrate that blacks owned and patronized neighborhood movie theaters in the silent era but also exemplify the particular and variegated ways in which the "masses" participated in mass culture. In Chicago's black community, the picture houses provided a space for consciousness and assertion of social difference as well as the consumption of mass amusements.

Numerous film historians have addressed issues of ethnicity, class, and urban geography in studies of early motion picture audiences and exhibition practices. Often, research concentrates on identifying changes in the class composition of nickelodeon and picture palace audiences, frequently focusing on European immigrants as audiences or exhibition in ethnic white neighborhoods.[3] For those concerned with a social history of exhibition, factoring in determinants of gender, ethnicity, and residential

From *Camera Obscura* 23 (May 1990). Reprinted by permission of the author and Indiana University Press.

patterns can nuance the monolithic categories of "working class" and "middle class." However, the emphasis on European immigrants presumes that the most significant shift in turn-of-the-century urban populations resulted from the second wave of European immigration. In fact, the nickelodeon era and the rise of the picture palace coincided with major population shifts among black Americans, as southern blacks moved to northern cities in a large-scale exodus known as the "Great Migration." In Chicago, the number of black residents increased nearly sevenfold between 1890 and 1910 and rose by 148 percent between 1910 and 1920, compared to a 21 percent rise in the non-black population.[4] These migrants also constituted an audience for the movies and, like their European counterparts, had a distinct ethnic and cultural heritage that influenced exhibition and moviegoing practices.

In scholarly work on early cinema, the tendency to neglect issues of black spectatorship is part of a more general theoretical problem. Most studies of mass culture employ theoretical models that downplay the possibility that minority groups can use commercial entertainment in culturally specific ways. As Lizabeth Cohen has argued, the "embourgeoisement thesis" emphasizes how mass culture blurs class lines and flattens ethnic distinctions, posing white, middle-class tastes and values as cultural norms to which all social groups aspire. In the embourgeoisement scenario, when workers or immigrants went to the picture house, listened to commercial radio, or purchased brand-name goods, they inevitably ceded their class identity or cultural autonomy to the agendas of those with economic and social power. Mass culture and commercial entertainment are seen as operating with inexorable force to integrate workers and immigrants into mainstream society.[5]

However, such models are often unable to account for historically specific actions of individual social groups. When Cohen investigated the lives of Chicago workers in the 1920s—workers who consumed mass culture in class and community-specific contexts—she discovered that their reactions to and use of commercial products and entertainment did not always play out the embourgeoisement scenario. Instead, immigrant, black, and working-class people often encountered mass culture under local and ethnic sponsorship that bolstered community identification and reduced the homogenizing impact of mass entertainment.[6] In addition, black Chicagoans, to a greater degree than their ethnic white co-workers, participated in mainstream commercial life by going to the movies, shopping at chain stores, and buying "race records" distributed by national companies. Although these activities did not pose an economic challenge to capitalism or to institutionalized racism, they need not be construed as evidence of cultural or ideological assimilation. Rather, Cohen argues, such acts of consumption were a means for blacks to feel more independent and autonomous as a race. By shopping at chain stores, black consumers could refuse to patronize white-owned establishments that failed to hire blacks or overcharged black customers. Purchasing blues and jazz recordings by black artists helped blacks develop and promote a culturally reaffirming African-American sound. Rather than evincing a desperate yearning for assimilation, consumption of mass culture yielded ingredients from which to construct a new, urban black culture.[7]

It is precisely this act of consumption as cultural production that John Fiske addresses in his work on popular culture. Invoking Michel de Certeau, Fiske distinguishes between mass culture—the distribution of mass-produced entertainment products—from popular culture, which arises from the interface of mass culture and the "practices of everyday life."[8] In creating popular culture, socially and economically subordinated people can use mass cultural products as material resources for oppositional activities and the assertion of social difference. While not always an articulated strategy of resistance, the practices of popular culture disturb and harass the hegemony of "mainstream culture" and prevent those with economic, social, or discursive power from molding the disenfranchised into their own image.[9]

Once the embourgeoisement model is nuanced by an emphasis on the cultural activities and everyday life of different social groups, the film text no longer serves as the prime site of meaning and instrumentality. This shift is useful when examining the relation between blacks and cinema because so few blacks have had access to the means of film production, with either financial or creative agency. While text-based work on black characters, stereotypes, and themes is revealing, the emphasis still usually rests with blacks as a minority in a predominantly white industry.[10] Moreover, few examples of black-cast film productions survive from the silent era. The paucity of such examples limits the ability of scholars to use these texts to construct a representative picture of black spectators in history.[11] An audience and exhibition-based study, centered in a particular black community, can ground its analysis in a context dominated by blacks, not as constructs of a text or victims of Hollywood racism but as workers and consumers, performers and spectators, and as people with the ability to invent their own cultural forms and practices.

The movie theaters and audiences of Chicago's Black Metropolis offer a particularly rich example of popular appropriation of commercial entertainment. In addition to witnessing the rationalization of the film industry and the codification of the classical Hollywood style, the pre-Depression era was one of heightened cultural activity, racial consciousness, and political activism on the part of black Americans. Patronizing a theater billed as the "Home of the Colored Race" was only one means by which the citizens of Black Metropolis constructed a black-oriented entertainment culture using products and venues most often controlled by white capital. As recorded in oral histories and contemporary black periodicals, the voices of this era reveal a number of ways that blacks exercised tactical consumption, incorporating motion pictures into specifically African-American cultural practices. Theater advertisements, reviews and accounts of audience response suggest that live performances by black acts, including vaudeville, blues, and jazz, featured prominently and even predominantly in community venues. The relations among black performers, black spectators, and mainstream white movies created a specific dynamic of reception that mitigated against the hegemony of mass culture. Black audiences "consumed" the movies in a context determined as much by the interests and tastes of the black community as by the economic and social agendas of the white majority.

The urban milieu in which black Chicagoans encountered mass culture was shaped by the Great Migration, which had a major effect on both the lives of black Americans and the development of northern cities. The impetus for this large-scale exodus of southern blacks has often been described in economic terms, with rural blacks responding to the promise of jobs in the industrial north and northeast. However, historians such as Jacqueline Jones, James Grossman, and Lawrence Levine have argued that the Great Migration was motivated by a number of interrelated factors, including the desire for better education, political franchise, equal treatment under the law, and hopes for a life free from racial violence and abuse.[12] As Grossman points out, the reasons for migration arose from a racially centered world view, and the process of migration itself strengthened and extended aspects of southern black culture, particularly the role of family and community. The first generation of black Americans to participate in the northern industrial economy did not abdicate their cultural or regional allegiances; rather, they maintained a consciousness shaped by living in a racially structured society.[13]

The influx of migrant blacks, which peaked in the mid- to late 1910s, had deep and far-reaching effects on community development, residential patterns, and class relations in Chicago's South Side neighborhoods. The majority of migrants settled in a 7.5-square-mile area known as Black Metropolis, or the "Black Belt," encompassing the Douglas, Grand, and Washington Park districts. Black Metropolis began just south of Chicago's downtown, known as the "Loop," and stretched thirty blocks southward along State Street, parallel to the stockyards. While Chicago's black population increased from 30,150 in 1900 to 233,903 in 1930, the borders of Black Metropolis remained fairly constant. During this period, over 90 percent of black Chicagoans remained in the increasingly congested black neighborhoods. Racial hostility discouraged most blacks from venturing into white or ethnic European neighborhoods, and migrants instead gravitated toward the "cultural/social matrix" of black institutions and familial networks on the South Side.[14] Competition for jobs and housing, and the choice of some blacks to cross picket lines of unions that refused them membership, contributed to bloody race riots in the summer of 1919.[15]

Not surprisingly, Grossman found little evidence that migrant blacks were interested in integration per se; rather, they often looked forward to freedom from whites in everyday life. The growing vitality and self-consciousness of black neighborhoods attracted those who preferred to avoid whites and their prejudices. Mahalia Jackson, who came to Chicago in the 1920s, described the South Side as a place where a black worker "could lay down his burden of being a colored person in the white man's world and lead his own life."[16] What Grossman terms a "dynamic of choice and constraint," strongly determined by economic factors, shaped the social and geographic boundaries of the district where black people from a range of social classes and regional backgrounds lived, shopped, and participated in leisure activities. Blacks were less likely than most Chicagoans to share public space with other ethnic groups of similar socio-economic status. In the face of historic discrimination and marginality, Chicago blacks enjoyed a certain autonomy in constructing a cultural "black world," relatively free from overt white intervention.[17]

The urban black class structure in this era has been described as a markedly truncated pyramid, with the majority of black men and women laboring in low-paying industrial or service occupations. While most black Chicagoans did not have significant contact with whites outside of the workplace, connections to white sources of power and middle-class values did influence social relations within the black community. According to David Nielson, the few members of the black professional elite saw themselves as more "class akin" to the white majority than "race akin" to the black minority and in some respects looked forward to acceptance and validation by white society.[18] In addition, caste, as related to skin color, figured into the social organization of black communities, reflecting whites' preferential treatment of lighter blacks and the connection between light skin and economic success.[19]

However, in other respects, black class distinctions depended less on relations with whites, or majority definitions of income and occupation, than on a "functional index" of respectability, i.e., a stable income, property ownership, church and club membership, and appropriate leisure habits.[20] Grossman describes notions of respectability—and, by extension, class—as influencing relations between the "Old Settlers" of Black Metropolis and newly arriving migrants. Institutions such as the Urban League and YMCA, as well as the black churches and press, organized campaigns to instruct newcomers in the norms and values of respectability, encouraging cleanliness, sobriety, and restrained behavior in public places. However, most working-class and migrant blacks chose "enthusiastic worship" and a "lively nightlife" as respite from tedious, physically draining occupations. Boisterous recreation in clubs, saloons, dance halls, and picture houses attracted the scorn of the staid "respectables" but was integral to the leisure activities of most urban black workers.[21]

Class and regional differences did not preclude racial consciousness and identification from acting as significant sources of cohesion in the community. Nielson characterizes racial solidarity, in terms of "we-group" or "participant identification," as operating across class lines in urban black society of this era.[22] Although the elite may have had an investment in the values of the white bourgeoisie, they also provided political and economic leadership based in the black community. Successful professionals and entrepreneurs sponsored the black press, fostered institutions such as the Urban League and the NAACP, and promoted an independent black marketplace.[23] In particular, the notion of a separate black economy was an articulated strategy of opportunity and resistance with historical precedents.[24] However, despite visible successes, such as black insurance or cosmetics companies, a lack of experience and capital hampered most black entrepreneurs and prevented them from offering goods and services competitive with those of white-owned stores or national chains. While black consumers did enact boycotts to force chain stores to hire black clerks, most residents of Black Metropolis were still dependent on white-owned businesses for food and other basic goods.[25]

The black press flourished in the 1910s and 1920s and was instrumental in sustaining the ethos of black economic autonomy as well as setting other agendas for its readership. Chicago-based black newspapers and periodicals included the Chicago *Defender*, the Chicago *Bee*, the Chicago *Whip*, the Chicago *Light*, the *Broad Axe*, and *Half-Century Magazine*.[26] Nielson describes such black newspapers as exhibiting a definitive "within-the-group" tenor, sustained by the fact that few whites knew of their existence. In this era, the black press provided a unique discursive arena where blacks could "talk without whites listening."[27]

The *Defender* was particularly influential and widely read. Founded in 1905 by Robert S. Abbott, it had a circulation of 33,000 by 1916, which jumped to 130,000 in 1919, a peak year of the Great Migration. Over two-thirds of the *Defender*'s circulation was outside of Chicago, and the newspaper played an important role in encouraging the migration of black southerners.[28] While the *Defender* highlighted the activities of the black bourgeoisie, featuring news of their business ventures and European travels, its coverage of employment and housing discrimination, city government, black sports, entertainment and political figures, and white violence against southern blacks pertained to readers with a range of class and regional affiliations. The editorial stance of the paper was consistently militant, exhibiting a strong rhetoric of race pride, separatism and political activism, and the terms *Race* or *Race Men* were used instead of *Negro*, which Abbott saw as derogatory. Particularly to black southerners, the *Defender* represented "unapologetic Black pride, dignity and assertiveness."[29]

In addition, the *Defender* was one of the first black newspapers to include a full entertainment section, with "Musical and Dramatic" pages that featured the nightlife on South State Street.[30] Colloquially known as the "Stroll," South State, between 26th and 39th streets, was the focus of business, shopping, and leisure activities in Black Metropolis. Centered on the intersection with 35th Street, the Stroll was the physical site of community expression on a variety of levels. Prominent symbols of black success, such as the Jesse Binga Bank, the Defender Building, and the Overton Hygenic Building, shared the streets with the Plantation Cafe, the Lincoln Gardens, and the Monogram, Grand, and Vendome movie theaters.[31] On the Stroll, the institutions and enterprises of the black bourgeoisie, as well as popular sites for recreation by working and migrant blacks, drew on what Grossman describes as the "familiarity and relief" of a black world.[32] It is in this context, imbued with a consciousness of cultural autonomy, social difference, and struggle, that black Chicagoans encountered commercial entertainment in the movie theaters.

Movie theaters proliferated on the Stroll, and the number of venues supported by the community reflects the strong interest in motion pictures on the part of black Chicagoans. From 1905–1913, there were at least twelve theaters in a four-block stretch of South State Street, offering movies along with vaudeville and musical performance. The number of theaters increased to sixteen in the mid- to late 1910s, paralleling the years of the greatest influx of southern migrants. By the mid-1920s, the number of theaters had climbed to more than twenty, as the focal point of nightlife shifted to the corner of 47th and South Parkway, and the South Side became renowned as a showcase for black music.[33] Musician and businessman Dempsey Travis remembers that "there were more movie theaters in the 3100 block of State Street during that period than on Randolph or North State Street" in Chicago's downtown.[34]

Changes in type and location of exhibition venues were in part determined by community-specific, socio-economic factors. Most of these theaters had seating capacities between 300 and 700 in the early 1910s and between 700 and 1,200 in the late 1910s and 1920s.[35] Throughout the silent era, advertisements and reviews in the *Defender* gave vaudeville a high profile.[36] In the early 1910s, theaters such as the Grand, the Monogram, and the States advertised "Light Vaudeville and Photo-Plays," "Big Musical Program—Pictures That Move," or "Vaudeville de Lux and Best Motion Pictures."[37] Available documentation on theaters in the 1920s indicates that virtually all were independently owned and operated, with the exception of the Owl and the Pickford, owned by Chicago Theaters Corporation.[38] Although some theaters promoted first-run features, in general, advertisements indicate that these venues carried second-run films that came "Straight from the Loop." The major theater chains did not expand into the area until 1928, with the construction of the Regal theater (seating capacity 3,000) by Balaban & Katz.[39] Unlike the upwardly mobile outlying areas and ethnic neighborhoods described by Douglas Gomery, the majority of the residents of black Metropolis did not enjoy the kind of discretionary income that motivated expansion and picture palace construction by the major chains during the 1910s.[40]

Nevertheless, movie theaters were popular sites of leisure and recreation for black Chicagoans, particularly workers and migrants. The *Defender*'s "Musical and Dramatic" pages were crowded with theater advertisements, reviews, and theatrical listings. In 1910, one columnist noted that "the moving picture theater craze has developed a wonderful stampede among the Negro. . . . [T]he young people and those who are impressed with love, romance, and innocence again thronged to the theater in large numbers."[41] As part of their promotional strategies, theater notices reported good attendance, e.g., "our big feature every day policy brings them in. . . . We have been taxed to capacity every night during this week," or "as far as attendance is concerned, we have cause to be jubilant."[42] For the most part, community audiences sustained the small, independently owned theaters on the Stroll, in which live entertainment functioned as an autonomous entertainment form throughout the silent era. In these modest second-run theaters, the practices and products of a national industry were incorporated into both the cultural strategies of the black middle class and the popular activities of black workers.

A consciousness of the cultural and geographic boundaries of Black Metropolis informed the advertising and business strategies of local theaters, as well as discourses about these theaters in the black press. In keeping with the ethos of independent black enterprise, the community press encouraged patronage of the two black-owned theaters, the Pekin and the Star.[43] In a 1912 *Defender* column entitled "In Union Is Strength," Minnie Adams chided readers for less than satisfactory support of the Pekin, the "name that made all Negro theaters possible."[44] Although Adams noted that the quality of the offerings at the Pekin might not compare to those of white-owned theaters, she exhorted "the Race" to "show our pride and loyalty by patronizing the house that was dedicated to us," and which had given "local talent so much consideration." Adams urged community members to "help the Pekin live forever" as a reward for promotion of black performers, and she stated that supporting the theater was a means for "the Race" to "upbuild its own and feel a pride in doing so."[45] Adams's comments allude to the problem faced by other black ventures, i.e., a lack of capital, which hampered black entrepreneurs in competing with white-owned businesses.

Writing in *Half-Century Magazine*, Juli Jones castigated blacks for failing to recognize the social and economic potential of motion picture exhibition. "If our colored people with an interest in the race at heart would pool their money, stop fighting each other, and get down to business, they would not only reap unlimited returns, but would do the race a great service."[46] His comments apply the strategy of economic independence to theater ownership, placing faith in communal capitalist enterprise as a unifying force. The *Defender* carefully noted the progress of blacks who became theater owners and managers, and it implied that theaters employing blacks would draw larger crowds. For example, in 1914, the *Defender* reported that the Star theater, owned and operated "by a member of our Race," was doing "landslide business" and quoted the manager as saying the theater might have to expand to accommodate the influx of patrons.[47] The *Defender*'s treatment of black-owned theaters exemplifies the positioning of business enterprise and selective consumption as political and cultural tools of the black middle class.

However, it is unclear to what extent black theater patrons, particularly workers and migrants, were motivated in their moviegoing habits by the strategy of an independent black marketplace. Despite the support for black ownership of theaters in the press, the majority of the theaters in the community were owned and operated—though not necessarily staffed—by whites. While movie patrons may have wished to support black-owned venues, the relative lack of such establishments meant that the majority of moviegoers on the Stroll encountered mass culture in theaters controlled by whites. These theaters deployed standard advertising and promotional strategies but inflected them with an awareness of their black audiences. Advertisements in the *Defender*, for example, incorporated many of the strategies attributed to Balaban & Katz's picture palaces, including the comfort of roomy seats, washed-air ventilation, luxurious appointments, perfect projection, and a select orchestra, all available "Just Off the Big Time" or in the "Finest Outside the Loop."[48] The latter phrase, consistently featured in advertisements for the States and Owl theaters, would have had particular meaning to black audiences (figure 25).

Chicago's *de facto* segregation extended to movie venues. Those blacks who attempted to attend theaters downtown or in outlying communities encountered Jim Crow seating practices or were denied access altogether. Blacks interviewed in 1919–1921 by the Chicago Commission on Race Relations reported that they were turned away from big downtown theaters, guided to second-rate seats, or forced to move at the request of white patrons.[49] Although Balaban & Katz's policy was to let in whoever could pay,[50] a manager of one big Loop theater stated that "the ticket sellers give [blacks] tickets in the balcony or gallery on the side aisles. . . . If negroes present tickets for the best main-floor seats, ushers try to put them in less conspicuous places."[51] The *Defender* urged blacks to "sue every time you are refused in theaters. . . . [B]uy your seat anywhere in Chicago theaters and sit there."[52] Despite a successful lawsuit filed by a black Chicagoan in 1910, which won the right to seating in any part of theaters in Illinois,[53] discriminatory practices persisted. In 1928, Travis and friends attempted to buy tickets at the Oakland Square theater, just outside the "border" of Black Metropolis at 39th and Drexel. They were told "Blacks not admitted here" and were subjected to threats of racial violence.[54] For black audiences,

Figure 25. Ad in Chicago Defender *(21 August 1915).*

simple access to theaters, and thus, to mainstream commercial entertainment, was qualified and determined by race in a way it was not for whites.

Even if blacks did gain entrance to downtown theaters, white-oriented business practices pervaded the exhibition context. Not only were black patrons required to move at the whim of whites, but as Gomery has described, Balaban & Katz had a specific policy of racial segregation among its employees, relegating blacks to more servile jobs such as messengers, maids, or porters rather than uniformed ushers or ticket-takers. Balaban & Katz even specified the racial characteristics acceptable in their black employees, requiring "the smaller type of negro boy. . . , not [the] markedly Negro type with heavy features."[55] Such discriminatory employment practices perpetuated a caste hierarchy of jobs and service based on white physiognomic ideals and were as much a part of the business strategies of downtown picture palaces as were lavish surroundings and high-quality entertainment. Moreover, such practices illustrate why many blacks chose to avoid integrated settings for leisure activities. For black audiences, the location of streetcar lines and access to downtown theaters affected movie-going patterns far less than the "dynamic of choice and constraint" that inflected everyday life in Black Metropolis.

Advertisements for theaters in black neighborhoods allude to the discriminatory practices of other Chicago exhibitors. Theaters in Black Metropolis were conscious of the need to assure their patrons a full welcome. The Pekin billed itself as the "Home of the Colored Race", the Grand as "Built for Colored People", and the Lux as the "Home Theater of the

South Side."[56] Accounts in the *Defender* promised that blacks could find courteous service in white-owned theaters on the Stroll as opposed to being "admitted on sufferance" and "relegated to the rear of the house" in other parts of the city.[57] While not picture palaces, the theaters displayed an awareness that black patrons were not likely to be welcome in the opulent and comfortable Loop theaters and instead sought "high-class" service in their own neighborhoods. In the modest "home theaters" of Black Metropolis, audiences could lay claim to the same kind of entertainment as whites by attending theaters that advertised highest quality surroundings and service in the "Finest Equipped Theater Outside the Loop" or the "Finest Picture House Outside the Loop."[58]

Black-oriented advertising made for good business in white-owned theaters on the Stroll. However, such business practices also tapped into the growing racial consciousness in the community and served as evidence of the impact of blacks as consumers. Moreover, discourses about theaters in the *Defender* indicate that blacks invested a proprietary interest even in the white-owned neighborhood theaters. One *Defender* columnist referred to "*our* Race picture houses, mostly controlled by white capital [emphasis added],"[59] implying that theaters were identified as belonging to the "Race" because of the composition of the audience, not the race of the owner. In Chicago, black audiences affected industry practices in the exhibition venue, if not at the point of film production. Theater advertising involved a specific construction of the moviegoing experience—not as a wholesale embrace of mainstream white tastes and values but as an encounter with mass entertainment framed with reference to racism and the desire for black cultural autonomy. While inviting blacks to become consumers of commercial entertainment, theater advertisers also addressed their audience as "outside" the dominant cultural and geographic center of Chicago. The reception of the films that played in the theaters was cued to take place in a context rooted in the neighborhood and the Race.

Most of the films exhibited were standard Hollywood fare: Westerns, newsreels, melodramas, serials, and spectaculars. Certainly, theaters in Black Metropolis heralded the arrival of black productions, such as Oscar Micheaux's *The Homesteader* (1918) and *Within Our Gates* (1920), which were produced by the Chicago-based Micheaux Film Corporation.[60] Often, these films played at several venues consecutively, with advertisements in the *Defender* clearly invoking the specific way such films would speak to a black audience. For example, the Vendome's advertisement for *Within Our Gates* billed the film as "a story of the Race with an all star Colored cast. . . . The Greatest Preachment against Race Prejudice . . . full of details that will make you grit your teeth in silent indignation."[61] Such films were described in opposition to standard Hollywood products, as featuring black performers and as referring to the everyday lives and struggles of a black, rather than white, audience. However, in comparison with Hollywood releases, such productions were few and far between. The notices for *Within Our Gates* shared the page with almost-as-large advertisements for "the sensation of the season," *Why I Would Not Marry*, a Fox drama, or for Theda Bara in *Salome*, a "Spectacle Incomparable," also playing at the Vendome.[62] The advertisements in the *Defender* indicate that exhibitors appealed to racial identity and common experiences as a strategy for marketing black-produced, black-oriented features, while continuing to capitalize on the popularity that mainstream, high-production-value releases had with black audiences.

Thomas Cripps has argued that black audiences preferred "slick Hollywood product" over "'race' movies ineptly produced by Blacks."[63] In large part, this pattern was the result of economic factors related to discrimination in the industry, which tipped the balance in favor of Hollywood product even in black venues. D. Ireland Thomas, a *Defender* columnist who championed black film production, expressed frustration at audience preferences and the difficulties faced by black and black-cast productions. With a distribution potential limited to southern segregated theaters and northern black neighborhood theaters, even low-budget "Race movies" were more expensive to book than those offered by national chains, and theaters passed this cost on to patrons. Ireland chastised black moviegoers for attending theaters owned by "the man who refused to show our own people upon the screen in the theater that we and only we patronize." However, in monetary terms, Race productions were less accessible than mainstream entertainment for the majority of black moviegoers, who were poor and working class. Ireland complained bitterly that theaters refused to book black productions because they could instead "exploit a big western picture and fool our people into [the] theater and make a profit."[64] The economic constraints imposed on the production and exhibition of black films meant that black patrons had to pay higher prices for infrequent, low-production-value entertainment. As a result, the moviegoing preferences of black audiences tended to parallel the overall consumption patterns in Black Metropolis, i.e., shopping for "name-brand" goods available through national chains at affordable prices.[65]

In general, black cultural presence was asserted in the theaters not through the entertainment on screen but by the performance on stage. While certain economic strategies on the part of theaters mitigated against the success of black film productions, other business strategies, in the form of promotion of live entertainment, provided an opportunity for the Race to "show our own people" in the space of the theater. Black vaudeville and musical performance figured prominently in the same neighborhood theaters that showed William Hart and Hoot Gibson westerns, Sennett and Arbuckle comedies, Pathé newsreels, and the *Perils of Pauline*.[66] Theatrical notices made a point to identify the acts as African-American, advertising the "Greatest Array of Colored Talent Ever Assembled" or "America's

Foremost Colored Organization."[67] Both the Monogram and Grand theaters on South State Street were part of the Theater Owners Booking Association vaudeville circuit (T.O.B.A.), which brought black acts to black audiences across the South and Midwest. Organized in 1909 by a white businessman who recognized a new and lucrative urban market for black performance, T.O.B.A. operated in a fashion analogous to a movie distribution chain, scheduling acts for theaters belonging to its network in cities such as Chicago, Oklahoma City, Memphis, and Atlanta. Although the Keith, Pantages, and Columbia circuits booked some black vaudeville and variety for white audiences in the Midwest, T.O.B.A. was known as the "colored circuit" because of the predominance of black acts and audiences in its theaters.[68]

In Chicago, Martin Klein, T.O.B.A.'s Western Office manager, operated out of the Overton Hygenic Building and managed the Grand theater. S. H. Dudley, the Eastern Office booker, was a black entertainer, whose newspaper column appeared in the *Defender*.[69] However, despite these strategic ties to the black business and entertainment communities, T.O.B.A. was known as a grueling and humiliating circuit, albeit one that provided opportunities for black performers to work on a regular basis. White control and exploitation of black stage life earned the circuit the appellation "Tough on Black Acts," and complaints against low wages, bad treatment, and promotion of degrading performance stereotypes were often aired in the black press. However, T.O.B.A. did allow black performance to become a regular feature in movie theaters on the Stroll. T.O.B.A. headliners such as Butter Beans and Susie, S.H. Dudley, Kid & Coot, and Sweet Mama Stringbean (a.k.a. Ethel Waters) frequently performed at the Grand and Monogram.[70] In addition, acts such as the Georgia Minstrels, the Darktown Follies, King and Bailey, Bert Williams, Tutt and Whitney's "Smart Set Revue," and Sissieretta Jones's "Black Patti Musical Company" consistently headlined at neighborhood theaters.[71]

As early as 1910, the *Defender* featured news on the T.O.B.A. circuit and the progress of black acts, promoting the "regular season of colored vaudeville" on the Stroll.[72] Performers sent notices from their stops on the circuit, noting changes of address and availability for bookings and exchanging news about the black entertainment community. In addition, the *Defender*'s extensive coverage of black acts prompted stage performers to sign on as traveling salespeople for the newspaper.[73] Columnists regularly reviewed black vaudeville, and even the *Defender*'s movie and theater critic, Tony Langston, frequently gave live acts top billing over movies in the theaters. In 1914, a *Defender* column asserted that "what the public wants and what the public pays for" are "real Afro-American shows and acts" and stated that the popularity of motion picture venues had "brought the narrow-minded vaudeville manager to his senses" in booking black acts.[74] In another instance, it was noted that "patrons of the Grand who do not go in time to see the 'movies' which always precede the vaudeville many times miss a rare treat,"[75] implying that motion pictures were not always the focal point of the theatrical program at theaters on the T.O.B.A. circuit.

In addition to vaudeville and variety, blues artists such as Bessie Smith, Mamie Smith, Ma Rainey, and Ethel Waters were likely to perform in routines on the T.O.B.A. circuit as early as 1914.[76] Travis recalls that the great "blues belters" of the era were frequent attractions at the Grand and Monogram.[77] Blues as well as jazz drew on a distinctly African-American musical heritage, and the blues incorporated traditions of West African music, with rhythmic counterpoint, call and response patterns, and diatonic "blues scales" as preserved through black folk music, work songs, and spirituals.[78] The blues related directly to black migrants' experiences, blending musical traditions from the rural South into an urban milieu. In her history of blues queens of the 1910s and 1920s, Daphne Duvall Harrison offers a definition of the blues, drawn from blues artists and black writers:

> The blues artist speaks directly to and of the folks who have suffered pain and assures them they are not alone; someone understands. . . . [T]he blues is about life: it has the power to reaffirm the values and worth of the people; and it is a wellspring of solace and hope.[79]

According to Levine, blues served as a group-oriented means of communication and expression, stressing interaction with the audience and often embodying elements of protest and resistance against whites. Moreover, blues performance functioned beyond popular entertainment, combining elements of charisma, catharsis, and solidarity into the manner of a church service. In the dynamic between blues performers and audiences, there were, "properly speaking, . . . no audiences, just participants."[80] These elements of black musical performance, which involved the audience in articulating common problems (including the experience of racism), shared the exhibition venue with mainstream Hollywood entertainment and added a culturally specific and possibly oppositional facet to the context for reception of such movies by a black audience.

Thus, in the "home theaters" of the South Side, the dynamic of reception was inflected with the dynamic of black performance, which addressed and involved the audience in a manner quite different from the motion picture. Even though the exhibition and performance context was imbricated in a national industry and circumscribed by white capital, black Chicagoans brought their cultural practices and expectations to the theaters. The motion picture venue was used as a space for development and display of a new urban black culture, which had both a commercial and popular component. In addition, new migrants could reaffirm their ties to the South at the same time that they encountered mass entertainment by attending the picture show in the same venue that showcased blues artists, the Georgia Minstrels, or a "Jubilee Week of Sunshine in Music," featuring the "Music Born in Our Own Southlands."[81] A performance context was layered over the film reception context, and the thematics and content of Hollywood movies were set against specifically African-American practices, which addressed the experiences of the black community.

The available descriptions of audience behavior in the 1910s often focus on the class composition of audiences and reflect the fact that blacks of all social classes attended theaters on the Stroll. Accounts in the *Defender* employed the discourses of the black middle classes and institutions that attempted to impart values of restraint and respectability to the migrant population. They also reveal the class-stratified response to more boisterous forms of popular entertainment. Noting the "craze" for motion pictures, Sylvester Russell bemoaned the fact that "the best class of people of the colored race are compelled to be mixed in with the undesirable element [in theaters] or remain home in seclusion."[82] In a review of Stewart and Wallace, a vaudeville team, Russell criticized a "falling off of the respectable element," resulting from "Miss Wallace's disreputable dance. . . . It is no wonder that Dr. Fischer extols the people of his church not to go to these wicked moving picture theaters."[83] Reviewing a variety, comedy, and acrobatic show at the Grand, Adams noted that "the 'Dance of the Rose' elicited the greatest applause, or, might I say, the loudest applause, not because a larger number applauded, but because the rough and frenzied style of the dance appealed to certain classes of the people, and that class is the noisiest, though they be few in numbers."[84] Furthermore, contemporaries viewed the blues and jazz music performed in black theaters as a rebellion against the strictures of middle-class mores.[85] In his work on the Harlem Renaissance, Bruce Kellner refers to the ambivalence the black middle classes may have felt toward this explosion of black music, and to blues in particular, which he describes as "frankly erotic and nothing that respectable, middle-class, cultured 'colored people' wanted to disclose."[86] As an institutional voice of the community, the black press sought to promote black performance at the same time it endeavoured to downplay the appeal of lively and bawdy entertainment and the predominance of "certain classes" of migrant and working blacks in the audience.

As Chicago became the major showcase for black music in the late 1910s and black musicians moved up river from New Orleans and St. Louis, blues and, increasingly, jazz dominated the popular nightlife on the Stroll. By the late 1910s, movie theaters in Black Metropolis shared the streets with night spots such as the Sunset, Entertainer, and Plantation Cafes, the Paradise Club, and the De Luxe and Lincoln Gardens, which featured "Jazzaway Jazzcopation" as well as "All-Star" blues and musical reviews, with performers such as Sammy Stewart and the Knights of Syncopation, King Oliver, Slick White, Shakey Beasely, and Jelly Roll Morton.[87] However, black jazz musicians did not simply share the entertainment district with movies; they participated directly in motion picture exhibition through the pit orchestra. The arrival of the jazz age had a marked effect on all aspects of motion picture exhibition in Black Metropolis, from advertising practices, to musical accompaniment of films and audience response, to debates about exhibition in the black press. Often, the insertion of black musical performance into the theatrical venue eclipsed the mass-entertainment component, and the picture house served as a center for the development and appreciation of popular black music.

During the 1920s, the "Musical and Dramatic" section of the *Defender* underwent a noticeable change. Advertisements for "First-Class Motion Picture Theaters" and "Feature Pictures Changed Daily" were overshadowed by advertisements for jazz and blues recordings on "Race" labels such as Columbia, Okeh, Black Swan, and Paramount.[88] The "picture house orchestra" began to dominate theater promotion, and critics and reviewers shifted their emphasis from movies and vaudeville to live music. A typical theatrical listing no longer even named the films playing at the theaters. Instead, for example, one finds notes on Jamie Bell's Orchestra at the Twentieth Century Theater ("the bunch are real picture players, and keep a line of anxious movie fans waiting") or the Sammy Stewart Orchestra, described as "drawing good crowds" at the Metropolitan. Theaters such as the Willard were commended for installing "Race" orchestras because "it means more work for musicians in the theaters."[89] As a performance and employment opportunity for black musicians, the picture house orchestra became a focal point of articles on movie theaters in the *Defender*. Moreover, while whites were part of the audience for jazz in the "Black and Tan" clubs on the South Side, they generally did not patronize the movie theaters or more modest clubs, most likely because they had access to both movies and jazz in other venues. Thus, the movie theaters offered a culturally autonomous setting for jazz performance, where black musicians played for black audiences.[90]

In a *Defender* column entitled "Orchestras as Theater Assets," Dave Peyton, a pit orchestra leader, described the musicians as a "supreme" attraction at the picture house and credited Race orchestras for pulling in an "avalanche of business" at movie theaters on the Stroll. According to Peyton, community members felt "as if they had won a battle of recognition by the placing of their own . . . in these theaters."[91] These musicians did not simply offer conventional piano or symphonic accompaniment for silent films.[92] Rather, they played in quintessential jazz bands—featuring saxophones, trumpets, banjo, tuba, and snare drum, or jazz instrumentation mixed with strings—and were led by popular figures such as Erskine Tate, Jamie Bell, Sammy Stewart, Clarence Black, and Clarence Jones.[93] A member of the Tate orchestra, Louis Armstrong, recalled that he and Fats Waller

> used to play in the symphony orchestra in Chicago in 1925. It was at the Vendome theater, a motion picture house. That was in the days of the silent films. We used to play for the films, and during the intermission we would

play a big Overture and a Red Hot number afterwards. And folks, I'm telling you, we used to really romp.[94]

Cripps has argued that blacks suffered a major disadvantage during the silent era because the lack of sound restricted the strong musical element of traditional black entertainment, which depended on audience reaction and participation for full effect.[95] However, accounts of the effect of Race orchestras on the exhibition context suggest exactly the opposite: the need for orchestras to accompany silent films provided an opportunity for black musical performance and audience participation to a far greater degree than in the sound era.

The black picture house orchestra offers a prime example of the cooptation of the practices, venues, and economic strategies of the motion picture industry by the cultural and economic interests of a minority population. The Race orchestra not only provided employment for black musicians but also infused the exhibition and reception context with a direct expression of black cultural invention. While not an avenue to power and influence in the movie industry, the pit orchestra was a means for blacks to maintain a visible and institutionalized presence in the community exhibition venue. As regular components of theater programs and marketing strategies, black performers could, in some sense, determine and "own" the "means of production" of the exhibition context. In addition, accounts from the period indicate that the pit orchestra was viewed as a means of cultural legitimation for black musicians. But beyond giving some blacks institutional power and respectability in a racist society, the pit orchestra, with its improvisatory jazz performance, altered and disrupted the mainstream exhibition scenario and, at times, flouted black middle-class notions of "proper" music and behavior.

Peyton's column, "The Musical Bunch," a regular *Defender* feature in the 1920s, testifies to the sometimes disruptive function of jazz performance in the picture houses, as well as the response of the black audience. In contrast to many jazz musicians, Peyton could be considered a member of the black professional elite; he was described as holding a doctorate in music, conducted a black symphony orchestra, and led pit orchestras at the Peerless and Regal movie theaters.[96] Furthermore, Peyton's writings reveal the struggle between "respectable" and "popular" culture in the black community as it was played out in the space of the theater and negotiated by the band leader himself.

As implied by the title "The Musical Bunch," Peyton's columns display a definite "within the group" tenor, in terms of both race and the entertainment community. He often counseled black musicians on proper behavior according to ideals of respectability and cultural legitimacy. In addition, Peyton advised black musicians to study European classical music, and he urged black orchestra leaders to set a "Christian and wholesome example" for their band members.[97] However, he also warned black musicians against whites who would steal and exploit their musical talents:

> It has been the custom for many years for the white musicians to come around our orchestras, spending a few dollars for drinks, getting our players to feeling good, and then having our players show them the different jazz tricks. . . . Hold onto your ideas. Don't show them a thing. There is the slap-tongue, the brass cry, the flutter tongue, and the 'wa-wa,' and many other tricks that our group originated. . . . Hold onto our stuff, boys, we can commercialize it just as the white brother is doing.[98]

Peyton's columns exhibit a double-edged strategy for enhancing black opportunity and cultural identity: on one hand, pursuing the legitimacy of European music and respectable behavior while, on the other, guarding black musical invention from appropriation and exploitation by whites.

Peyton held definite opinions about correct performance for picture house orchestras and the limited role that jazz and popular music ought to play. During 1926, he wrote numerous columns criticizing "inappropriate" music in the theaters, indicating that the theater was a terrain of contention between mainstream and popular cultural practices and between certain classically trained band leaders and popular musicians. Peyton's comments are usually framed in terms of cultural legitimacy, often equating "standard" (i.e., white, commercial entertainment practices) with "high" culture and "proper" musical expression. For example:

> The picture industry today requires proper musical settings to bring out its theme. Standard music must be employed to render picture accompaniment. . . . In Chicago, the great metropolis of Western America, the race musician is about to go over the top. We have been playing too much 'hokum' and jazz music. Some of our leaders have the idea in their heads that jazz is all the music the public wants. . . . [J]azz has its place on the [movie] programs, it has its moments, but the general music policy is standard musical portrayal. . . . [M]ix some good music in with your organization in the legitimate class.[99]

The "standard music" and "proper settings" to which Peyton refers are the conventions of piano or orchestral accompaniment for silent feature films. Silent movie accompaniment often incorporated European orchestral music and opera as well as popular tunes and may have been performed according to an original or compiled score. As early as 1910, movie companies, music publishers, and the trade press distributed cue sheets for accompaniment of individual films. Whether arranged or not, movie accompaniment was usually intended to run along with the images, reinforcing the storyline, punctuating the action, heightening emotional affectivity, and supporting character and thematic development.[100] David Bordwell has described musical accompaniment as one of the earliest and most overt "continuity factors" of cinematic narrative. While theaters often showcased musical performance before or between screenings, conventional accompaniment did not function as an autonomous entertainment form or focal point of attention during the film.[101]

The musical trade press often criticized overwrought, ill-paced, or obtrusive musical interpretation for interfering with the audiences' ability to attend to or appreciate the cinematic narrative. Significantly, popular unit organ accompaniment, which drew on a vaudevillian musical style, was accused of being too loud, vulgar, and disruptive of the exhibition context.[102] Peyton's discussions of "inappropriate" music echo these debates but place particular emphasis on popular black music. In Peyton's view, black musical expression was to be integrated into "standard" mainstream practices and thus into the ranks of artistic legitimacy. Jazz and "hokum" could be played before the film or with certain genres such as comedy but not during a drama when "standard" music should be subsumed to the flow of the narrative.[103] According to Peyton, black musical forms had to be kept within certain boundaries, and popular expression needed to be restrained. Otherwise, the Race musician might "go over the top" and jeopardize black cultural "legitimacy." Mainstream commercial entertainment was not to be disrupted by excessive displays of improvisatory, "nonstandard" musical expression.

However, the persistence of Peyton's criticisms and advice to orchestra leaders and musicians indicates significant deviation from his vision of proper integration of black popular music into mainstream cultural practices. Peyton repeatedly admonished picture house orchestras for changing the "atmosphere" that should prevail in the theater by failing to accompany the screen drama with "appropriate classical musical settings."[104] In one column, he chided Race orchestras for "discordant playing," explaining:

> I mean certain so-called jazz artists getting away from the score and the unqualified leader not being aware that the jazz artist is ruining the composition. . . . [T]he 'hokum' player, with jaws poked out, mouthpiece of his instrument buried deep into his lips and making all kinds of weird squawks, is given preference over a first-class schooled musician. . . . This ranting and shimmying in the pit is disgraceful to music. What would Nathaniel Finston, the director of Balaban & Katz's orchestra, look like shaking and ranting over his musicians?[105]

While Peyton's descriptions are intended to criticize the intrusion of unrestrained physical performance and unschooled musical techniques into the "legitimate" arena, he unwittingly reveals the extent to which black performance altered the standard context for motion picture exhibition. Picture house musicians were not heeding Peyton's call for motion picture accompaniment in the dominant style of white downtown theaters. Rather, the pit orchestra was described as erupting into the spectators' consciousness, both visually and aurally, in "discordant" moments of improvisatory performance unsubordinated to the narrative progression of the film. The exhibition context was imbued with a style of black musical performance that drew attention away from the screen, to the "ranting, shimmying" musicians. The theater was transformed from a venue for mass entertainment into a site of exuberant musical invention and expression of difference. And, much to Peyton's dismay, audiences responded to jazz with enthusiasm. "Of course," he wrote, "a few dozen in the audience rave when this jazz player's feature is over, and the word goes out that boy can certainly jazz." On one occasion, Peyton described the "freakish high-registered breaks" in a solo by Louis Armstrong as bringing movie "patrons to a howl." In another instance, Peyton conceded: "Of course, more noise is made by the jazz fiends and popular music lovers [in the audience] because that class of music invites noise and frivolity."[106]

Peyton's grudging acknowledgement of popular enthusiasm for "inappropriate music" echoes earlier critics' disavowal of audience response to the "falling off of the respectable element" in vaudeville performance. Peyton's views on both musical performance and audience behavior deploy notions of "high art" and class-bound behavior identified by Lawrence Levine as central to the "sacralization of culture" operative in the late nineteenth century.[107] Levine describes the bifurcation of public entertainment, such as theater and symphonic music, into "serious" versus popular forms, with a concomitant division of audiences and venues along socioeconomic lines, especially in large urban centers. In particular, Levine identifies a trend toward the sacralization of orchestral music, as endowed with unique spiritual properties. As a form of "high culture," classical music was to be performed by highly trained musicians on a program free from contamination by popular entertainment or interference from a "disrespectful" audience.[108] These values are echoed in Peyton's description of "standard," classical, European music, which "carries in its theme a moral lesson, it recites history, it appeals. It's absolutely essential to the gallery of the world's arts."[109] Moreover, according to Levine, audience behavior was increasingly circumscribed, both by official protocols and informal social controls. Behavior patterns that had once characterized Shakespearean playhouses (smoking, "audible dramatic criticism," talking, whistling, stomping, hand-clapping) were deemed inappropriate for a "highbrow" cultural context and were increasingly transferred to venues for "lowbrow" popular entertainment, such as vaudeville and burlesque.[110]

Peyton's columns incorporate these values, revealing class friction and differing cultural aspirations within the black community. Peyton tended to position the motion picture as a "highbrow" cultural product, which demanded the respect of the audience and deserved the "standard" accompaniment of classical music. Motion pictures were a link with a powerful white culture, with which Peyton hoped the Race would achieve legitimacy. By narrowly defining the role of black music and disowning "certain classes" who responded to popular music with "noise and frivolity," Peyton hoped to bring the behavior of both performers and audiences in line with the mainstream. Peyton's multiple identification as a popular and classical musician, defender of black musical invention and institutional voice of the black middle class, led him to promote a gradual and unobtrusive introduction of black popular music into the space of the theater. However, he was fighting a losing battle.

After repeatedly advocating conventional orchestral accompaniment for movies, Peyton responded to the continued "jazzing" of motion pictures with a special column in 1926, entitled "The Picture House Orchestra," which the *Defender* reprinted in 1927. It reads, in part:

> The orchestra in the picture house, with its extensive library, has the advantage over the vaudeville orchestra. They have plenty of opportunity to rehearse and prepare their programs. . . . In most of our Race picture houses, mostly controlled by white capital, the Race orchestras discolor the atmosphere that should prevail in the picture house by not characterizing the photoplay, although having all the above-mentioned advantages. During a death scene flashed on the screen, you are likely to hear the orchestra jazzing away on 'Clap Hands, Here Comes Charlie.' I blame the leader for this carelessness. He should watch his pictures more closely and make his settings to harmonize.
>
> Another bad feature in the picture orchestra is the improper line-up of the instrumentation. The big brass tuba, banjo and saxophones have no business in the legitimate picture orchestra during the showing of a dramatic screenplay. The regular legitimate orchestral line-up should be employed. The leaders should visit the larger Loop and outlying houses, see the system, and employ it in their theaters. . . .
>
> There is entirely too much 'hokum' played in our Race picture houses. It only appeals to a certain riff-raff element who loudly clap hands when the orchestra stops, misleading the leader to believe that his efforts are winning the approval of the entire audience. . . .
>
> Polite syncopation during a comedy or newsreel picture dealing in the popular syncopated melodies is delightful to hear, but the awful, low-down, so-called blues should be eliminated entirely from the pit.[111]

Peyton's diatribe encapsulates the various elements of the exhibition and reception context in theaters in Black Metropolis, from the issue of white economic control, to the pit musicians' disregard of "orthodox" practices, to the contradictory responses of "respectables" and "riff-raff" in the audience. Performing in white-owned, commercial venues, black musicians appropriated the place and role of the picture house orchestra for culturally specific and even oppositional practices. Jazz performed during the exhibition of films offered black spectators a lively demonstration of ethnic difference and invention, quite separate from the entertainment on the screen. In the Race picture houses, movie music often functioned as an autonomous entertainment form and significantly altered the dynamic between film text and spectator. Peyton's reference to the discontinuity between a cinematic death scene and its musical "accompaniment" suggests that Race orchestras might have gone beyond simply ignoring the narrative or the sheet music library to read films against the grain, undermining "preferred readings" with satirical interpretations. As manifest displays of African-American culture, jazz and blues subverted the influence of mainstream entertainment, in a prime example of the semiotic opportunism of popular culture. The imposed system of exhibition and industry practices offered black musicians and spectators the chance actively to undermine the homogenizing force of mass entertainment.

Doubtless, some audience members agreed with Peyton and were unhappy with the disruption of Hollywood movies by "ranting, shimmying" musicians and the loudly clapping "riff-raff." Yet, even for spectators who wanted a mainstream cinematic experience or who simply wanted to follow the film, the reception context was altered by the presence of black performers. In a sense, the ideological operations of white-produced commercial films were uncovered by the interplay between screen and stage entertainment. Live black performance may have pointed out the exclusion and stereotyping of blacks in Hollywood cinema, and white ideals of glamour, stardom, and performance were perceived in relation to those exemplified by black entertainers who had an altogether different relation to their audience than did the stars on the screen.

The prevailing exhibition context in Chicago's South Side did not play out an embourgeoisement scenario or foster the uncomplicated assimilation of black workers and migrants into the American mainstream. Rather, the movie theater was a place where racial identity could be asserted in the face of mass culture, as well as a space where class and regional allegiances could be forged within the black community. Unfortunately, the particular historical circumstances that enabled black culture to maintain a strong presence in Chicago's Race theaters were dissolved by the onset of the Depression and the conversion to sound. The stock market crash dealt a severe blow to black businesses and financial resources, facilitating inroads by white-owned chains and effectively halting the struggle for an independent black marketplace. Black workers and the unemployed no longer had the discretionary income to spend on leisure activities, and their influence as movie consumers diminished. Moreover, the financial impact of the Depression on theaters and the introduction of the "talkies" greatly reduced employment and performance opportunities for black musicians and entertainers.[112] But throughout the silent era, the movie theater provided the inhabitants of Black Metropolis with the opportunity to construct a specifically African-American, urban, popular culture. More than just a site of unqualified hegemony for white, commercial culture, the South Side theater was a place where black performers and spectators could "really romp."

Appendix: Motion Picture Theaters, 1909–1928

Below are picture houses, movie theaters, and other venues advertising or listed as featuring movies, "photoplays," or "pictures that move" in the Chicago *Defender* (1909–1928). Seating capacities are supplied in parentheses when available (*Film Daily Yearbook* 1926–1929). Information on theaters of the 1920s is also from listings in *The Official Theatrical World of Colored Artists*.

Theaters, 1909–1913

Byron's Temple of Music, 3230 S. State St.

Chateau Gardens, 5318–26 S. State St.

Grand (716), 3110–3112 S. State St.

Lincoln (299), 3132 S. State St.

Lux, 35th and Michigan Ave.

Majestic

Merit

Monogram (432), 3028 S. State St.

Mott's Pekin Temple, 27th and S. State St.

Phoenix, 3104 S. State St.

States (686), 35th and S. State St.

Washington, 3440 S. State St.

Theaters, 1915–1917

Apollo (669), 47th and Forrestville

Atlas (650), 4711–17 S. State St.

Elba, 3115 Indiana

Fountain, 344 E. 35th St.

Grand (716), 3110–3112 S. State St.

Lincoln (299), 3132 S. State St.

Monogram (432), 3028 S. State St.

Mott's Pekin Temple, 27th and S. State St.

Owl (944), 4653 S. State St.

Phoenix, 3104 S. State St.

Pickford (754), 35th and Michigan Ave.

Star, 3837 S. State St.

States (686), 35th and S. State St.

Vendome (1265), 3143 S. State St.

Washington, 3440 S. State St.

Theaters, 1925–1928

Apollo (669), 47th and Forrestville

Caruso's Virginia (276), 43rd and Indiana

Franklin (739), 31st and Calumet

Grand (716), 3110–3112 S. State St.

Groveland (400), 31st and Cottage Grove

Harmony (593), 411 E. 43rd St.

Indiana (786), 219 W. 43rd St.

Lincoln (299), 3132 S. State St.

Lyceum (700), 3851 Cottage Grove

Metropolitan (1384), 4622 Grand
Boulevard/South Parkway

Michigan (1345), 110 E. 55th St.

Monogram (432), 3028 S.
State St.

Owl (944), 4653 S. State St.

Peerless (904), 3955 Grand
Boulevard/South Parkway

Pickford (754), 35th and Michigan
Ave.

Regal (3000), 47th and Grand
Boulevard/South Parkway

States (686), 35th and S. State St.

20th Century (932), 4708 Prairie

Vendome (1265), 3143 S. State St.

Western (298), 2311 West Lake St.

Willard (1195), 51st and Calumet

NOTES

I am grateful to the members of the University of Wisconsin-Madison Historiography Seminar (spring 1988), who provided stimulating discussion and commentary on an earlier version of this paper. Thanks also to Lynn Spigel and Michael Friend for their help in preparing this manuscript for publication.

1. Dempsey Travis, *An Autobiography of Black Jazz* (Chicago: Urban Research Institute, 1983), p. 34.

2. Ibid., p. 2.

3. See, for example, Robert C. Allen, "Motion Picture Exhibition in Manhattan, 1906–1912: Beyond the Nickelodeon," *Cinema Journal* 28:2 (1979), 2–15; Douglas Gomery, "The Growth of Movie Monopolies: The Case of Balaban and Katz," *Wide Angle* 3:1 (1979), 54–63, and "Movie Audiences, Urban Geography, and the History of the American Film," *The Velvet Light Trap* 19 (1982), 23–29; Garth Jowett, "The First Motion Picture Audiences," *Journal of Popular Film* 3:1 (1974), 39–54; Judith Mayne, "Immigrants and Spectators," *Wide Angle* 2 (1982), 32–40; Russell Merritt, "Nickelodeon Theaters, 1905–1914: Building an Audience for the Movies," in Tino Balio, ed., *The American Film Industry*, rev. ed. (Madison: University of Wisconsin Press, 1985), pp. 83–102.

4. Chicago Commission on Race Relations, *The Negro in Chicago: A Study of Race Relations and a Race Riot* (Chicago: University of Chicago Press, 1922), p. 22; James R. Grossman, *Land of Hope: Chicago, Black Southerners, and the Great Migration* (Chicago: University of Chicago Press, 1989), pp. 127, 135, 278; Jacqueline Jones, *Labor of Love, Labor of Sorrow: Black Women, Work and the Family from Slavery to the Present* (New York: Vintage, 1985), pp. 153–6. Between 1900 and 1930, over 2 million blacks left the South for northern cities. From 1916 to 1921, an estimated half million blacks headed north, almost 5 percent of the total southern black population. Between 1880 and 1910, Chicago's black population rose from 6,480 to 44,103; in 1920, the census put the number of blacks at 109,458, an increase of over 65,000. However, Grossman notes that the 1920 census probably undercounted blacks, and sources such as the Urban League estimated that the black population increased by 50,000 between 1916 and 1917 alone and by 75,000 between 1913 and 1919.

5. Lizabeth Cohen, "Encountering Mass Culture at the Grassroots: The Experience of Chicago Workers in the 1920s," *American Quarterly* 41:1 (1989), 7. Cohen refers to Daniel Bell, *The End of Ideology* (New York: Harvard University Press, 1962); Stuart Ewen, *Captains of Consciousness: Advertising and the Social Roots of Consumer Culture* (New York: McGraw, 1976); Stuart and Elizabeth Ewen, *Channels of Desire: Mass Images and the Shaping of American Consciousness* (New York: McGraw, 1982); Richard W. Fox and T. Jackson Lears, eds., *The Culture of Consumption* (New York: Pantheon, 1983); John Goldthorpe and David

Lockwood, *The Affluent Worker in the Class Structure* (London: Cambridge University Press, 1969).

6. Cohen, "Encountering Mass Culture," pp. 7, 16.

7. Ibid., pp. 21–26.

8. John Fiske, "Popular Forces and the Culture of Everyday Life," *Southern Review* 21 (1988), 288–306. Also see Michel de Certeau, *The Practice of Everyday Life* (Berkeley: University of California Press, 1984). Fiske uses de Certeau's model of military strategies and tactics to distinguish between mass and popular culture. According to this model, those in possession of social or institutional power exercise strategies, which are visible and regularized manipulations of power, with recognizable agents, discourses, and means and places of operation. Accordingly, the distribution of mass entertainment through the channels and venues of the motion picture industry is a strategic operation in the consumer society of late capitalism. Tactics, on the other hand, are deployed by those without access to social or institutional power. Tactics consist of sporadic, unsystematic acts, which resist or evade the "occupying forces" in their own places of operation. In creating popular culture, socially and economically subordinated people exercise *tactical* consumption, a form of semiotic opportunism characterized by de Certeau as trickery, ruse, or even "guerilla warfare," in which the cultural products of the imposed system are used for oppositional purposes. However, this opposition between strategies and tactics as deployed by distinct social groups is not borne out by an examination of the moviegoing practices and cultural activities of black Chicagoans in the silent era. Although black Chicagoans had limited access to social and institutional power in the larger society, different sectors of the black community deployed strategies as well as tactics to utilize movie exhibition for culturally specific purposes.

9. Fiske, "Popular Forces," pp. 288–91.

10. See Thomas Cripps, *Slow Fade to Black: The Negro in American Film, 1900–1942* (New York: Oxford University Press, 1977); Cripps, "'Race Movies' as Voices of the Black Bourgeoisie: *The Scar of Shame*," in John E. O'Connor and Martin A. Jackson, eds., *American History/American Film* (New York: Ungar, 1979), pp. 39–56; Cripps, *Black Film as Genre* (Bloomington: Indiana University Press, 1978); Cripps, "Black Films and Filmmakers: Movies in the Ghetto, B.P. (Before Poitier)," *Negro Digest* (February 1969); Cripps, "The Dark Spot in the Kaleidoscope: Black Images in American Film," in Randall M. Miller, ed., *The Kaleidoscope Lens: How Hollywood Views Ethnic Groups* (New York: Jerome S. Ozer, 1980), pp. 15–35. Also see Donald Bogle, *Toms, Coons, Mulattoes, Mammies and Bucks: An Interpretive History of Blacks in American Films* (New York: Viking, 1973); Daniel J. Leab, *From Sambo to Superspade: The Black Experience in Motion Pictures* (Boston: Houghton Mifflin, 1975); Edward Mapp, *Blacks in American Films: Today and Yesterday* (Metuchen: Scarecrow, 1974); Peter Noble, *The Cinema and the Negro, 1905–1948* (London: S. Robinson, 1948) and *The Negro in Films* (London: S. Robinson, 1948); Gary Null, *Black Hollywood* (New York: Citadel, 1975); Lindsay Patterson, *Black Films and Filmmakers* (New York: Dodd, 1975).

11. See Jane Gaines, "*Scar of Shame:* Skin Color and Caste in Black Silent Melodrama," *Cinema Journal* 26:4 (1987), 3–21. Gaines addresses the historical black spectator as constructed by the mode of address and textual operations of silent melodrama.

12. Grossman, *Land of Hope*, p. 5; Jones, *Labor of Love*, pp. 153–6; Lawrence W. Levine, *Black Culture and Black Consciousness: Afro-American Folk Thought from Slavery to Freedom* (New York: Oxford University Press, 1977), p. 265.

13. Grossman, *Land of Hope*, pp. 4–8.

14. Chicago Commission, *Negro in Chicago*, pp. 22, 106; St. Clair Drake and Horace R. Clayton, *Black Metropolis: A Study of Negro Life in a Northern City* (New York: Harcourt, 1945), pp. 8–12, 174; Grossman, *Land of Hope*, pp. 123–7, 177–80. Also see *Black Metropolis Historic District* (Chicago: Commission of Chicago Historical and Architectural Landmarks, 1984); Otis and Beverly Duncan, *The Negro Population of Chicago: A Study of Residential Succession* (Chicago: University of Chicago Press, 1957); Allan Spear, *Black Chicago: The*

Making of a Negro Ghetto, 1890–1920 (Chicago: University of Chicago Press, 1967). The area encompassed by Black Metropolis began around 22nd St. and extended southward past 51st St. in the 1910s and between 63rd and 71st Sts. in the 1920s. To the west, the district was bounded by the Rock Island and New York Central tracks (between Wentworth and S. Dearborn), beyond which lived working-class ethnic whites. Across Cottage Grove Ave., the eastern border, were white middle-class neighborhoods and the University of Chicago area. Drake and Clayton, *Black Metropolis*, pp. 15, 63; Grossman, *Land of Hope*, pp. 124–6. Also see Homer Hoyt, *Forty-Four Cities in the City of Chicago* (Chicago: Chicago Plan Commission, 1942); and Louis Wirth and Eleanor H. Bernert, *Local Community Fact Book of Chicago* (Chicago: University of Chicago Press, 1949).

    15. See Chicago Commission, *Negro in Chicago*, pp. 1–16; Grossman, *Land of Hope*, pp. 177–80; and William M. Tuttle, Jr., "Contested Neighborhoods and Racial Violence: Prelude to the Chicago Riot of 1919," *Journal of Negro History* 15:4 (1970), 266–88.

    16. Mahalia Jackson and Evan M. Wylie, *Movin' On Up* (New York: Hawthorne, 1966), p. 46, quoted in Grossman, *Land of Hope*, p. 261.

    17. Grossman, *Land of Hope*, pp. 127–8, 161, 260–1.

    18. Ibid., pp. 28–9, 184; David Gordon Nielson, *Black Ethos: Northern Urban Negro Life and Thought, 1890–1930* (Westport, Conn.: Greenwood, 1977), pp. xv, 2, 51. Also see Leroi Jones (Amiri Baraka), *Blues People: Negro Music in White America* (New York: William Morrow, 1971), pp. 53–54, 130–3.

    19. Gaines, *"Scar of Shame,"* pp. 11–13.

    20. Grossman, *Land of Hope*, pp. 128–9; Nielson, *Black Ethos*, p. 56.

    21. Grossman, *Land of Hope*, pp. 131, 143–50.

    22. Nielson, *Black Ethos*, p. 196.

    23. Grossman, *Land of Hope*, pp. 128–31; Nielson, *Black Ethos,* p. xv.

    24. "Black Capitalism" had been central to Booker T. Washington's doctrine of self-help and was integral to the separatist program of Marcus Garvey's United Negro Improvement Association, which had particular currency with black workers. Cohen, "Encountering Mass Culture," pp. 21–23; Nielson, *Black Ethos*, pp. 102–6. For an example of contemporary discourses on economic independence, see Kathryn M. Johnson, "Observations About the Need of Business Enterprises Among Colored People," *Half-Century Magazine* (December 1916), 12.

    25. Cohen, "Encountering Mass Culture," p. 23.

    26. Grossman, *Land of Hope*, pp. 357–58; *The Official Theatrical World of Colored Artists* (New York: Theatrical World Publishing, 1928), p. 16.

    27. Nielson, *Black Ethos*, p. 11.

    28. Grossman, *Land of Hope*, pp. 74, 78. For a detailed discussion of the *Defender* and its role in the migration process, see Grossman, *Land of Hope*, pp. 66–97.

    29. Ibid., p. 75.

    30. Ibid., p. 86.

    31. Ibid., p. 86; *Black Metropolis Historic District*, pp. 1–16.

    32. Grossman, *Land of Hope*, p. 132.

    33. See Appendix for listings of community movie theaters.

    34. Travis, *Autobiography of Black Jazz*, p. 30.

    35. Seating capacities drawn from *The Film Yearbook* (New York: Film Daily, 1926), pp. 496–8; *Film Yearbook* (1927), pp. 530–2; *The Film Daily Yearbook* (1928), pp. 545–679; *Film Daily Yearbook* (1929), pp. 599–601.

    36. This corroborates and extends Robert C. Allen's argument that small-time vaudeville, as an autonomous entertainment form, was a major factor in motion picture exhibition in the early 1910s. Allen, "Motion Picture Exhibition," p. 10.

    37. *Defender* (31 July 1909), 3; (20 July 1913), 5.

    38. *Official Theatrical World*, p. 66.

    39. Ibid.; Travis, *Autobiography of Black Jazz*, p. 145.

40. See Gomery, "Movie Audiences," pp. 26–28.

41. Sylvester Russell, "Musical and Dramatic," *Defender* (9 April 1910), 3; (5 August 1911), 4.

42. "Musical and Dramatic," *Defender* (4 September 1915), 6.

43. Both these theaters were identified as having black proprietors. Available accounts indicate that the Pekin was owned and operated by Robert T. Motts from 1905 until his death in 1913 or 1914 and that the Star was owned by Teenan Jones from the mid- to late 1910s. "Musical and Dramatic," *Defender* (4 February 1912), 6; (24 February 1914), 6; (31 January 1916), 6; Junius Wood, "The Negro in Chicago," report from the Chicago *Daily News* (11–27 December 1916), 25.

44. Minnie Adams, "In Union Is Strength," *Defender* (24 February 1912), 6.

45. Ibid.; "Musical and Dramatic," *Defender* (31 January 1916), 6.

46. Juli Jones, "Motion Pictures and Inside Facts," *Half-Century Magazine* (July 1919), 16.

47. "Musical and Dramatic," *Defender* (31 January 1914), 6.

48. Gomery, "Movie Monopolies," pp. 57–61; advertisements, *Defender* (17 January 1917), 3; (17 April 1917), 3.

49. Chicago Commission, *Negro in Chicago*, pp. 317–20.

50. Cohen, "Encountering Mass Culture," p. 16.

51. Chicago Commission, *Negro in Chicago*, pp. 317–20.

52. *Defender* (11 July 1910), 1.

53. Ibid.

54. Dempsey Travis, *An Autobiography of Black Chicago* (Chicago: Urban Research Institute, 1981), p. 32.

55. Gomery, "Movie Monopolies," p. 59.

56. *Defender* (17 June 1911), 3; (8 March 1913), 5; (21 August 1915), 6.

57. Adams, "In Union Is Strength," p. 6.

58. *Defender* (17 January 1917), 3; (17 April 1917), 3.

59. Dave Peyton, "The Picture House Orchestra," *Defender* (3 April 1926), 6.

60. Established in Chicago, the Micheaux Film Corp. moved its studio and production operations to New York in 1921. For a detailed account of black and black-cast productions, see Henry T. Sampson, *Blacks in Black and White: A Sourcebook on Black Films* (Metuchen: Scarecrow, 1977). According to Sampson, there were approximately 95 independent film companies that produced black-cast films in the silent era, 10 of which were Chicago-based. Approximately 40 of these companies were black-owned and -operated. Sampson estimates 135 silent-era black-cast productions, noting 1921 as the peak year with 30 releases.

61. Advertisement, *Defender* (17 January 1920), 7.

62. Ibid.

63. Cripps, *Slow Fade to Black*, p. 5.

64. D. Ireland Thomas, *Defender* (10 January 1925), quoted in Sampson, *Blacks in Black and White*, pp. 6–7.

65. See Cohen, "Encountering Mass Culture," 21–24, for a discussion of consumption patterns in Black Metropolis.

66. *Defender* (26 January 1918), 7; Travis, *Autobiography of Black Jazz*, p. 30.

67. *Defender* (30 July 1910), 4; (28 October 1911), 6.

68. Daphne Duvall Harrison, *Black Pearls: Blues Queens of the 1920's* (New Brunswick: Rutgers University Press, 1988), pp. 24–29.

69. Ibid., p. 27; *Official Theatrical World*, 66, 75. Besides performing with the Georgia Minstrels and Smart Set Comedians, S.H. Dudley organized the first black theater circuit in 1913 and became a major stockholder in T.O.B.A. in 1920. Bruce Kellner, ed., *The Harlem Renaissance: A Historical Dictionary for the Era* (New York: Methuen, 1984), p. 107.

70. Harrison, *Black Pearls*, pp. 29–30.

71. Ibid., p. 72; advertisements, *Defender* (12 August 1911), 3; (26 January 1918), 7; Travis, *Autobiography of Black Jazz*, p. 30. Comic Billy King organized and toured with a number of minstrel troupes and staged weekly shows, often with dancer Bill Bailey, at the Grand until 1923. Actor, comic, and dancer Bert Williams performed with the Ziegfeld Follies and appeared in two films, *Darktown Follies* (1914) and *A Natural Born Gambler* (Biograph, 1916). Actor and producer Salem Tutt Whitney staged shows with brother Homer Tutt on the T.O.B.A. circuit and in Harlem theaters, and he toured with the Smart Set Revue and Sissieretta Jones. Jones, known as "Black Patti" after Italian prima donna Adelina Patti, studied at the New England Conservatory as well as headlining the Black Patti Troubadors and Black Patti Musical Comedy Company. Langston Hughes, *Black Magic: A Pictorial History of the Negro in American Entertainment* (New York: Prentice-Hall, 1967), pp. 54–56, 96, 337; Kellner, *Harlem Renaissance*, pp. 204–5, 210–1, 338, 387.

72. "Musical and Dramatic," *Defender* (10 February 1910), 4; (23 April 1910), 4; (7 May 1910), 4.

73. Grossman, *Land of Hope*, p. 103.

74. "Musical and Dramatic," *Defender* (29 August 1914), 6.

75. Ibid.

76. Harrison, *Black Pearls*, p. 23.

77. Travis, *Autobiography of Black Jazz*, p. 30.

78. See Ernest-Borneman, "The Roots of Jazz," in Nat Hentoff, ed., *Jazz: New Perspectives on the History of Jazz by Twelve of the World's Foremost Critics and Scholars* (New York: Rinehart, 1959); Leonard Feather, *The Encyclopedia of Jazz* (New York: Horizon, 1960); W. C. Handy and Abbe Niles, *Blues: An Anthology* (New York: A. & C. Boni, 1926): Harrison, introduction, *Black Pearls*; Jones (Baraka), *Blues People*; Levine, *Black Culture*, Chap. 4; Stephen Longstreet, *The Real Jazz, New and Old* (Baton Rouge: University of Louisiana Press, 1956); Gunther Schuller, *Early Jazz: Its Roots and Musical Development* (New York: Oxford University Press, 1968); Bruce Kellner, ed., *Keep A-Inchin' Along: Selected Writings of Carl Van Vechten about Black Arts and Letters*, (Westport, Conn.: Greenwood, 1979).

79. Harrison, *Black Pearls*, pp. 6–7.

80. Levine, *Black Culture*, pp. 234–7.

81. *Defender* (17 September 1921), 8.

82. Russell, "Musical and Dramatic," *Defender* (9 April 1910), 3.

83. Russell, "Musical and Dramatic," *Defender* (12 February 1910), 3.

84. Adams, "Musical and Dramatic," *Defender* (22 June 1912), 6.

85. Levine, *Black Culture*, pp. 239, 293.

86. Kellner, *Harlem Renaissance*, p. xix.

87. *Defender* (11 March 1922), 6; (25 March 1922), 7.

88. As Levine and Cohen argue, the success of "Race" records exemplifies the impact of blacks as consumers of mass culture. Between 1920 and 1942, 5,500 blues records, featuring black artists, were issued on record labels owned and controlled by whites (except for Black Swan) and marketed exclusively to black audiences. An estimated 5 to 6 million Race records were sold each year in the 1920s, at a time when the entire black population in the US numbered no more than 15 million. Cohen, 24–25; Levine, 225–9. Also see Ronald Clifford Foreman, "Jazz and Race Records, 1920–32: Their Origins and Their Significance for the Record Industry and Society," dissertation, University of Illinois, 1969.

89. "Musical and Dramatic," *Defender* (15 May 1926), 6. Orchestras and leaders appeared to have migrated between theaters. In 1921, advertisements and notices placed the Erskine Tate Orchestra at the Vendome; the Clarence Lee Orchestra at the Owl; the Clarence Black Orchestra at the Pickford (at the Savoy Ballroom by 1928), and the Clarence Jones Orchestra at the Avenue, a vaudeville theater. In 1926, Dave Peyton was listed at the Peerless Theater. *Defender* (17 December 1921), 6; (15 May 1926), 6. *Official Theatrical World* lists the following as "established orchestras" in 1928: Verona Biggs Orchestra, Owl; Billy Butler

Orchestra, Grand; Clarence Jones Orchestra, Vendome; Dave Peyton Orchestra, Regal; Sammy Stewart Orchestra, Willard; Erskine Tate Orchestra, Metropolitan (p. 64).

90. Cohen, "Encountering Mass Culture," p. 24.

91. Peyton, "Orchestras as Theater Assets," *Defender* (16 October 1926), 6.

92. See Gillian B. Anderson, *Music for Silent Films, 1894–1929* (Washington, D.C.: Library of Congress, 1988), p. xv–xviii.

93. Orrin Keepnews and Bill Brauer, Jr., *A Pictorial History of Jazz* (New York: Crown, 1955), p. 37; *Official Theatrical World,* p. 64; Travis, *Autobiography of Black Jazz,* p. 131.

94. Nat Shapiro and Nat Hentoff, eds., *Hear Me Talkin' to Ya: The Story of Jazz by the Men Who Made It* (New York: Rinehart, 1955), p. 256. I am grateful to Johnine Ornelas for pointing out this quote and source.

95. Cripps, *Slow Fade to Black,* p. 4.

96. Adams, "Musical and Dramatic," *Defender* (29 January 1916), 6.

97. Peyton, "Musical Bunch," *Defender* (5 June 1926), 6; (14 August 1926), 6; (26 September 1926), 6.

98. Peyton, "Musical Bunch," *Defender* (23 October 1926), 6.

99. Peyton, "Musical Bunch," *Defender* (9 October 1926), 6.

100. Anderson, *Music for Silent Films,* xiii–xli; David Bordwell, Janet Staiger, and Kristin Thompson, *The Classical Hollywood Cinema: Film Style and Mode of Production to 1960* (New York: Columbia University Press, 1985), pp. 33–5.

101. Bordwell et al., *Classical Hollywood Cinema,* pp. 33–5.

102. Anderson, *Music for Silent Films,* pp. xxvi–ii.

103. Peyton, "Standard Music," *Defender* (5 June 1926), 6; "Modern Orchestra Formation," *Defender* (15 May 1926), 6.

104. Peyton, "Modern Orchestra," p. 6.

105. Peyton, "Musical Bunch," *Defender* (3 July 1926), 6; (9 October 1926), 6.

106. Peyton, "Musical Bunch," *Defender* (3 July 1926), 6; (17 September 1927), 6; "Standard Music," p. 6.

107. Lawrence W. Levine, *Highbrow/Lowbrow: The Emergence of Cultural Hierarchy in America* (Cambridge: Harvard University Press, 1988).

108. Ibid., pp. 68, 132.

109. Peyton, "Standard Music," p. 6.

110. Levine, *Highbrow/Lowbrow,* p. 77.

111. Peyton, "Picture House Orchestra," p. 6; reprinted in *Defender* (23 September 1927), 6.

112. *Black Metropolis Historic District,* pp. 1–16; Cohen, "Encountering Mass Culture," pp. 26–7.

Gaylyn Studlar

The Perils of Pleasure?
Fan Magazine Discourse as
Women's Commodified
Culture in the 1920s

The hand that shakes the chatelaine rules the screen. She may not count for much at the polls, but at the box office her two-bit ballot controls the situation, making and unmaking stars.
—Herbert Howe, "What are Matinee Idols Made of?" *Photoplay, April 1923*

What is the matter with the movies today? . . . This daydream stuff, and sex problems, have killed the pictures.
—*Letter to the Editor,* Motion Picture Magazine, *December 1921*

In the 1920s, the American film industry clearly operated on the assumption that women formed their single most important audience. Even though the notion of a female box-office majority—at any time in American film history—has been dismissed as an erroneous "impression," the significance of the female film audience was reaffirmed by Hollywood throughout the decade. A *Photoplay* article from 1924 suggests that the American film audience was 75 percent women while a *Moving Picture World* article of 1927 cites women's 83 percent majority at the movies. A 1928 article from *Exhibitors Herald/Moving Picture World* asserts: "It has become an established fact that women fans constitute the major percentage of patronage or at least cast the final vote in determining the majority patronage."[1]

In its assessment of the relationship between female viewers and Hollywood cinema, current theory proposes that the industry's appeal to

From *Wide Angle* 13:1 (1991). Reprinted by permission of the author and The Johns Hopkins University Press.

women is so overwhelmingly consumer-oriented that it is usually more apparent in the extratextual cinematic discourse attached to films than in the films themselves. I do not believe that this generalized view holds true of the 1920s, an era marked by an impressive number of film romances, female-centered and domestic melodramas, often adapted by women screenwriters from popular literature aimed directly at women. But in this article, my interests are focused on the well-orchestrated exploitation of a star system aimed largely at women. This system provided the most obvious (and controversial) extratextual (as well as textual) evidence of American women's impact on the cinema in the 1920s. For this was the decade in which movie palaces were turned into what theater manager Arthur Mayer vilified as "Valentino traps" (figures 26a and 26b.)[2]

In pursuing the issue of women's spectatorship and its relationship to star discourse during Hollywood filmmaking practice of the 1920s, this paper has two broadly conceived and related purposes: first, to explore the relationship of the American cinema of the 1920s to historically constructed notions of femininity; and second, to complicate speculative theories of spectatorship and gender that posit classical Hollywood cinema as a relatively transhistorical and monolithic entity subjecting women to predictably powerful and oppressive effects. These two goals are formulated as a response to Miriam Hansen's call for an alternative history of film culture that will locate the "traces" of female subjectivity heretofore ignored and account for the effect of different historical periods and social formations on the positioning of women in relation to dominant cinema.[3]

In responding to the need of which Hansen speaks, I am addressing the historical and cultural specificity of ideological configurations of gendered subjectivity as they appear in one unlikely extratextual cinematic discourse: the fan or movie magazine. I will argue that the fan magazine is a crucial index of the ideological and historical dimensions of the cinematic field of the 1920s and a neglected source for assessing how women were positioned as viewers/readers/consumers within discourses specifically aimed at influencing women's reception of Hollywood film. In fact, the fan magazine may be a more demographically reliable indicator of what women actually experienced of extratextual film mechanisms than those tie-ups ("tie-ins") and exhibition ploys suggested by press books and exhibitors trade magazines. Press books served as guides to exhibitors, but they are no guarantee of what was actually used in practice to address women moviegoers. We can also assume that—at 5 to 25 cents a copy—fan magazines were widely accessible to a much broader segment of the female population than were tie-in purchases or contests aimed at specific groups at selected times and exhibition locations. In 1922, *Photoplay* alone claimed a circulation of over two million copies per month. In addition, beginning in the 1920s, most fan magazines adopted a policy of including direct feedback from readers in their editorial pages that further distinguished them from many other largely "one-way" promotional mechanisms.[4]

The
SHEIK

The
popular romance
lives again
on the screen,
with
Agnes Ayres
and
Rudolph Valentino
in the
leading roles.

Photographs by Donald Biddle Keyes.

Below—A scene from
"The Sheik," with
Valentino and Agnes
Ayres.

HAVE you read it? The chances are that you
have. The story of a handsome Arab Sheik,
and the English woman whom he kidnaps and
holds for his own, is peculiarly adaptable to
pictures. For the glamor and the beauty of the
desert, the colorful costumes, the real love story lend
themselves to the shadows. Rudolph Valentino, the
Latin lover of "The Four Horsemen," plays the
Sheik. Agnes Ayres is *Diana*, the heroine. The
whole is more or less a tangible version of "Pale hands
I love, beside the Shalimar, where are you now, who
lies beneath thy spell?" But we wonder what the
censors will do to it.

Figure 26a.

Mr. Valentino
with Agnes
Ayers in "The
Sheik"

Mr. Valentino
Demonstrates
cave-man love and
tenderness. His article
tells his preference

With Gloria
Swanson
"Beyond the
Rocks"

Woman and Love

By RUDOLPH VALENTINO

WHEN you ask me to write for you what I think about woman, I feel that I must produce for you something that would look like the Encyclopedia Britannica. Yet when I should be through with his great work, I shall still have said less than nothing about oman.

We cannot know woman because she does not know herself. She is the unsolvable mystery, perhaps because there is no olution. The Sphinx has never spoken—perhaps because she has nothing to say.

But since woman is the legitimate object of man's thoughts, and mine have been somewhat distilled in the alcohol of experience, I may be able to give to you a little draft of truth.

English is not my own tongue as you know. In Italian, French, Spanish, I might express myself better, for there we have such little words that have fire and understanding and delicate shades of meaning to which I know not yet the English translations.

My point of the view on woman is Latin—is continental. The American man I do not understand at all. I have lived much in Paris, in Rome, in New York, and from this traveling, which is of the finest to develop the mind and understanding soul, I have composed my little philosophy about woman.

For there is only one book in which you may read about Woman. That is the Book of Life. And even that is written in cipher.

But those who refuse to read it are generally more deeply wounded than those who digest it thoroughly.

What comes to my mind first as I try to put into some order my ideas on this all-important subject, I will tell you first of all this: Which of the

women I have known, have perhaps loved a little, do I remember instantly, and which have I forgotten, so that I must think and think to recall them at all?

The most difficult thing in the world is to make a man love you when he sees you every day. The next is to make him remember that he has loved you when he no longer sees you at all.

Strangely enough, I remember the women who told me perhaps their little lonelinesses, who spoke in close moments true and sweet and simple heart throbs.

Even the highest peak of emotion is finished. It has flamed, gone out, and told us very little about life. It was to enjoy, to drink deeply. But never is even that treasured in the heart as are those moments of simple, tender confidences, when a gentle, loving sigh opened the treasure house of a woman's heart and she spoke truly of those things within.

A man likes even the bad women he knows to be good.

To a woman who has revealed her soul, who has given a brief glimpse of her heart, no man ever pays the insult to forget; he pays her homage. I remember a little Italian girl I once knew. She was very beautiful —so young. We used to sit in a tiny cafe we knew in Naples, and hold hands quite openly. I do not think I ever kissed her. We talked little, for she was not educated. It was not her magnificent eyes, nor the glory of her hair that was like a blackbird's wing, nor the round white curves of her young body—I remember her because of those little intimate moments when our thoughts were bound together by her simple, tender, gentle words. We were intimates, and the soul is such a lonely thing that it treasures those moments of companionship.

I do not like women who know too much.

The modern woman in America tries to destroy romance. Either it must be marriage or it must be ugly scandal.

No other woman can ever mean to a man what his children's mother means to him.

A love affair with a stupid woman is like a cold cup of coffee.

I would not care to kiss a woman whose lips were mine at our second or third meeting.

One can always be kind to a woman one cares nothing about.

The greatest asset to a woman is dignity.

Figure 26b.

266

Despite the indisputable culpability of the fan magazine in constructing star discourse as a "cult of personality," it produced a paradoxical position of reader/spectator subjectivity that complicates the notion of the female spectator condemned to narcissistic overidentification or collusion with classical cinema in a stereotypical "feminine" confusion of sign and signified. Contemporary feminist film theory has often suggested that perilous positions of female subjectivity are inscribed in classical Hollywood cinema. Mary Ann Doane writes that this patriarchal system constructs "a female spectator whose nonfetishistic gaze maintains a dangerous intimacy with the image." Doane posits this cinematic peril as part of a socialization practice in which women are lured into the role of "over-involved female spectator" and "deprived of a gaze, deprived of subjectivity and repeatedly transformed into the object of a masculine scopophiliac desire."[5]

Doane's remarks evidence how contemporary theory's description of Hollywood's construction of female subjectivity resembles the accusations once directed at movie magazines, which were sometimes accused of encouraging a stereotypically "feminine" relationship between the fan and the filmic process. Writing in 1939, Carl F. Cotter refers to movie magazines as "cinematic scriptures" for fans who "literally govern their lives by them." Although he does not refer directly to these fans as women, his target is clear:

> Not only do they pattern their hair styles, their clothes, their cookery, and their behavior after those of their favorite actors and actresses as interpreted by the sob-sisters; most of them also base their most profound thinking on the words of the same authorities.

Not surprisingly, the fan magazine continues to be dismissed in passing as one more example of women's "excessive collusion with the cinematic imaginary." This collusion, of which Doane speaks, might appear to gain its most credible evidence from the 1920s, in the infamous excesses of the Valentino cult and the fan magazine's culpability in sustaining a so-called hysterical female desire "misplaced" onto Hollywood stars.[6]

Certainly, fan magazines of the era, like trade magazines and film exploitation materials, are not entirely absent of commentary that might support such a view of the female spectator. But the fan magazine was not a purely repressive form nor did it collapse all distinctions between cinematic signifier and signified. Instead of automatically reinforcing female powerlessness and marginalization before a patriarchal system, it explored, albeit in ideologically contradictory terms, the historically specific locus of women in American cinema, culture, and society during the 1920s.

Extratextual Temptation and the "Daughters of Eve"

Within the context of the apparent widespread industry belief in American women's unrivaled box office power, virtually all fan magazines of the 1920s textually inscribed a female reader in their address: in their fiction stories, talent searches, editorials, star interviews, and advice to readers columns. Like other women's magazines of the era, fan magazines featured the work of a number of women including editors (Adele Whiteley Fletcher and Elsie Seeligman), writers (Adela Rogers St. Johns, Ruth Waterbury, Hazel Simpson Naylor, Ruth Hall, and Katherine Ann Porter), as well as photographers (Helen MacGregor and Ruth Harriet Louise). And, in keeping with the most popular magazine in the United States, *The Ladies Home Journal*, fan magazines relied on advertising to sustain a low cover price and maximum circulation. As a result, fan magazines of the 1920s displayed a myriad variety of beauty and home products. Wedged between "Friendly Advice on Girls' Problems" and contests for new screenplays were ads for everything from "Romance Chocolates" to automobiles that would prove that "In these modern days . . . the daughters of Eve . . . thrill to the power of the big Overland engine as keenly as any man." But, whatever it might sell in its back pages and margins, the fan magazine could never forget its primary focus: selling stars.[7]

Even though it assumed its place as a component process in the commodification of Hollywood cinema during the 1910s, the fan magazine proliferated during the 1920s, with numerous entries into the market such as *Screen Secrets, Screen Play, Screenbook, Pantomime, Shadowland, Screen Stories, Movie Weekly, Film Fun,* and *Screenland* joining *Motion Picture Classic* (1915), *Motion Picture Magazine* (1911), *Photoplay* (1911), and *Picture Play* (1915). The fan magazine's appeal to women in the 1920s confirms Diane Waldman's generalization that Hollywood's extratextual practice assimilates women's experiences and channels their interests into "marriage, romance, and consumerism." The representation of stars for an anticipated female reader was offered within a formula that paid obeisance to this triumverate of "traditional" American femininity. However, the unprecedented rise of the fan magazine's popularity in the 1920s took place within a broader ideological framework marked by women's growing economic and sexual emancipation and the widespread belief that changes in women's behavior were contributing to a radical subversion of American gender ideals. As a result of the specific socio-historical and discursive circumstances of its emergent growth, fan magazine discourse of this decade reveals complications and contradictions to received opinion about the extratextual cinematic construction of female subjectivity.[8]

In this respect, fan magazines of the 1920s demonstrate the need to more carefully document and decipher the contradictions and ambiguities in Hollywood's extratextual (and textual) address as well as the need to challenge assumptions regarding the cultural "construction" of the female audience at any given historical moment. For example, in "From Midnight Shows to Marriage Vow," Waldman argues that press books from 1929–1943 "reveal that those responsible for marketing films thought in terms which rewarded the traditional woman as defined by a patriarchal culture, and ignored and excluded those who deviated from that norm." Waldman is persuasive regarding the years she considers, but we must resist the temptation to assume that the "traditional woman" in the United States was defined (even by the cinema) in exactly the same way in 1943 as in the 1920s. It would have been difficult for fan magazines to ignore *all* American women who deviated from "traditional" gender assumptions in the 1920s because throughout the decade large numbers of American women were perceived as departing from longstanding gender norms in courtship behaviors, in the dynamics of marriage, and in their expression of economic independence. Although women's newly realized freedoms may seem limited in retrospect, they became the subject of intense public debate. Ultimately the Victorian models of woman as sacrificing mother or passively chaste maiden were eclipsed in the 1920s as American ideals of femininity changed in profound ways. The structures of American society remained patriarchal, but they were not impervious to change.[9]

Although it may have depended on romance, marriage and consumerism as primary appeals to women, fan magazine discourse of the 1920s, as the product of an era of intensified (and anxious) gender awareness, was neither static nor simple. Fan magazines were in no sense ideologically "radical," but in comparison with general cultural discourses aimed at men, they often evidenced a progressive view of women's changing sexual and economic roles. And, contrary to the expectations of much of contemporary theory, the female subjectivity that is inscribed in fan magazines of this era is hardly over-identificatory, passive and mindlessly consumerist, but distanced, skeptical, and active as well as being relational, intimate, and empathetic. In fact, I will seek to show that the fan magazine of the 1920s allowed if not encouraged a type of so-called fetishistic, "I-know-but-nevertheless" balancing of knowledge and belief that is often considered to be impossible for women spectators. I will also argue that fan magazines functioned to encourage women to guiltlessly pursue cinema as an experience resonant with the possibilities of familiar pleasures. These pleasures, as "degraded" by consumerism as we may now be tempted to label them, emanated from and shared in a cultural arena privileging women's interests and agency.

Going Fishing: Private Lives as Public Pleasures

Assumed to be a veritable smorgasbord of gossip, glamour, and romantic fodder dished out for women's naively credulous consumption, the fan magazine has long been denigrated as inaccurate history and shameless publicity sham. With regard to the fan magazines of the 1920s, this blanket condemnation is unwarranted. In addition to star interviews, articles, and photo layouts, fan magazines provided a forum for candid film reviews and instructive articles on art direction, costuming, and cinematography. They even offered serious glimpses into the history of film exemplified by *Photoplay*'s commissioning of a series of articles from Terry Ramsaye that became the basis of his pioneering work, *A Million and One Nights*.

Almost all the fan magazines were published independently of the studios, but they had a vested interest in maintaining a harmonious relationship with the film industry to guarantee access to star material. They did not uncritically reprint publicity releases in the same manner as many newspapers, nor were they gossip rags. With the startling exception of *Movie Weekly*, the majority of fan magazines conservatively guarded the boundaries of an emerging star discourse whose guiding principles, as Richard deCordova has shown, were established during the mid 1910s. In 1912 *Photoplay*'s "Answers to Inquiries" column told readers that "information as to matrimonial alliances and other purely personal matters will not be answered"; by 1915, however, the boundaries of fan magazine discourse had expanded to include a revelation of the star's professional/private life, but only within the limits of a discourse emphasizing marriage, family, and clean living.[10] DeCordova has argued that the boundaries of star discourse shifted radically in the 1920s. He notes that "the press during the twenties depended as much on a fascination with scandal as a revulsion by it." Indeed, the stars' transgressions were, as he says, "regularly and intensely covered." But while this was true of newspapers, it was not the case with the overwhelming majority of fan magazines. In keeping with the formula of extracinematic appeal suggested by Waldman, myths of traditional romantic love rather than revelations of sexual transgression fueled the fan magazines in the 1920s (just as they had in the 1910s). In articles such as *Screen Secrets'* "Why Not Get Married: Happy Husbands of Hollywood Answer the Bachelors" and *Picture Play*'s "Love Makes the Man," this preoccupation (with love) was elaborated within a carefully controlled discourse centered on the stars' domestic bliss as happily married heterosexual couples. In the early 1920s, the courtship rituals of the stars were the subject of commentary but generally only after the participants were engaged or married, as in *Photoplay*'s "Untold Love Stories of the Stars" (1923). Around 1926 a gradual relaxing of discursive boundaries regarding extramarital relations occurred, but the fan magazine continued to legitimate the stars' love affairs within narratives that usually ended either with the promise of marriage or the tragedy of true lovers' separation, as in Dorothy Manner's recounting of three unlikely celebrity pairings in "Love Stories Behind the Cameras" for *Motion Picture Magazine* (1926).[11]

The fan magazine's careful balancing of the appeals of intimacy, sensationalism, and specularity appears motivated less by the need to protect the delicate sensibilities of its female readership than by the demands of an era in which Hollywood was rocked by scandals, including the Fatty Arbuckle trials, the William Desmond Taylor murder, Wally Reid's drug-related death, and Valentino's divorce problems (including accusations of bigamy). Adhering to the tone of *Motion Picture Magazine*'s 1915 promise "to be more than a mere entertainment . . . to instruct and uplift," *Photoplay* announced its intention to ignore scandal in a 1922 editorial, "Moral House Cleaning: What's It All About?," in which editor James Quirk refused to refer to Arbuckle and Taylor by name but blamed the public, a "scavenger press," and "seekers for cheap and lurid publicity" for dragging "an entire community . . . into the mire." He continued: "*Photoplay* is not posing as a defender of the motion pictures. . . . [It] prefers, in fact, to refrain from all discussion on the subject. But it can not sit by silently and behold both public and press besmirch with lies the entire rank and file of a great industry."[12]

Photoplay kept its promise of refusing to discuss Hollywood star scandals; most other fan magazines followed suit. Events might be alluded to long after their occurrence, but through a strategy of indirection that relied heavily on the reader's preexistent knowledge of events gleaned from *other* sources, not the magazines themselves. For example, Wally Reid's drug-related death was treated in *Photoplay* as "a brave and splendid fight" in "The Unhappy Ending of Wally Reid's Life Story: A Tribute from a Friend." Pictures of Reid with his wife and son confirmed his place within a family discourse that could not utter the words "drug addiction." With no explanation of the circumstances of Reid's death, author Herbert Howe praised Reid's last real life role as "his greatest" in order to recuperate the star as heroic victim: "Reid died with the whispered hope that he might save at least a few from the agony that was his." Thus, Reid's transgressions are resituated by Howe within the assimilable categories of humanity and domesticity. The same strategy is repeated in "The Butterfly Man and the Little Clown" appearing in *Photoplay* in 1929. Author Adela Rogers St. Johns resituates Mabel Normand's "hot-headed, wild, young foolishness" within a domestic narrative of marital devotion defying disgrace and impending death: Mabel lies ill, wasting away, forgotten by a "very self-protective" and "smug" Hollywood, but cherished by the husband who understands and adores her. By way of contrast, those star transgressions that were unrecuperable within the boundaries of a family discourse (like the alleged sexual irregularities of Fatty Arbuckle) were only occasionally allowed to "leak" into the fan magazine, usually through readers' letters.[13]

Such a policy of restraint with regard to sex-charged sensationalism ostensibly protected the economic interests of the magazines by protecting their chief commodity: the stars. But despite their protective attitude toward that commodity, fan magazine articles often crucially depended on their readership being well versed in the sensational details of the film colony's behavioral excesses. This mode of discursive restraint suggests that the fan magazines did not seriously attempt to prevent gossip mongering or to shield the female audience.

Of necessity, fan magazines had to sustain the long-term loyalty of the female film audience, and they assumed a readership of ongoing interest, knowledge—and skepticism. Writing in *Photoplay* in 1924, Frederick James Smith commented on what fan magazine readers already knew: "The public frequently gets an added fillip of interest from a player's private life—or what it believes it to be." Smith's remark is characteristic of the way in which fan magazines spoke to their readership as an audience once removed from "the public" and more sophisticated in its recognition of Hollywood illusionism, on and off the screen.[14]

According to one source, some fan magazine writers worked as stars' press representatives, and in all likelihood many articles and interviews were composed without the participation of the actors who are either generously quoted or credited with authorship. There is ample proof that fan magazines were well aware that their readers might not believe the stars actually participated in disclosing their most private thoughts and actions. In 1923, *Movie Weekly* announced that Rudolph Valentino would edit an upcoming issue. To allay any doubt as to Valentino's participation, *Movie Weekly* dutifully reproduced a photo of the editor-in-chief overseeing Valentino hard at work behind a desk. Similarly, *Motion Picture Magazine* asked actress and avowed feminist Alla Nazimova a loaded question: "Does old age hold terrors for you?" Lest readers dismiss her reply as inauthentic, her handwritten response was photographically reproduced for all to read.[15]

The strategy evidenced in *Motion Picture Magazine*'s query to Nazimova is characteristic of most fan magazines, which actually offered very little information as to what the stars did or how they lived unless it was presented as the star's personal chronicle of his or her life. Instead, they provided much more intimate information: they revealed what the stars "thought," as stated directly in the title of a 1926 *Cinema Art* article, "What Mrs. Barthelmess Thinks of Richard." This led one female reader to ask "why the Limelight Divinities so often feel it incumbent upon them to advise us (the plain people) regarding love, marriage and the everafter. The ones who seem especially keen about this are those who have been themselves conspicuously unsuccessful."[16]

By providing glimpses of the stars' most personal thoughts and relying on the reader's wealth of preestablished knowledge, the fan magazine posited the reader in a discursive relationship of complicity with the stars even while it simultaneously offered continual demystification of the manufactured nature of the star system. This system, as one fan magazine article admitted, was dependent on rubber-stamped personal autographs and exaggerated claims. The lack of veracity of Hollywood publicity and the constructed nature of the star system became the object of tongue-in-cheek satire, amused tolerance, and occasional denunciation in fan magazines. Typical in its tone is the lead for a *Pantomime* photo layout of 1921: "Strange that so many movie beauties take up fishing as a pastime, isn't it. But here's triple proof on this page. . . . And, of course, the camera doesn't lie." A photo of Bebe Daniels is accompanied by the caption: "Sh-h-h! This is a secret—this particular bit of fishing was done in the backyard outside Bebe's California bungalow, and the lake is nothing but a sublimated puddle caused by heavy rain." Author Mary Winship takes a more cynical tone in discussing starlet Marguerite de la Motte in "Out of Arabian Nights." Winship says de la Motte's posings remind her "of a high school girl with social ambitions": "She is very young. I can never remember just how old these girls are . . . but [her] eyes are so perfect . . . that they make you forget her conversation completely—which is perhaps just as well." A gentler tone is restored in a *Photoplay* question-and-answer column, which told a reader from Indiana: "Well, Mary Miles Minter was nineteen the last I heard, but then that was almost a year ago, so she must be eighteen now." However, fan magazines also regularly published letters that spoke openly with resentment of the "manufacture" of stars and with disgust for the industry's transparent promotional ploys. One letter asked: "Is it right that stars should be manufactured for our use?" Another declared that "the idea of Novarro resembling Valentino originated for advertising purposes only," and yet another complained of "so-called 'Producer-made' and 'beauty-winner' stars (that are forced before the public)."[17]

The fan magazines offered their readers a superior, distanced awareness of the star-making process while simultaneously perpetuating an illusion of intimacy with the stars. This strategy may have activated a reading process that is in many ways analogous to that theorized for modern romance novels. Tania Modleski interprets the inscribed position for romance readers as one that permits women to be "superior in wisdom to the heroine at the same time that they emotionally identify with her." Fan magazine readers could easily achieve a similar, distanciated yet intimate "double perspective" with regard to Hollywood illusionism and the stars with whom they were encouraged to identify. Although Modleski has suggested that the double-perspective inscription of the romance reader leads to "a continual sensation of being in bad faith," Janice Radway describes the process in more positive terms. In Radway's words, such a perspective "allows the reader to have it both ways." In keeping with romance reader's experience, the fan magazine reader was also allowed the "imaginative space to express her reservations and negative feelings," in this instance, concerning the construction of the Hollywood star system. She could indulge in the fantasy of possessing intimate, "true" knowledge about the stars while at the same time continue to control and overrule that emotional investment "with the voice of her greater knowledge" (about their manufacture).[18]

It is not surprising that the manufactured nature of the star system frequently was revealed in the contradictory inscriptions of star personality. Slippage in the actor or actress's offscreen persona was typical of the development of the picture personality in the 1910s when, as deCordova has observed, the extrafilmic identity "merely reproduced the representations of personality already produced in films." The policy of conflating actor personality and screen image continued to be used in the 1920s, chiefly to promote minor stars or new actors and actresses. Some conflation or intermingling was, of course, inevitable in the star system's confusion of the actor with the screen persona in order to construct the "star" persona, a marketable commodity, but fan magazines increasingly encouraged a distanciation between screen persona and actor-identity. For example, a caption in *Photoplay* notes how Betty Compson's photograph illustrates how "her 'still' camera personality," "her moving picture camera self," and "the real Betty Compson" are all different. It concludes by noting that "she shares this versatility with most of the other stars."[19]

The growing reluctance of the fan magazines to conflate players and parts in the 1920s may reflect a defensive posture, "damage control," in the face of the increasing inability of the Hollywood system to maintain control over star discourse as well as its inability to predict volatile public reaction to changing standards of sexual conduct. In *Photoplay*'s "Does Decency Help or Hinder?" (1924), Frederick James Smith suggests that Mary Miles Minter's screen image of innocence had made it impossible for her to professionally survive the sexual revelations of the William Desmond Taylor affair. Appearing to anticipate Smith's advice regarding the dangers in adhering to extremes of innocence or vice, a 1922 article features Lew Cody telling *Photoplay* readers of his year-long tour of personal appearances that was meant to prove that "Lew Cody was not the dallying dilettante, the nonchalant heart-breaker . . . but just Lew Cody." In typical fan magazine fashion, the article's title and byline: "A Reformed Villain," *By Himself*, promise a titillating convergence between the onscreen, sexually transgressive persona and the offscreen one. Despite this, the contents proceed to reestablish the difference between Lew Cody the actor and Cody the screen's best known "male vamp" and redeem them from a conflation "created by an over-zealous press agent" and believed, the article implies, by a public not nearly as knowledgeable as *Photoplay*'s readers.[20]

At the same time fan magazines encouraged a certain skepticism toward the stars, then, they also cultivated a paradoxically false and true intimacy that encouraged a relational, "feminine" mode of emotional investment. The fan magazine's "double perspective" of reading suggests that women's emotional investment in stars should not automatically be equated with a collapse of identity into object. Instead, what is evoked by both the tone and content of the fan magazines is more on the order of an identification with stardom as a kind of "masquerade," a play with identity. This is not a defensive masquerade of lack (as theorized by Riviere and adapted by Doane), but a playful one bringing elements of make believe and pretense into play—on both sides of the screen. Such a masquerade, with its suggestion of a "fetishistic" balance of belief and disbelief, no doubt would have elicited the understanding of many women in the 1920s who themselves were engaged in an attempt to resituate themselves in relation to changing concepts of female social and sexual identity.[21]

"Promiscuity's Coming World" and the Necessities of Containment

In a popular marriage manual of 1922, *Married Life and Happiness (or Love and Comfort in Marriage)*, Dr. William J. Robinson observed that the "rigid anesthetic [sic]" woman was becoming rare. That condition, he noted, was a "nuisance" and a "misfortune though a bearable one." It was, he warned, "the opposite type of woman who is the greatest danger to the health and even life of her husband . . . the hypersensual woman . . . with an excessive sexuality." Robinson's comments serve both as evidence of the freer discussion of sexuality in American popular discourses in the 1920s and an example of how that freedom of expression was marked by an increasing anxiety with regard to the regulation of women's sexuality.[22]

In the 1920s, women's sexual desire, dismissed a few short years before as "mainly a pretense," was quickly becoming *the* national preoccupation, as the politically focused, prewar feminism appeared to be superceded by a "new feminism" grounded in sexual self-expression. Single women were not the only vanguard for this trend, as Dorothy Bromley told readers of *Harper's* in "Feminist-New Style." She noted that married women were refusing to be consigned exclusively to the domestic role and expected to be satisfied "as a lover and a companion"; they were also insisting on "more freedom and honesty within the marriage." The advent of reliable birth control, the childless "companionate" model of marriage, and a new sexual consciousness linked to Freudianism all contributed to the legitimation of women's sexual demands.[23]

The marital expectations cited by Bromley may hardly appear to herald an erotic awakening with radical social implications, but, in combination with the movement of women into the work force, these expectations signalled a change in attitudes toward normative middle-class standards of male domestic authority and gender norms beyond the sexual sphere. By actively seeking sexual pleasure, American women of the 1920s were widely believed to be usurping a male prerogative more powerful and precious than the vote. In response, countless doctors, psychologists, anthropologists, and social commentators accused American women of destroying the norms of heterosexual relations, eroding the boundaries between the sexes, and sending American masculinity into rapid decline. Universal suffrage and female employment were not cited as the chief culprits in these distressing trends; women's assertion of their right to seek sexual gratification was. Women of the 1920s were shattering the sexual double standard, with desultory effects. "Promiscuity's coming world," warned Will Durant in 1927, would be one absent of marriage and, therefore, home and family. History would look back on the behavior of women in the 1920s to observe how "[a]n institution which had lasted ten thousand years was destroyed in a generation." Durant's dire predictions support social historian Paula Fass's observation that "gazing at the young women of the period, the traditionalist saw the end of American civilization as he had known it." However, "traditionalists" were not alone condemning the apparent change in women; archfeminist Charlotte Perkins Gilman dismissed women of the 1920s who confused feminine values by refusing to acknowledge that they were made to be mothers and "not, as seems to be widely supposed, for [the] enjoyable preliminaries."[24]

The American public perceived women's changing desire as being explicitly and problematically encouraged by the cinematic institution. As one *Photoplay* reader remarked: "I hear all the evils of the age, dancing, smoking, petting, loose morals, laid to the movies." Writing in *The New Republic*, Lloyd Lewis suggested that the atmosphere of the movie theater, or as he phrased it, the "blue dusk" of the "twilit [sic] palace," gave free reign to a woman's sexual fantasies and "dissolved the Puritan strictures she has absorbed as a child." In "What the Films Are Doing to Young America," sociologist Edward Alsworth Ross declared that the movies were making young women (and men) more "sex-wise, sex-excited, and sex-absorbed than . . . any generation of which we have knowledge."[25]

Payne Fund sociologist Herbert Blumer's 1933 study, *Movies and Conduct*, confirmed what numerous critics, censors, and reformers had been saying throughout the 1920s: movies and movie stars were playing havoc with the sexual fantasies of young American women of all classes and races. Although equally concerned with the behavior of males, Blumer cites innumerable testimonials detailing young women's reaction to Hollywood cinema of the 1920s. Typical was the response of a sixteen-year-old high school sophomore: "I've been thrilled and deeply stirred by love pictures . . . I know [they] have made me more receptive to love-making . . . and I kiss and pet much more than I would otherwise." From such revelations, Blumer decides that the film spectator "becomes malleable to the touch of what is shown. Ordinary self-control is lost." Not surprisingly, Blumer believes that "emotional possession induced by passionate love pictures represents an attack on the mores of our contemporary life." The viewer, says Blumer, can be psychologically induced to imitate the behavior shown on the screen either in a pattern of temporary experimentation or as a permanent change. His evidence is found, in part, in the testimony of an eighteen-year-old who recounts: "It seems on the screen that the wild girl or the one that pets gets the one she loves. I am now trying that method and am going to see how it will work."[26]

In an era in which the public pleasures women took from "Valentino traps" seemed almost as dangerous to society as the private pleasures they were assumed to be demanding elsewhere, the fan magazine's marketing of stars in relation to the construction of female subjectivity was a complex enterprise, more complex than merely rewarding "the traditional woman as defined by a patriarchal culture" and ignoring and excluding "those who deviated from that norm." Fan magazines of the 1920s did emphasize the apparently conventional aspects (romance/marriage) of the domain of "feminine" interpersonal relations, but at the same time they sought to channel women into nominally normative models of female subjectivity, fan magazines attempted to satisfy sexually and socially transgressive aspects of women's desire. As the 1920s wore on, that task of negotiation proved to be difficult, but not only because of the many, well-publicized star scandals. The task was made much more arduous by the widespread perception that American women were challenging the "natural" constitution of masculinity and femininity, both in real life and in Hollywood's "screen life."[27]

Jazz Queens and Victorian Visions

In fulfilling the distinct agendas of being a "woman's magazine" and existing as a supporting mechanism for the film industry, fan magazines participated in discursive practices derived from women's mass produced popular culture even as they extended beyond the concerns of marketing one film or studio into the wider arena of marketing stars. The fan magazine did not operate in a cultural vacuum but was inextricably imbricated in the web of popular discourses created about—and for—women. One consequence of this intertextually influenced negotiation of the spectator/reader was that fan magazines, like other women's magazines, continually compromised and equivocated in their discursive regulation of female sexual and social subjectivity. In particular, the fan magazine's approach to romance, sex, and marriage resembled that offered in women's fiction, including the numerous short stories and serials offered in *The Ladies Home Journal, McCalls,* and *Redbook.* Many of these stories are narratives of liberation and repression in which marriage is promised to be enabling rather than constraining. Even though women's right to erotic choice might be affirmed by these stories, female sexual pleasure was subsumed into a discourse of romantic love and legitimated by a traditional gender arrangement, with marriage as a precondition for the most meaningful and sexually pleasurable choices. Although this containment of female sexuality in marriage follows a predictable patriarchal agenda, the stories must be placed within their historical context: readers likely would have known that American marriage was widely recognized as changing, invigorated by women's right to increased erotic and economic choice.[28]

Addressing the problem of women's sexual subjectivity in terms repeated throughout the decade is the story "Irmalee and the Mid-Victorian Age" appearing in *McCalls* in July 1925. The story's first-page teaser asks: "Which do our American men really prefer—the bold modern flapper, or the demure girl of yesteryear?" The answer was both. Irmalee initially is represented as the archetypal flapper who brags: "[We] out-smoked and out-drank and out-danced and out-petted the rest of the world. We nabbed all the young chaps and we accumulated all the older ones. We didn't even stay off the married women's preserves." Jealous of her divorced thirty-seven-year-old mother, Irmalee steals away her mother's boyfriend, Shawn. She accomplishes this by appearing to him as a Victorian vision in billowing flock and rose-draped hat. When he asks her ". . . do you go in for the new poetry? Or is it psycho-analysis?" she replies: "Tennyson." Shawn is smitten, but Irmalee cannot sustain the masquerade, for she is "the jazz queen of her set." She decides to show up for a dinner date as the scantily clad, cigarette-smoking "ultra-modern person" she believes herself to be. Rather than being disillusioned, as she anticipates, Shawn helps her to realize her true self, neither the passive Victorian ideal nor the sensation-seeking flapper, but the "very modern girl" who wants "all that the game" has given her but wants it honestly. Shawn assumes they will be immediately wed, but Irmalee warns him that she is not "to be won so easily."[29]

As part of a cinematic lure that was susceptible to charges of encouraging a new, dangerous model of feminine sexuality, fan magazines steered a similar course between the old and new sexual ideologies. Like Irmalee, the fan magazine reader was called on to negotiate the bind between the old standard of sexual restraint and the "new" possibility of sexual desire. The fan magazine's ideal new woman, like that of women's magazines, vacillated constantly between asserting her newly realized social and sexual freedoms and retreating from her autonomy. Marriage was ostensibly the primary means of containing women's freedom, but American marriage was also being destabilized in the 1920s; no longer did it occupy "the supreme place in the interest and life of women." As psychologist Beatrice Hinkle noted: "A complete change in attitude, often in the form of a violent revolt against the former ideals and customs affecting the marriage relations, is in full swing and the general uncertainty and instability in the relation is probably more marked [in the United States] than in any other country." Rejecting conservatives' relentlessly reiterated demands that women return to child-centered domesticity, the ideological compromise promoted in women's fictions promised that women's happiness resided in finding sexual satisfaction, not in inappropriate assertiveness that made women like men in a single sexual standard, but in an accomodation that might offer companionship, equality, and good sex.[30]

Anticipating "Irmalee," [*Motion Picture*] *Classic* told its readers in 1924 that "no topic of the day, including the most eminent of the murders . . . [is] so eagerly pursued as that of the Modern Girl: what she is doing and why she is doing it; and what she is thinking, if at all; and why she is as she is." This sarcastically tinged appraisal of the "modern girl" served the purpose of introducing the opinions of actress Doris Kenyon. In "There are No More Mothers," Doris is described as a girl "gently born and bred"; she is compared to daffodils, "snowy anemones," and "budding spring." Suddenly, the article takes an unexpected turn to reveal that Doris is not so old fashioned after all. She actually thinks there are no more mothers "of the kind there used to be." The new mother, she says, "looks as young as her daughters, frequently acts younger and spends most of her time having as good a time as she can manage to achieve." Doris sees this trend as "a sign of healthy common sense," showing that traditions can be abandoned when they "no longer serve a purpose." She ends by praising the "courage and comradeship" that have come to exist between the generations because of a "modern generation [that] isn't afraid any longer."[31]

"There are No More Mothers" demonstrates the fan magazine's most common strategy of addressing the question of the modern woman and her sexuality: through their "personal" statements, stars became aligned with certain social positions and attitudes. In 1921, Wallace Reid's "personal" opinion of the modern girl was voiced in the article "How to Hold a Wife." He remarks: "Now she has acquired pretty much the same right to amuse herself as a man . . . and if her new freedom has gone to her head a bit, let's cheer her on. It won't hurt her and it will probably do her good." The specific star context for these comments was established by Wally Reid's easygoing screen personality constructed by such "modern" marriage films as Cecil B. DeMille's *The Affairs of Anatol*, but Reid's tolerant attitude toward women's newfound freedom would have been out of place in general interest magazines that were filled with reactionary articles such as "Evils of Woman's Revolt against the Old Standard" and "Are Women Inferior or Are They Trying to Side-Track Nature?" His opinion, however, was quite at home in the fan magazine's discourse, not only because of its appeal to women but also because of the editorial precedent set by other women's magazines, such as *The Ladies Home Journal*, which, as early as 1920, defended "the wonderful women who now surround us on every side" and refused, like Doris Kenyon, to look nostalgically on "the old-fashioned charming young miss and the old-fashioned broody-type of mother [who] have all but disappeared."[32]

Addressing controversial issues of female subjectivity (flapperdom, bobbed hair, careers for women), fan magazines often relied on a single star to express a contradictory position or employed the pronouncements of several stars to offer opposing viewpoints within a single article. Vacillating widely between approval and condemnation of controversial female behavior, the stars became the voices of authority to be best contradicted by other stars. These opposing visions sometimes were left to stand on their own as evidenced in *Photoplay*'s "The Battle of Bobbed Hair: National Opinion of Those For and Against Clipped Locks" (1924), but often they were coopted into the larger project of selling the movies by incorporating controversy into an assimilable (and palatable) ideological category, as in "What the Screen Idols Think of the Flapper."[33]

In this 1927 *Motion Picture Classic* article, author Dorothy Wooldridge canvasses male stars to report that Ronald Colman "smiles tolerantly at flapperdom," but Gilbert Roland's ideal is "an old fashioned, modern girl,"—in other words, another Irmalee. Wooldridge quotes Richard Barthelmess as saying of the flapper: "She's a bit mad and a bit ugly, but effective in bringing life out of its rut to a greater freedom. . . . I know they [women] do not think that ultra-modernism is becoming or attractive or even quite sane. They know better." His references to the flapper as "mad" and "ugly" resemble numerous other conservative reactions to the flapper's lack of traditional feminine restraint as well as to her "mannish" fashion aesthetic regarded, ironically, as unfeminine but also openly solicitous of male sexual response. Wooldridge manages to redirect Barthelmess's disparaging comment by representing it as the consensus opinion of the screen lovers. Echoing Wallace Reid's "How to Hold a Wife," she interprets this opinion as: "The flapper doesn't mean any harm, is having a good time, but she knows the limit." Wooldridge goes on to describe the typical flapper as a woman who could take care of herself and tell the world: "I've got my 'mad money' to pay car fare home tonight if things get too rough." By reaffirming the flapper's adherence to the old sexual standard, Wooldridge turns aside Barthelmess' conservative resistance even as women's potentially transgressive sexual behavior is neutralized. Although Wooldridge provides ideological closure with her "consensus" description of the flapper, the article is provided with a more open ending. "There is what your screen stars think of 'flaming youth,'" it proclaims. "Who is right?"[34]

Wooldridge's description of the flapper could be taken as the fundamental starting point for flapper films of the 1920s, but the films appear more conservative than the fan magazines. Absolutely formulaic, they typically tell the story of a young woman ("girl") from the country, the convent, or a cloistered home who is enamoured with the wild jazz scene. Her life as a "chaste young hell cat" ends when she is almost date raped or killed in a speeding roadster. Rather than rescuing herself with her "mad money," the erstwhile flapper is saved by a former fiance or boyfriend; she returns to his arms and promises to become a good, old-fashioned wife.[35]

This basic pattern is repeated throughout the decade in films from virtually every studio: *Why Girls Leave Home* (1921), *Nice People* (1922), *The Perfect Flapper* (1924), *Wine of Youth* (1924), *Wild, Wild Susan* (1925), *We Moderns* (1925), *The Adventurous Sex* (1925), and *Joy Street* (1929). In a typical example, William De Mille's *Nice People* "Teddy" (Theodora) Gloucester (Bebe Daniels) is saved from the intoxicated advances of a "flapperooster" acquaintance by Billy (Wallace Reid), the boyfriend she abandoned to take up flapperdom. *Screenland* (a fan magazine published for a chain of Paramount theatres in Dallas, Texas) described the plot for its readers: "Typical modern girl, one filled with life and overflowing with vitality and the jazz spirit of the present day realizes that the conventions are matters of importance. . . . She also learns that modesty can be something besides a mere word and that tender chivalry is infinitely preferable to jazzy familiarity." In *The Perfect Flapper*, "Tommie" Lou Pember (Colleen Moore) is an old-fashioned girl whose unpopularity leads her to resort to jazz attitudes to improve her social life. Her flirtations provoke a couple into a divorce suit, but marital disaster is averted when Tommie falls in love with the wife's lawyer and vows to reform.[36]

These films tend to support Paula Fass's observation that the flapper became the basis of "fictionalized, emotion-packed distortions of a type that was meant to evoke rather than to describe and finally to comfort through rebuke." However, like "What the Screen Idols Think of the Flapper," most of the films represent their heroines as uninhibited and ungovernable but do not rebuke them for trying "to live the codeless existence of the male" (i.e., promiscuity), since, unlike women's magazine heroines, film heroines rarely forfeited their virginity to flappermania. Instead, the sexual act was displaced onto a girlfriend (as in *Dancing Daughters* and *IT*) so that the flapper's actions can be viewed as a rather benign, temporary erotic experimentation from which she (like Irmalee) can be rescued and reclaimed for married domesticity.[37]

Conspicuously absent from these films is any clue as to how the heroine's eroticized behavior would be curbed in marriage (figures 27 and 28). There is also some evidence that the narrative closure regulating female sexuality was not necessarily what young women remembered of the films. Blumer attempts to suggest just this from the numerous testimonials that he cites, such as the one from a young woman who admitted that she emulated Clara Bow to advantage: "I have learned from the movies how to be a flirt, and I have found out that at parties and elsewhere the coquette is the one who enjoys herself the most."[38]

The weakness in the films' containment of the flapper's symbolic eroticism is particularly evident in a Clara Bow vehicle, *IT* (1927). Bow's

Figure 27. Clara Bow, whose overwhelming dynamic eroticism (i.e., her "It") remains uncurbed by narrative closure.

working-class character aggressively demonstrates the right of erotic choice that is absent in many of the other films. In *IT*, Clara Bow plays Bette Lou, a sales clerk working in the world's largest department store. Bette Lou sees Cyrus Waltham (Tony Moreno), the eligible son of the store's owner, and immediately declares: "Sweet Santa Claus, give me *him*!" She chooses not to wait for Christmas; with singleminded determination, she pursues him. Cyrus ultimately proposes, even though the combination of Bette Lou's (and Bow's) overwhelming erotic dynamism (i.e., her "It") and her loyalty to her roommate, a single mother, has resulted in a mixup: he thinks that she is an unwed mother. Bette Lou rejects his proposal of marriage, but he vows to ask her again when he discovers that she is really not "that kind of girl." At a yachting party, Cyrus's snooty society girlfriend dismisses Bette Lou's

Gloria Swanson is one of the only two actresses on
the screen who has IT, avers Madame Glyn

Vilma Banky is the other. Fewer women than
men have this priceless gift, says its discoverer

What Is IT?

Elinor Glyn discovered IT. Some players have
risen to stardom because of IT. Equally
talented ones have failed through lack of IT

By
Dorothy Spensley

I*T!*
It used to be such a meek and
dignified little word that the
tongue would slip easily over
without even causing a tremor when
it was uttered.

And in your school days when you
played "tag," *It* was the tagger and
you ran not to be *It.*

It is different in this day and age.
Now you run to get *It.*

What is this quivering—pulsating
—throbbing—beating—palpitating
It?

Undeniably *It* is a product of this
decade. Indeed, you might say *It* is
a product of this hour. But what is
It?

It dripped from the pen of a writer
of glowing words, glowing deeds and
glowing acts. And as it dripped, it
spread until everyone in the world
knew that *It* had suffered a re-birth.

If you have *It,* the world is your
peanut to crack and digest at your
leisure.

It is the "Open Sesame" to success
in life and love.

The peculiar thing about *It* is that

Elinor Glyn, who transformed an insignificant pronoun into a world-
discussed word

no doctor can place a thermometer in
your mouth and his fingers upon your
pulse and, after a grave moment, say
"You have 98.9 degrees of *It.*" *It* is
not located that way—you radiate *It.*

It is a sort of invisible aura that
surrounds your being and bathes you
in its effulgence.

Is *It* personality? Magnetism?
Hypnotism? Sex appeal?—oh, hack-
neyed term! Fascination? Charm?
What is It?

You will find *It* in actors, directors,
and writers—*It* will blossom among
coal miners, truck drivers and book
sellers. *It* is not restricted to class or
creed. *It* is not dependent on beauty
of face or form—wealth or degree of
station.

But what is *It?*

The woman who should know the
most in the world about *It* is Elinor
Glyn. It was she who transformed
this unobtrusive pronoun into a
world-discussed noun. Madame
Glyn, as you will recall, is the lady
who introduced the tiger skin into
fiction. And the tiger skin was apparent in this interview. In fact, we

Figure 28. "What is this quivering—pulsating—throbbing—beating—palpitating It?"

"lack of reserve," but he declares that "she has plenty in reserve." Bette Lou proves him to be right in more than the sexual sense, as she demonstrates her moxy and her moral worth by rescuing her society rival when they both fall overboard. The film ends with Bette and Cyrus in a soaked and sexy embrace, the visual promise that Bette's choice of a husband may legitimate her lower-class sexual expressivity but will not curb it.

Stepping Out of Her Place

Like the sexualized flapper, the increased visibility of the "working woman" in American society complicated the cinematic construction of female subjectivity. The need to justify women working was necessitated by heightened fears evident at the end of World War I. Conservatives such as William Howard Taft predicted that the "great army of women" who had joined the work force during the war would return to their homes, and if readers of *The Ladies Home Journal* were not so inclined, he warned them that the "Industrial use of the labor of women" was a threat to basic American values. Taft declared that female labor was aligned with "the anarchists, the Bolshevists, [and] the radical socialists [who] do not believe in home." In defiance of these warnings, the influx of middle-class wives as well as young, single women into the work force prompted *The Nation* to warn that "the world is now fast becoming woman-made. . . . Men still hold the big jobs and get the big rewards, but their confidence is going."[39]

Rejecting the notion that women's growing economic independence was usurping men's authority and destroying the family, numerous fictional stories in women's magazines approved of women's work outside the family but still as a prelude to marriage or as an extension of the family role, not as a career. In bolder terms, *The Ladies Home Journal*'s nonfiction encouraged women's professionalism in numerous articles such as "Doctor? Lawyer? Merchant? Chief," "How Can I Really Learn a Profession?" "Should a Woman Get a Man's Pay?" "The After-the-War Women in New Fields," and even "Women Directors of Plays and Pictures."[40]

Fan magazines represented the working woman in terms similar to other female-oriented discourses and extended their ambiguous construction of female sexual subjectivity into their discussion of the working woman. Throughout the decade, two patterns were repeated. In the first, fan magazines praised Hollywood's women writers, directors, and stars. In the second, female stars—the very epitome of successful working women—either lauded or denounced the modern working woman. In both instances, the terms of these sometimes opposing arguments could be appropriated into the more important imperative of encouraging the consumption of the star/commodity.

In 1922, Dorothy Gish went on record denouncing the "New Woman" for assuming she was "a man's mental equal" and for "trying now to step out of her place," but zealous protestations against the working woman were actually fairly rare in fan magazines and counterpointed by numerous other articles that praised both the "new" woman and Hollywood's working women. This praise was not initiated in the 1920s but actually anticipated in the late 1910s, as in Madame Petrova's 1918 declaration to *Motion Picture Classic:* "The only women I want to play are women who *do* things. I want to encourage women to do things—to take their rightful part in life."[41]

With the industry's own investment in a number of women stars who influenced their productions, and more women screenwriters than at any time before or since, fan magazines of the 1920s usually praised rather than denounced female professionalism. *Motion Picture Classic* carried an article on screenwriter June Mathis that remarked on her envied status as a woman to whom men went to be made—professionally. The magazine described her as a professional who commanded "more respect for her pronouncements than anyone else in the business." Another article on Mathis in *Motion Picture Stories* called her "virtual dictator of a great film company." *Photoplay* attacked the rampant industry prejudice that had made Dorothy Arzner only the first woman director in ten years but softened her possible threat by recounting the early history of "little Dorothy Arzner," who as a child was "a playmate of the movie great [sic]" at her father's cafe. In similar fashion, actress Corinne Griffith was dubbed "an amazing contradiction" with "the face of an early Italian angel and the hands of a twentieth-century business woman. Her hands are large and thin and sturdy. . . . They prove that beauty was not the only reason for her present fame and fortune. These are working hands."[42]

Just as the fan magazine mediated Corinne's beauty with business savvy, when possible they also marketed the stars as exemplars of the balancing of careerism and modern marriage. Typical of fan magazine discussion is an article "Profession and Marriage," appearing in *Screenland* of August 1920. It is worth quoting at length:

> Can a woman be a successful wife and business woman at the same time, is a question that arises a thousand times a day in the lives of various people. . . . Indeed it is possible. Woman has her sphere of work to do and a place of her own in the world, the same as a man. She may be a lawyer, movie star, or manicurist. Her husband may be a broker, chauffeur, movie idol or bank president. What difference does it make? To be successfully married and have a career is to share each other's joys and sorrows, successes and failures in business, or else leave all suggestions of one's business at the office, bank or studio, when entering the home.

Marked exceptions to this trend do occur, as in a *Photoplay* article of 1922 entitled "Confessions of a Modern Woman." Heralded by Adela

Rogers St. Johns as "the screen's greatest exponent" of the "ultra-advanced American female," Gloria Swanson distances herself from both her roles and her remarks by stating that "It is as the actress, the student of human character and emotions, that I speak—and not as myself." She tells readers that women with careers should never marry because "it's impossible to achieve a happy marriage and to be a free agent at the same time." In studying to portray the "bodily-beautiful, selfish, emancipated, restless, intolerant [and] unhappy" modern woman, Swanson says she has observed that modern woman's unhappiness stems mainly from her refusal to accept the fact that "no woman in the world is every happy with a man unless that man is her master."[43]

On the one hand, Swanson's remarks might reassure some readers that even successful, independent women stars such as Gloria still believed in the "traditional" social directives that upheld home and family as the undisputed primary feminine values. But Swanson's emphasis on women's need for "mastery" did not fall within the fan magazine's normative definition of heterosexual relations. Instead, it served the function of adding fuel to the fire of a heated controversy then occupying both fan magazine and newspaper star discourse. This controversy was initiated by publicity surrounding Rudolph Valentino and his portrayal of the "masterful" Ahmed Ben Hussain in *The Sheik*, released in late 1921 and adapted from a bestselling novel by Edith M. Hull[44] (figure 29).

Hull's novel, detailing the story of an independent Englishwoman who is kidnapped and raped by a tribal prince of the desert, was dismissed by one reviewer as "the cheapest and tawdriest novel ever written." Many reviewers of the film version actually predicted that it would fail because Valentino's Sheik did not rape the heroine. After all, the assumption was that the appeal of a rape fantasy was the key to the book's success.[45]

Valentino's sheik was considered by most reviewers to be only marginally masterful, a "Continental gentleman" in comparison with his literary counterpart. Therefore, the ensuing emphasis on mastery in extra-textual discourses surrounding the film version was quite obviously the result of a carefully orchestrated strategy to stir interest by stirring up controversy. One newspaper article issued an explicit warning: "Don't read this if you don't like a controversy." *Baltimore News* offered "Do Women Like Masterful Men?" which quoted Valentino as saying: "No matter whether they are feminists, suffragettes, or so-called new women, they like to have a masterful man make them do things." In another newspaper article, Valentino is quoted as saying: "I believe that the modern woman is unhappy. Her sudden economic liberation has created a false and hectic bloom."[46]

This specific intertextual reference clarifies the reason for Swanson's reactionary remarks within the context of the fan magazine. Rather than endorsing her view, "Confessions of a Modern Woman" demonstrates

Figure 29. *Valentino's Sheik was considered only to be marginally masterful.*

the need to situate stars within the consumerist imperative of selling pictures. Swanson's remarks in *Photoplay* appeared at the time that Valentino and Swanson were currently co-starring in *Beyond the Rocks* and in the same *Photoplay* issue Valentino blames the restlessness of the "modern woman in America" on the American man who "cannot hold a woman, dominate and rule her."

As might be expected, fan magazines quickly dropped the conflation of Valentino and the masterful sheik, but they could not drop the controversy surrounding Valentino.[47]

Woman-Made Men

To many observers, women's challenge to traditional sexual relations and American ideals of masculinity was given its greatest evidenciary support in the stardom of and controversy surrounding Valentino. His rise to fame seemed to personify the "woman-made man" and women's perverse search for a new model of masculinity that transgressed normative American models. As Lorine Pruette told readers of *The Nation* in 1927, "If it is true that man once shaped woman to be the creature of his desires and needs, then it is true that woman is now remodeling man." The American cinema was not considered to be the only pervasive disseminator of "pernicious" ideals of manhood. Women's literature was also denounced as supplanting the influence of the "manly man" who understood "woman's love of petty power." These new pernicious fictional ideals were said to be providing the model for real-life counterparts, for the "lounge lizards," "cake eaters," "boy flappers," and "flapperoosters" who indulged feminine sexual impulses either for money or for the lack of anything better to do.[48]

The visual objectification of the male in film and its surrounding discourses was not new in the 1920s, but it gained enormous public attention (and notoriety) as the act of women looking at men became symbolic of the tumultuous changes believed to be taking place in the system governing American sexual relations. Although women stars originally dominated its pages, the fan magazine of the postwar years began to cater more to women's express demand to see (as well as read about) male stars. By 1921, one male fan magazine writer was already complaining of the prevalence of "young and pretty heroes" in motion pictures, but Valentino epitomized the "woman-made man" for several reasons: He had been financially dependent on women in his stint as a paid dancing companion; his first wife Jean Acker publicly despaired of her effort "to make a man of him," and he had been brought to film fame by a woman, screenwriter June Mathis. These facts led many (men, in particular) to conclude that he was a typical "lounge lizard" who pursued the distinctly unmasculine goal of living off women, in this instance, the millions of women fans who packed the theaters to see him.[49]

The problematic issue of Valentino's "woman-made" status tied the apparent contradictions in the fan magazine's construction of femininity and female desire to its desperate attempt to define an image of masculinity both socially acceptable and sexually persuasive. As a consequence, the fan magazine's specific assignment of defining female fantasy surrounding the stars became increasingly controversial. Fan magazines did not ignore the negative publicity surrounding the star but eagerly participated in the debate over the reasons for Valentino's popularity. Taking a break from defending other unpopular causes, Clarence Darrow defended Valentino as a harmless diversion for married women, and *Motion Picture Classic* called on a prominent psychologist to discuss whether Valentino represented an "indictment" of the American businessman in "The Vogue of Valentino." *Screenland* pictured Valentino muscle flexing and demanded to know "Who Said Lounge Lizard?"; *Photoplay* offered the star posed like "The Thinker" in seminude photos as well as the delightful details of Mary Winship's "When Valentino Taught Me How to Dance."[50]

Even as fan magazines appeared to acquiesce to women's perceived desire for an exotic model of masculinity exemplified by Valentino, they also worked to undercut the star. Instead of unequivocally endorsing him as a profitable film commodity, *Photoplay* attempted to demystify Valentino as the center of women's personal fantasy scenarios: Adela Rogers St. Johns noted that he may represent "the lure of the flesh" to women in his screen image, but in real life he was an "ordinary young man, with atrocious taste in clothes, whose attributes render him devoid of physical charm." His leading ladies, she told readers, got absolutely no thrill playing love scenes with him. Similarly, Herbert Howe warned readers not to "confuse the man with his stellar shade. He [Valentino] . . . is the pilgrim boy as far as trifling with hearts is concerned."[51]

Clearly, the undercutting of Valentino's popularity evidenced the perceived need to bring fan magazine discourse into some kind of alignment with ideological imperatives at odds with and more important than one film star's popularity with women. Valentino incited socially transgressive sexual implications that could hardly be depoliticized within a xenophobic culture. As a result, even the fan magazine could no longer completely trust women in their appreciation of a film idol, despite numerous fan letters that suggested little more than women's appreciation of his "personality" and his acting ability. As the debate over Valentino raged, one fan magazine reader wrote:

> It is true that our feminine hearts go pit-a-pat when we see Valentino up on the screen. . . . But when the lights go up on every day life once more, how perfectly splendid it is for American women to have one hundred percent, plain American husbands, who treat them as pals and equals and love them for saving pennies for the children's future, instead of spending them on sunken marble baths . . .

Another fan letter reacted to criticism of Valentino as a foreigner by reminding the magazine and its readers that the concern over the actor's ethnic origins was nonsense because "we are speaking of actors and their acting and not of intermarriage with them." But it was the fear of intermarriage (at worst) and sexual arousal (at best) that shaped the response to Valentino as a representative of those new immigrants from southern and eastern Europe, that "slag in the melting pot" that many feared would lead to "race suicide" and a "mongrelization" of the Nordic-Anglo-Saxon race in the United States.[52]

Fan magazines adopted strategies to channel women into ethnically, racially, and nationally normative models of heterosexual romance in a nativist culture. In particular, they attempted to foster an appreciation of stars who were exemplars of "the fine, upstanding, typical American," the "man's man" type who would, unlike Valentino, be liked by men as well as women. *Photoplay* promoted Ronald Colman in a 1924 article entitled "A Ladies' Man Who Is Regular Guy; Ronald Colman is a Favorite of Both Sexes." Real men, articles such as this implied, would never be content to be mere matinee idols but wanted to be directors, gentleman farmers, or merely good actors. At the same time, in an apparent effort to defuse and still satisfy women's apparent desire for a foreign fantasy lover, Anglo-Saxon actors increasingly co-opted the roles of swarthy, passionate foreigners in films such as *The Night of Love*, in which Ronald Colman masquerades as a vengeful gypsy chief who, in sheiklike fashion, kidnaps a princess.[53]

The backlash against the foreign lover in fan magazines never reached the extremes of other forms of popular culture, but after Valentino's death, *Photoplay* did not hesitate to publish a letter from a male reader who praised actor William Boyd and remarked: "It is gratifying to note the return of the American hero. . . . What a relief, after the foreign invasion." An article by Adela Rogers St. Johns in the same year suggested that "child-like, picturesque" Valentino had allowed himself to be totally dominated by his second wife, a confirmation of his woman-made status long discussed in newspapers but suppressed in the fan magazines. "Such men make romantic figures on the screen," St. Johns continued, but in real life they proved to be unsatisfactory husbands who "need to be taken care of, protected, surrounded and helped." By 1928, even "It," that quality of sex appeal once bestowed by Elinor Glyn on Valentino, Clara Bow and Rex the Wild Horse, was no longer regarded as a coveted quality without limitations of gender or species but something, as director Wesley Ruggles told readers of *Motion Picture Classic*, that "No real he-man living ever had . . . or ever will."[54]

The Fan Magazine and the Hysterical Female Spectator

"The death of Rudolph Valentino is the culminating point of the stars' great epoch," writes Edgar Morin in *The Stars*. He describes the response elicited by the star's death in August 1926: "Two women commit suicide in front of the hospital where Valentino has just died; his funeral rolls by in an atmosphere of collective hysteria; his grave is still covered with flowers." As inaccurate as the specific details Morin's account of Valentino's death may be, his impression of female fans shares much with contemporary film theory's prevailing image of women spectators—and their intense, excessive, hysterical investment in Hollywood cinema and its stars.[55]

In *The Desire to Desire*, Mary Ann Doane compares the female spectator of classical Hollywood film to the female hysteric. She states: "Unable to negotiate the distance which is a prerequisite to desire and its displacements, the female spectator is always, in some sense, constituted as a hysteric." "She can only futilely and inelegantly . . . desire to desire." Following the oft-expressed notion that woman cannot help but be con-

structed by the patriarchal cinematic gaze, Doane describes a female spectator aligned by cinematic enunciation with "an excess of emotion, sentiment, affect, empathy"; her gaze is closely bound to the image in a
proximity that virtually condemns her to emotional overinvestment and
overidentification. Her body becomes vulnerable to an inscription of hysterical symptoms that demonstrates her lack of any real "access to a desiring
subjectivity." Unless she can somehow manufacture a distance through a
defensive "masquerade," her desire is engaged in the narcissistic and
masochistic imperatives of self-commodification; she will lose herself in
"becoming" an image that is too close.[56]

Yet, by continuing to use terms such as *overidentification* and *collapse*
in relation to issues of female spectatorship, Doane posits a problematic notion
of female subjectivity. Such a theory reifies androcentric values. As a result, as
Patrice Petro observes, "women's closeness to the image can only be conceived
as a 'deficiency' within a masculine epistemology." Within Doane's perpetu-
ation of a "masculine epistemology," woman's desire for closeness can only
be equated with a collapse of identity. Empathy is always dangerous, and
emotion is antithetical to comprehension.[57]

In their inelegant behavior, the largely female crowds attempting
to view Valentino's body at Campbell's Funeral Church would seem to have
demonstrated the essence of hysteria as described by Doane. However, if
one looks at the newsreels of the event, they show festive rather than
mourning crowds and an atmosphere more reminescent of a premiere than
a funeral. Women recounted to *The New York Times* reporter that they
brought flowers, not in tribute, but with a calculated interest in being given
access to the chapel, and Valentino's manager finally closed the proceedings
because the crowds "showed the most gross irreverence." In this respect,
these many fans of Valentino who stood for hours to get a glimpse of the
star's corpse might be accused of a paradoxically "unfeminine" element of
detachment from their object of adoration.[58]

Likewise, the fan magazine and its readers might be accused by
contemporary theory of indulging in a paradoxically "unfeminine" element
of distanciation from their object(s) of adoration, particularly in the endless
discussion of the disparities between star image and actor personality and
of the mechanisms of filmic construction. As I have shown, the fan magazine encouraged a disavowing relationship, a balancing of intimacy and
distance, sensationalism and empathy, knowledge and belief in its readers.

The fascinations of the fan magazine also evidence a desire for
intensification of the cinematic signifier, for a revelation of the "truth"
behind the screen. Admittedly, fan magazines of the 1920s offered a contradictory unveiling of cinematic truth because the knowledge they offered
was both illusionary and real. Nevertheless, fan magazine readership may
have given women the sense of a privileged status in reading the film text
through their understanding of a "truth" not immediately revealed on

screen, beyond mere sight and visual representation. Revealing what was hidden from sight on the screen, fan magazines of the 1920s proclaimed both the lack in the image in relational terms (its one-sided perversity) and its fullness of expression, a fullness (of the star) that the screen could not at any one time capture, that eluded the immediate field of vision.[59]

As a consequence of this process, the fan magazine may have helped to derail women's spectatorship from "normal" male visual orientation, although as I have argued elsewhere, we should not be too quick to assume the rigidity of identifications set into play by the "patriarchal gaze." Fan magazines contributed to this visual reorientation with their shift to the invisible (the extratextual, the biographical), and with the highly detailed plot synopses that magazines such as *Motion Picture Classic* and *Motion Picture Magazine* regularly offered for much anticipated pictures. Rather than substitute for the film, this preparation in narrative left women free to contemplate other elements of the text: the stars. As a result, fan magazines activated strategies of textual reading that diversified the possibilities of women's looking as well as their intellectual and emotional response. Interest across a range of cinematic signifiers could be refocused to permit an intensification of visual fascination.[60]

With its rampant ideological contradictions and ambiguities, the fan magazine of the 1920s might be read as a sign of women's subordination to patriarchal relations in the extratextual "marginalization" and "commodification" of the female spectator as consumer. Doane has suggested that the coercive power of consumerism inevitably makes the woman into a passive subject whose desire is reduced to a narcissistic and/or masochistic position of self-commodification. She also argues that consumerism "requires a transformation in modes of perception" such that women participate in a free-floating consumer gaze, "alienated from narrative" and focused on "possession." Somehow escaping the enunciative constraints of the patriarchal gaze, the female spectator becomes engaged in a process in which "the desire to possess displaces comprehension as the dominant mechanism of reading."[61]

Engaged not in an hysterical split, but in a double perspective balancing closeness and distance, readers were not likely to be completely satisfied in an urge to vicariously "possess" the star constructed by the fan magazine. As strong as the fan magazine's "consumer appeal" may have been in the increasingly consumer-oriented 1920s, women did not go to the movies or read fan magazines merely to "possess" the luxurious furnishings or the clothes or the stars that might be displayed. They went for an experience, one whose terms of fascination could be altered by the extratextual process. As a consequence, it is unlikely that the complex activity of the female spectator or the fan magazine reader of the 1920s can be fully explained by a model of consumerism, such as that advanced by Doane, that depends on a binarism in which women can only either possess *or* comprehend.[62]

Even if, for reasons of scholarly prudence, we would hesitate to automatically confirm the fan magazine as a significant influence *on* women's spectatorship, we can certainly consider it as one consistent indicator of an industry-related reading *of* the socially determined female audience. Despite its contradictions, fan magazine discourse of the 1920s did not encourage a total investment in an illusion but appears largely predicated on the assumption that women could participate in an engagement with the cinema that might include, for lack of a better term, a "fetishistic" pleasure taken from the play of text and intertext, discovery and disavowal, make believe and transparent marketing mechanism. As such, the humble fan magazine may provide a privileged site for understanding the historical and theoretical complexity of women's reception of the American cinema—especially in the 1920s, when many of them braved the perils of female pleasure, plunged into "Valentino traps," and emerged beyond the text—in the fan magazine's "no-man's land" of intertextual fascination.

NOTES

The research for this paper was funded, in part, by an Emory University Research Grant. My thanks to participants in the Columbia Film Seminar (April 1990) for their helpful comments on an earlier draft of this paper and to Ned Comstock of the Archives of the Performing Arts, University of Southern California, for his assistance in locating fan magazine articles. Thanks also to Matthew Bernstein for his astute editorial advice.

1. Frederick James Smith, "Does Decency Help or Hinder?" *Photoplay* 26 (November 1924), 36; Beth Brown, "Making Movies for Women," *Moving Picture World* (26 March 1927), 34. The quotation from *Exhibitors Herald/Moving Picture World* is cited in Charlotte Herzog. "'Powder Puff' Promotion: The Fashion Show-in-the-Film," *Fabrications* (New York: Routledge, 1990), p. 157. Regarding a female box-office majority, Leo Handel suggests that the Hollywood film industry often operated "under the impression" that women were a majority of the American film audience and notes that "it is even possible, though not probable, that this proportion (of 65–70% women) held true at some time in the past." See Handel, *Hollywood Looks at its Audience* (Urbana: University of Illinois, 1950), p. 90. See also Diane Waldman, "From Midnight Shows to Marriage Vows," *Wide Angle* 6 (1984), p. 41.

2. On Hollywood's extratextual appeal, see Mary Ann Doane, *The Desire to Desire* (Bloomington: Indiana University, 1987), p. 26; and Waldman, "From Midnight Shows," p. 41. The quotation is from Arthur Mayer, *Merely Colossal* (New York: Simon & Schuster, 1953), p. 178.

3. Miriam Hansen, "Adventures of Goldilocks: Early Cinema, Consumerism and Public Life," *Camera Obscura* 22 (1990), 51–72.

4. *Editorial*, "What Do You Want?" *Photoplay* 21 (May 1922), 19. A more realistic circulation figure is probably 500,000.

5. Doane, *Desire to Desire*, pp. 31, 32.

6. Carl F.Cotter, "The Forty Hacks of the Fan Mags," *The Coast* (February 1939), 1. On collusion with the image, see Doane, *Desire to Desire*, pp. 1–2. On spectatorial hysteria, see Doane, *Desire to Desire*, pp. 66–69. For a discussion of female reaction to Valentino, consult Miriam Hansen, "Pleasure, Ambivalence, Identification: Valentino and Female Spectatorship," *Cinema Journal* 25 (Summer 1986), 6–32 and Gaylyn Studlar "Discourses of

Gender and Ethnicity: The Construction and De(con)struction of Rudolph Valentino as Other," *Film Criticism* 13 (Winter 1989), 18–35.

7. For circulation figures and an analysis of the dynamics of early twentieth-century magazine publishing in relation to advertising, see Theodore Peterson, *Magazines in the Twentieth Century* (Urbana: University of Illinois, 1956).

8. Waldman, "From Midnight Shows," p. 48.

9. Ibid., p. 42. Martin Pumphery offers a provocative analysis of the role of 1920s consumerism in the emergence of a new feminine ideal divorced from the past and tradition in "The Flapper, the Housewife and the Making of Modernity," *Cultural Studies* 1 (May 1987), 179–94.

10. *Movie Weekly* was published by Mcfadden Publications (which also published *True Confessions*). It went so far as to publish testimony from the Valentino divorce trial in which Jean Acker Valentino testifies as to the consummation of her marriage to "The World's Greatest Lover." (She could not remember anything regarding the event.) *Movie Weekly* (ca. November 1921), unpaginated clipping, New York Public Library Theater Arts Collection (hereafter cited as NYPLC). In his useful survey of the history of fan magazines, Anthony Slide calls *Movie Weekly* (1921–1925) "the nearest equivalent to contemporary fan magazines" with their "gossip articles." See Slide, *International Film, Radio, and Television Journals* (Westport, Conn: Greenwood, 1985), pp. 384–5. Richard deCordova, *Picture Personalities: The Emergence of the Star System in America* (Urbana: University of Illinois, 1990). The quote is from "Answers to Inquiries," *Photoplay* (March 1912), 72, quoted in deCordova, *Picture Personalities*, p. 105–6.

11. DeCordova, *Picture Personalities*, pp. 119–21. Jack Wooldridge, "Why Not Get Married: Happy Husbands of Hollywood Answer the Bachelors," *Screen Secrets* 6 (November 1928), 66+; Alma Tally, "Love Makes the Man," *Picture Play* (May 1929), 56+; "Untold Love Stories of the Stars," *Photoplay* 22 (March 1923), 30+; Dorothy Manner, "Love Stories Behind the Cameras," *Motion Picture Magazine* 32 (December 1926), 20+.

12. Editorial, *Motion Picture Magazine* (March 1915), 1; James Quirk, "Moral House Cleaning: What's It All About?" *Photoplay* 21 (April 1922), 52.

13. Herbert Howe, "The Unhappy Ending of Wally Reid's Life Story: A Tribute from a Friend," *Photoplay* 22 (March 1923), 32+; Adela Rogers St. Johns, "The Butterfly Man and the Little Clown," *Photoplay* 36 (July 1929) 38+; "Brickbats and Bouquets: Letters to the Editor," *Photoplay* 22 (September 1922), 113, (hereafter cited as "Letters to the Editor").

14. Smith, "Does Decency Help," p. 36.

15. Slide, *International Film*, p. 383; *Movie Weekly* (11 August 1923), unpaginated clipping, NYPLC; *Motion Picture Magazine* 26 (December 1918), 101.

16. Burt Knight, "What Mrs. Barthelmess Thinks of Richard," *Cinema Art* (April 1926), unpaginated clipping, NYPLC; "Letters to the Editor," *Photoplay* 22 (July 1922), 115.

17. Dorothy Wooldridge, "What the Screen Idols Think of the Flapper, *Motion Picture Classic* 25 (July 1927), 20; "How They Play," *Pantomime* (12 October 1921), 1; Mary Winship, "Out of Arabian Nights," *Photoplay* 22 (April 1922), 40+; The Answer Man, "Questions and Answers," *Photoplay* 21 (January 1922), 122; "Letters to the Editor," *Photoplay* 22 (March 1923), 62; "Letters to the Editor," *Movie Weekly* (7 October 1922), unpaginated clipping, NYPLC; "Letters to the Editor," *Photoplay* 23 (October 1922), 113.

18. Tania Modleski, "The Disappearing Act: A Study of Harlequin Romances," *Signs* 5 (Spring 1980), 446; Janice Radway, *Reading the Romance* (Chapel Hill: University of North Carolina, 1984), pp. 140–1.

19. "Who is this? Bebe Daniels?" *Photoplay* 21 (January 1922), 37.

20. Smith, "Does Decency Help," p. 36; Lew Cody, "A Reformed Villain: *By Himself*," *Photoplay* 22 (July 1922), 50.

21. Doane, *Desire to Desire*, pp. 30–33; Doane, "Film and the Masquerade: Theorising the Female Spectator," *Screen* 23 (September–October 1982), 74–87; See also Joan Riviere,

"Womanliness as Masquerade," *International Journal of Psychoanalysis* 10 (1929), reprinted in Victor Burgin, James Donald, Cora Kaplan, eds., *Formations of Fantasy* (London: Methuen, 1986), pp. 35–44.

22. William J. Robinson, *Married Life and Happiness (or Love and Comfort in Marriage)*, 4th ed. (New York: Eugenics Press, 1922), pp. 89, 93.

23. On the change in opinion regarding women's sexual desires, see Editors, "Sex O'Clock in America," *Current Opinion* (August 1913), 113–4, and Phyllis Blanchard and Carlyn Manasses, *New Girls for Old* (New York: The Macaulay Co., 1930), p. 78. Dorothy Bromley quote is from Bromley, "Feminist-New Style," *Harper's* 155 (1927), 552. For the origins of companionate marriage, see Ben Lindsey and Wainwright Evans, *Companionate Marriage* (New York: Boni & Liveright, 1927).

24. On the unparalleled influence exerted by women exercising the "privilege of living with the same license" as men, see Cora Harris, *Flapper Anne* (Boston: Houghton Mifflin, 1925), quoted in *New York Times Book Review* (5 May 1926), 8; Joseph Collins, "Woman's Morality in Transition," *Current History* 27 (1927), 33–40; and Edward Sapir, "The Discipline of Sex," *American Mercury* 16 (1929), 413–20. The quotations are from Will Durant, "The Modern Woman: Philosophers Grow Dizzy as She Passes By," *Century Magazine* 113 (February 1927), 421; Paula Fass, *The Damned and the Beautiful: American Youth in the 1920s* (New York: Oxford, 1977), p. 25; and Charlotte Perkins Gilman, "Vanguard, Rear-guard, and Mud-guard," *Century Magazine* 104 (1922), 351.

25. "Letters to the Editor," *Photoplay* 31 (February 1927), 12; Lloyd Lewis, "The Deluxe Picture Palace," *The New Republic* 58 (March 1929), 174–5; Edward Alsworth Ross, *World Drift* (New York: Century, 1928), p. 179.

26. Herbert Blumer, *Movies and Conduct* (New York: Macmillan, 1933), pp. 108, 109, 52.

27. The quotation is from Waldman, "From Midnight Shows," p. 42.

28. Some women's magazine stories dealing with romance, sex, and marriage in typical fashion are Sarah Lindsay Coleman's "Invisible Cords," *McCalls* 53 (November 1925), 8+; Gerald Beaumont's "The Sporting Venus," *Red Book* 43 (June 1924), 58–61; and Zane Grey's "The Bee-Hunter," *The Ladies Home Journal* 42 (March 1925), 22+.

29. Vivian Bretherton, "Irmalee and the Mid-Victorian Age," *McCalls* 53 (July 1925), 16, 17, 61.

30. Quotations are from Beatrice Hinkle, "The Chaos of Modern Marriage," *Harper's* 157 (December 1925), 5, 1. Those many tracts calling for a return to motherhood as the dominant ideal of women's lives included Gina Lombroso-Ferrero's *The Soul of Woman* (New York: E.P. Dutton, 1923); Anthony M. Ludovici's *Woman: A Vindication* (New York: Alfred A. Knopf, 1923); and Knight Dunlap's *Personal Beauty and Racial Betterment* (St. Louis: C. V. Mosby, 1920).

31. Faith Service, "'There are No Mothers Any More' says Doris Kenyon," *Classic* 29 (March 1924), 23, 86. *Classic* was alternately titled (and is hereafter cited) as *Motion Picture Classic*.

32. Wallace Reid, "How to Hold a Wife," *Photoplay* 19 (January 1921), 28; McMenamin, "Evils of Woman's Revolt against the Old Standard," *Current History* 19 (1927), 30–32; Louis E. Bisch, "Are Women Inferior or Are They Trying to Side-Track Nature?" *Century Magazine* 113 (1927), 674–81. Quotation is from Editorial, "What Do We Mean by 'Nice'?" *The Ladies Home Journal* 42 (November 1920), 1.

33. "The Battle of Bobbed Hair: National Opinion of Those for and against Clipped Locks," *Photoplay* 26 (June 1924), 32–33; Wooldridge, "What the Screen Idols Think," pp. 20+.

34. Wooldridge, "What the Screen Idols Think," pp. 21, 20, 86.

35. The phrase *chaste young hell cat* is from Harris, *Flapper Anne*, p. 8.

36. There were at least two magazines entitled *Screenland*. One was a national publication in print from 1921–1927. The other, cited here, was a fan magazine printed in Dallas, Texas, and distributed at six Paramount theaters in Dallas, although newsstand availability

is also suggested. Paramount stars and films were the exclusive subject of this otherwise typical fan magazine. Quotation from *Screenland* 1 (10 September 1922), 9.

37. The "codeless existence" quote is from Allan Leigh, *Women Like Men* (New York: Macaulay, 1926), p. 214.

38. Blumer, *Movies and Conduct*, p. 52.

39. William Howard Taft, "As I See the Future of Women," *The Ladies Home Journal* 36 (March 1919), 27, 113; Lorine Pruette, "Should Men Be Protected?" *The Nation* 125 (31 August 1927), 201.

40. See Harriet Abbott, "Doctor? Lawyer? Merchant? Chief?" *The Ladies Home Journal* 42 (July 1920), 43+; Anonymous, "How Can I Really Learn a Profession?" *The Ladies Home Journal* 36 (August 1919), 39+; Emily Newell Blair, "Should a Woman Get a Man's Pay?" *The Ladies Home Journal* 36 (April 1919), 39+; Isaac Marcosson, "The After-the-War Women in New Fields," *The Ladies Home Journal* 35 (June 1918), 13+; Henry MacMahon, "Women Directors of Plays and Pictures," *The Ladies Home Journal* 42 (December 1920), 12+.

41. Dorothy Gish, "Largely a Matter of Love," *Photoplay* 21 (March 1922), 38; Frederick James Smith, "Petrova and Her Philosophy of Life," *Motion Picture Classic* 7 (September 1918), 77.

42. Gladys Hall, "A Maker of Young Men," *Motion Picture Classic* 29 (March 1924), 22; Dorothy Dannell, "The Troubles of a Star Maker," *Motion Picture Magazine* [n.d.], 3, clipping, NYPLC; Ivan St. Johns, "Good-Bye to Another Tradition," *Photoplay* 31 (March 1927), 40; Delight Evans, "The Girl on The Cover," *Photoplay* 21 (January 1922), 38.

43. "Profession and Marriage," *Screenland* (Dallas) 1 (13 August 1920), 13; Adela Rogers St. Johns, "The Confessions of a Modern Woman—as Told by Gloria Swanson," *Photoplay* 21 (March 1922), 21, 22.

44. Edith M. Hull, *The Sheik* (New York: A. L. Burt, 1921).

45. Anonymous, *New York World* [n.d.], quoted in *Exhibitor's Trade Herald* (19 November 1921), 1763. For discussions of the film's restraint in comparison to the book, see "Movie Denatures Tale of *The Sheik*," *Cleveland Press* (28 November 1921), 16; and Adele Whiteley Fletcher, "Across the Silversheet," *Motion Picture Magazine* [n.d.], 108, clipping, NYPLC. Fletcher says of the film: "Remembering censorship, we wondered why they ever bought the motion picture rights in the first place."

46. The phrase, *a Continental gentleman* is from Fletcher, "Across the Silversheet," p. 108; N.E.A. Service, "A Love Recipe That Is Almost Sure to Start a Controversy," *Evening Examiner-New Era* (29 September 1921), unpaginated clipping, NYPLC; "Do Women Like Masterful Men?" *Baltimore News* (22 October 1921), unpaginated clipping, NYPLC; Valentino's comment on women's economic liberation is in "Is the American Girl Playing a Losing Game?" *Metropolitan* (January 1923), unpaginated clipping, NYPLC.

47. Rudolph Valentino, "Woman and Love" *Photoplay* 21 (March 1922), 106.

48. Pruette, "Should Men Be Protected?" p. 200; on women's literature, see Ludovici, *Woman*, pp. 12–13. For an outraged reaction to the effect of flapperdom on male behavior, see Freeman Tilden, "Flapperdames and Flapperoosters," *The Ladies Home Journal* 40 (May), 16+.

49. "Letters to the Editor," *Photoplay* 29 (January 1926), 12; Bert Lytell, "A Lesson in Love," *Photoplay* 19 (February 1921), 43. For Jean Acker's account of her attempt to make a man of Valentino, see "Wedded, Found Spouse Broke?" *Los Angeles Times* (24 November 1921), unpaginated clipping, NYPLC. For a stereotypical male reaction to Valentino, see Dick Dorgan's "Giving 'The Sheik' the Once Over from the Ringside," *Photoplay* 21 (April 1922), 90–92 and Dorgan's "I Hate Valentino," *Photoplay* 22 (July 1922), 26. The issue of Valentino's needing to be made into a man was actually taken up in the promotion of at least one of his films. *Moran of the Lady Letty* (1922) was advertised as the story of "a soft society dandy whom [sic] love made into a man." ca. 1922, unpaginated clipping, NYPLC.

50. Clarence Darrow, "The Screen Sheik Is a Blessing to Married Men," *Motion Picture Classic* (May 1924), unpaginated clipping, NYPLC; Guy Rowe [pseudonym], "The Vogue of

Valentino," *Motion Picture Classic* 25 (February 1923), 23+; "Who Said Lounge Lizard?" *Screenland* (February 1923), unpaginated clipping, NYPLC; "The Thinker," *Photoplay* 25 (April 1924), 43; Mary Winship, "When Valentino Taught Me How to Dance," *Photoplay* 21 (May 1922), 45+.

51. Adela Rogers St. Johns, "What Kind of Men Attract Women Most?" *Photoplay* 25 (March 1924), 110–11; Herbert Howe, "What Are Matinee Idols Made of?" *Photoplay* 23 (April 1923), 41.

52. Quotation on American men is from "Letters to the Editor," *Photoplay* 22 (July 1922), 115; the quotation on intermarriage is from "Letters to the Editor," *Photoplay* 23 (September 1922), 113. "Slag in the melting pot" and subsequent phrases are from an article on the new immigrants, George Creel's "Close the Gates," *Collier's* (6 May 1922), 9. For a discussion of the dimensions of xenophobia in the United States during the 1920s, consult John Higham, *Strangers in the Land: Patterns of American Nativism, 1860–1925*, 2nd ed. (New Brunswick, N.J.: Rutgers, 1988).

53. St. Johns, "What Kind of Men Attract Women Most?" p. 111; Arthur Brenton, "A Ladies' Man Who Is a Regular Guy," *Photoplay* 27 (December 1924), 66, 132. See also Nancy Pryor, "The Sheik Stuff Is Out: Hugh Allen Says It Leaves Him Cold," *Motion Picture Classic* 27(June 1928), 26+.

54. "Letters to the Editor," *Photoplay* 32 (June 1927), 84; Adela Rogers St. Johns, "Why Do Great Lovers Fail as Husbands," *Photoplay* 32 (July 1927), 116; Hal K. Wells, "The He of It," *Motion Picture Classic* 27 (May 1928), 18.

55. Edgar Morin, *The Stars*, trans. Richard Howard (New York: Grove Press, 1961), p. 16.

56. Doane, *The Desire to Desire*, pp. 13, 66, 67. See also Doane, "Film and the Masquerade," p. 87.

57. Patrice Petro, *Joyless Streets* (Princeton, N.J.: Princeton University Press, 1989), p. 48. On overidentification and the "collapse" of subject into object, see Doane, *The Desire to Desire*, esp. pp. 9, 13, 153, 168–9, 176–7. Doane dismisses the possibility that women spectators could engage in a fetishistic balancing act with the cinema: "Fetishism—the ability to balance knowledge and belief and hence to maintain a distance from the lure of the image—is also inaccessible to the woman, who has no need of the fetish as a defense against a castration which has already taken place" (p. 12). For an extended discussion of the interpretation of fetishism in feminist film theory, see Studlar, *In the Realm of Pleasure* (Urbana: University of Illinois, 1988).

58. "Public Now Barred at Valentino's Bier," *The New York Times* (26 August 1926), 1, 5. In "Thousands in Riot at Valentino Bier," *The New York Times* (25 August 1926), 3, *The Times* suggested of the mourners: "They were merely curious, and looked it. Hardly one looked even sorrowful, much less reverent."

59. DeCordova takes a similar position with regard to the star system's channeling of the spectator towards the "truth" that lies behind a screen. DeCordova, *Picture Personalities*, esp. pp. 145–6.

60. On the possibilities of identification in relation to the "patriarchal gaze," see Studlar, *In the Realm of Pleasure*.

61. Doane, *Desire to Desire*, pp. 31–2.

62. On the appeal of "ownership by viewing," see Jeanne Allen, "The Film Viewer as Consumer," *Quarterly Review of Film Studies* 5 (1980), 481–99. One example of the unfortunate excesses that can occur when applying consumer culture theory to film is evident in Jane Gaines' otherwise admirable article, "The Queen Christina Tie-Ups: Convergence of Show Window and Screen," *Quarterly Review of Film and Video Studies* 11 (1989), 35–60. Gaines reads the famous scene of Garbo's postcoital touching of objects in the room that has served as the site of her sexual encounter with Don Antonio as a sign of Christina's "initiation into consumer desire . . . heterosexuality *makes her want things.*" See p. 50. Gaines says the encounter is the character's first heterosexual one, but the film's early scenes imply otherwise.

Selected Bibliography

I have chosen to provide a "selected" rather than "annotated" bibliography in order to cover as many research avenues as possible, especially given the recent work on silent cinema. Because this bibliography is designed primarily for readers in the United States, references to languages other than English have been excluded.

Abel, Richard. *French Cinema: The First Wave, 1915–1929*. Princeton, N.J.: Princeton University Press, 1984.

———. *French Film Theory and Criticism: A History/Anthology, I. 1907–1929*. Princeton, N.J.: Princeton University Press, 1988.

———. *The Ciné Goes to Town: French Cinema, 1896–1914*. Berkeley: University of California Press, 1994.

Abel, Richard. "Pathé Goes to Town: French Films Create a Market for Nickelodeon," *Cinema Journal* 35 (Fall 1995).

Allen, Robert C. "Motion Picture Exhibition in Manhattan, 1906–1912: Beyond the Nickelodeon," *Cinema Journal* 18 (Spring 1979), 2–15.

———. *Vaudeville and Film, 1895–1915: A Study in Media Interaction*. New York: Arno Press, 1980.

Allen, Robert C., and Douglas Gomery. *Film History: Theory and Practice*. New York: Knopf, 1985.

Anderson, Gillian B. "The Presentation of Silent Films, or Music as Anaesthesia," *The Journal of Musicology* 5 (1987), 257–95.

———. *Music for Silent Films (1894–1927): A Guide*. Washington, D. C.: Library of Congress, 1989.

Anderson, J. L. "Spoken Silents in the Japanese Cinema; or Talking to Pictures: Essaying the Katsuben, Contextualizing the Texts," in Arthur Nolletti, Jr., and David Desser, eds., *Reframing Japanese Cinema: Authorship, Genre, History*. Bloomington: Indiana University Press, 1992, pp. 259–311.

Balides, Constance. "Scenarios of Exposure in the Practice of Everyday Life: Women in the Cinema of Attractions," *Screen* 34 (Spring 1993), 19–37.

Balio, Tino, ed. *The American Film Industry*, 2nd ed. Madison: University of Wisconsin Press, 1985.

Ball, Robert Hamilton. *Shakespeare on Silent Film: A Strange Eventful History*. London: George Allen & Unwin, 1968.

Balshofer, Fred and Arthur C. Miller. *One Reel a Week*. Berkeley: University of California Press, 1967.

Barnes, John. *The Rise of the Cinema in Great Britain*. London: Bishopsgate Press, 1983.

Barnouw, Eric. *The Magician and the Cinema.* New York: Oxford University Press, 1981.

Belton, John, ed., *Film History* 6 (Winter 1994)—special issue on audiences and fans.

Bernardini, Daniel, ed., *The Birth of Whiteness: Race and the Emergence of United States Cinema.* New Brunswick, N. J.: Rutgers University Press, 1995.

Bordwell, David. *French Impressionist Cinema: Film Culture, Film Theory, Film Style.* New York: Arno, 1980.

Bordwell, David, Janet Staiger, and Kristin Thompson. *The Classical Hollywood Cinema: Film Style and Mode of Production to 1960.* New York: Columbia University Press, 1985.

Bordwell, David, and Kristin Thompson. "Linearity, Materialism and the Study of the Early American Cinema," *Wide Angle* 5:3 (1983), 4–15.

Bottomore, Stephen. "Shots in the Dark: The Real Origins of Film Editing," *Sight and Sound* 57 (Summer 1988), 200–4.

Bowser, Eileen. "The Brighton Project: An Introduction," *Quarterly Review of Film Studies* 4:4 (Fall 1979), 509–38.

———, ed., *The Slapstick Symposium.* Brussels: FIAF, 1987.

———. *A History of the American Cinema, II: The Transformation of Cinema, 1908–1915.* New York: Scribner's, 1991.

Bratton, Jacky, Pam Cook, and Christine Gledhill, eds., *Melodrama.* London: British Film Institute, 1994.

Brewster, Ben. "A Scene at the Movies," *Screen* 23 (July–August 1982), 4–15.

———. "*Traffic in Souls:* An Experiment in Feature-Length Narrative Construction," *Cinema Journal* 31 (Fall 1991), 37–56.

Brownlow, Kevin. *The Parade's Gone By.* London: Paladin, 1968.

———. *Hollywood the Pioneers.* London: Collins, 1979.

———. *Behind the Masks of Innocence. Sex, Violence, Prejudice, Crime: Films of Social Conscience in the Silent Era.* Berkeley: University of California Press, 1990.

Bruno, Giuliana. *Streetwalking on a Ruined Map: Cultural Theory and the City Films of Elvira Notari.* Princeton, N.J.: Princeton University Press, 1993.

Burch, Noël. "Porter, or Ambivalence," *Screen* 19 (Winter 1978–1979), 91–105.

———. "Film's Institutional Mode of Representation and the Soviet Response," *October* 11 (Winter 1979), 77–96.

———. "How We Got into Pictures: Notes Accompanying *Correction Please,*" *Afterimage* 8/9 (1981), 24–38.

———. "Primitivism and the Avant-Gardes: A Dialectical Approach," in Philip Rosen, ed., *Narrative, Apparatus, Ideology: A Film Theory Reader.* New York: Columbia University Press, 1986, pp. 483–506.

———. *Life to Those Shadows.* Berkeley: University of California Press, 1990.

Cassady, Ralph, Jr. "Monopoly in Motion Picture Production and Distribution, 1908–1915," *Southern California Law Review* 32:4 (Summer 1959), 25–67.

Chanan, Michael. *The Dream That Kicks.* London: Routledge & Kegan Paul, 1980.

Charney, Leo, and Vanessa Schwartz, eds., *Cinema and the Invention of Modern Life.* Berkeley: University of California Press, 1995.

Cherchi Usai, Paolo. *Burning Passions.* Trans., Elizabeth Sansone. London: British Film Institute, 1994.

Cherchi Usai, Paolo, and Lorenzo Codelli, ed., *The Path to Hollywood*. Pordenone: Edizioni Biblioteca dell'Immagine, 1988.

————, ed., *Before Caligari: German Cinema, 1897–1920*. Pordenone: Edizioni Biblioteca dell'Immagine, 1990.

————, ed., *The DeMille Legacy*. Pordenone: Edizioni Biblioteca dell'Immagine, 1991.

Cherchi Usai, Paolo, and Yuri Tsivian, ed., *Silent Witnesses: Russian Films, 1908–1919*. London: British Film Institute, 1989.

Cosandey, Roland, and André Gaudreault, eds., *Images across Borders*. Lausanne: Editions Payot, 1995.

Cosandey, Roland, André Gaudreault, and Tom Gunning, eds., *An Invention of the Devil?: Religion and Early Cinema*. Lausanne: Editions Payet, 1992.

Crafton, Donald. *Before Mickey: The Animated Film, 1898–1928*. Cambridge, Mass.: MIT Press, 1982.

————. *Emile Cohl, Caricature, and Film*. Princeton, N.J.: Princeton University Press, 1990.

————, ed. *Iris* 11 (Summer 1990)—special issue devoted to early cinema audiences.

deCordova, Richard. *Picture Personalities: The Emergence of the Star System in America, 1907–1922*. Champaign: University of Illinois Press, 1990.

Deutelbaum, Marshall, ed., *"Image" on the Art and Evolution of the Film*. New York: Dover, 1979.

Dibbets, Karel and Bert Hogenkamp, eds., *Film and the First World War*. Amsterdam: Amsterdam University Press, 1995.

Eisner, Lotte. *The Haunted Screen: Expressionism in the Cinema and the Influence of Max Reinhardt*. Berkeley: University of California Press, 1969.

Elsaesser, Thomas. "Film History and Visual Pleasure: Weimar Cinema," in Patricia Mellencamp and Philip Rosen, eds., *Cinema Histories, Cinema Practices*. Washington, D. C., American Film Institute, 1984, pp. 47–84.

————, ed., *Early Cinema: Space, Frame, Narrative*. London: BFI, 1990.

Everson, William K. *American Silent Film*. New York: Oxford University Press, 1978.

Fell, John, ed., *Film before Griffith*. Berkeley: University of California Press, 1983.

Fielding, Raymond. *A Technological History of Motion Pictures and Television*. Berkeley: University of California Press, 1967.

————. *The American Newsreel, 1911–1967*. Norman: University of Oklahoma Press, 1972.

Flitterman-Lewis, Sandy. *To Desire Differently: Feminism and the French Cinema*. Urbana: University of Illinois Press, 1990.

Friedberg, Anne. *Window Shopping: Cinema and the Postmodern*. Berkeley: University of California Press, 1993.

Gartenberg, Jon. "The Brighton Project: The Archives and Research," *Iris* 2:1 (1984), 5–16.

————. "Vitagraph before Griffith: Forging Ahead in the Nickelodeon Era," *Studies in Visual Communication* 10:4 (1984), 7–23.

Gaudreault, André. "Detours in Film Narrative: Cross-Cutting," *Cinema Journal* 19 (Fall 1979), 39–59.

————. "The Infringement of Copyright Laws and Its Effects (1900–1906)," *Framework* 29 (1985), 2–14.

————. "Theatricality, Narrativity, and 'Trickality': Reevaluating the Cinema of Georges Méliès," *Journal of Popular Film and Television* 15:3 (1987), 110–9.

Gledhill, Christine, ed., *Home Is Where the Heart Is: Studies in Melodrama and the Women's Film*. London: BFI, 1987.

Gomery, Douglas. *Shared Pleasures: A History of Movie Presentation in the United States*. Madison: University of Wisconsin, 1992.

Gunning, Tom. "Non-Continuity, Continuity, Discontinuity: A Theory of Genres in Early Film," *Iris* 2:1 (1984), 100–12.

————. "The Cinema of Attraction: Early Film, Its Spectator and the Avant-Garde," *Wide Angle* 8:3/4 (1986), 63–70.

————. "An Aesthetics of Astonishment: Early Film and the (In)credulous Spectator," *Art & Text* 34 (Spring 1989), 31–45.

————. "Primitive Cinema—A Frame Up? or The Trick's on Us," *Cinema Journal* 28 (Winter 1989), 3–12.

————. "Film History and Film Analysis: The Individual Film in the Course of Time," *Wide Angle* 12:3 (1990), 4–19.

————. *D. W. Griffith and the Origins of American Narrative Film*. Urbana: University of Illinois Press, 1991.

————. ed., *Persistence of Vision* 9 (1991)—special issue devoted to early cinema.

Hake, Sabine. *The Cinema's Third Machine: Writing on Film in Germany, 1907–1933*. Lincoln: University of Nebraska Press, 1993.

Hansen, Miriam. "Early Silent Cinema: Whose Public Sphere?" *New German Critique* 29 (Spring–Summer 1983), 147–84.

————. "Reinventing the Nickelodeon: Notes on Kluge and Early Cinema," *October* 46 (Fall 1988), 179–98.

————. "Adventures of Goldilocks: Spectatorship, Consumerism and Public Life," *Camera Obscura* 22 (1990), 51–71.

————. *Babel and Babylon: Spectatorship in American Silent Film*. Cambridge, Mass.: Harvard University Press, 1991.

————. "Early Cinema, Late Cinema: Transformations of the Public Sphere," *Screen* 34 (Autumn 1993), 197–210.

Hendricks, Gordon. *Origins of American Film*. New York: Arno, 1972.

Hertogs, Daan and Nico de Klerk, eds., *Nonfiction From the Teens: The 1994 Amsterdam Workshop*. Amsterdam: Stichung Nederlands Filmmuseum, 1994.

Higashi, Sumiko. *Cecil B. DeMille and American Culture: The Silent Era*. Berkeley: University of California Press, 1994.

High, Peter B. "The Dawn of Cinema in Japan," *Journal of Contemporary History* 19:1 (1984), 23–57.

Hiroshi, Komatsu. "Some Characteristics of Japanese Cinema before World War I," in Arthur Nolletti and David Desser, eds., *Reframing Japanese Cinema*. pp. 229–58.

Holman, Roger, ed., *Cinema 1900–1906: An Analytical Study*. 2 vols. Brussels: FIAF, 1982.

Jacobs, Lea. "The Woman's Picture and the Poetics of Melodrama," *Camera Obscura* 31 (1993), 121–147.

Jacobs, Lewis. *The Rise of the American Film*. New York: Teachers College Press, 1968.

Kauffmann, Stanley, and Bruce Henstell, eds., *American Film Criticism: From the Beginnings to Citizen Kane*. New York: Liveright, 1972.

Keil, Charlie. "Reframing *The Italian:* Questions of Audience Address in Early Cinema," *Journal of Film and Video* 42 (Spring 1990), 36–48.

Kenez, Peter. *Cinema and Soviet Society, 1917–1953.* Cambridge: Cambridge University Press, 1992.

Kerr, Walter. *The Silent Clowns.* New York: Knopf, 1975.

Kirby, Lynne. "Male Hysteria and the Early Cinema," *Camera Obscura* 17 (1988), 113–31.

———. "Gender and Advertising in American Silent Film: From Early Cinema to *The Crowd,*" *Discourse* 13 (Spring–Summer 1991), 3–20.

Korszarski, Richard. *An Evening of Entertainment: The Age of the Silent Feature Picture, 1915–1928.* New York: Scribner's, 1991.

Kracauer, Siegfried. *From Caligari to Hitler: A Psychological History of the German Cinema.* Princeton, N.J.: Princeton University Press, 1947.

Kuenzli, Rudolf, ed., *Dada and Surrealist Film.* New York: Willis Locker & Owens, 1987.

Lant, Antonia. "The Curse of the Pharaoh, or How Cinema Contracted Eyptomania," *October* 59 (Winter 1992), 87–112.

Larue, Kalton. *Continued Next Week: A History of the Moving Picture Serial.* Norman: University of Oklahoma Press, 1964.

Lawder, Standish. *The Cubist Cinema.* New York: New York University Press, 1975.

Leyda, Jay. *Kino: A History of the Russian and Soviet Film,* 3rd ed. Princeton, N.J.: Princeton University Press, 1983.

Leyda, Jay, and Charles Musser, ed., *Before Hollywood: Turn-of-the-Century Film from American Archives.* New York: American Federation of the Arts, 1986.

Liebman, Stuart. "French Film Theory, 1910–1921," *Quarterly Review of Film Studies* 8 (Winter 1983), 1–23.

Lindsay, Vachel. *The Art of Moving Pictures.* New York: Liveright, 1970.

Lounsbury, Myron O. *The Origins of American Film Criticism, 1909–1939.* New York: Arno Press, 1973.

Low, Rachel. *The History of the British Film.* 6 vols. London: George Allen & Unwin, 1948–1979.

Marks, Martin. "The First American Film Scores," *Harvard Library Bulletin* 2:4 (1991), 78–100.

Mast, Gerald, ed., *The Movies in Our Midst: Documents in the Cultural History of Film in America.* Chicago: University of Chicago Press, 1982.

May, Lary. *Screening Out the Past: The Birth of Mass Culture and the Motion Picture Industry.* New York: Oxford University Press, 1980.

Mayne, Judith. "Immigrants and Spectators," *Wide Angle* 5:2 (1982), 32–41.

———. *Private Novels, Public Films.* Athens: University of Georgia Press, 1988.

———. *The Woman at the Keyhole: Feminism and Women's Cinema.* Bloomington: Indiana University Press, 1990.

Mottram, Ron. *The Danish Cinema before Dreyer.* Metuchen, N. J.: Scarecrow, 1988.

Munsterberg, Hugo. *The Photoplay: A Psychological Study.* New York: Dover, 1970.

Musser, Charles. "The Eden Musée: Exhibitor as Creator," *Film and History* 11 (December 1981), 73–83.

———. "The Nickelodeon Era Begins: Establishing the Framework for Hollywood's Mode of Representation," *Framework* 22/23 (Autumn 1983), 4–11.

———. "Another Look at the Chaser Theory," *Studies in Visual Communication* 10:4 (1984), 24–44.

———. *The Thomas Edison Papers: A Guide to Motion Picture Catalogs by American Producers and Distributors, 1894–1908.* Frederick, Maryland: University Publications of America, 1985.

———. *Before the Nickelodeon: Edwin S. Porter and the Edison Manufacturing Company.* Berkeley: University of California Press, 1991.

———. *The Emergence of Cinema, I: The American Screen to 1907.* New York: Scribners, 1991.

Musser, Charles, and Carol Nelson. *High-Class Moving Pictures: Lyman H. Howe and the Forgotten Era of Traveling Exhibition, 1880–1920.* Princeton, N.J., Princeton University Press, 1991.

Nasaw, David. *Going Out: The Rise and Fall of Public Amusements.* New York: Basic Books, 1993.

New German Critique 40 (Winter 1987)—special issue on Weimar film theory.

Nielsen, Michael C. "Labor Power and Organization in the Early U.S. Motion Picture Industry," *Film History* 2:2 (1988), 121–31.

Niver, Kemp. *The First Twenty Years.* Los Angeles: Artisan Press, 1968.

Pearson, Roberta. "Cultivated Folks and the Better Classes: Class Conflict and Representation in Early American Film," *Journal of Popular Film and Television* 15 (Fall 1987), 120–8.

———. *Eloquent Gestures: The Transformation of Performance Style in Griffith Biograph Films.* Berkeley: University of California Press, 1992.

Pearson, Roberta, and William Uricchio. "How Many Times Shall Caesar Bleed in Sport: Shakespeare and the Cultural Debate about Moving Pictures," *Screen* 31 (Fall 1990), 243–61.

Peiss, Kathy. *Cheap Amusements: Working Women and Leisure in Turn-of-the-Century New York.* Philadelphia: Temple University Press, 1986.

Petro, Patrice. *Joyless Streets: Women and Melodramatic Representation in Weimar Cinema.* Princeton, N.J.: Princeton University Press, 1989.

Pratt, George C. *Spellbound in Darkness: A History of the Silent Film.* Greenwich: New York Graphic Society, 1973.

Rabinovitz, Lauren. "Temptations of Pleasure: Nickelodeons, Amusement Parks, and the Sights of Female Sexuality," *Camera Obscura* 23 (1990), 71–88.

Ramsaye, Terry. *A Million and One Nights.* New York: Simon & Schuster, 1926.

Robinson, David. "Music of the Shadows: The Use of Musical Accompaniment with Silent Films, 1896–1936," supplement to *Griffithiana* 38/39 (1990).

Rosenbloom, Nancy. "Progressive Reform, Censorship, and the Motion Picture Industry, 1909–1917," in Ronald Edsforth and Larry Bennett, eds., *Popular Culture and Political Change in Modern America.* Buffalo, NY: SUNY Press, 1991, pp. 41–59.

Rosenzweig, Roy. *Eight Hours for What We Will: Workers and Leisure in an Industrial City, 1870–1920.* Cambridge: Cambridge University Press, 1983.

Salt, Barry. *Film Style and Technology: History and Analysis,* 2nd ed. London: Starword, 1993.

Schlüpmann, Heide. "Melodrama and the Social Drama in the Early German Cinema," *Camera Obscura* 22 (1990), 72–89.

Singer, Ben. "Manhattan Nickelodeons: New Data on Audiences and Exhibitors," *Cinema Journal* 34 (Spring 1995), 5–35.

Sklar, Robert. "Oh! Althusser!: Historiography and the Rise of Cinema Studies," in R. Sklar and C. Musser, eds., *Resisting Images: Essays on Cinema and History.* Philadelphia: Temple University Press, 1990, pp. 12–35.

Slide, Anthony. *Early Women Directors.* London: A. S. Barnes, 1976.

Slide, Anthony. *Early American Cinema.* 2nd ed. Metuchen, N. J.: Scarecrow, 1994.

Sloan, Kay. *The Loud Silents: Origins of the Social Problem Film.* Urbana, Illinois: University of Illinois Press, 1988.

Spehr, Paul. *The Movies Begin: Making Movies in New Jersey, 1887–1920.* Newark, N.J.: Newark Museum, 1977.

Staiger, Janet. "Combination and Litigation: Structures of US Film Distribution, 1896–1917," *Cinema Journal* 23 (Winter 1983), 41–71.

———. "The Eyes Are Really the Focus: Photoplay Acting and Film Form and Style," *Wide Angle* 6:4 (1983), 14–23.

———. *Interpreting Films: Studies in the Historical Reception of American Cinema.* Princeton, N.J.: Princeton University Press, 1992.

———. *Bad Women: The Regulation of Female Sexuality in Early American Cinema, 1907–1915.* Minneapolis: University of Minnesota Press, 1995.

Streible, Dan. "A History of the Boxing Film, 1894–1915: Social Control and Social Reform in the Progressive Era," *Film History* 3:3 (1989), 235–57.

Taylor, Richard. *The Politics of the Soviet Cinema, 1917–1929.* Cambridge: Cambridge University Press, 1979.

Taylor, Richard, and Ian Christie, eds., *The Film Factory: Russian and Soviet Cinema in Documents, 1896–1939.* Cambridge, Mass.: Harvard University Press, 1988.

———. eds., *Inside the Film Factory: New Approaches to Russian and Soviet Cinema.* London: Routledge, 1991.

Thompson, Kristin. *Exporting Entertainment: America in the World Film Market, 1907–1934.* London: BFI, 1985.

———. ed., *Film History* 5 (December 1993)—a special issue devoted to institutional histories of early cinema.

Toulet, Emmanuelle. "Cinema at the Universal Exposition, Paris 1900," *Persistence of Vision* 9 (1991), 10–36.

Tsivian, Yuri. "Cutting and Framing in Bauer's and Kuleshov's Films," *KINtop* 1 (1992), 103–13.

———. *Early Cinema in Russia and Its Cultural Reception.* London: Routledge, 1994.

Turim, Maureen. "French Melodrama: Theory of a Specific History," *Theater Journal* 39 (October 1987), 307–27.

———. "Seduction and Elegance: The New Woman of Fashion in Silent Cinema," in Sheri Benstock and Suzanne Ferris, eds., *On Fashion,* New Brunswick, N.J.: Rutgers University Press, 1994, pp. 140–58.

Uricchio, William and Roberta Pearson. "Constructing an Audience: Competing Discourses of Morality and Rationalization During the Nickelodeon Period," *Iris* 17 (Autumn 1994), 43–54.

———. *Reframing Culture: The Case of the Vitagraph Quality Films.* Princeton, N.J.: Princeton University Press, 1993.

Vardac, A. Nicholas. *Stage to Screen: Theatrical Method from Garrick to Griffith.* Cambridge, Mass.: Harvard University Press, 1949.

Wagenknecht, Edward. *The Movies in the Age of Innocence.* Norman: University of Oklahoma Press, 1962.

Waller, Gregory. "Situating Motion Pictures in the Prenickelodeon Period: Lexington, Kentucky, 1897–1906," *Velvet Light Trap* 25 (Spring 1990), 12–28.

———. *Main Street Amusements: Movies and Commercial Entertainment in a Southern City.* Washington, D. C.: Smithsonian Institution Press, 1995.

———. "Another Audience: Black Moviegoing, 1907–1916," *Cinema Journal* 31 (Winter 1992), 3–25.

Walsh, Michael, ed., *Velvet Light Trap* 37 (Spring 1996)—special issue devoted to Feuillade and the serial.

Williams, Linda. "Film Body: An Implantation of Perversions," *Ciné-Tracts* 12 (1981), 19–35.

Youngblood, Denise. *Movies for the Masses: Popular Cinema and Soviet Society in the 1920s.* Cambridge: Cambridge University Press, 1992.

Contributors

RICHARD ABEL is a Professor of English at Drake University. Currently he is working on a project entitled *The "Red Rooster" Scare, or the Americanization of Early American Cinema.*

RICK ALTMAN is a Professor of French and Communication Studies at the University of Iowa. Currently, he is completing a book, *Doing Things with Genre,* and doing research on sound theory and the history sound in American cinema.

MARY CARBINE is the Film Librarian at the University of Chicago Film Studies Center. She has worked as a film archivist, librarian, and consultant for the Academy of Motion Picture Arts and Sciences as well as other archives.

PAOLO CHERCHI USAI is Curator of Film at the George Eastman House, co-director of the Pordenone Silent Film Festival, and editor of the *Journal of Film Preservation.* He has written extensively on early cinema.

TOM GUNNING is an Associate Professor in the Department of Radio, Television, and Film at Northwestern University. His current project is a study of early cinema and modernity.

NORMAN KING is a Senior Lecturer in Film and Television Studies at the University of Glasgow and an editor of *Screen.*

CHARLES MUSSER is a documentary filmmaker, editor, and Assistant Professor of American Studies and Film Studies at Yale University. One of his current projects is *Filmmaking for Edison's Kinetoscope, 1890–1895: A Filmography with Documentation.*

ROBERTA PEARSON teaches at the Centre for Journalism Studies, University of Wales–Cardiff. With William Uricchio, she is writing *The Nickel Madness: The Struggle Over New York City's Nickelodeons* (forthcoming from Smithsonian Institution Press).

HEIDE SCHLÜPMANN teaches film theory and film history at Frankfurt University. She is co-editor of *Frauen und Film* and author of *Unheimlichkeit des Blicks: Das Drama des Frühen Deutschen Kinos.*

BEN SINGER is an Assistant Professor teaching film studies at Smith College. He is completing a book on popular audiences and the "lowbrow" aesthetic in early cinema.

GAYLYN STUDLAR is Director of the Program in Film and Video at the University of Michigan. Her most recent book, co-edited with David Desser, is *Reflections in a Male Eye: John Huston and the American Experience* (Smithsonian Institute, 1993).

YURI TSIVIAN is a Senior Researcher Fellow in the Institute of Folklore, Literature and Art at the Latvian Academy of Sciences; he also teaches silent film history at the University of Southern California.

WILLIAM URICCHIO is a Professor of Film and Television History at the University of Utrecht and has written widely on the emergence of representational systems. With Roberta Pearson, he is writing *The Nickel Madness: The Struggle over New York City's Nickelodeons* (forthcoming from Smithsonian Institution Press).

MIKHAIL YAMPOLSKY teaches in the Department of Comparative Literature and Russian and Slavic Studies at New York University. Among his books in Russian, *Tiresias' Memory* soon will be published in English translation by the University of California Press.

Index